ALSO BY SUSAN G. PURDY

Have Your Cake and Eat It, Too
    (Winner of IACP Julia Child Cookbook Award)
A Piece of Cake
As Easy as Pie
Christmas Cooking Around the World
Christmas Gifts Good Enough to Eat!
Jewish Holiday Cookbook
Halloween Cookbook
Christmas Cookbook
Let's Give a Party
Christmas Gifts for You to Make
Books for You to Make
Costumes for You to Make
Jewish Holidays
Holiday Cards for You to Make
If You Had a Yellow Lion
Be My Valentine
Christmas Decorations for You to Make
My Little Cabbage

Let Them EAT CAKE

140 SINFULLY
RICH DESSERTS—
WITH A FRACTION
OF THE FAT

SUSAN G. PURDY

WILLIAM MORROW AND COMPANY, INC.
New York

Text and illustrations copyright © 1997 by Susan G. Purdy
Color photographs copyright © 1997 by Dennis Gottlieb,
with the exception of Fresh Orange Wedding Cake,
copyright © *Cooking Light*, Howard L. Puckett, photographer
Food styling by Delores Custer

Library of Congress Cataloging-in-Publication Data

Purdy, Susan Gold, 1939–
    Let them eat cake : 140 sinfully rich desserts—with a fraction of
the fat / Susan G. Purdy.—1st ed.
        p.   cm.
    Includes bibliographical references (p.   ) and index.
    ISBN 0-688-14039-4
    1. Desserts. 2. Low-fat diet—Recipes.   I. Title.
TX773.P986   1997
641.8'6—dc21   96–45469
                                                            CIP

Printed in the United States of America

First Edition

1 2 3 4 5 6 7 8 9 10

BOOK DESIGN BY RACHEL MCBREARTY

*F*or my sister,
Nancy Gold Lieberman,
with love and admiration

Acknowledgments

The preparation of this book has continued over a period of years and involved many members of my family, friends, professional colleagues, and technical experts in a variety of fields. In addition, since this book is a continuation of the material in my first work on fat-reduced baking, *Have Your Cake and Eat It, Too*, I have drawn again on the expertise of those who helped me the first time around. More than most projects, then, this book is a community effort, and I want to offer my deepest gratitude to all who helped.

For valor in the line of duty, tasting my continual test efforts, and offering moral support, I thank my husband, Geoffrey, our daughter, Cassandra, and my mother, Frances Joslin Gold, who suggested this project in the first place. I also thank Nancy, Stephan, David, and Scott Lieberman, my mother-in-law Lucille Purdy, as well as Tabitha and Jason Song.

Several talented young chef/bakers helped me develop and test new recipes and techniques. I thank especially my daughter, Cassandra; also Lynnia Milliun and Ann Martin. Lana Jurigian and Kristin Eycleshymer began working with me as student assistants in my classes at the Cambridge (Massachusetts) School of Culinary Arts. Since their graduation, they have become good friends, inspired recipe testers, and chefs: Lana at Pentimento in Belmont, Massachusetts, and Kristin at Heart's Delight Cafe in Framingham, Massachusetts.

For tasting a new morsel each time they entered our home, I thank all our friends and family, including especially Scott Hanna, Fran Brill and Bob Kelly, Ann Swift, Lee and Jessie-Leigh Lord, Scott Williams and Jim King, Elizabeth and Pirie MacDonald, Charley Kanas, Katia Kanas, and Leonard and David Roberts.

For testing recipes in their own homes and providing careful comments, I am indebted to Claire Rosenberg, Lee Rush, Judy Perkins, Jolene Mullen, Janie Peterson, and Tracy Glaves Spalding. Food stylists/chefs Aliza Green, Katie Keck, and Elizabeth Duffy tested and prepared my recipes for television and photographic appearances; their comments were invaluable.

For providing special recipes as well as information about diabetes, I thank Nancy Mowbray and Susan Kinsolving. Harold J. Holler, R.D., Position Development Specialist of the American Dietetic Association, answered queries with thoughtful attention to detail and reviewed the text on dietary regulations for individuals having diabetes. For information, recipes, and advice about celiac disease and gluten-free products, I thank Beth Hillson and her colleague Liz Reed, of the Gluten-Free Pantry in Glastonbury, Connecticut.

For literary quotations used in this text, I thank three California friends, Edna R.S. Alvarez, Gail Humphreys, and Helen Chrostowski. For continuing work on fat-reduction techniques, answering countless questions, and offering continual encouragement, I thank my friend Patsy Jamieson, test kitchen director of *Eating Well* magazine, as well as Susan Herr, test kitchen manager, and Elizabeth Hiser, M.S., R.D., nutrition editor. Registered dietician Marsha Hudnall, R.D., M.S., reviewed and revised my Nutritional Analysis figures, Light Touch notes, and Understanding Ingredients chapters with great skill and thoughtful good humor. For technical advice and generous gifts of time and talent, I thank Atlanta-based food scientist and writer Shirley O. Corriher. Harold McGee, writer and food scientist reviewed technical questions regarding baking equipment, as did my good friend, kitchen designer and writer Deborah Krasner.

For holding my hand through the early stages of this project, I am indebted to editor Harriet Bell (now at Broadway Books) and Skip Dye, formerly of William Morrow Special Sales. For wholeheartedly "adopting" me and following the completion of the book with good grace, warmth, and skill, I am grateful to Ann Bramson and my new editor, Pam Hoenig, at William Morrow. For book design, I thank Rachel McBrearty, and for the jacket design, Iris Jeromnimon.

Lusciously creamy chocolate cakes go to photographer Dennis Gottlieb and food stylist Delores Custer for their technical brilliance, patience, and good humor. We shared seven days I will treasure.

I thank my literary agent, Susan Lescher, for her putting me in such good hands as well as for offering me thoughtful advice; my friend and publicist, Lisa Ekus, for her continual good ideas and enthusiastic support. Merrilyn Siciak, of Lisa Ekus Public Relations, has held my hand, answered queries, and offered friendship and advice beyond the call.

As my computer skills slowly improve under their careful guidance and incredibly patient tutelage, I thank Jan Pieter Hoekstra, Bill Chin, Scott Lieberman, and Scott Williams.

I thank Ginnie Sweatt Hagan, Vermont friend and neighbor, for sharing both the fruits of her berry-picking labors and the overflowing recipe files of her kitchen. I thank Pat Schoenfeld for sharing her Apple Brown Betty recipe, Ann Amendolara Nurse for always being there for me with encouragement, new ideas, and kind words, and Arthur Schwartz for his enthusiastic recommendation of my work on his WOR radio program, "Food Talk."

For responding to technical queries, I gratefully thank: Dr. Paul D. Doolan; Sandra Nuño, Nutrition IV, First DataBank, San Bruno, California; Bonnie G. Hinkson, Product Information, Hershey Foods Corporation; Anna Moses, Manager, Public Relations, The Dannon Company, Tarrytown, New York; Lois Levine, Test Kitchen Coordinator, Wilton Industries, Woodridge, Illinois; Linda M. Braun, Consumer Services Manager, American Egg Board; Jerry Huard, Grace Cocoa Company; King Arthur Flour Company; Rob Byrne, Ph.D., Director of Product Safety and Technology, International Dairy Foods Association; Rena Cutrufelli, American Dietetic Association; Gail Bellamy, Senior Editor, *Restaurant Hospitality* magazine; Nancy Kervin, National Restaurant Association Information Services and Library; Susan Mack, President, Cutting Edge Enterprises, Atlanta; and Mary Evans, Byerly's School of Culinary Arts, Minneapolis.

For suggesting their favorite pie recipes and ordering special ingredients for me at the M&B IGA in New Milford, Connecticut, I thank Tom Mitchell, grocery manager; Frank Benham, owner; and John Grant, produce department. For supplying me with special produce at the Washington, Connecticut, Food Market, I thank Pat Maiorino, perishables manager.

For the original sketches I used for the wedding cake drawings, I thank Susan Martin.

CONTENTS

Cakes, Plain and Fancy

NTRODUCTION

In my family, we are nearly as devoted to our desserts as we are to each other. A few years ago, when my mother was advised for medical reasons to go on a low-fat diet, there was no question that the cake problem would have to be solved—the only question was by whom and how fast. As the designated baker in the family, I quickly set out to learn all I could about the theory and practice of reducing total fat, saturated fat, and cholesterol in baking. That two-year study, and its practical application, formed the basis of my first book on this subject, *Have Your Cake and Eat It, Too*. At that time, there were many books about heart-healthy, low-fat cooking but, with the exception of meringue cakes, poached fruits, and sorbets, very few ventured into the difficult business of reducing the fat in cakes and pastries.

Out of necessity, I studied the chemistry of dietary fat, learning why it should be reduced and experimenting with how to do it. My primary goal was to learn, within the baking repertoire, how to make the recipes more heart-healthy, cutting the fat but keeping the taste.

By the time I finished *Have Your Cake and Eat It, Too*, I

discovered several things had happened. First, my family and I had many low-fat recipes that we loved and ate by choice—chocolate buttermilk cake, yogurt-crumb coffee cake, blueberry muffins, reduced-fat pie crust—new favorites. We had actually learned a new pattern of eating: We preferred less richness, less butter and cream in our baked goods (and in general cooking as well), and we tasted and felt the difference when we ate something containing an overload of butter. Sure, it tasted luxurious, but as a sometime thing. We still love rich treats, understand. In a heartbeat, I will cross the street for a slice of chocolate truffle cake . . . but it will be a smaller slice than before (and that heartbeat is the steadier for it, too).

The second thing I noticed was that although my book was at the publisher, my desk was still heaped with notes for cakes and pies I wanted to work on, ideas I had not yet tried or thought needed more time. There seemed no end to my obsession with tinkering and testing to transpose every recipe to another, lower-fat key without losing its melody. This book is the result of my continued work on this subject. And the work mounts. I continue to receive consultation requests and mail from individuals and from restaurants trying to revamp high-fat recipes.

The third thing I noticed was that nutritional awareness had become a national fact of life rather than a novelty, a way of thinking, of eating, of living. Research indicates that the general public wants healthy choices available yet harbors the fear that foods that are "good for you" will not taste good.

While that is a fine argument for using the delicious recipes in this book when dining at home, it may pose a serious dilemma when you are dining out. When chefs put a cholesterol-free, low-fat dessert on the menu with a "heart-healthy" insignia, it turns out that few actually order it. We deserve a break from the kitchen cops and dietary spin doctors and we need more great-tasting healthy pastries when we dine out.

The restaurant and food service industry has been studying and theorizing about our behavior for some time. They observe many diners ordering a Spartan salad entree followed by chocolate caramel cake. In the February 1996 issue of *Perspectives*, an International Association of Culinary Professionals (IACP) Foundation Report, editor Susan Mack poses the question "Does this schizophrenic eating reflect nutritional misinformation or is it simply an effort on the part of the diner to balance the 'good' with the 'bad'? Food service professionals can't decide. . . . "

A 1995 study of five hundred food service operators conducted by the food industry research firms Thomas Food Industry Register and Find/SVP reported that 95% of their customers are concerned about the nutritional content of food they order. Major concerns were: dietary fat (52%); cholesterol (20%); calories and other issues (9%). Nearly three-quarters of the restaurant operators in this study reported adding healthful menu items in response to public demand, with 49% serving low-fat desserts. Public interest and awareness have only increased since these studies were done.

Developing fat-reduced baked goods is amazingly difficult; altering fat and carbohydrate ratios is a perilous process. A cake recipe, for example, is actually a chemical formula of carefully orchestrated elements harmoniously proportioned to create a certain degree of rise, a characteristic texture, fine grain, delicate taste, and moist crumb. When you upset the balance of these elements, every single thing changes. If you drop a series of notes in a sonata, a lovely theme becomes mere noise; similarly, if you take all the fat and sugar out of a cake recipe, you will create a rubbery tasteless pancake if you are lucky.

If excellence is your goal, it is never all or nothing. Fat cannot be entirely removed, sugars cannot be slashed, salt cannot be omitted. A small amount of fat, in fact, is essential to good health; a small amount of sugar and salt are essential for flavor, color, texture. I have learned to cut back, not cut out: that is the secret of success. Great taste depends upon keeping a little of all the good stuff . . . including butter, nuts, chocolate, cream. I do alter the ratio of ingredients, enhancing flavors naturally by adding more pure extracts, citrus zest, ripe fruit, fine-quality cocoa. I add fruit purées and yogurt, vary the type of flour, and use the best-tasting, least "chemically engineered" fat-reduced dairy products I can find. Most important, I do it all with readily available, easy-to-find natural ingredients, without any artificial fat, sugar, or egg substitutes.

I am often asked how I test my recipes. The answer is: very thoroughly. It can take a dozen trials, forty or more in some cases, and occasionally, with tears of frustration, I feed the sorry results to the raccoons in the woods. When I am successful, I prepare the recipe for my family (the front line of testers), then a few hardy friends. Sometimes I have a "blind tasting" party, without specifying which desserts are classic and which are reduced in fat and/or cholesterol. Finally, I pass the recipes along to other home bakers to test and comment upon in their own kitchens.

What are my criteria? First and foremost, great taste. The recipes must stand on their own and taste wonderful, not "okay because they are low fat." If I hear the comment "I guess I should like it if it's good for me," out it goes. While it is true that a low-fat cake will not taste the same as one made with all butter, neither does it, by definition, have to be boring. No one wants to devote the time or expense required to make a dessert unless the results are sure to be delicious. A dessert has to taste fabulous and the recipe has to be fun, easy, and work every time.

Since *Have Your Cake* was first published, a plethora of commercial low-fat products has appeared on the market along with many new books and articles on the subject. At the same time, two glaring problems have emerged in the spotlight: first, as fat (which both contributes and carries flavor) is dropped, calories (in the form of carbohydrates) often stay the same or even rise (no surprise here, this is done to restore taste and improve texture); second, in spite of technical juggling, the taste and texture of many of the commercial products are still abysmal. The public complains that they are eating more low-fat products but still gaining weight. The reality: because products are low-fat, people may be eating more of them without realizing that excess calories from any source will still make you fat. The national focus on obesity has shifted attention to include total calorie count as well as saturated fat and cholesterol reduction. This concern must be seen in context, however.

Even with home baking, it is a common misapprehension that a low-fat recipe will also be low-calorie. Not necessarily. My recipes are certainly lower in percentage of calories from fat, but not *necessarily* lower in percentage of calories from carbohydrates (sugars and starches) or proteins, though I try to limit calories *whenever possible without sacrificing flavor* (see Fat, Dietary Fat, Cholesterol, and Calories, page 359).

The balance between calories from fat and calories from carbohydrates must be carefully weighed when developing a recipe. In a dessert, sugar and fat cannot be equally reduced or there will be no taste left at all. Remember that this is, after all, a book of desserts, not a total menu plan for everyday eating. Desserts should be exceptionally delicious and rewarding; the dessert course should be an interlude of sublime relaxed pleasure, neither an exercise in mathematical calculation nor an act of self-denial.

That said, if the calorie count in a particular recipe in this book seems high to you at first glance, notice how few of the calories come from fat. If your concern with personal weight management necessitates numbers watching, the nutritional analysis for each recipe is there for you to study. Finally, if you're still concerned, cut your dessert portion in half and eat it very slowly, enjoying the full-bodied flavor of each and every morsel.

If you have any doubt that healthy desserts are here to stay, you have only to look at your local Girl Scout or school bake sale. There on the table between brownies and pound cakes sits the proudly labeled low-fat bar cookie or cholesterol-free coffee cake.

It is also interesting to consider the response of students in my entertaining and baking classes. I often make one or two low-fat cakes in addition to some rich classics. I bake, and the students taste, before I delve too far into my comparative grams-of-fat-per-serving lecture. I love to see their surprise and delight at finding a delectable reduced-fat dessert; their enthusiasm is contagious, and inspiring. My students' expectations that low-fat desserts would taste disappointing are typical of the public in general. My hope is that the big flavors and satisfying home-tested treats in this collection will restore their faith and yours.

In selecting these recipes, I relaxed and had a good time. In *Have Your Cake and Eat It, Too*, I learned the technique of fat reduction and tried to present a well-balanced collection of recipes. This time, I went for fun and personal favorites: Peach Pizza (a free-form pie without a pie plate), Tortilla Tarts (fruit and sugar baked on tortillas), homey puddings (Upside-down Apple Bread Pudding with Bourbon Cream Sauce, Grandma's Noodle Pudding, homemade

Chocolate Pudding), luscious silky Tiramisù, dreamy Drop-Dead Chocolate-Espresso Mousse Cake, and (sigh) Chocolate-Caramel Turtle Tartlets. I have also included many American regional recipes (Sweet Potato Pie, Chess, and Pecan Pie) and all-American favorites like Lemon Meringue Pie, rich, gooey Coconut Cream Pie, and Chocolate Cream Pie. The cookie collection includes a wonderful crisp Chocolate Chip Cookie, cinnamon-nut Rugelach with apricot glaze, and classically creamy Lemon Squares, to name a few I can't live without.

A small number of recipes, which are basic to the baker's pantry, previously appeared in *Have Your Cake and Eat It, Too*. They are: All-Purpose Pie Crust, Graham–Grape-Nuts Crumb Crust, Chocolate Crumb Crust, Chocolate Sponge Roll, Vanilla Cream, Shortcut Vanilla Pastry Cream, Fromage Blanc, Ricotta Cream, Homemade Yogurt Cheese, Lemon Curd, Vanilla Custard Sauce, Caramel Sauce, Berry Sauce, Raspberry Sauce, All-Purpose Glaze and Firm Fruit Glaze, Vanilla Icing Glaze and Variations, Cookie Frosting, Light Cream Cheese Frosting, Seven-Minute Icing and Variations, Boiled Icing and Variations, and Oat Streusel Topping.

I am often asked the origin of the phrase "Let them eat cake." According to the *Oxford Dictionary of Quotations*, it was a common saying in the eighteenth century, made famous by a cynical retort attributed to Marie Antoinette during the French Revolution (1789). On hearing that the populous had no bread to eat, the queen is said to have replied "*Qu'ils mangent de la brioche*" (Let them eat brioche). While I'm willing to borrow her words, I know I am on the *right* side of the (low-fat) revolution. So, yes, let them eat cake—and puddings, cobblers, pies, and cookies!

About "The Numbers" and Nutritional Analysis

The nutritional analyses of the recipes in this book should be viewed as guide rather than gospel, even though every attempt was made to ensure accuracy. The analyses have been calculated using the Nutritionist IV Diet Analysis software from First DataBank, San Bruno, California.

The data are supplied by various sources, from the FDA to manufacturers. Rarely, information is incomplete or even unknown; in those cases, substitutions of similar ingredients are made. The analysis for each recipe is per serving, and lists total calories, proteins, total fat, saturated fat (satfat), carbohydrates, sodium, and cholesterol. When yield varies (6 to 8 portions), analysis is calculated on the first, smaller figure (that is, 6 portions); when there are several suggested ingredients, analysis is made on the first mentioned. Fractions are rounded off to the nearest whole number except fat, satfat, and trace amounts which are so noted; when total fat is less than 0.5 g, it is considered a trace amount. Note: If you try to calculate the percentage of calories from fat in these recipes using the printed rounded-off figures, your results will not always agree with mine. This is because my calculations were done by computer using figures carried to three decimal places instead of being rounded off.

Portions are based on average-size servings and have not been shaved to "cook" the numbers. In the Light Touch notes following the recipes, I give the percentage of calories from fat to show the contrast between traditional full-fat and fat-reduced recipes.

When looking at the percentage of calories from fat for a single recipe, one should bear in mind that the American Heart Association recommends, for people over two years of age, a guideline of 30% calories from fat for *total daily caloric intake*; this means that not every recipe or single food must be below 30%. It is the balance that counts; thus, a low-fat meal might be capped off with a dessert that is relatively high in fat.

Sometimes a particular recipe, in order to have proper taste and texture, will be over 30% calories from fat even in its reduced-fat version. The great majority of recipes in this book are well below this standard and all are significantly below the fat content of conventional recipes. But in some recipes, even a small amount of fat will register as proportionally high, while the actual per-serving figures are low in grams of fat. This is because there are relatively few ingredients in the recipe and/or those that are there contribute few calories. In a few cases, the total fat will be above 30% simply because the recipe requires more fat to achieve the proper taste and texture—it will still be below the fat content of a conventional version of the same recipe. While accommodating as healthy a regime as possible, it is my priority to offer baked goods that give pleasure rather than to adhere to strict numerical rules.

ABOUT THE RECIPES IN THIS BOOK

- Before baking from this book, read the sections on ingredients and equipment starting on page 295. The information and the techniques described will help you achieve success.

- Read each recipe from beginning to end before starting to cook. This will help you plan your time efficiently and enable you to discover whether or not you have all the ingredients and equipment on hand before beginning.

- Use ingredients specified in the recipe. (This is not the place to be creative.) When fat is reduced, the importance of every element retained is increased. In many recipes, skim milk will produce a markedly different result than 2% milk; use unsalted butter where specified; never substitute soft margarine or margarine "spread" which is totally unreliable for baking.

- All dry measurements are level.

- All eggs are U.S. Grade A Large (2 ounces).

- "Grated zest" of citrus fruits refers to the brightly colored outer layer of the peel, not the bitter white inner layer, or pith.

- When a recipe says "$^1/_2$ cup chopped nuts," the nuts are chopped *before* measuring; "$^1/_2$ cup nuts, chopped" means they are chopped *after* being measured.

- When a recipe says "$^1/_2$ cup *unsifted* flour," it means that the flour is simply stirred in the canister to fluff it up, then spooned or scooped from the canister into a measuring cup and leveled off with a knife. When it says "$^1/_2$ cup *sifted* flour," it is sifted, then spooned into a measuring cup and leveled off with a knife.

- For reliable baking results, use the type of flour (cake or all-purpose) specified in each recipe. Flours differ in (gluten-producing) protein content, acidity, and absorb moisture differently.

- If baked in an aluminum pie plate or baking pan, fruit can pick up an off flavor or metallic taste. It is best to use a nonaluminum, ceramic, or ovenproof glass (Pyrex) pie plate or dish.

- If you find you don't have the baking pan recommended, turn to the Pan Volume and Serving Chart (pages 340–341) for substitutions. When a recipe can be baked in a different type of pan, the recipe will include total batter volume in the Yield; use this figure to calculate pan size following the guide.

- Room temperature means about 68°F. It is important to have baking ingredients at room temperature so they will blend together properly.

- Check your oven temperature. Inaccurate oven temperature is one of the most common causes of baking failure. Use a separate oven thermometer (page 346) purchased in a hardware or gourmet food store. Set it on the oven rack; adjust your oven dial as necessary for the correct internal temperature. External oven calibrations are frequently incorrect.

- When two times are given for doneness (e.g., 10 to 15 minutes), check the oven at the first time, then watch closely until the second. Your oven may vary from mine; the most important thing is to watch the baked product instead of the clock to observe signs of doneness: cake springy, tester comes out clean.

- Where alternative ingredients are listed (e.g., skim or 1% milk) the nutritional analysis has been calculated on the first-mentioned item.

- When measuring yogurt, pour off the excess liquid before measuring. Drain yogurt through a sieve only if directed in the recipe.

- Use pure flavoring extracts whenever possible; they do not leave any chemical aftertaste, unlike some chemically formulated "imitation" flavors. Some flavors are, however, only widely available in "imitation" form, such as banana.

- In instructions for freezing baked goods, the terms "airtight" and "double-wrapped" refer to the following procedure: Cool the product completely, set it on a stiff foil-covered cardboard disk, and wrap it first in an airtight layer of plastic wrap, then in a layer of aluminum foil (preferably heavy-duty with double-folded edges to keep out air) or in a heavy-duty plastic bag. Label carefully and include date.

Cookies,
BARS, AND BROWNIES

Cookies are private, individual treats you don't have to share. A reward, a nosh, a midnight snack. So cookies had better be good. Very good.

You will not be disappointed by this collection. Unlike many reduced-fat cookies, these are big and bold in taste and texture. The crisp cookies (Chocolate Chip, Peanut Butter) are crisp, the soft (Berry Bars, Brownies) are supposed to be that way. You get what you expect, and then some. Cookies depend upon different fats for their taste and texture. Solid fats differ in melting points, volumes of water, and the amount of flour they require to hold dough together. While butter is ideal for a crisp thin cookie, a blend of butter and solid white shortening makes a fatter cookie that holds its shape and is a little chewy. Reducing fat alters the balance among fat, starch, and sugar.

Commercially successful low-fat cookies tend to be soft and chewy, with the fat replaced entirely or in large part by fruit purée, which replicates some of the qualities of fat: it holds in moisture, contains pectin which tenderizes gluten, adds flavor, and traps air when whipped. Nonetheless, commercial bakers go too far, and often spoil their results, by using extra sugar and chemically engineered additives to enhance flavor lost when fat is removed.

My secret is to use only natural ingredients, including a little butter, often browned in advance to enhance its flavor, plus a little oil and light cream cheese for rich mouth-feel. Brown sugar is often called for because it contributes flavor. Extra vanilla or good fruit preserves add taste, as does grated ginger or citrus peel.

Watch baking times carefully and bake Oatmeal-Raisin-Walnut Cookies, for example, slightly longer if you want them really crisp, or slightly less if you prefer them chewy. The plain Chocolate Cookies are satisfying by themselves (and can be used to make Chocolate Crumb Crust) but when sandwiched with Marshmallow Fluff, create a sublime low-fat version of Nabisco's Oreos™.

I have been seeking the best fat-reduced brownie for years. Here are three that I love: basic Fudge, rich Cream Cheese Marbleized Brownie, and a non-chocolate Blondie that is buttery and irresistible. Classic Luscious Lemon Squares have finally found a home in a fat-reduced but flavor-unchanged format; this is now my preferred version of the recipe and no one guesses it's not the original. With the development of a good fat-reduced Cream Cheese Pastry, I have devised New York deli–worthy Rugelach, rich, tasty, and glazed with apricot preserves.

Walnut Crumb Bars and Berry Bars with Streusel Topping are quick and easy to put together, perfect to take on a picnic, as are gingerbread-like Bionic Bars and Orange Biscotti. For the sophisticated guests at your dinner party, pass a tray of unusual Glazed Ginger Tartlets or Ginger-Date Wedges, or molded Chocolate Tulip Shells filled with fruit or Vanilla Cream. And for Passover, try the matzoh meal version of Tulip Cookies filled with fruit.

CHOCOLATE CHIP COOKIES

At last, fat-reduced but honestly great... rich old-fashioned flavor, lots of chips, and very crisp. The secret of the fat reduction with full flavor is to intensify the butter taste by browning a small amount before blending with low-fat cream cheese. Mini chocolate chips give more bursts of chocolate than would bigger chunks scattered farther apart, and high-fat nuts are omitted. Unlike many low-fat cookies, these will stay crisp for a week (if there are any left by then).

My search for a crisp cookie led to endless variations which ultimately brought me very close to a recipe developed by the test kitchen of Eating Well *magazine. Though my adaptation differs somewhat, we have worked together, agree in theory, and I give them a grateful nod of thanks.*

Advance Preparation

Before use, the butter must be browned, then chilled about 5 minutes in the refrigerator. Dough can be made 1 day ahead and chilled. Cookies can be baked and frozen, wrapped airtight, for up to 3 weeks.

Special Equipment

Cookie sheet(s), preferably nonstick

Temperature and Time

350°F for 11 to 12 minutes

Butter-flavor no-stick cooking spray

3 tablespoons unsalted butter

1 cup sifted cake flour

¹/₄ teaspoon baking soda

¹/₂ teaspoon salt

¹/₃ cup plus 1 tablespoon packed dark brown sugar

¹/₃ cup plus 1 tablespoon granulated sugar

¹/₃ cup low-fat cream cheese, at room temperature

1 large egg plus 1 large egg white

2 teaspoons vanilla extract

¹/₂ cup (3 ounces) semisweet mini chocolate chips or chopped block chocolate

1. Position racks to divide the oven in thirds and preheat the oven to 350°F. Lightly coat cookie sheet(s) with cooking spray and set aside.

2. In a small saucepan or syrup pan, melt the butter and cook over low heat until the butter begins to turn a golden brown and has a nutty aroma, about 4 minutes. Watch carefully so the butter does not burn. Set aside to cool slightly, then place in a metal bowl (to avoid thermal shock) and freeze or refrigerate about 5 minutes to solidify butter.

3. Whisk together in a mixing bowl the cake flour, baking soda, and salt. Set it aside.

4. In a large bowl with an electric mixer, cream together both sugars, the solid butter, and the cream cheese. Beat until smooth. Add the egg plus white and vanilla and beat well. With the mixer on slow speed, add the dry ingredients, then the chocolate chips or chopped chocolate. The dough will be soft but not runny; it does not need to be chilled before use but can be made ahead and chilled for convenience.

5. Drop the dough by tablespoonfuls on the prepared cookie sheets; allow a couple of inches between cookies for spread during baking. Bake for 11 to

12 minutes, until golden with a slightly darker edge. The longer the cookies bake, the crisper they will be. Transfer with a spatula to a wire rack; when cool, store in an airtight container.

Nutritional Analysis (per cookie): 68 calories; 1 g protein; 2.8 g fat; 0.8 g satfat; 10 g carbohydrate; 59 mg sodium; 11 mg cholesterol

COWBOY CRUNCH COOKIES

Prepare Chocolate Chip Cookies as above, but add 3 tablespoons water along with eggs. Along with the chocolate chips, beat in 1/2 cup old-fashioned rolled oats (not the quick-cooking type).

Nutritional Analysis (per cookie): 73 calories; 1 g protein; 2.9 g fat; 0.8 g satfat; 11 g carbohydrate; 60 mg sodium; 11 mg cholesterol

Light Touch

I developed this recipe with Ann Martin, who was at the time a baking student at the Culinary Institute of America in Hyde Park, New York. Ann entered these cookies in a comparison tasting with other chocolate chip cookies developed by her CIA classmates. Ann was pleased to report back that they liked this version and were surprised by their low fat content and good taste; the competition had between 48% and 50% calories from fat.

The 1930 classic Toll House Cookie recipe weighs in at 52% calories from fat. Each of those cookies has 105 calories, 6.4 g fat, and 2.1 g saturated fat. Our enlightened chocolate chip cookie is proud to announce a 31% reduction in fat, to 36%, dropping 37 calories and slightly more than half the fat and saturated fat per cookie. You can cut further (with a resultant slight loss in taste and texture) to 30% calories from fat by using only 2 tablespoons butter and 1/4 cup mini chips. In my tests, any deeper cut in fat or changes in liquid and flour proportions produced a cakey texture that was unacceptable.

In the Cowboy Crunch variation, the addition of oats brings the calories from fat to 34% and adds 5 calories per cookie but does not significantly alter the fat content.

PEANUT BUTTER COOKIES

These crisp cookies have a strong peanut butter flavor. The dough will be soft, but it is not necessary to chill it before using. This is one of the few recipes in the book that call for "light" margarine (not "soft spread"); the quality of that especially formulated fat is necessary for the proper texture in these cookies. Note: Taste your peanut butter; if it is salty, omit salt in the recipe.

1/4 cup light margarine or solid vegetable shortening

1/4 cup light cream cheese

2 teaspoons vanilla extract

1/2 cup granulated sugar

1/2 cup packed dark brown sugar

1 large egg

1/2 cup chunky peanut butter

1 1/2 cups sifted all-purpose flour, plus extra for shaping cookies

1/2 teaspoon salt (see Note, above)

1/2 teaspoon baking soda

Advance Preparation

Cookies are best on the day they are baked but will stay crisp a few days in an airtight container.

Special Equipment

Cookie sheet(s); baking parchment or aluminum foil

Temperature and Time

375°F for 12 to 14 minutes

1. Position racks to divide the oven in thirds and preheat the oven to 375°F. Cover cookie sheet(s) with baking parchment or aluminum foil and set aside.

2. In a large mixing bowl, beat together the margarine or shortening and cream cheese until completely smooth. Blend in the vanilla and both sugars, then add the egg and peanut butter and beat well.

3. Sift together the flour, salt, and baking soda, add to the peanut butter mixture, and beat just until blended. The dough will be soft.

4. Drop the dough by tablespoonfuls on the covered baking sheet, spacing them 1 inch apart. Flatten each cookie with a table fork dipped into flour, making a traditional crisscross pattern (excess flour can be brushed off after the cookies are baked). Bake the cookies for 12 to 14 minutes, until browned. Cool on a wire rack. The cookies will become crispier as they cool.

Nutritional Analysis (per cookie): 43 calories; 1 g protein; 1.7 g fat; 0.3 g satfat; 6 g carbohydrate; 46 mg sodium; 4 mg cholesterol

continued

I have resisted working with peanut butter cookies because their essence is the richness of nuts, which are high in fat. Most attempts to lower fat in these cookies result in a soft, cakey product. I found that by replacing butter with a combination of light margarine and light cream cheese, there was enough solid fat to make the cookie crisp. I found the cookie not worth making with less than $^1/_2$ cup of chunky peanut butter, which brings the calories from fat to 35%. If solid vegetable shortening (Crisco) is used in place of the margarine, calories from fat go to 40%, but this shortening has half the saturated fat of butter and gives excellent texture. Our recipe is a 33% reduction in calories from fat compared to a classic full-fat peanut butter cookie (52%), with half the fat and cholesterol per cookie.

CHOCOLATE COOKIES

Yield: About thirty 2$^1/_2$-inch cookies

These flavorful cookies stay crisp (unlike most low-fat cookies, which are soft) because they contain some fat: butter, browned for extra flavor, and light cream cheese.

Butter-flavor no-stick cooking spray
1 cup sifted cake flour
$^1/_4$ cup unsifted unsweetened Dutch-processed cocoa
$^1/_4$ teaspoon baking soda
$^1/_2$ teaspoon salt
3 tablespoons unsalted butter
$^1/_2$ ounce unsweetened chocolate, finely chopped
$^1/_2$ cup packed dark brown sugar
$^1/_2$ cup granulated sugar
$^1/_3$ cup light cream cheese, at room temperature
1 large egg plus 1 large egg white
2 teaspoons vanilla extract

Advance Preparation

Cookies can be baked and frozen, wrapped airtight, for up to 3 weeks.

Special Equipment

Cookie sheet(s), preferably nonstick

Temperature and Time

350°F for 11 to 12 minutes

1. Position racks to divide the oven in thirds and preheat the oven to 350°F. Lightly coat cookie sheet(s) with cooking spray and set aside.

2. Whisk together in a mixing bowl the cake flour, cocoa, baking soda, and salt. Set aside.

3. In a small saucepan, melt the butter over medium heat for several minutes until it begins to turn golden brown and have a nutty aroma. Watch carefully so it does not burn. Stir in the chopped unsweetened chocolate and set aside off the heat until the chocolate is melted. Stir until smooth.

4. In a large bowl with an electric mixer, cream together both sugars and the cream cheese. Scrape down the bowl and beaters. Add the melted butter–chocolate mixture, the egg plus white, and the vanilla; mix well. Beat in the flour-cocoa mixture. Scrape down the bowl and beaters again. The dough will be quite soft; this is all right.

5. Drop the dough by the tablespoonful on the prepared cookie sheet(s). Leave a couple of inches between cookies so they can spread during baking. Bake for 11 to 12 minutes, until slightly darkened at the edges; for an extra-crisp cookie, bake about 1 minute longer. Cool the cookies on the baking sheet for a few minutes, then use a spatula to transfer cookies to a wire rack. Cool completely, then store in an airtight container.

Nutritional Analysis (per cookie): 63 calories; 1 g protein; 2 g fat; 0.8 g satfat; 10 g carbohydrate; 68 mg sodium; 11 mg cholesterol

CHOCOLATE SANDWICH COOKIES

Marshmallow fluff holds two chocolate cookies together to make this delight. Let the kids help assemble these; it's half the fun.

Make one recipe Chocolate Cookies, above (30 cookies), to make 15 sandwich cookies (2 each). To make more, double the cookie recipe. Make one half recipe (2¹/₂ cups) Marshmallow Fluff (page 252).

To assemble the cookies, spread 1 generous tablespoon of fluff between 2 cookies. Press lightly on the top cookie to spread the filling nearly to (but not over) the edge. Filling should be a scant ¹/₄ inch thick. Set the filled cookies on a tray so the fluff can air-dry, about 30 minutes. Note: If you have just made the marshmallow fluff, it may still be warm but can be used right away to fill the cookies.

Nutritional Analysis (2 cookies filled with 1¹/₄ tablespoons fluff): 157 calories; 2 g protein; 4.5 g fat; 1.7 g satfat; 28 g carbohydrate; 145 mg sodium; 23 mg cholesterol

Light Touch

Although these delicious cookies contain butter and light cream cheese as well as solid chocolate, each one has very small amounts of fat and cholesterol; they have 31% calories from fat. The sandwich cookies made with marshmallow fluff have more ingredients (which contain neither fat nor cholesterol) so the calories from fat drop to 25%.

OATMEAL-RAISIN-WALNUT COOKIES

Yield: About twenty-five to thirty 2-inch cookies

The crispness of these cookies depends upon the length of time they are baked. You can leave out the walnuts if you prefer.

Butter-flavor no-stick cooking spray
2 tablespoons unsalted butter
1/3 cup light cream cheese, cold
1/2 cup packed dark brown sugar
1/4 cup granulated sugar
2 large egg whites
1 tablespoon vanilla extract
2 tablespoons skim or 1% milk
3/4 cup plus 2 tablespoons sifted cake flour
1/4 teaspoon baking soda
1 teaspoon salt
1 1/2 teaspoons ground cinnamon
1 1/4 cups old-fashioned rolled oats (not quick-cooking type)
1 cup seedless raisins
1/3 cup walnuts, chopped (optional)

Advance Preparation

Before use, the butter must be browned, then chilled; this can take 5 to 8 minutes in the refrigerator. This step can be done up to 2 days ahead. Cookies are best when freshly baked; however, they keep a day or two when wrapped airtight.

Special Equipment

Metal bowl; 2 cookie sheets, preferably nonstick

Temperature and Time

375°F for 15 minutes

1. Position two racks to divide the oven in thirds and preheat the oven to 375°F. Lightly coat baking sheets with cooking spray.

2. In a small saucepan, melt the butter over medium heat for several minutes, until it begins to turn golden brown and have a nutty aroma. Watch carefully so butter does not burn. Set it aside to cool, then place in a metal bowl (to avoid thermal shock) and refrigerate for 5 to 8 minutes, until the butter is solidified.

3. In a large bowl, using an electric mixer or wooden spoon, combine and beat the cream cheese, both sugars, and the browned and chilled butter. Add and beat in the egg whites, vanilla, and milk. Whisk together the flour, baking soda, salt, and cinnamon and stir into the sugar–egg white mixture. Stir in the oats, raisins, and walnuts, if used. The dough will be slightly softer than that in a classic recipe and will thicken on chilling, but chilling is not necessary; you can use it right away.

4. Drop the dough by the level tablespoonful on prepared baking sheets, spacing the cookies 1 inch apart. With dampened fingers, press slightly on the cookies to flatten the tops a little (the thinner they are, the crispier and more toasted the oats, the better the taste).

5. Bake the cookies about 15 minutes, until golden brown with slight darkening around the edges. The more they bake, the crispier they will be. Cool the cookies on a wire rack.

Nutritional Analysis (per cookie, with walnuts): 99 calories; 2 g protein; 3 g fat; 1 g satfat; 17 g carbohydrate; 97 mg sodium; 4 mg cholesterol

Light Touch

Most reduced-fat oatmeal-raisin cookies contain applesauce or another fruit purée to replace part of the fat; this produces a soft, rather sticky cookie with less than wonderful texture and taste. I finally settled on a formula similar to that used in my chocolate chip cookie: browned butter plus light cream cheese. The classic oatmeal-raisin cookie weighs in with about 33% calories from fat. This version (with walnuts) is only 25%; without the nuts, it is nearly half the original (18%). The only cholesterol comes from the cream cheese and the small amount of butter (plus 1% milk if used). The addition of walnuts contributes texture and flavor as well as 10 calories and 1 g fat per cookie.

Luscious Lemon Squares

Yield: Sixteen 2-inch squares

To succeed with this recipe you only need to know two quick steps and one important tip. First step: The crust mixture is blended together, pressed into the pan with your fingers, and prebaked. The tip: Be sure to press the pastry up the pan sides, forming a lip to contain the custard and prevent its leaking onto the bottom. Second step: The lemon custard is whisked up, poured onto the prebaked crust, and baked, but at a lower heat than before, to ensure a creamy texture. This is everyone's favorite recipe, every bit as good as the classic full-fat version.

Butter-flavor no-stick cooking spray

Pastry Crust

1¹/₂ cups sifted all-purpose flour

¹/₂ cup plus 2 tablespoons sifted confectioners' sugar

¹/₄ teaspoon salt

3 tablespoons unsalted butter, at room temperature

1 tablespoon plus 1 teaspoon canola oil

1 tablespoon fresh lemon juice

2 tablespoons water, or as needed

Filling

1 teaspoon packed grated lemon zest

3 tablespoons fresh lemon juice

1 cup granulated sugar

Pinch of salt

2 large eggs

Topping

2 tablespoons sifted confectioners' sugar

1. Position a rack in the lower third of the oven and preheat the oven to 350°F. Lightly coat a baking pan with cooking spray, line the bottom with wax paper or baking parchment, and spray the paper. Set aside.

2. Make the crust. In a large mixing bowl, whisk together the flour, confectioners' sugar, and salt. Use a fork or a wooden spoon to work in the butter, then the oil, lemon juice, and water. When pinched in your fingers, the dough should cling together like a pie crust; if too dry, add a few more drops of water. Turn out the dough into the prepared pan and use your fingers to press it into an even layer across the pan bottom and up the sides, making a lip about ¹/₂ to ³/₄ inch deep. If the dough sticks to your fingers, cover it with a sheet of plastic wrap before pressing.

Advance Preparation

Can be prepared 1 day ahead. Lemon Squares can be baked ahead, wrapped airtight, and frozen, but they never taste as delicate as when fresh-baked.

Special Equipment

8-inch square baking pan (not black metal); baking parchment or wax paper; small sifter

Temperature and Time

Pastry alone: 350°F for 20 minutes. Lemon Custard added to pastry: 325°F an additional 20 minutes

---

3. Set the pan in the oven and bake at 350°F for 20 minutes, until the pastry is opaque and the edges are golden brown. Remove the pan to a wire rack to cool and reduce the oven heat to 325°F.

4. Prepare the filling. Combine the lemon zest and juice with the sugar, salt, and eggs in a large mixing bowl and whisk until blended well. Note: If you prefer to use an electric mixer for this step, you will create a foam on the custard which will bake into a crisp, chewy top layer. This is also good, but makes it harder to cut neat slices.

5. Pour the custard over the still-hot pastry (it is also fine if pastry is cold, in case you prefer to bake it in advance) and set the pan in the 325°F oven to bake about 20 minutes, until the custard top is lightly golden and dry to the touch. No imprint of your finger should remain on the top. Cool on a wire rack.

6. When completely cool, sift confectioners' sugar evenly over the top of the lemon filling. Cut into 16 squares (4 on each side); to cut neatly, dip the knife in water and shake off excess before cutting.

Nutritional Analysis (per square): 143 calories; 2 g protein; 4 g fat; 1.7 g satfat; 25 g carbohydrate; 59 mg sodium; 33 mg cholesterol

---

Light Touch

The classic recipe for lemon squares has nearly the same number of calories per slice, but weighs in at 41% calories from fat, as opposed to my streamlined 26%. I have cut over one third of the total fat, half the saturated fat, and 10 mg of cholesterol from each slice, yet retained the rich flavor and appealing silken texture. Note: If you wish a richer crust, you can add 1 more tablespoon butter to it (use a little less water) to raise calories from fat to 29%.

RUGELACH

Rugelach are bite-sized crescent-shaped confections made of either a rich yeast dough or a cream cheese pastry rolled over a variety of sweet fillings.

I like to make rugelach with cream cheese pastry; my favorite fillings are Cinnamon-Nut and Chocolate, but you can be creative and invent your own using the proportions below as a guide. I prepare several different types of filling for one batch of dough, although you can triple any one of the filling mixtures to use with the entire pastry recipe. For the richest taste and appearance, be generous with the apricot glaze inside and on top of each piece, and don't forget to line the baking sheet with foil or parchment so the glaze doesn't stick. Note: I prefer to make the pastry for rugelach with all-purpose rather than cake flour to give it a little extra strength.

Butter-flavor no-stick cooking spray

Pastry

Double recipe Reduced-Fat Cream Cheese Pastry (page 47), made with 2 cups unsifted *all-purpose* flour (not cake flour)

Glaze

¹/₃ cup apricot preserves

1 tablespoon fresh orange juice or water

Topping

¹/₃ cup granulated sugar

Fillings *(each fills about 10 triangles)*

Cinnamon-Nut

2 tablespoons packed dark brown sugar

2 tablespoons chopped walnuts

¹/₄ teaspoon ground cinnamon

¹/₈ teaspoon ground nutmeg

Chocolate

1¹/₂ teaspoons unsifted unsweetened Dutch-processed cocoa

2¹/₂ tablespoons packed dark brown sugar

¹/₄ teaspoon grated semisweet chocolate

Apricot-Raisin

1 teaspoon granulated sugar

¹/₄ teaspoon ground cinnamon

8 dried apricot halves, finely chopped

2 tablespoons seedless raisins, finely chopped

Advance Preparation

Rugelach can be baked a day or two in advance, or wrapped airtight and frozen up to 3 weeks. The prepared but unbaked rugelach can also be wrapped airtight and frozen; bake, without thawing, for 5 to 10 minutes longer, until golden brown. They are best when freshly baked.

Special Equipment

2 cookie sheet(s) or other flat baking pans; aluminum foil or baking parchment; pastry brush

Temperature and Time

350°F for 20 to 25 minutes

---

1. Line the baking sheet(s) with foil or parchment, lightly coat with cooking spray, and set them aside. Prepare the pastry, divide it in half, wrap each portion in plastic wrap or foil, and refrigerate until fillings are prepared. Leave one half wrapped and refrigerated while working with the other.

2. Make the glaze by combining the preserves and juice or water in a small saucepan. Set over medium heat and stir until liquefied. Remove from heat. Strain into a small bowl if you wish (it looks more professional when strained, but I like the small bits of fruit). Place the glaze and a pastry brush near your work area. In a separate small bowl, set out the granulated sugar for topping.

3. Select your filling mixtures, noting that each mixture fills 10 or 11 pieces. Combine each mixture in a small bowl, tossing the ingredients together. Set a teaspoon beside each mixture.

4. Position racks to divide the oven in thirds and preheat the oven to 350°F. Working with one half of the dough, roll it out on a lightly floured surface to a 12-inch circle about 3/16 inch thick. Don't worry if the edges are a little uneven. With a large sharp knife, divide the circle into 16 even wedges (cut in half, then quarters, then eighths, then sixteenths). Leave the dough triangles in place where cut. Working with half the pieces at one time, simply brush the glaze over all, spread filling over glaze, then roll up from the wide end to the tip and place on the prepared baking sheet with the tip on the bottom. Brush more glaze over the top of each piece and sprinkle on a little granulated sugar. Repeat with the other half of the dough. Turn the ends down to make crescent shapes. Bake the rugelach for 20 to 25 minutes, until they are a rich golden brown and the sugar on top is caramelized. Cool on a wire rack.

Nutritional Analysis (per piece, glazed and sugared):

Cinnamon-Nut: 90 calories; 2 g protein; 5 g fat; 1 g satfat; 10 g carbohydrate; 95 mg sodium; 6 mg cholesterol

Chocolate: 87 calories; 1 g protein; 4 g fat; 1 g satfat; 11 g carbohydrate; 101 mg sodium; 6 mg cholesterol

Apricot-Raisin: 86 calories; 2 g protein; 4 g fat; 1 g satfat; 11 g carbohydrate; 95 mg sodium; 6 mg cholesterol

Light Touch

Cinnamon-walnut rugelach made with classic cream cheese pastry contains 66% calories from fat; by contrast, my lightened cinnamon-nut version with reduced-fat cream cheese pastry drops to 49% calories from fat and cuts out 27 calories, a little more than half the fat, four fifths of the saturated fat, and three quarters of the cholesterol per piece. The other fillings vary just slightly in fat content, ranging from 43% calories from fat (apricot-raisin) to 44% (chocolate). While these are all over 30% calories from fat, the per-serving figures are low and fit well into a reduced-fat diet.

WALNUT CRUMB BARS

Yield: Eighteen 2 × 2¹/₂-inch bars

This easy-to-make bar cookie is inspired by a popular 1950s cracker nut pie made with walnuts and crushed Ritz crackers mixed into meringue and topped with ice cream. The idea is good, but it makes a better cookie than a pie: chewy, quite sweet, and nutty. Hold the ice cream and serve with a dollop of store-bought cappuccino frozen yogurt. If you have a food processor or blender, process the crumbs first, then add and chop the nuts.

Cinnamon graham crackers are the most flavorful for this recipe; you can also make chocolate walnut crumb bars using chocolate graham crackers. To make the chocolate crumb bars without chocolate graham crackers, add about 3 tablespoons of Dutch-processed cocoa to the regular graham cracker crumbs.

Butter-flavor no-stick cooking spray (optional)

¹/₂ cup walnuts, finely chopped

Fifteen 2¹/₂-inch low-fat cinnamon graham cracker squares, crushed (1 cup crumbs)

1 teaspoon baking powder

4 large egg whites

Pinch of salt

Pinch of cream of tartar

³/₄ cup packed light or dark brown sugar

1 teaspoon vanilla extract

¹/₂ teaspoon almond or maple extract (optional)

Advance Preparation

The cookies can be baked a day ahead or wrapped airtight and frozen for a week or two.

Special Equipment

8 × 12-inch baking pan

Temperature and Time

350°F for 35 to 40 minutes

1. Position a rack in the center of the oven and preheat the oven to 350°F. Lightly coat a baking pan with cooking spray or line the bottom with baking parchment.

2. Place the nuts in a small frying pan and stir over medium heat for 3 to 4 minutes, until toasted and fragrant; don't burn. Transfer to a medium-sized bowl and toss with the crumbs and baking powder. Set aside.

3. In a large grease-free bowl, with clean beaters, whip the whites with the salt and cream of tartar until foamy. Gradually crumble in the brown sugar and whip until the whites are nearly stiff, but not dry. Beat in both vanilla and almond or maple extract if used.

4. Fold the nut-crumb mixture into the whites in several additions. Spread the mixture evenly in the prepared pan and bake 35 to 40 minutes, until the top is golden and slightly springy and dry to the touch; a knife inserted in the center will come out clean. Cool on a wire rack. Cut into 18 bars; for neat slices, dip the knife in water and shake off excess before each cut.

Nutritional Analysis (per bar): 81 calories; 2 g protein; 2 g fat; 0.2 g satfat; 14 g carbohydrate; 76 mg sodium; 0 mg cholesterol

Low-fat graham crackers are available in supermarkets. A little almond or maple extract is used to bring up the flavor, since the original 1 cup of nuts must be reduced by half for our purposes. This flavorful cookie has no cholesterol at all and just 25% calories from fat; if you cut down the nuts to $1/3$ cup, you drop to 19% and eliminate 7 calories and a little over half a gram of fat per bar.

BERRY BARS WITH STREUSEL TOPPING

Yield: 12 medium-sized or 9 large bars

Quick, easy, and delicious, this is nothing more than your favorite jam sandwiched between layers of crunchy crumbs. Don't tell the kids these tasty snacks also happen to be nutritious; just tuck them into their lunchboxes. Note: Use any type of jam or preserves, homemade or all-fruit and sugar-free. Once I ran low on jam and successfully substituted for half the quantity ¹/₂ cup of drained crushed canned pineapple blended with 1 tablespoon of flour.

Butter-flavor no-stick cooking spray

Streusel

³/₄ cup sifted all-purpose flour

¹/₄ teaspoon salt

¹/₄ cup granulated sugar

¹/₃ cup packed light brown sugar

¹/₂ cup old-fashioned rolled oats (not quick-cooking type)

¹/₃ cup toasted wheat germ

¹/₃ cup Grape-Nuts cereal

2 tablespoons chopped walnuts

¹/₂ teaspoon ground cinnamon

1 teaspoon vanilla extract

¹/₂ teaspoon almond extract

2 tablespoons canola or walnut oil

1 tablespoon skim milk or fruit juice

1 large egg white

Filling

¹/₂ cup raspberry preserves

¹/₂ cup blueberry preserves

1 tablespoon grated lemon zest

1 tablespoon fresh lemon juice

¹/₂ teaspoon ground cinnamon

1. Position a rack in the center of the oven and preheat the oven to 350°F. Lightly coat a baking pan with cooking spray and set it aside.

2. In a large bowl, toss together all the streusel ingredients to form crumbs. Add 1 more tablespoon of skim milk if the crumbs are too powdery. Press 1³/₄ cups of the crumbs into an even layer on the bottom of the pan. Bake 18 minutes, until golden brown.

3. In a medium-sized bowl, blend together the filling ingredients, then spread the filling over the hot prebaked streusel. Top with the remaining

---

Advance Preparation

The bars can be baked a couple of days ahead, or double-wrapped and frozen up to 1 week.

Special Equipment

8- or 9-inch square baking pan

Temperature and Time

350°F for 18 minutes for bottom layer of crumbs, plus 15 to 18 additional minutes after adding topping

---

streusel crumbs in a more-or-less even layer; don't pack down, and don't worry if some jam peeks through crumbs on top.

4. Bake 15 to 18 minutes longer, until the top is golden brown. Cool on a wire rack. Cut into squares or bars while still warm, but don't try to lift squares from the pan until completely cold or they will crumble.

Nutritional Analysis (per medium-sized bar): 209 calories; 4 g protein; 4 g fat; 0.4 g satfat; 41 g carbohydrate; 76 mg sodium; 0 mg cholesterol

Light Touch

The trick here was to create a tasty butter-free, cholesterol-free crumb blend that held together well and remained crisp. The binding is now supplied by the egg white, the butter is replaced by a little oil, and flavor is enhanced with extracts, cinnamon, and just a few nuts. We have dropped about 100 calories, all the cholesterol, and nearly two thirds the fat per bar. Calories from fat are reduced 63% (to 16% from the original 43%), with a bonus of 2 g dietary fiber in each bar.

PINEAPPLE BARS

Yield: 4 cups batter; 24 bars (1¹/₂ × 3 inches)

This moist chewy bar cookie is perfect for a quick energy pick-up or a lunchbox snack. Children love to make this recipe because it is so easy to beat with a wooden spoon, and the not-too-sweet pineapple flavor is appealing; don't tell them that the whole wheat flour and wheat germ are nutritious. You can also make this as a sheet cake, glazed with confectioners' sugar mixed with pineapple juice.

Butter-flavor no-stick cooking spray

1 cup unsifted whole wheat flour

1¹/₄ cups sifted all-purpose flour

2 teaspoons baking powder

¹/₂ teaspoon salt

³/₄ cup granulated sugar

³/₄ cup packed light brown sugar

¹/₄ cup toasted wheat germ or regular oat bran

3 tablespoons canola oil

1 large egg plus 1 large egg white

1 tablespoon vanilla extract

1 teaspoon pineapple or orange extract (optional)

One 20-ounce can unsweetened crushed pineapple (do not drain; 2 cups including juice)

Topping

2 tablespoons confectioners' sugar

Advance Preparation

The bars will keep a week, wrapped airtight.

Special Equipment

9 × 13-inch baking pan

Temperature and Time

350°F for 30 to 35 minutes

1. Position a rack in the center of the oven and preheat to 350°F. Lightly coat the baking pan with cooking spray.

2. In a large mixing bowl, whisk together both flours, the baking powder, salt, both sugars, and the wheat germ.

3. In a medium-sized bowl, combine and mix well the oil, egg plus white, extracts, and pineapple. Pour this mixture over the dry ingredients and beat until well blended. The batter will be quite soft.

4. Pour the batter into the prepared pan and bake 30 to 35 minutes, until golden brown and springy to the touch and the cake begins to pull away from the sides. A cake tester inserted in the center will come out dry.

5. Cool the cake on a wire rack, then cut into 24 bars and serve from the pan. Sift a little confectioners' sugar over the top just before serving.

Nutritional Analysis (per bar): 87 calories; 2 g protein; 2 g fat; 0.3 g satfat; 15 g carbohydrate; 57 mg sodium; 9 mg cholesterol

This recipe was inspired by a Pineapple Amish Cake I first tasted in a restaurant in Lancaster County, Pennsylvania. Sometime later I found a similar "Amish Cake" in a cookbook published by The Shipley School of Bryn Mawr, Pennsylvania (*Food for Thought: Just Desserts*, Wimmer, 1988). That plain, fairly spartan cake was made without fat, but it had a secret weapon: icing made with confectioners' sugar plus 1/2 cup butter and 8 ounces cream cheese, to rate 34% calories from fat. Without the cream cheese icing, and with adjustments including the addition of a small amount of oil to improve the texture, I cut more than half the calories, three quarters of the fat, and all but a trace of the satfat to reach 23% calories from fat.

Liz's Gluten-Free Bionic Bars

Yield: sixteen 2-inch-square bars

Liz Reed and Beth Hillson create special recipes for customers at Beth's mail-order company, the Gluten-Free Pantry (see page 373). Gluten-free baking, which substitutes a blend of nonwheat flours, can often be high in fat; however, these clever ladies have managed to lower the fat content of many gluten-free recipes including Liz's gingerbreadlike Bionic Bars, which are moist, soft, and lightly spiced. Liz points out that brown rice flour (sold in natural foods stores and available from the Gluten-Free Pantry) is the best choice here because its granular texture gives a good mouth-feel while white rice flour tends to get gummy. The unusual addition of puréed beans contributes moisture, body, and fiber.

Butter-flavor no-stick cooking spray

One 19-ounce can cannellini beans (white kidney beans), drained but not rinsed

1 large egg

¼ cup canola oil

⅔ cup unsweetened applesauce

⅓ cup nonfat dry milk

⅓ cup lightly packed light brown sugar

¾ cup brown rice flour

¼ cup potato flour (potato starch)

1 teaspoon baking soda

½ teaspoon salt

2 teaspoons ground cinnamon

¼ teaspoon ground cloves

½ teaspoon ground nutmeg

½ teaspoon ground allspice

¼ cup Zante currants or seedless raisins

¼ cup golden raisins

Advance Preparation

Bars can be double-wrapped and refrigerated 3 to 4 days or frozen up to 2 weeks.

Special Equipment

8 × 8-inch baking pan

Temperature and Time

350°F for 30 minutes

1. Position a rack in the center of the oven and preheat the oven to 350°F. Lightly coat a baking pan with cooking spray.

2. In a large bowl with a fork or potato masher, or in a food processor or blender, finely mash or purée the beans to a paste. Transfer them to a large mixing bowl and beat in the egg, oil, and applesauce. Mix in all the remaining ingredients.

3. Spoon the batter into the prepared pan and bake about 30 minutes, until the top is springy, the cake begins to pull away from the pan sides, and a

toothpick inserted in the center comes out with just a few clinging crumbs. Don't overbake or the bars will be dry. Cool in the pan on a wire rack for about 10 minutes, then cut into bars.

Nutritional Analysis (per bar): 141 calories; 4 g protein; 4 g fat; trace satfat; 23 g carbohydrate; 67 mg sodium; 14 mg cholesterol

Light Touch

These are not only gluten free, but they contain only 26% calories from fat. The applesauce replaces a portion of the fat and also supplies moisture and flavor; the bean purée and brown rice flour increase the dietary fiber to 1 g per bar.

GLUTEN-FREE ORANGE BISCOTTI

Yield: Twenty-two to twenty-four
1/2-inch-thick biscotti

These flavorful, crisp biscotti are a little denser than is traditional because they are free of gluten, a protein found in wheat flour. The recipe was created by my friend Beth Hillson, owner of the Gluten-Free Pantry (see page 373). Beth sells special foods and develops recipes for individuals who cannot digest gluten. Another common allergy is to wheat in general. Gluten-free recipes are helpful for both dietary restrictions.

Gluten-free recipes are characterized by blends of several types of starch, combined with respect to their individual qualities and flavors. White rice flour is available in natural food stores, many supermarkets, or from the Gluten-Free Pantry. Be sure to check the label on your baking powder, because some brands are not gluten free. Xanthan gum, available from the same supplier, is a powder used sparingly to bind gluten-free baked goods; guar gum, available in natural food stores, may be substituted. The gum makes the biscotti slightly less dry, but the recipe will also work without it.

Advance Preparation

Biscotti can be stored for a month in an airtight container or wrapped airtight and frozen.

Special Equipment

Cookie sheet; baking parchment or aluminum foil; pastry brush; serrated knife

Temperature and Time

First baking: 350°F for 25 minutes; second baking: 325°F for 15 to 20 minutes

Dough

1¼ cups white rice flour

2 tablespoons cornmeal

¾ cup cornstarch

1½ teaspoons baking powder

½ teaspoon xanthan gum or guar gum (optional)

Pinch of salt

½ cup granulated sugar

¼ cup (½ stick) unsalted butter, melted

¼ cup nonfat orange or vanilla yogurt, drained 15 minutes

2 tablespoons honey

Grated zest of 1 orange (2 to 3 tablespoons)

1 large egg

1 teaspoon orange extract, gluten free (optional)

¼ cup walnuts, coarsely chopped

Topping

2 tablespoons skim milk

1 tablespoon granulated sugar or packed brown sugar

1. Position a rack in the center of the oven and preheat the oven to 350°F. Line a baking sheet with parchment paper or foil and set it aside.

2. In a large mixing bowl, whisk together the rice flour, cornmeal, cornstarch, baking powder, xanthan or guar gum if used, and salt. Set aside.

3. In a second large bowl, beat together the sugar, melted butter, yogurt, honey, orange zest, egg, and orange extract, if desired. Stir in the nuts. Add the flour mixture and stir until smooth; add a tablespoon more cornstarch if the dough feels too sticky to touch. The dough will be quite soft; scrape it into a ball and divide in half. Set both portions on the lined baking sheet and cover with plastic wrap (so the dough won't stick to your fingers).

4. Working through the plastic wrap, shape each portion of dough into a log about 7 × 2$^1/_2$ inches; set the logs about 2$^1/_2$ inches apart on the baking sheet. In a cup, stir together the skim milk and sugar to make a topping glaze. Brush the top of each log with the glaze. Bake for 25 minutes, until golden. The dough spreads when it bakes. Cool the logs in the pan set on a wire rack. Reduce the oven heat to 325°F.

5. When the logs are cool enough to handle but still warm, remove to a cutting board and use a serrated knife to cut them crosswise into $^1/_2$- to $^3/_4$-inch-thick diagonal slices. Return the slices, cut side up, to the same baking sheet and return the pan to the oven to bake 15 to 20 minutes longer, just until golden. The longer biscotti are baked, the crispier and more crumbly they become. Cool the biscotti on a wire rack and store in an airtight container.

Nutritional Analysis (per biscotti): 112 calories; 1.4 g protein; 3 g fat; 2 g satfat; 19 g carbohydrate; 37 mg sodium; 16 mg cholesterol

---

Light Touch

With 27% calories from fat, these delicious biscotti are heart healthy and low fat as well as gluten free.

GLAZED GINGER TARTLETS

Yield: About fifteen 3¹/₂-inch oval barquette molds, or similar-sized tartlet molds

It is a temptation to call these "Surprising" Ginger Tartlets, because the sliver of fresh gingerroot layered between the crisp spice cookie and the shiny golden lemon glaze first surprises your tongue, then delights it. This Zen experience is the creation of one of my baking assistants, Lynnia Milliun, who assures me you can omit the fresh gingerroot if it is unavailable, though the result is not nearly as much fun. Lynnia bakes this dough in oval barquette molds, which are about 3¹/₂ inches long and approximately the size of a cookie. If you don't have a mold in this shape, any small round tartlet mold will do, or you can simply roll out the dough, cut it with any kind of cookie cutter, then bake on a lightly greased cookie sheet.

Dough

- 3 tablespoons unsalted butter, at room temperature
- ¹/₄ cup packed light brown sugar
- ¹/₄ cup dark corn syrup
- 2 teaspoons vanilla extract
- 2 cups sifted cake flour
- ¹/₂ teaspoon baking soda
- ¹/₄ teaspoon salt
- ¹/₂ teaspoon ground cinnamon
- 1¹/₂ teaspoons ground ginger or 1 teaspoon peeled and grated fresh gingerroot
- 1 tablespoon water, or as needed

- 1 small piece fresh gingerroot (about 1 × 4 inches), peeled
- Butter-flavor no-stick cooking spray

Glaze

- 1 large egg white
- 1¹/₂ cups sifted confectioners' sugar
- 1 teaspoon fresh lemon juice

1. Make the dough. In the large bowl of an electric mixer, cream together the butter, sugar, corn syrup, and vanilla. In a separate bowl, combine and whisk together all the dry ingredients, including ground or grated ginger. With the mixer on low speed, gradually add the dry mixture to the creamed mixture, alternating with water. Add a drop or two more water if needed to form a dough ball. The dough will be sticky. Remove the dough from the bowl and wrap the dough in plastic wrap or place in a plastic bag. Refrigerate about 1 hour, or overnight, to firm.

Advance Preparation

The dough should chill about 30 minutes to firm before use. It can be made 1 or 2 days in advance. Once baked, these cookies keep a week at room temperature; as they air-dry, they harden but then are delicious dipped in sweet dessert wine or coffee.

Special Equipment

Barquette molds, 3¹/₂ inches long, or similar-sized small tartlet molds in any shape; vegetable peeler; cookie sheet (optional)

Temperature and Time

375°F for 20 minutes

2. With a vegetable peeler or sharp paring knife, slice 15 long thin strips of gingerroot, each the length of a mold. Wrap the ginger strips in plastic wrap until needed.

3. Position a rack in the center of the oven and preheat the oven to 375°F. Coat individual barquette or tartlet molds lightly with cooking spray. Work with half the dough at one time, leaving the remainder in the refrigerator. On a floured surface, roll the dough about ⅛ inch thick. Gather several molds together side by side, set a sheet of rolled dough over the molds, then press the dough down into the molds and cut off the dough at the mold tops with your fingers. Repeat. Set one strip of ginger on top of the dough in each mold. Note: If you don't have enough molds, bake the ones you have, then cool them and continue.

4. Make the glaze. In a small bowl, cut the white of one egg with two cross-cutting knives to break up the albumen. Then measure half the white (1 tablespoon) and discard the remainder. Beat the half white with the sugar and lemon juice until completely smooth, thick, and spreadable, about the consistency of sour cream; add a few drops of lemon juice if too thick. With a knife or small spatula spread about ¾ teaspoon of glaze over the fresh ginger strip on each mold, covering the top completely.

5. For ease in handling, set a group of prepared molds on a cookie sheet. Bake about 20 minutes, until the glaze on top of the tart is golden brown. Peek in the oven after about 10 minutes; if the glaze is browning too fast, cover the molds lightly with a tented piece of aluminum foil.

6. Cool the molds on a wire rack. Remove the tarts from the molds, coaxing them out if necessary with the tip of a paring knife. Store in an airtight tin.

Nutritional Analysis (per barquette): 147 calories; 1 g protein; 3 g fat; 2 g satfat; 29 g carbohydrate; 71 mg sodium; 7 mg cholesterol

Light Touch

These high-taste cookies contain only 16% calories from fat. Although they have 147 calories, they deliver so much flavor that one is a satisfying serving.

GINGER-DATE WEDGES

This sophisticated lemon-glazed cookie is created from a flavorful mixture of ground dates and orange peel sandwiched between two crisp layers of ginger-spiced dough. I like to prepare it in a round cake pan, then slice it into thin wedges. You could also sandwich the filling between two rolled-out rectangles of dough and, after baking, slice it into diamonds or squares. If you love ginger, add 1 tablespoon peeled and grated fresh gingerroot or chopped candied ginger to the date filling.

Butter-flavor no-stick cooking spray

Pastry

1 recipe dough for Glazed Ginger Tartlets (page 26)

Filling

One 8-ounce package pitted dates

Grated zest of 1 orange, about 3 tablespoons

¹/₄ cup dark corn syrup

1 tablespoon water or any type fruit juice

1 tablespoon orange liqueur (Cointreau or Grand Marnier) or ¹/₂ teaspoon orange extract

Glaze

1 large egg white

1¹/₂ cups sifted confectioners' sugar

1 teaspoon fresh orange or lemon juice

Advance Preparation

The dough needs 1 hour to chill before being rolled out; can be prepared 1 day ahead. The recipe can be prepared several days ahead; it keeps 1 week at room temperature or, wrapped airtight, up to 2 weeks in the freezer.

Special Equipment

8 × 1¹/₂-inch round cake pan

Temperature and Time

350°F for 30 to 35 minutes

1. Prepare the dough and chill at least 1 hour, until firm enough to roll out. Lightly coat an 8-inch cake pan with cooking spray. Position a rack in the center of the oven and preheat the oven to 350°F.

2. On a well-floured surface, roll half the dough into a circle about ¹/₈ inch thick and fit it neatly into the bottom and up the sides of the cake pan. Or simply press half the dough into an even layer over the bottom and up the sides of the pan. Chill the remaining dough.

3. In a food processor fitted with the steel blade, combine all the filling ingredients and purée until a thick paste. Spread the filling over the pastry in the pan. Roll out the remaining dough and press over the filling.

4. Make the glaze. In a small bowl, cut the white of one egg with two cross-cutting knives to break up the albumen. Then measure half the white (1 tablespoon), discarding the remainder, and beat with the sugar and lemon juice until completely smooth, thick, and spreadable, about the consistency of sour cream. With a spatula or knife, spread all the glaze over the top layer of pastry.

5. Bake for 30 to 35 minutes, until the top glaze is golden. Check the pastry after 15 minutes; if it is browning too quickly, cover the top lightly with a tented piece of foil. Cool about 10 minutes on a wire rack; while still warm, cut into 12 wedges.

Nutritional Analysis (per wedge): 258 calories; 2 g protein; 3 g fat; 2 g satfat; 56 g carbohydrate; 94 mg sodium; 8 mg cholesterol

---
Light Touch

A small slice of this "grown-up" cookie packs lots of taste and texture but has only 11% calories from fat.

CHOCOLATE TULIP SHELLS

Yield: Ten to twelve 6-inch diameter tulips

*These crisp wafer cookies—*tulipes *in classic French confectionery—are quick and easy to make. In a matter of minutes you can mold them into dramatic tulip-shaped containers for berries or cream fillings. Tulips can be baked in the oven or made on a frying pan or electric griddle. Tulips made in humid weather may soften and lose their shape; to re-form the cup shape, see step 6. Note: Tulip shells are quite fragile: if you need to transport or store them, leave them in muffin cups or stack them carefully in a sturdy covered box. For decorative effects, you can "draw" with tulip batter to make flowers, stars, or other shapes to use as garnishes for desserts.*

Advance Preparation

To avoid the problem of the shells softening and losing their shape in hot moist weather, it is safest to make them a couple of hours before serving if possible. In cool dry weather, tulips can be baked ahead and stored 24 hours in an airtight container; or they can be frozen up to a week.

Special Equipment

Cookie sheets or electric frying pan or electric griddle; muffin tin with 2¹/₂-inch-diameter cups or 4 or 5 small juice glasses (1³/₄- to 2¹/₂-inch-diameter base); broad spatula or pancake turner

Temperature and Time

Oven baking: 400°F for 4 to 6 minutes. Electric frying pan: 350°F for about 5 minutes total

Butter-flavor no-stick cooking spray

¹/₃ cup unsifted cake flour

2 tablespoons unsifted unsweetened cocoa, preferably Dutch-processed

¹/₈ teaspoon salt

¹/₂ cup granulated sugar

2 tablespoons unsalted butter, melted

2 tablespoons canola oil

3 large egg whites

1 tablespoon water, or as needed

1 teaspoon vanilla extract

¹/₄ teaspoon almond extract (optional)

1. If wafers are to be made in the oven, position a rack in the center and preheat the oven to 400°F. Coat cookie sheets with cooking spray. (For making the wafers on a griddle, see step 6.)

2. Whisk together the flour, cocoa, salt, and sugar in a bowl.

3. In another bowl, whisk together the butter, oil, egg whites, water, and extracts. Add the dry ingredients and whisk until smooth.

4. Make only 2 to 3 wafers per cookie sheet, so they have room to spread. For each one, drop a very generous tablespoon of batter onto the sheet, then use the back of the spoon to spread it evenly into a 5- to 6-inch (or larger) round wafer without any holes or air bubbles. Leave several inches of space between wafers.

5. Bake the wafers 4 to 6 minutes, until the tops are dry and the edges are slightly darker than the center. Immediately remove the baking sheet from the oven. Place the sheet on a wire rack and use a broad spatula to lift each warm wafer, center it over an inverted jelly glass, and pinch the bottom into a cup form; or ease it down into a muffin cup, gently crimping the edges to form the cupped shape. Let the wafers set until completely cool and crisp (just a few minutes). (Note: Make one to test the correct baking time; if underbaked, they will not get crisp when cold.) Repeat, using up the remaining batter. If the wafers stick to the pan before you have time to lift them off, return the pan to the oven briefly to warm. Add a few drops of water if the batter thickens.

6. If making the wafers on an electric griddle, set the heat to 350°F; the cocoa makes them tend to burn if the surface is too hot. Coat the surface lightly with cooking spray. Spread the batter as in step 4, but don't make the wafers too thin or they will tear when turned; experiment until you get the feel for the correct thinness. Bake the wafers 2½ to 3 minutes on the first side—the top should be dry. Lift one edge and peek under—the bottom should be browned. Flip the cookie over and bake 2 minutes longer. Shape into cups as in step 5 above; allow to cool completely.

7. If the wafers soften and flatten because of humidity, position them in muffin cups, easing them down into the cup shape, and rewarm them in a preheated 350°F oven for 3 to 5 minutes. Place the muffin pan on a wire rack and allow the wafers to cool completely in the cups; remove when crisp.

Nutritional Analysis (per tulip shell, unfilled): 106 calories; 2 g protein; 5 g fat; 1.8 g satfat; 14 g carbohydrate; 53 mg sodium; 7 mg cholesterol

Light Touch

Butter is basic to tulip shells, giving proper taste as well as texture. When half the butter is replaced by predominately monounsaturated canola oil, only 15% of the fat is saturated, but the calories from fat rise slightly from the classic 43% to 44% (because oil is 100% fat while butter is only about 80%).

While this recipe may seem high in fat compared to others in the book, it has only a few ingredients, and few of these contribute calories, so a high percentage of calories appears to come from fat. When the tulip shell is filled with fruit and yogurt or other low-fat ingredients as part of an assembled dessert (see Tropical Dreams, page 207), the total calories come from all the ingredients, and fat grams per serving will drop.

PASSOVER TULIP COOKIES WITH FRUIT

Yield: 10 to 12 tulip cookies about 5 inches in diameter; recipe can be doubled exactly

Made with matzoh meal and potato flour, these crisp cookie cups are suitable for the Passover holiday. They are made in a few minutes and can be baked on an electric frying pan or in the oven. You can drape them over a glass or press them in a muffin pan to form cups in which to serve fresh fruit. Note: Tulip cookies flatten and soften if the weather is humid. To recrisp, see step 5.

Butter-flavor no-stick cooking spray

Tulip Cookies

¹/₄ cup matzoh meal

3 tablespoons unsifted potato flour (potato starch)

¹/₈ teaspoon salt

¹/₄ cup plus 2 tablespoons granulated sugar

2 tablespoons unsalted butter, melted and cooled

2 tablespoons canola oil

2 large egg whites

2 teaspoons vanilla extract

1 teaspoon almond, lemon, or orange extract

2¹/₂ tablespoons water (only if using electric frying pan)

Fruit

3¹/₂ to 4 cups cut-up fresh (or well-drained canned) fruit or fresh berries (raspberries, for example)

¹/₄ cup granulated sugar, or to taste

2 to 3 tablespoons fruit-flavored liqueur or rum (optional)

Topping

1 tablespoon confectioners' sugar

Advance Preparation

In dry weather, tulips can be stored airtight at room temperature about 2 days. They can be stored frozen in an airtight container for up to a week.

Special Equipment

Cookie sheets or electric frying pan; 3 or 4 juice glasses with bottom diameter 1³/₄ to 2 inches or muffin tin with 2¹/₂-inch-diameter cups; pancake turner; sifter

Temperature and Time

Oven baking: 400°F for 4 to 6 minutes. Electric frying pan: 350°F about 5 minutes total

---

1. If using the oven, position a rack in the center and preheat the oven to 400°F. Lightly coat cookie sheets with cooking spray. (If using an electric frying pan, see step 4.)

2. In a large mixing bowl, whisk together all the dry ingredients. In a smaller bowl, whisk together all the wet ingredients. Then add the wet to the dry and whisk until smooth. Let the batter stand about 10 minutes, so the matzoh meal can absorb the moisture. If it stands longer and becomes too thick, whisk in 1 or 2 tablespoons more water.

3. If baking in the oven: Make only 2 to 3 cookies per sheet, because they spread. For each one, drop 1 level tablespoon of batter onto the sheet and spread it with the back of a spoon to a 5-inch round wafer without any air bubbles or holes. Leave about 3 inches between wafer. The thinner you spread the batter, the crispier and more tender the cookie. The bigger the diameter, the more graceful the cup shape (but the fewer you will get from the batter). Bake 4 to 6 minutes, until the cookies are dry on top and the edges are golden brown. Do not overbake. As soon as the cookies are done, use a broad spatula to lift each one and place it over an inverted juice glass or press it down to fit inside a muffin cup. Allow to cool in this position. Repeat with the remaining batter.

4. If using an electric frying pan, preheat the pan to 350°F and coat lightly with cooking spray. Spread 1 level tablespoon of batter into a 5-inch disk as above, and bake 2½ to 3 minutes on the first side. The top should be dry. Lift one edge and look under—the bottom should be golden brown. Flip the cookie over and bake the bottom until browned, about 2 minutes longer. Shape into cups as in step 3; allow to cool completely.

5. If the cookies flatten because of humidity, set them on a baking sheet and return to the 350°F oven for about 5 minutes and make flat cookies. To recrisp cup-shaped cookies, set them back into the cups of a muffin pan before returning to the oven. Cool cookies in the muffin cup pan on a wire rack.

6. Prepare the fruit. In a mixing bowl, toss the fruit with the sugar and liqueur, if used.

7. To assemble: Just before serving, spoon about ⅓ cup of fruit into each cup and sift on a tiny bit of confectioners' sugar. Note: Serve within the hour because the cups will soften if fruit stands in them too long.

Nutritional Analysis (per tulip without fruit): 105 calories; 1 g protein; 5 g fat; 1.7 g satfat; 13 g carbohydrate; 26 mg sodium; 7 mg cholesterol

Nutritional Analysis (per tulip plus ⅓ cup berries): 154 calories; 2 g protein; 5 g fat; 1.7 g satfat; 24 g carbohydrate; 26 mg sodium; 7 mg cholesterol

FUDGE BROWNIES

What makes a perfect brownie? A crisp, crunchy top with dense, chewy-moist fudgy interior? A slightly gooey mouth-feel that begs for a glass of milk? That is my idea of perfection, and this recipe has it all. Watch baking times carefully—overbaked brownies are dried out. Gooey and fudgy is better. Note: Regular Baker's brand chocolate gives good results, but brands such as Lindt, Ghirardelli, or Callebaut give an even richer taste, as does alkalized Dutch cocoa (Droste or Poulain, for example), used instead of regular unsweetened (Hershey) cocoa. The extra vanilla and pinch of nutmeg and cinnamon bring out the chocolate flavor.

Butter-flavor no-stick cooking spray

$1/4$ cup ($1/2$ stick) unsalted butter, cut up

1 ounce unsweetened chocolate, chopped

1 cup minus 2 tablespoons sifted cake flour

$1/2$ cup unsifted unsweetened Dutch-processed cocoa

$1/4$ teaspoon baking powder

$1/4$ teaspoon salt

$1/8$ teaspoon ground cinnamon

Generous pinch of ground nutmeg

$1 1/4$ cups granulated sugar

1 large egg plus 2 large egg whites

1 tablespoon vanilla extract

3 tablespoons water

Advance Preparation

Brownies can be baked ahead, wrapped airtight, and frozen for up to 3 weeks without flavor loss.

Special Equipment

8- or 9-inch square baking pan, preferably metal

Temperature and Time

350°F for 22 to 25 minutes

1. Position a rack in the center of the oven and preheat the oven to 350°F. Lightly coat a baking pan with cooking spray.

2. In a small saucepan, combine the butter and chopped chocolate and set over very low heat until melted. Stir the mixture and set aside to cool.

3. In a medium-sized mixing bowl, whisk together the flour, cocoa, baking powder, salt, cinnamon, and nutmeg.

4. Measure the sugar into the large bowl of an electric mixer and beat in the cooled butter-chocolate mixture. Add the egg plus whites, vanilla, and water and beat well. Add the dry ingredients and mix on low speed just until blended. Don't overbeat. The batter will be thick.

5. Spoon the batter into the prepared pan, smooth the top, and bake for 22 to 25 minutes; 23 minutes is usually right for me. When done, the top will look dry and a wooden pick inserted near the edge will come out with a few crumbs but the center will look slightly gooey. Cool in the pan and cut into squares.

Nutritional Analysis (per brownie): 130 calories; 2 g protein; 4.8 g fat; 2 g satfat; 22 g carbohydrate; 70 mg sodium; 22 mg cholesterol

I have been trying for a couple of years to produce a brownie worthy of the name with less fat and less solid chocolate. My taste testers finally agree that this is it—a great brownie they would never suspect of being lower in anything. I have cut the classic 58% down to 31% calories from fat and eliminated 87 calories, 10 g fat, and 22 mg cholesterol from each brownie.

When traditional proportions are disrupted, textures become moist and cakey at best or dry, insipid, and tough at worst. Some trials, however, resulted in delicious cake like Midnight Chocolate Cake (page 147) and Cocoa Cake (page 149). One rule emerged clearly: The fewer ingredients, the better the brownie. Avoid the usual low-fat stand-ins: applesauce, yogurt, corn syrup, canola oil. Use butter, but less, and replace most of the solid chocolate with rich-tasting Dutch-processed cocoa; retain at least 1 ounce of solid chocolate, however, for a more complex chocolate taste. A few tricks: Cake flour produced a more tender crumb than all-purpose, and melting the butter with the chocolate, as opposed to creaming the solid butter with the sugar, gave a fudgier crumb. A touch of baking powder seems to enhance the crunch of the top crust.

Faced with the choice of adding high-fat chopped nuts or keeping the ¼ cup butter, there was no contest; nuts put us over the top in fat content. However, if you feel deprived without them, sprinkle about 3 tablespoons of finely chopped walnuts on top before baking; the changes are modest: 33% calories from fat, plus 9 calories and 1 g fat per brownie.

CREAM CHEESE MARBLEIZED BROWNIES

Yield: Sixteen 2-inch brownies

These rich, fudgy brownies are rippled with a creamy white filling that adds to their flavor and dramatic presentation.

Butter-flavor no-stick cooking spray

Chocolate Batter

¹/₄ cup (¹/₂ stick) unsalted butter, cut up

1 ounce unsweetened chocolate, coarsely chopped

1 cup minus 2 tablespoons sifted cake flour

¹/₂ cup unsifted unsweetened Dutch-processed cocoa

¹/₄ teaspoon baking powder

¹/₄ teaspoon salt

¹/₈ teaspoon ground cinnamon

Generous pinch of ground nutmeg

1¹/₄ cups granulated sugar

1 large egg plus 2 large egg whites

2 teaspoons vanilla extract

3 tablespoons water

Cream Cheese Filling

4 ounces light cream cheese, at room temperature

¹/₄ cup granulated sugar

1 tablespoon unsifted cake flour

1 large egg white

1 teaspoon vanilla extract

Advance Preparation

Brownies can be baked ahead, wrapped airtight, and stored at room temperature 3 days or frozen up to 3 weeks.

Special Equipment

8- or 9-inch square baking pan; wax paper or baking parchment

Temperature and Time

350°F for 22 to 25 minutes

1. Position a rack in the center of the oven and preheat the oven to 350°F. Lightly coat a baking pan with cooking spray, line the pan with wax paper or parchment, and spray the liner.

2. In a small saucepan, combine the butter and chopped chocolate and set over very low heat until melted. Stir the mixture well and set aside to cool.

3. In a medium-sized mixing bowl, whisk together the flour, cocoa, baking powder, salt, cinnamon, and nutmeg. Set aside.

4. Measure the sugar into the large bowl of an electric mixer and beat in the cooled butter-chocolate mixture. Add the egg plus whites, the vanilla, and water and beat well. Add the dry ingredients and mix on low speed just until blended. Don't overbeat.

5. Prepare the cream cheese filling. In a medium-sized or small mixing bowl, beat together well the cream cheese, granulated sugar, and flour.

When blended, add the egg white and vanilla and beat as smooth as possible. Don't worry if some tiny lumps of cream cheese remain.

6. Spread about two thirds of the chocolate batter in the prepared baking pan, covering the pan bottom. Spread the cream cheese batter on top. Swirl on the remaining chocolate batter, covering most but not all the white filling; it will not cover completely. With a table knife, draw S-shaped lines through the dark and light batters, creating a marbleized pattern.

7. Bake the brownies for 22 to 25 minutes, until the top is dry and springy to the touch. The cream cheese batter should still be white (not golden brown) and a wooden pick inserted about 1 inch from the edge should come out with just a few crumbs clinging to it; the center will still be slightly gooey. Do not overbake or the cream cheese batter will become tough. Cool in the pan on a wire rack, then cut into squares.

Nutritional Analysis (per brownie): 160 calories; 3 g protein; 6 g fat; 2 g satfat; 26 g carbohydrate; 113 mg sodium; 24 mg cholesterol

Light Touch

I have modified the classic brownie with 62% calories from fat by almost 50% (to 34%) and eliminated 198 calories, 20 g fat, 8 g satfat, and 70 mg cholesterol per bar. This is achieved by cutting back the chocolate and using cocoa, dropping the nuts, and drastically cutting the eggs, butter, and cream cheese. The result, however, is still luscious and dramatic.

BLONDIES

Yield: 25 bars about 1 1/2 inches square in 8-inch pan or 1 3/4 inches square in 9-inch pan

Thin chewy bar cookies with a rich, sweet buttery flavor, these are an updated version of old-fashioned blondies—brownies without chocolate. This is the essence of "high taste, low fat": you cannot eat just one, they are so irresistible.

To speed the procedure, you can chop and mix the ingredients in a food processor or blender, but they can also be mixed quickly by hand.

Butter-flavor no-stick cooking spray

1/3 cup halved or broken walnuts

1/3 cup vanilla wafer cookie crumbs (8 Nabisco 'Nilla Wafers, broken up)

1/3 cup Grape-Nuts cereal

1/2 cup sifted all-purpose flour

1 teaspoon baking powder

1/2 teaspoon salt

1 cup packed dark brown sugar

1 large egg plus 1 large egg white

2 tablespoons unsalted butter, melted

2 teaspoons canola oil

2 tablespoons Kahlúa, bourbon, brandy, or water

1 tablespoon vanilla extract

Advance Preparation

These can be made a day or two ahead, or wrapped airtight and frozen up to 2 weeks.

Special Equipment

8- or 9-inch square baking pan

Temperature and Time

350°F for 22 to 25 minutes

1. Position a rack in the center of the oven and preheat the oven to 350°F. Lightly coat a baking pan with cooking spray and set aside.

2. Combine the nuts, cookie crumbs, and Grape-Nuts in a food processor or blender and pulse until coarsely ground. Or chop the nuts and crush the cookies by hand, then mix them into the Grape-Nuts in a large bowl.

3. Add all the remaining ingredients and pulse 3 or 4 times, or stir together just to blend and moisten. Do not overwork.

4. Spread the batter evenly in the prepared pan and bake 22 to 25 minutes, just until the cake begins to pull away from the pan sides and a cake tester inserted about 1/2 inch from the edge comes out clean. The top will feel springy to the touch about 1/2 inch from the edge; the center may be a little softer. Cool in the pan on a wire rack. Cut into 25 bars (5 on a side); to get clean cuts, dip the knife in water first.

Nutritional Analysis (per blondie): 83 calories; 1 g protein; 2.7 g fat; 0.8 g satfat; 13 g carbohydrate; 74 mg sodium; 11 mg cholesterol

To cut the classic 47% calories from fat to 29%, eliminating half the cholesterol, half the fat, and more than half the saturated fat, I have dropped all but ¹/₃ cup nuts from my classic blondie recipe, substituted crushed cookies and Grape-Nuts for texture, and eliminated half the butter and one egg yolk to reduce the saturated fat.

To give the illusion of more nuts, you could put most of them in the batter but save a few to sprinkle on the top. If you cut out the top nuts and only use ¹/₄ cup, total calories from fat drops to 27%, but the amount of fat cut from each cookie is negligible.

Pastry

AND CRUMB CRUSTS, AND MERINGUE PIE SHELLS

Quick and easy, crumb crusts are the best choice for the beginner baker and the only choice for many reduced-fat nonbaked pie fillings. These fillings are creamy, and their total fat content usually cannot support the greater fat of a pastry crust.

I have included a variety of crumb combinations, some with little or no added sugar for those concerned with restricting sugar intake. I have varied the binding agents but usually include about two tablespoons of canola oil and a tablespoon or two of melted butter (for the incomparable flavor). Moistening is accomplished with honey, unsweetened apple juice or fruit juice, or water. Some crusts are also bound with egg whites and must be baked. Crumb crusts designed to hold nonbaked fillings must be firm enough themselves to withstand a cut and lift on the fork without crumbling. Most crumb crusts benefit from being baked a short time to give a toasted flavor and increased strength. They can, however, simply be pressed into place and chilled until firm.

To enhance the nutty flavor without using high-fat nuts, hazelnut or walnut oil may be combined with or used in place of canola oil, and half a teaspoon of almond or maple extract can be added to the mixture. For new flavors and textures, try experimenting with different crumb combinations, using healthy toasted breakfast cereals, homemade granola, crackers, and low-fat crisp cookies such as amaretti.

Crumbs tend to stick to your fingers when you are pressing them onto the pie plate. The old trick was to dampen your hands first; the new idea: spread a sheet of plastic wrap over the crumbs before pressing and spreading them out.

I do not indicate the nutritional analysis for pastry shells alone because they are always eaten together with a filling. However, for the sake of comparison, it is interesting to note that a classic crumb crust with about $1/3$ cup of butter has about 53% calories from fat. The recipes used here range from 41% to 48%, with a dramatic reduction in saturated fat.

REDUCED-FAT PIE PASTRY

When lowering fat in a pie crust, you quickly discover that you need a good proportion of fat for tenderness or you have flour and water, which makes a tough, stiff cracker. The one serious strike for health you can make, however, is to cut the saturated fat drastically by altering the amount of butter. A single conventional butter pie crust containing an egg yolk has about 60% calories from fat; one *unfilled* portion of pastry contains 141 calories, 9 g fat (4 g saturated), and 43 mg cholesterol. My All-Purpose Pie Crust contains zero cholesterol, 138 calories, and nearly the same amount of total fat, although only 0.6 g satfat.

In the search for this tender, flavorful, and low-fat pastry, the breakthrough worthy of celebration came when I learned about Elmira and Mary's Pie Pastry (*Have Your Cake and Eat It, Too*). This is a recipe that actually changes people's lives because it is so easy, tasty, and does not require a rolling pin. It is now one of my life's essentials and is included here as All-Purpose Pie Crust. Use it for everything.

I have tinkered with this recipe slightly to make a different version that is a little richer and easier to sculpt with the fingers. The result is Basic Pie Crust, which adds a small amount of low-fat cream cheese to the basic formula. Real Cream Cheese Pastry has always been a favorite of mine, and a requirement when making Rugelach. Since I was including these delightful pastries in this volume, my baking assistant Ann Martin and I developed Reduced-Fat Cream Cheese Pastry, which combines light cream cheese with a little oil plus butter in a new form: melted and browned to enhance its flavor, then chilled back into a solid. One year, a one-inch-thick file, and a few frayed nerves later, the taste and texture are splendid; this recipe has only about one third the fat of the original version.

ALL-PURPOSE PIE CRUST

Yield: Pastry for 1 single-crust 9-inch pie

This is my favorite reduced-fat pastry for nearly every occasion, unless otherwise specified in this book. This pastry is considerably easier to work with than any all-oil crust, and has a slightly flaky texture caused by the interaction of protein and sugar in the milk working with the starch in the flour. You can toss out your rolling pin—mix this dough right in the pie plate, and press it into place with your fingers! No work, no fail, quick and delicious every time! Note: In Have Your Cake and Eat It, Too, *this recipe was titled Elmira and Mary's Pie Pastry.*

1 cup unsifted all-purpose flour

$1/2$ teaspoon granulated sugar

$1/2$ teaspoon salt

$1/3$ cup canola or safflower oil

$1^1/2$ tablespoons skim milk, or as needed

Advance Preparation

Unbaked dough, wrapped airtight, can be stored in the refrigerator over-night. However, it is easiest to roll out when made immediately before use.

Special Equipment

9-inch pie plate

1. Combine the flour, sugar, and salt in a 9-inch pie plate or bowl and stir with a fork to blend. Drizzle the oil and milk over the mixture, and lightly toss it with the fork or your fingertips until crumbly. Pinch the mixture together; it should hold well. If too dry, add a few more drops of milk.

2. With the back of a spoon or your fingers, press or pat the dough evenly over the bottom, up the sides, and onto the rim of the plate; take care not to build it up in the corners but make the rim generous if you want to flute it. If the dough sticks to your fingers, cover it with a piece of plastic wrap before pressing out. You can also roll out this dough on a lightly floured surface or between two sheets of lightly floured wax paper.

3. Crimp the edges with the floured tines of a fork or pinch into a fluted pattern with your fingers. Refrigerate until ready to use per filling recipe.

To partially or completely prebake (blind-bake) the pie crust: Position a rack in the lower third of the oven, and preheat the oven to 425°F. Line the dough with a sheet of aluminum foil (shiny side down), and top it with a layer of pie weights (sold in bakeware shops) or dried rice or beans.

To partially prebake the shell: Bake for about 10 minutes. Remove the foil and weights and bake for an additional 3 to 5 minutes, until the dough is no longer translucent but has not yet begun to color.

To completely prebake the shell: Bake for about 10 minutes. Lower the oven heat to 350°F. Remove the foil and weights from the pie shell, and bake for an additional 10 to 15 minutes, until the pastry is golden brown.

BASIC PIE CRUST

A variation on my All-Purpose Pie Crust, this has the addition of a small amount of low-fat cream cheese that changes the taste and texture subtly and makes the pastry especially easy to handle and shape. The texture is tender and almost flaky, with fine taste. This can be mixed directly in the pie plate and pressed into place with your fingers (no rolling pin required!), or prepared in a bowl and rolled out on a lightly floured surface. To prebake, see page 45.

1¼ cups unsifted all-purpose flour

½ teaspoon salt

½ teaspoon granulated sugar

3 tablespoons light cream cheese or Neufchâtel cheese

⅓ cup canola oil

1½ tablespoons skim milk

Advance Preparation

Unbaked pastry can be wrapped and refrigerated overnight or wrapped airtight and frozen up to 1 month. Quality is best if made just before using and chilled 30 minutes before rolling out.

Special Equipment

9-inch pie plate

1. In the pie plate itself or in a bowl, combine and toss together the flour, salt, and sugar. Pinch in the cream cheese with your fingertips, blending it into small flakes with the flour. Add the oil to the milk and pour onto the dry ingredients. With a fork or your fingers, lightly stir the mixture until thoroughly moistened and crumbly. The dough should hold together like clay when pinched in your fingers; add a drop or two more milk if too dry. If you plan to roll out the dough, it is helpful to form the dough into a ball, cover with plastic wrap, and refrigerate about 30 minutes.

2. If you don't want to use a rolling pin, form the dough at this point without refrigerating. With your fingers, pat the dough into an even layer in the pie plate. If dough sticks to your fingers, place a sheet of plastic wrap over the dough before pressing. Take care not to build up extra thickness in the corners. Press enough dough onto the rim to allow for fluting, either by pinching with your fingers into a V shape or pressing with the floured tines of a fork.

REDUCED-FAT CREAM CHEESE PASTRY

Yield: Pastry for 1 single-crust 9-inch pie; for Rugelach, recipe can be doubled exactly, but use all-purpose flour

Classic cream cheese pastry, used for Rugelach and many other individual pastries, contains three ingredients: flour plus equal parts butter and whole-fat cream cheese. Obviously very rich (73% calories from fat), it is also delicious to taste and easy to handle. In short, too good to give up. I have been tinkering with a reduced-fat version for a long time, and finally have developed one with good taste and texture that handles well and has about one third the calories from fat (54%). Per serving (not counting any filling) it delivers 56 fewer calories, half the fat, a quarter of the saturated fat, and one third the cholesterol. The fat secret: butter that is melted, browned (to enhance its taste), then solidified, plus light cream cheese and a little monounsaturated canola oil. You can prepare this pastry any way you prefer—in a bowl, blended with fingers or fork, or in a food processor. The dough may crack slightly when blind-baked for a tart shell, but filling will cover this up. Note: Keep the cream cheese refrigerated until just before using.

2 tablespoons unsalted butter

1 cup unsifted cake or all-purpose flour

¹/₂ teaspoon salt

1 tablespoon granulated sugar

¹/₃ cup light cream cheese, cold

2 tablespoons canola oil

Advance Preparation

The browned butter must be chilled until solid—about 5 to 8 minutes in the refrigerator. The browning and chilling step may be done 1 or 2 days ahead. Unbaked dough can be made ahead, wrapped, and refrigerated up to 2 days.

Special Equipment

9-inch pie plate

1. In a small saucepan or frying pan, melt the butter over medium heat for several minutes until it begins to turn golden brown and have a nutty aroma. Watch carefully so it does not burn. Transfer it to a metal bowl (to avoid thermal shock) and place in the refrigerator for a few minutes until solidified.

2. In a large mixing bowl, toss together the flour, salt, and sugar. Scrape in the browned and solidified butter, add the cold cream cheese, and use your fingertips or a fork or pastry blender to work the fat into the dry ingredients, creating small flakes. Add the oil and stir with a fork until blended in. Alternatively, use the food processor. Pulse the dry ingredients, then add the cold butter and cream cheese and pulse until cut in. Add the oil and pulse just until the mixture looks sandy, beginning to form very small beads. Turn off the machine.

3. Pinch the dough between your fingers—it should hold together well. If made in the processor, it may at first look dry and crumbly, but the warmth of your hands will bring it together as you mold the dough into a ball. Wrap and chill the dough for later use, or roll it out on a lightly floured surface and fit it into a pie plate, or shape small pastries following individual recipes.

PHYLLO PIE SHELL AND PHYLLO CUPS

Yield: 9- to 11-inch pie shells, or 4-inch tartlet shells or phyllo cups

Phyllo (filo) is paper-thin pastry, a specialty of Greek and Middle Eastern bakers. It is sold frozen in supermarkets and specialty food stores in 1- or 1½-pound packages. When phyllo is layered with a little fat and sugar, it makes one of the best-tasting pastry shells I know, and is also one of the easiest to prepare; it actually takes more time to explain than to do. You can make regular pie-size shells or linings for tarts and tartlets, or you can shape cups baked in a muffin pan for individual servings. Don't be put off; once you get the idea, it's a snap to create a delicately flaky, elegant container for any unbaked pie filling or mousse.

When working with phyllo, be sure to keep the unused pastry leaves completely covered at all times with a sheet of plastic wrap or aluminum foil topped by a tea towel; phyllo dries out very quickly in the air.

The average sheet of phyllo is about 13 × 17 inches; depending upon the size of your baking container, you may be able to fold a sheet in half or even quarters before cutting. In any case, remove the number of sheets needed, then rewrap and refreeze extra sheets.

Phyllo Pie Shell

For each 9-inch pie shell: 6 circles phyllo dough, cut about 11½ inches in diameter

For each 10-inch pie shell: 6 circles phyllo dough, cut about 12½ inches in diameter

For each 11-inch tart shell: 6 circles phyllo dough, cut about 13 inches in diameter

For each 4-inch tartlet shell: 4 circles phyllo dough, cut about 6¼ inches in diameter

Butter-flavor no-stick cooking spray

3 tablespoons unsalted butter, melted (for 4-inch tartlet, use only 1½ tablespoons)

¼ cup confectioners' sugar (for 4-inch tartlet, use only 2 tablespoons)

1. Cut out the phyllo circles, selecting the size and number of phyllo sheets from the list above. Stack up the required number of sheets, place your pie plate or tart or tartlet pan upside down on the top sheet of phyllo, and, using the tip of a sharp paring knife, draw a freehand circle the size indicated, which is about 2½ inches beyond the rim of the container. Immediately cover the cut circles with plastic wrap or aluminum foil and a tea towel to prevent drying.

Advance Preparation

May be prepared a day ahead and stored air-tight.

Special Equipment

For pie shell: 2 baking pans of the same (or nearly the same) size to sandwich the layers in the oven so they do not lift in the heat; pastry brush. For phyllo cups: muffin tin; aluminum foil

Temperature and Time

Pie shell: 400°F for 10 to 15 minutes. Phyllo cups: 350°F for 7 to 10 minutes

2. Position a rack in the lower third of the oven and preheat the oven to 400°F. Coat the inside of the baking pan lightly with vegetable spray.

3. To assemble one shell of any size, place one cut circle of phyllo in the prepared baking pan. Spread the phyllo with a few dabs of melted butter, spray a couple of times with cooking spray, and sprinkle on a little of the sugar. Repeat, adding each layer and spreading with a little fat and sugar; do not coat and sugar the top layer.

4. Cover the top phyllo layer with a second pan of the same (or just slightly smaller) size to prevent puffing up. Bake for 5 to 7 minutes, until golden, then (using potholders) remove from the oven, flip the whole thing over so the bottom of the shell faces up, remove the top pan, and return to the oven to bake about 5 minutes longer, until the bottom of the shell is golden and crispy. Bake tartlet pans on a cookie sheet for easy handling. Cool on a wire rack. Return the shell to its original baking pan, bottom down. Cool completely before adding the filling.

Phyllo Cups (to make 8 individual cup-size servings)

Butter-flavor no-stick cooking spray

4 sheets phyllo dough

3 tablespoons granulated sugar

1. Position a rack in the lower third of the oven and preheat the oven to 350°F. Lightly coat the muffin cups with cooking spray.

2. Lay the sheets of phyllo flat on a work surface and cut them lengthwise in half. Then cut crosswise into thirds, making six pieces about $5^{1}/_{2} \times 6^{1}/_{2}$ inches from each full sheet. Cover the sheets with plastic wrap and a tea towel to prevent drying.

3. Place one of the phyllo squares into a muffin cup and press it down gently, easing it into the cup shape. Spray it lightly with cooking spray and sprinkle with a pinch of sugar. Add a second phyllo square, setting it on top of the first but slightly turned so the corners do not match up. Ease this second layer into the cup and spray and sugar it; be sure the spray reaches the edges of the phyllo. Add a third piece of phyllo, sprayed and sugared, completing one cup. Repeat, making a total of 8 cups each with 3 layers. Be sure the central cavity is as big as possible. To hold it in place, you can crumple a $2^{3}/_{4}$-inch-diameter ball of aluminum foil and set it into the bottom of each cup to hold space as it bakes.

4. Bake the cups for 7 to 10 minutes, until light golden brown and crisp. Remove from the oven and cool on a wire rack. Leave the fragile cups in the muffin pans until ready to serve.

5. Shortly before serving, carefully transfer each phyllo cup to an individual serving plate, spoon filling inside, and sift a little confectioners' sugar over the top.

MERINGUE PIE SHELLS AND INDIVIDUAL MERINGUE NESTS

Yield: One 9-inch pie shell or eight 3-inch meringue nests

Baked meringue can be shaped into a full pie shell, called a vacherin *in French, or made into individual cup or nest shapes (petits vacherins); both methods are given below. Pies made with meringue shells are also known as angel pies, presumably because the filling is surrounded by heavenly white clouds.*

Since this shell contains no fat, it is a good choice for a relatively high-fat filling. Select any nonbake filling or mousse, sorbet, or fresh berries (see Index).

Butter-flavor no-stick cooking spray

3 large egg whites, at room temperature

¹/₄ teaspoon cream of tartar

¹/₈ teaspoon salt

³/₄ cup superfine sugar

¹/₂ teaspoon vanilla or almond extract

1. Position a rack in the center of the oven and preheat the oven to 275°F. To make a full pie shell, lightly coat a 9-inch pie plate with cooking spray. To make individual meringue shells, line 2 baking sheets with parchment paper, brown paper, or aluminum foil and set them aside.

2. In the large grease-free bowl of an electric mixer, combine the egg whites, cream of tartar, and salt. Whip the whites until foamy, then gradually add the sugar and whip until the whites are shiny and soft peaks form. Add the extract and whip about 7 to 10 minutes longer, stopping occasionally to scrape down the bowl and beaters, until the sugar is dissolved and the meringue is stiff and shiny.

3. To form a full pie shell, spread the meringue onto the bottom and sides of the prepared pie plate. Using the back of a large spoon, spread some meringue up to the rim, forming a decorative edge. Alternatively, use a pastry bag fitted with a ¹/₂-inch star tip to pipe the meringue around the rim. Bake for 1 hour and 15 minutes, until firm and crisp. The meringue should remain white or pale beige; do not allow it to darken. Lower the oven temperature if browning starts. Cool the shell in the pie plate on a wire rack.

4. To form individual meringue nests, evenly space 8 large spoonfuls of meringue on the prepared baking sheets. With the back of the spoon, form into 3-inch-diameter nests with high sides. Or, alternatively, spoon and spread eight 3-inch-diameter disks of meringue, then use a pastry bag fitted with a ¹/₂-inch star tip to pipe high edges around each disk. Bake about 1 hour, until crisp and firm; do not allow meringues to darken in color. While still warm, remove them from the baking sheets and cool on a wire rack.

Advance Preparation

Meringue shells can be prepared ahead and stored, covered, in an airtight container for up to 1 week.

Special Equipment

Electric mixer with balloon whisk; 9-inch pie plate (for large shell) or 2 baking sheets and baking parchment, brown paper, or aluminum foil (for nests)

Temperature and Time

Pie shell: 275°F for 1 hour and 15 minutes. Meringue nests: 275°F for 1 hour

REGULAR AND LOW-FAT GRAHAM CRACKER CRUMB CRUSTS

Yield: About 2 cups crumbs; enough for 9- or 10-inch pie shell

Regular old-fashioned graham crackers are available in many flavors, from honey or cinnamon to chocolate; they have never been very high in fat. Recently, low-fat graham crackers have appeared in supermarkets. According to my analysis (with manufacturer-supplied nutritional data), one 2¹/₂-inch regular graham cracker square has 28 calories, 0.5 g fat, and 42 mg sodium; the same-size low-fat Keebler graham cracker has 24 calories, 0.3 g fat, and only 33 mg sodium. So there is some advantage in using the low-fat variety, though it is not great. The recipe made with low-fat crackers has only 1% fewer calories from fat; each slice has 0.4 g less fat and 7 fewer calories.

Low-fat and regular crackers can be used interchangeably in the crust; however, the flavor is brighter with the cinnamon graham rather than the plain or honey graham. Add a little cinnamon or nutmeg to your mixture if you can only find plain crackers. Store-bought regular graham cracker crumbs may also be used. For ease in measuring, four 2¹/₂-inch graham cracker squares makes ¹/₄ cup crumbs.

This recipe is designed for use with unbaked fillings. You can, however, fill this shell with fruit filling and bake the whole pie at one time.

The crumbs are bound with a little oil, butter, and just enough water to bring them together. The crust is baked for a few minutes so that it will hold together well when sliced. Baking is not absolutely essential, but it adds a toasty flavor and strengthens the crust.

Advance Preparation

Crust can be prepared, baked, wrapped, and refrigerated 1 day ahead or frozen for up to 2 weeks. Thaw before filling.

Special Equipment

9- or 10-inch pie plate or 8- or 9-inch spring-form pan

Temperature and Time

350°F for 8 to 9 minutes or chill to set instead of baking

Twenty-four 2¹/₂-inch regular old-fashioned or low-fat graham cracker squares (1¹/₂ cups crumbs)

2 tablespoons granulated sugar

¹/₄ teaspoon ground cinnamon (omit if using cinnamon crackers)

2 tablespoons canola oil

1 tablespoon unsalted butter, melted

2 tablespoons water, or as needed

1. Position a rack in the center of the oven and preheat the oven to 350°F.

2. Crumble the graham crackers into the workbowl of a food processor and pulse to form crumbs. Or place the crackers in a closed plastic bag and roll with a rolling pin to form crumbs. In the processor or in a bowl, combine the crumbs with all other ingredients and pulse or toss until crumbs are evenly moistened. They should hold together well when squeezed between your fingers; add a few more drops of water if needed.

continued

3. Turn the crumbs into a pie plate and use your dampened fingers or the back of a spoon to press the crumbs into an even layer around the pan sides. Spread the remaining crumbs evenly over the bottom and press flat. If crumbs stick to your fingers, cover the crumbs with a sheet of plastic wrap and press on the plastic to get a smooth, even layer. Freeze leftover crumbs.

4. Bake the pie shell in the center of the oven for 8 to 9 minutes, until *slightly* darkened in color. Cool completely on a wire rack before adding a chilled filling.

LOW-SUGAR GRAHAM CRACKER CRUMB CRUST

Yield: About 2 cups crumbs; enough for a 9- or 10-inch pie shell

There is no sugar added to this crust made with low-fat graham crackers (which do contain some sugar) flavored with unsweetened frozen apple juice concentrate. This pie shell may be prebaked before being filled with an unbaked filling, or it may be chilled until firm without being baked.

> **Twenty-four 2¹/₂-inch low-fat honey or cinnamon graham cracker squares (1¹/₂ cups crumbs)**
>
> **1 tablespoon unsalted butter, melted**
>
> **2 tablespoons canola oil**
>
> **1 tablespoon frozen unsweetened apple juice concentrate, thawed but not diluted**

Advance Preparation

Crust can be prepared 1 day ahead.

Special Equipment

9- or 10-inch pie plate

Temperature and Time

350°F for 8 to 9 minutes or chill to set instead of baking

1. If you are to bake the pie shell, position a rack in the center of the oven and preheat the oven to 350°F.

2. Crumble the graham crackers into the workbowl of a food processor and pulse to form crumbs. Or place crackers in a closed plastic bag and crush with a rolling pin. In the processor or in a bowl, combine the crumbs with all the other ingredients and pulse or toss until crumbs are evenly moistened. They should hold together well when squeezed between your fingers; add a drop or two more juice if needed.

3. Turn the crumbs into the pie plate, cover with a piece of plastic wrap (to keep crumbs from sticking to your fingers), and press the crumbs into an even layer in the pan.

4. Chill the shell or bake it for 8 to 9 minutes, until *slightly* darkened in color. Cool completely on a wire rack before adding a chilled filling.

GINGERSNAP–GRAHAM CRACKER CRUMB CRUST

Yield: About 1¹/₂ cups crumbs; enough for a 9-inch pie shell

The bright flavor of this crust comes from blending graham crackers with gingersnaps. Grape-Nuts cereal is added in place of nuts for a little crunch; their toughness is cut by pulsing them in the food processor while making the crumbs.

Seven 2¹/₂-inch low-fat or regular graham cracker squares, preferably cinnamon flavored (about ¹/₂ cup crumbs)

8 gingersnaps

¹/₂ cup Grape-Nuts cereal

1 tablespoon unsalted butter, melted

2 tablespoons canola oil

2 tablespoons honey

1 tablespoon water, only if needed

Advance Preparation

Crust can be prepared 1 day ahead.

Special Equipment

9-inch pie plate

Temperature and Time

350°F for 8 to 9 minutes or chill to set instead of baking

1. Position a rack in the center of the oven and preheat the oven to 350°F.

2. Crumble the graham crackers and gingersnaps into the workbowl of a food processor, add the Grape-Nuts, and pulse to form crumbs. Or place the crackers, gingersnaps, and Grape-Nuts in a closed plastic bag and roll with a rolling pin to form crumbs. In the processor or in a bowl, combine the crumbs with the melted butter, oil, and honey and pulse or toss until the crumbs are evenly moistened. They should hold together well when squeezed between your fingers; add the water if needed.

3. Transfer the crumbs to a pie plate and use your dampened fingers or the back of a spoon to press them into an even layer around the pan sides. Spread the remaining crumbs evenly over the bottom and press flat. If crumbs stick to your fingers, cover the crumbs with a sheet of plastic wrap and press on the plastic to get a smooth, even layer.

4. The crust can be chilled to firm, but holds its shape best when sliced if baked slightly. Bake the pie shell in the center of the oven for 8 to 9 minutes, until just *slightly* darkened in color. Cool completely on a wire rack before adding a chilled filling.

GRAHAM–GRAPE-NUTS CRUMB CRUST

Yield: 1¹/₃ cups crumbs for 9-inch pie crust; 1²/₃ cups crumbs for 10-inch pie crust or 8-inch springform pan

The egg white in this recipe binds the crumbs well, but its presence also means the crust must be baked before serving. You can prebake the crust and use it with unbaked fillings, or partially prebake it, then bake it again with a filling that needs to be baked. The challenge is to keep the crumb crust from overbrowning, and the solution, depending upon the type of filling and length of time it is baked, is to avoid building up the crumbs into a high rim; they will brown less if they extend only a short distance above the top of the filling.

Note: The recipe calls for half an egg white; to measure, put the white in a dish and cross-cut it with 2 knives; reserve 1 tablespoon white.

Ingredients for making a 10-inch pie crust or 8 × 2-inch springform crust follow the basic recipe; the procedure is the same.

Advance Preparation

The unbaked pie shell can be prepared a day ahead, wrapped, and refrigerated. The baked shell can be prepared a day in advance and kept covered at room temperature.

Special Equipment

9- or 10-inch pie plate or 8 × 2-inch spring-form pan

Temperature and Time

Bake unfilled pie shell: 350°F for 7 minutes, then longer if needed according to specific recipe

Twelve 2¹/₂-inch low-fat or regular graham cracker squares (about ³/₄ cup crumbs)

¹/₃ cup Grape-Nuts cereal

2 tablespoons granulated sugar

1 tablespoon canola, hazelnut, or walnut oil

1 teaspoon unsalted butter, melted

¹/₂ large egg white (see Note, above)

1 to 2 teaspoons fruit juice or water, as needed

1. If the crust is to be prebaked, position a rack in the center of the oven and preheat the oven to 350°F.

2. Crumble the graham crackers into the bowl of a food processor and pulse until some crumbs begin to show. Add the Grape-Nuts and process until crackers are completely reduced to crumbs. Add the sugar, oil, melted butter, egg white, and 1 teaspoon of juice. Pulse until the crumbs are evenly moistened. Pinch a spoonful of crumbs together and test to see if they are moist enough to hold the print of your finger. If necessary, add a drop or two more liquid and pulse once or twice to blend.

3. Turn the crumbs out into a pie plate or springform pan and cover with a piece of plastic wrap (to prevent crumbs from sticking to your fingers). Spread the crumbs in an even layer around the sides of the pan and across the bottom.

4. If you will be using an unbaked pie filling, bake the shell now for 7 minutes, then cool completely. The crust firms and crisps as it cools.

5. If you will be using a filling that must be baked, refrigerate the pie shell until ready to fill and bake. Or partially prebake it, for extra firmness, at 350°F for about 5 minutes.

Ingredients for 10-inch Pie Shell or 8 × 2-inch Springform Crust

Sixteen 2¹/₂-inch graham cracker squares (about 1 cup crumbs)

¹/₂ cup Grape-Nuts cereal

2 tablespoons granulated sugar

1 tablespoon canola, hazelnut, or walnut oil

2 teaspoons unsalted butter

1 large egg white

1 tablespoon fruit juice or water

CHOCOLATE CRUMB CRUST

Yield: About 1¹/₂ cups crumbs; enough for a 9-inch pie shell or six 3-inch tartlet shells

You can make this crumb crust with homemade crisp Chocolate Cookies (see page 8) or with Nabisco chocolate wafers or chocolate graham crackers, which are also quite low in fat. This crust can be filled without baking or, for added strength, it can be baked at 350°F for 8 minutes, then chilled before adding a cold filling. Note: For a 10-inch pie shell, use about 30 chocolate wafers or 28 chocolate graham cracker squares (about 1³/4 cups crumbs) and add 1 or 2 tablespoons more water, as needed.

Twenty-five crisp chocolate wafer cookies (about 8 ounces), or twenty-four 2¹/₂-inch low-fat chocolate graham cracker squares, broken up (about 1¹/₂ cups crumbs)

2 tablespoons canola or sunflower oil

1 tablespoon unsalted butter, melted

¹/₈ teaspoon ground cinnamon

1 tablespoon skim milk or water, or as needed

Advance Preparation

Crust can be prepared several hours ahead and refrigerated before being filled. It does not need to be baked.

Special Equipment

9-inch pie plate

Temperature and Time

350°F for 8 minutes or chill to set instead of baking

1. Place broken cookies in the workbowl of a food processor and pulse to form crumbs. Or place cookies in a closed plastic bag and roll with a rolling pin to form crumbs. In the processor or in a bowl, combine the crumbs with all the other ingredients and pulse or toss until the crumbs are evenly moistened. They should hold together well when squeezed between your fingers; add a few drops more liquid if needed.

2. Turn out the crumbs into the pie plate, cover with a piece of plastic wrap if desired (to prevent crumbs from sticking to your fingers), and press the crumbs into an even layer around the pan sides. Spread the remaining crumbs evenly over the bottom and press flat. Chill the crust until ready to fill or bake as indicated above.

Cobblers,
CRISPS, CRUMBLES,
AND PIES

Add a few pastry crumbs to the top of some sweetened fruit, shake on a tad of cinnamon, and you create irresistible magic. Strong men weep. "Motherhood and apple pie" is not a cliché for nothing. Remember the young thing who "baked Billy Boy a cherry pie quick as you could wink an eye"? I was reminded of those song lyrics recently when I heard some friends in Vermont refer to blueberry pie as "Boycatcher Pie." Just to confirm popular wisdom, a 1996 study by the Smell and Taste Treatment and Research Foundation in Chicago exposed a group of male volunteers to a selection of scents while monitoring blood flow to their erogenous zones. The most stimulating fragrance: pumpkin pie with cinnamon and nutmeg, and pumpkin pie mixed with lavender (a pie idea there?).

Few can resist a pie, or anything in its family, including cobblers, crisps, and crumbles. What is the difference between them? A cobbler has a biscuit dough simmered directly on top of the sweetened fruit, giving it a "cobbled" or patched appearance. Crisps and crumbles have sweet crunchy crumbs baked onto the fruit filling.

All of these are quick and easy to make, just a slap-dash to assemble with any combination of fruit available. These are the treats for lazy morning brunches or easy family get-togethers; for best flavor, serve these treats warm from the oven and add a dollop of vanilla or plain yogurt alongside. With slightly more effort and a touch of class, you can top your fruit with pastry and call it a pie . . . that's where the boycatching part comes in.

The following recipes are guaranteed to win your lover's heart but not stop it! To reduce fat without losing flavor, start by eliminating the bottom crust, automatically halving the fat from pastry. Or make a wide-spaced lattice pastry, or bake a decorative pie crust "cookie" or two to set on top of the fruit mixture instead of a solid top crust. Instead of thin two-crust pies, make hearty deep-dish fruit mixtures.

Fruit pies in every form are my favorites, so this is a section with over twenty-eight recipes and lots of variety. First the quick and casual: Apple-Pear-Plum Low-Sugar Fruit Crisp and a couple of cobblers (Strawberry-Rhubarb and Deep-Dish Blueberry-Honey), and an Apple and Honey Crumble for Passover made with matzoh meal crumbs that taste delicious. Apples are essential, from classic Brown Betty and rich Apple–Golden Raisin–Honey Pie to a basic but tasty apple pie with no sugar added. I have taken an "enlightened" look at regional American pie favorites, including Pecan, Vermont Maple Walnut, Buttermilk Chess, Southern Sweet Potato, and a drop-dead Mississippi Mud Pie. In the "old favorites" department there are two pumpkin pies, Lemon Meringue, Key Lime, Fresh Cherry Clafouti, and Vermont Blueberry Pie. To answer a challenging reader who defied me to make a scrumptious creamy *and* low-fat pie, I created Banana Split Pie, Chocolate Cream Pie with Meringue Topping, Coconut Cream, Strawberry Cream, Mandarin Mousse, Peaches 'n' Cream, and romantic Valentine Heart Tarts, plus decadent Chocolate-Caramel Turtle Tartlets.

If you want something dazzling and delectable but made in minutes, try Tortilla Tarts or Burrito Blintzes. Last but not least, for Independence Day, try my Red-White-and-Blue Fourth of July Pie or the Fourth of July Firecracker Pie—it contains a secret ingredient that will bite you back!

STRAWBERRY-RHUBARB COBBLER

Yield: One 10-inch cobbler; 8 or 9 servings

An old-fashioned favorite: flavorful fruit compote topped by tender lemon-scented biscuits. This easy family-style dessert can also be served warm from the oven.

The technique for preparing cobblers can vary. Some are made entirely in a skillet, with the dough added to the fruit, then covered and cooked on the stovetop; the dough remains soft on top. I prefer to cook the fruit in a saucepan, then put it in a pie plate, top it with the cobbler dough, and bake it in the oven so the top is a crisp golden brown. The texture of the baked topping perfectly complements the soft juiciness of the fruit. For Old-Fashioned Deep-Dish Blueberry-Honey Cobbler, see the variation.

Advance Preparation

The fruit can be prepared and simmered ahead, then reheated just before adding the biscuit topping, baking, and serving.

Special Equipment

10-inch deep-dish pie plate

Temperature and Time

375°F for 30 minutes

Fruit

- ³/₄ pound rhubarb stalks, scrubbed, trimmed, and cut into 1-inch pieces (generous 2¹/₂ cups)
- 1 quart (about 4 cups) whole ripe strawberries, rinsed, hulled, and patted dry
- ¹/₄ cup packed dark brown sugar
- ¹/₂ cup granulated sugar, or to taste depending on sweetness of berries
- ¹/₂ teaspoon ground cinnamon
- 1 teaspoon grated orange zest (optional)
- ¹/₂ cup fresh orange juice, divided
- 2 tablespoons cornstarch

Cobbler Dough

- 1 large egg
- 1 tablespoon unsalted butter, melted
- 1 tablespoon canola oil
- ¹/₂ cup buttermilk, or ¹/₂ cup 1% milk plus 1 tablespoon fresh lemon juice
- 1 teaspoon grated lemon zest
- 1¹/₄ cups unsifted all-purpose flour
- 1 teaspoon baking powder
- ¹/₈ teaspoon baking soda
- ¹/₄ teaspoon salt
- 3 tablespoons granulated sugar
- ¹/₂ teaspoon ground nutmeg

Topping

- 2 tablespoons granulated or pearl sugar

continued

1. Position a rack in the center of the oven and preheat the oven to 375°F.

2. Prepare the fruit and place it in a large nonreactive saucepan. If the berries are large, cut them in half. Add to the fruit the sugars, cinnamon, grated orange zest, and ¼ cup of the orange juice. Set the pan over medium heat, cover, and simmer 10 to 15 minutes, until the fruit is soft.

3. While the fruit simmers, prepare the cobbler dough: In a large mixing bowl, beat together the egg, melted butter, oil, milk, and grated lemon zest. Add the dry ingredients all at once, then stir just until moistened and combined; don't overbeat. Set aside.

4. Dissolve the cornstarch in the remaining ¼ cup of orange juice and stir it into the fruit mixture. Boil for 1 minute, stirring, until the juice is thickened and no longer cloudy. Remove from the heat and pour the mixture into an ungreased 10-inch pie plate.

5. Drop the dough by the tablespoonful onto the top of the fruit mixture. You should have about 9 mounds of dough, with a little space between each. Sprinkle a bit of granulated or pearl sugar on top of the dough, then set the pie plate in the preheated oven to bake about 30 minutes, until the top is golden brown. Set on a wire rack to cool until it stops bubbling. Serve warm, spooning the cobbler directly from the baking pan. Add yogurt if desired.

Nutritional Analysis (per serving): 274 calories; 5 g protein; 4.5 g fat; 1 g satfat; 56 g carbohydrate; 150 mg sodium; 31 mg cholesterol

OLD-FASHIONED DEEP-DISH BLUEBERRY-HONEY COBBLER

Yield: One 9-inch crisp; 10 servings

Note: Individuals with diabetes can omit the sugar in the berry mixture, biscuit dough, and topping; use very sweet berries. Prepare Strawberry-Rhubarb Cobbler with the changes below:

Fruit

6 cups fresh blueberries, picked over, rinsed, and patted dry

¼ **cup honey**

2 tablespoons granulated sugar, or to taste, depending on sweetness of berries

Generous pinch of ground cinnamon

1 teaspoon grated lemon zest

1 tablespoon fresh lemon juice

2¼ tablespoons cornstarch

½ **cup fresh orange or apple juice**

Dough

Same as on page 61

Topping

1 tablespoon granulated sugar plus ¼ teaspoon ground nutmeg

1. In a large nonreactive saucepan, combine the berries, honey, sugar, cinnamon, and lemon zest and juice. Set on medium heat and stir without mashing the fruit for about 3 minutes. Dissolve the cornstarch in the orange juice and add to the berries. Bring to a boil and boil for 1 minute, stirring, until the sauce thickens and is no longer cloudy. Taste and adjust sweetness if desired.

2. Turn the fruit into a 10-inch deep-dish pie plate. Prepare the dough, sprinkle on the sugar-nutmeg topping, and complete the recipe as above. Bake at 375°F for 30 minutes.

Nutritional Analysis (per serving): 279 calories; 5 g protein; 4.6 g fat; 1 g satfat; 57 g carbohydrate; 153 mg sodium; 31 mg cholesterol

---

Light Touch

Both the Strawberry-Rhubarb and the Blueberry-Honey cobblers have a mere 15% calories from fat. The per serving figures reduce slightly in the unlikely event that you want to share this with any more friends (thereby making your portion smaller).

APPLE-PEAR-PLUM LOW-SUGAR FRUIT CRISP

—Yield: One 9-inch crisp; 10 servings

You can use this as a master recipe to make fruit crisp with seasonal apples, berries, peaches, and/or plums, whatever is available. Select only the sweetest and ripest fruit; quality is even more important than usual because no sugar is added, just apple juice concentrate. This recipe may be helpful to individuals with diabetes or those on sugar-restricted diets; if you wish, however, use 3 tablespoons of any sugar-free all-fruit preserves or Steel's honey-flavor Nature Sweet (see page 323).

Fruit *(about 5 cups fresh fruit and raisins before cooking)*

2 Golden Delicious apples, peeled, cored, and thinly sliced

2 ripe Bosc, Anjou, or Bartlett pears, peeled, cored, and sliced 1/4 inch thick

2 or 3 large purple plums or 4 to 6 Italian prune plums, pitted and sliced (skins on)

1/2 cup packed golden raisins

1 teaspoon ground cinnamon

1/2 teaspoon ground nutmeg

1/4 cup frozen unsweetened apple juice concentrate, thawed but not diluted

2 tablespoons water or any type of fruit juice

1/3 cup all-fruit (sugar-free) fruit preserves (optional)

Topping *(makes 1 2/3 cups)*

3/4 cup unsifted whole wheat or all-purpose flour

3/4 cup low-fat graham cracker crumbs (made from twelve 2 1/2-inch squares)

1/2 cup unsweetened shredded wheat cereal (1 large biscuit, crushed) or old-fashioned rolled oats (not quick-cooking type)

1 teaspoon ground cinnamon

1/8 teaspoon salt

1/2 teaspoon almond extract

1 tablespoon unsalted butter, melted

1/3 cup frozen unsweetened apple juice concentrate, thawed but not diluted

1. Position a rack in the center of the oven and preheat the oven to 375°F.

2. Combine in a large nonreactive saucepan all the cut-up fruit, raisins, cinnamon and nutmeg, apple juice concentrate, and water. Cover and bring to a boil. Reduce the heat and simmer about 8 minutes, until the apples are

---

Advance Preparation

The crumb topping mix-ture may be prepared a day ahead, wrapped, and refrigerated. The fruit crisp tastes best the day it is baked.

Special Equipment

9-inch pie plate

Temperature and Time

375°F for 35 minutes

fork tender, but not mushy. (Cooking time will vary depending upon type of fruit used.) When done, pour the fruit through a strainer set over a bowl. Reserve the fruit (you should have about 4 cups); return the juice to the saucepan, stir in fruit preserves if used, and set it aside.

3. While the fruit cooks, prepare the topping. In a large bowl, combine all the topping ingredients and toss together until crumbs form. Add a drop or two more juice if needed.

4. Put all the drained fruit into the ungreased pie plate and set it aside. Place the reserved fruit juice over medium-high heat and boil it about 3 minutes, until it reduces to 3 to 4 tablespoons of thick syrup (watch carefully so it does not burn). Pour this syrup over the fruit in the pie plate. Sprinkle about half the crumb mixture over the filling and pat it down very gently. Scatter the remaining crumbs over the top.

5. Set a piece of aluminum foil (shiny side down) on the oven shelf (or on the floor of the oven if possible) to catch any drips of juice. Bake the pie for about 35 minutes, until the top crumbs are golden brown and the fruit below is tender when pierced with the tip of a sharp knife. Cool the pie on a wire rack.

Nutritional Analysis (per serving): 210 calories; 4 g protein; 2.6 g fat; 0.9 g satfat; 47 g carbohydrate; 84 mg sodium; 3 mg cholesterol

---

Light Touch

This fruit crisp has a very satisfying natural sweetness and really doesn't leave you craving more sugar. The topping adds 4.5 g dietary fiber per serving. Instead of moistening the crumbs with fat, I have used a tablespoon of butter for flavor and apple juice concentrate for moisture; only 11% of the calories come from fat.

PASSOVER APPLE AND HONEY CRUMBLE

Yield: One 9-inch crumble; 10 servings

Matzoh meal (instead of flour) is mixed with chopped walnuts to make the crumb topping; the texture is crisp and crunchy, and not too sweet. I use apples and pears for the fruit, but any fruit will do and dried fruits can be added: dried pears, apricots, or peaches are good with sliced apples, for example. Honey adds a mellow, rich flavor, but 3 tablespoons of granulated sugar can be substituted. Note: For Passover, be sure the margarine is marked "Kosher for Passover." Matzoh meal is available in supermarkets in the kosher foods section.

Fruit Filling

4 cooking apples, peeled, cored, and thinly sliced

3 ripe Bartlett, Bosc, or Anjou pears, peeled, cored, and thinly sliced

$^1/_4$ cup peach, apricot, or other fruit preserves

$^1/_4$ cup honey

$^3/_4$ teaspoon ground cinnamon

$^1/_4$ teaspoon ground nutmeg

3 tablespoons matzoh meal

2 tablespoons fresh lemon juice

3 tablespoons packed dark brown sugar

3 tablespoons currants or golden raisins

Crumb Topping (makes 1$^2/_3$ cups)

$^1/_3$ cup chopped walnuts

$^1/_2$ cup matzoh meal

$^1/_2$ cup packed dark brown sugar

Pinch of salt

$^1/_2$ teaspoon ground cinnamon

2 tablespoons cholesterol-free margarine, marked "Kosher for Passover"

2 tablespoons canola oil

1 tablespoon apple or other fruit juice

1. Position a rack in the center of the oven and preheat the oven to 350°F.

2. In a large nonreactive mixing bowl, combine and toss together all the fruit filling ingredients. Arrange the mixture in an ungreased pie plate and gently flatten the top.

3. To make the crumb topping, combine in a mixing bowl the walnuts, matzoh meal, brown sugar, salt, and cinnamon. Add the margarine and blend it in with your fingers (pinching it into flakes) or a fork. Add the oil

---

Advance Preparation

The crumb mixture can be prepared a day ahead, covered, and refrigerated. The crumble is best served the day it is baked.

Special Equipment

9-inch pie plate

Temperature and Time

350°F for 50 minutes

---

and juice and stir until crumbs form; add a drop or two more juice if needed. Spread the crumbs on top of the fruit.

4. Bake the crumble about 50 minutes, until the topping is golden brown and the fruit is tender when pierced with the tip of a knife. Cool on a wire rack.

Nutritional Analysis (per serving): 277 calories; 2 g protein; 8 g fat; 0.8 g satfat; 53 g carbohydrate; 46 mg sodium; 0 mg cholesterol

Light Touch

With just 25% calories from fat, this is a healthful and delicious dessert. It is made with matzoh meal for the Passover holiday, but it tastes good all year long. I have reduced the fat by about half from a classic crumb topping made with butter (53% calories from fat).

APPLE BROWN BETTY

Yield: 12 servings

Who, exactly, was Betty? As hard as I've tried to find out, her identity is still hidden under a mound of apple peelings. The recipe, however, is clearly related to fruit crisps, cobblers, and crumbles, as well as bread puddings. Betty became quite popular in America in the late nineteenth century, a warm, homey layering of sweetened, spiced fruit and crumbs. Variations abound: Some cooks use a blend of apples and pears, some mix tart and sweet apples, some use toasted bread crumbs, others leftover cookie or cake crumbs. Clearly this is a dessert where your own creativity can shine.

The following recipe is my adaptation of a brown betty shared by a very creative friend, Pat Schoenfeld, who likes to prepare easy but elegant desserts that can be presented in her own decorative handmade pottery. Pat combines different types of apples with raisins, brown and white sugars, spices, and a secret ingredient: vanilla extract.

This old-fashioned dessert is best served warm from the oven, with a dollop of vanilla yogurt (hold the whipped cream).

Butter-flavor no-stick cooking spray

Crumbs

About 3 cups low-fat or regular cinnamon graham cracker crumbs (from forty-four 2$^{1}/_{2}$-inch squares; 2 packages)

1 cup seedless raisins

$^{1}/_{4}$ cup ($^{1}/_{2}$ stick) unsalted butter, melted

$^{1}/_{4}$ cup fresh lemon juice

2 tablespoons apple or orange juice plus 1 tablespoon more juice or water, if needed

Fruit

8 or 9 large apples (half Golden Delicious or McIntosh and half Greening or Granny Smith), peeled, cored, and thinly sliced (about 8 or 9 cups)

3 tablespoons fresh lemon juice

Grated zest of 1 lemon

1 cup packed light brown sugar

$^{1}/_{3}$ to $^{1}/_{2}$ cup granulated sugar, depending on sweetness of apples

1$^{1}/_{2}$ tablespoons ground cinnamon

2 teaspoons ground nutmeg

$^{1}/_{4}$ teaspoon ground cloves

1 tablespoon vanilla extract

Advance Preparation

The betty is best served the day it is made. It can be rewarmed before serving at 350°F for 15 to 20 minutes.

Special Equipment

8 × 12-inch baking pan (5- to 6-cup capacity)

Temperature and Time

350°F for 30 minutes covered with foil, then 20 minutes, or longer if needed, uncovered

1. Position a rack in the center of the oven and preheat the oven to 350°F. Lightly coat a baking pan with cooking spray.

2. Prepare the crumbs. If making your own, break the crackers into the food processor (or into a heavy-duty self-sealing plastic bag). Crush into crumbs in the processor (or with a rolling pin). Turn the crumbs out into a large bowl and toss with the raisins, melted butter, and both types of juice. The mixture should form medium-sized crumbs that are neither pasty nor powdery; add a tablespoon of juice or water if necessary.

3. Prepare the fruit. In a large nonreactive mixing bowl, toss the sliced apples with the lemon juice and zest, both sugars, the spices, and vanilla.

4. Reserve about 1⅓ cups of crumbs for the topping. Sprinkle about ¾ cup of the crumbs on the bottom of the baking pan, top with a layer of apples, then alternate layers of crumbs and apples, ending with the reserved crumbs sprinkled evenly over the top.

5. Cover the pan with foil crimped lightly around the edges and bake for 30 minutes. Remove the foil and bake an additional 20 minutes, until the apples are tender when pierced with the tip of a knife and the top crumbs are golden brown. Baking time depends upon the type of apples.

Nutritional Analysis (per serving): 308 calories; 2 g protein; 5.6 g fat; 3 g satfat; 66 g carbohydrate; 162 mg sodium; 11 mg cholesterol

Light Touch

Pat's original recipe uses 1 stick of melted butter and contains only 24% calories from fat. By cutting out half the butter and using low-fat cracker crumbs, I have reduced the fat by 34%, to 16%, with a savings of 46 calories, 4 g fat, and 11 mg cholesterol. If you want a more severe cut, use just 2 tablespoons of butter and the result will be 11% calories from fat, 290 calories, and 4 g fat per serving.

APPLE–GOLDEN RAISIN–HONEY PIE

Yield: One 9-inch pie; 10 servings

A richly satisfying old-fashioned single-crust fruit pie heaped with apples and flavored with naturally sweet golden raisins, honey, brown sugar, cinnamon, and nutmeg. When juicy plums of any variety are in season, I like to add about a cup of unpeeled plum slices to this pie—they contribute a burgundy hue and extra flavor. There is only one crust, on the pie top. For a dazzling presentation, don't forget to brush the crust with egg white glaze and sprinkle with sugar just before baking.

Pie Shell

1 recipe Basic Pie Crust (page 46) but made with 1¹/₂ cups flour and just a few extra drops of skim milk to hold it together

Fruit Filling

8 large cooking apples (Granny Smith, for example), peeled, cored, and thinly sliced

¹/₂ cup golden raisins

¹/₃ cup honey

¹/₄ cup packed light or dark brown sugar

3 tablespoons cornstarch

1 teaspoon ground cinnamon

¹/₂ teaspoon ground nutmeg

¹/₈ teaspoon salt

Glaze

1 large egg white

1 tablespoon skim milk or water

1 tablespoon granulated or coarse-grain sugar

Advance Preparation

Pie is best served the day it is made.

Special Equipment

9-inch pie plate; wax paper; pastry brush

Temperature and Time

425°F for 15 minutes, then 350°F for 30 to 40 minutes

---

1. Prepare the pastry as directed, gather it into a ball, wrap in foil, and refrigerate while preparing the fruit.

2. Make the filling. In a large mixing bowl, toss together all the filling ingredients. Arrange the fruit in the pie plate, carefully packing the apples together compactly into a firm domed shape; if they are tossed in haphazardly, they tend to collapse more during baking.

3. Roll out the pastry between two 14-inch pieces of lightly floured wax paper, lifting and repositioning the paper if necessary to prevent wrinkles; you should have a circle of pastry about 11¹/₂ inches in diameter. Peel off the top paper, invert and center the pastry over the apple dome, and peel off the backing paper. With your palms, gently mold the pastry over the fruit. If the pastry tears, moisten the edges and press on scraps to patch. If you wish, cut decorative leaves from leftover pastry and apply them to the egg-glazed surface before sugaring. Leaving a generous 1-inch overhang, trim away excess pastry, then fold under the 1-inch border and crimp it along the rim of the plate.

4. To make the glaze, beat together the egg white and milk or water. With a pastry brush, coat the pastry with the glaze, then sprinkle evenly with sugar. With the tip of a paring knife, cut a 1/2-inch steam hole out of the center of the pastry, then cut 5 steam vents around it. Refrigerate the pie to firm and relax the pastry (preventing shrinkage) while oven preheats.

5. Position a rack in the center of the oven and preheat the oven to 425°F. Bake the pie for 15 minutes, then reduce the heat to 350°F and bake 30 to 40 minutes longer, until the pastry top is golden brown and the fruit is tender when pierced with a long thin knife blade through a vent hole. Cool the pie on a wire rack. Serve warm. Note: Check the pie after the first 20 to 25 minutes of baking; if the top is overbrowning, cover it loosely with a tent made of aluminum foil (page 342).

Nutritional Analysis (per serving): 309 calories; 3 g protein; 10 g fat; 1 g satfat; 53 g carbohydrate; 199 mg sodium; 0 mg cholesterol

Light Touch

Simply by dropping one buttery crust, you eliminate a lot of the calories, fat, and cholesterol from a pie. A classic apple pie with two crusts contains about 34% calories from fat. By contrast, this pie has 30% calories from fat, but only 2% of those are saturated and there is no cholesterol; most of the calories here (67%) come from carbohydrates.

LOW-SUGAR APPLE PIE

This recipe was given to me by Ginnie Sweatt Hagan, a Vermont friend and neighbor. A nurturer as well as a nurse, Ginnie is famous for bringing home-baked treats to all those under her care. This recipe is a favorite of her patients with diabetes. Ginnie prefers to use sweet apples such as Delicious or McIntosh, and I like to add golden raisins as well. Instead of sugar, frozen unsweetened apple juice is the sweetener of choice in this pie. The mixture is baked in a sugarless pastry shell or a reduced-fat graham cracker crust. The graham cracker crust contains no added sugar but has a small amount of sugar in the crackers. See Light Touch on the next page.

Advance Preparation

Pie is best served on the day it is baked.

Special Equipment

9-inch pie plate

Temperature and Time

For pie with all-purpose pie shell: 425°F for 15 minutes, 350°F for 35 minutes. For pie made with crumb crust: 350°F for 45 to 50 minutes

Pie Shell

1 recipe unbaked All-Purpose Pie Crust (page 45), made *without* sugar, or Low-Sugar Graham Cracker Crumb Crust (page 52)

Fruit Filling

6 ounces ($^3/_4$ cup) frozen unsweetened apple juice concentrate, thawed but not diluted

2 tablespoons fresh lemon juice

2 tablespoons unsifted all-purpose flour

1 teaspoon ground cinnamon

$^1/_2$ teaspoon ground nutmeg

$^1/_4$ teaspoon ground ginger (optional)

$^3/_4$ cup golden raisins

6 or 7 large sweet apples (Golden Delicious or McIntosh, for example), peeled, cored, and sliced

1. Prepare the pie crust and line a pie plate. Flute the edge if using pastry, or press the crumbs into the plate. Do not prebake the shell. Set the prepared pastry shell in the refrigerator while you prepare the fruit. Position a rack in the lower third of the oven and preheat the oven to 425°F if using the pastry crust, 350°F for the crumb crust.

2. Make the fruit filling. In a medium-sized nonreactive saucepan, combine the apple juice concentrate, lemon juice, flour, cinnamon, nutmeg, ginger if used, and raisins. (Cooking the raisins in the sauce plumps and softens them while also drawing out their sweetness.) Whisk over medium heat for 2 to 3 minutes, until it thickens like a pudding. You will have about $^3/_4$ cup.

3. In a bowl, toss the apples with the thickened sauce, to coat all slices. Turn the fruit into the pie crust. If using the pastry crust, bake at 425°F for 15 minutes, then reduce the heat to 350°F and continue baking an additional 35 minutes, until the fruit is tender when pierced with a knife. If using the crumb crust, bake the pie at 350°F for the full 45 to 50 minutes.

Nutritional Analysis (per serving with sugar-free All-Purpose Pie Crust): 235 calories; 2 g protein; 7.7 g fat; 0.6 g satfat; 41 g carbohydrate; 115 mg sodium; 0 mg cholesterol

Nutritional Analysis (per serving with Low-Sugar Graham Cracker Crumb Crust): 216 calories; 2 g protein; 5 g fat; 1 g satfat; 44 g carbohydrate; 91 mg sodium; 3 mg cholesterol

---

Light Touch

When the pie is made with the pie crust (without any sugar), the calories from fat (which are all in the crust) are 29%. With the graham cracker crumb crust, total calories from fat fall to 20%; no sugar is added but there is some sugar already in the crackers. If additional sugar-free sweetener is desired, use Steel's Vanilla Nature Sweet (see page 373) or any all-fruit sugar-free preserves.

PECAN PIE

Yield: One 9-inch pie; 10 servings

Advance Preparation

The partially prebaked pie shell can be prepared 1 day ahead. Once filled, the bottom crust tends to soften on standing longer than 24 hours.

Special Equipment

9-inch pie plate; pie weights

Temperature and Time

Partially prebake pie shell: 425°F for 15 minutes. Filled pie: 400°F for 10 minutes, then 350°F for 30 to 35 minutes

A classic of the American South, pecan pie is known for its rich, sweet taste. I have toned it down slightly but kept all the flavor, adding a touch of molasses for complexity and lemon juice to reduce the cloying sweetness. The taste of butter is still here, but reduced in quantity; to add more, read Light Touch on the next page. The pie looks more traditional when the pecans are halved, but since only a small quantity is used, the pecans go farther when chopped; the crunch is enhanced by the addition of a little Grape-Nuts cereal. As a variation, add 3/4 cup of whole cranberries to the filling; their tartness is a good counterpoint to the sugar.

Pie Shell

1 recipe All-Purpose Pie Crust (page 45)

Filling

2/3 cup packed dark brown sugar

1 large egg plus 2 large egg whites

1 teaspoon unsalted butter, melted

2/3 cup dark corn syrup

2 tablespoons unsulfured molasses

1 tablespoon fresh lemon juice

2 teaspoons vanilla extract

1/4 teaspoon salt

1/3 cup Grape-Nuts cereal

1/3 cup pecans, chopped

continued

Cobblers, Crisps, Crumbles, and Pies 73

1. Prepare and partially prebake the pie shell according to the directions on page 45. Set aside to cool. Position a rack in the center of the oven and preheat the oven to 400°F.

2. In a large mixing bowl, combine the brown sugar and egg plus whites and beat with an electric mixer or whisk until smooth. Add the melted butter, corn syrup, molasses, lemon juice, vanilla, and salt; beat until blended.

3. Pour the filling into the prepared pastry shell, sprinkle on the Grape-Nuts, then press them gently below the surface with a spatula (they bob back up). Sprinkle the pecans on top. Bake at 400°F for 10 minutes, then reduce the heat to 350°F and bake 30 to 35 minutes longer, until a knife inserted about 1 inch from the edge comes out clean. Cool on a wire rack.

Nutritional Analysis (per serving): 284 calories; 3 g protein; 10.6 g fat; 1.1 g satfat; 45 g carbohydrate; 214 mg sodium; 22 mg cholesterol

---

Light Touch

One bite of classic pecan pie and your taste buds know the facts: 52% calories from fat, 401 calories, and 24 g fat in a slice, not to mention 118 mg cholesterol. My taste buds are still happy. In this new recipe the flavor is intense but the calories from fat are reduced by 37% (to 34%). Cutting out 2 yolks, two thirds of the nuts, and all but a touch of the butter makes a difference, but the biggest drop comes from substituting a reduced-fat pastry crust. Personally, I prefer the richness of extra butter, so I use 2 tablespoons instead of 1 teaspoon, adding about 20 calories and 2 g fat per serving.

VERMONT MAPLE WALNUT PIE

Yield: One 9-inch pie; 10 servings

This is the pie you see on the sideboard when smoke curls from the chimney and frost begins to tinge the burgundy leaves that cover the yard. When it is fall in Vermont, this is it! The essence of home and harvest, the maple syrup surely from the sugar bush out back. I found the original version of this recipe at a church fair near our summer home in northern Vermont.

For authentic flavor, it is important to use pure maple syrup, dark amber or even Grade B, deep in color and intense in flavor. A pastry crust is traditional but pushes the fat content up slightly; if you are concerned, use the Graham–Grape-Nuts Crumb Crust and read Light Touch on the next page.

Pie Shell

1 recipe Graham–Grape-Nuts Crumb Crust (page 54) or All-Purpose Pie Crust (page 45)

Filling

1 large egg plus 2 large egg whites

1/4 teaspoon salt

1/3 cup granulated sugar

2 tablespoons unsalted butter, melted

1 tablespoon dark corn syrup

1 cup pure maple syrup

1/2 teaspoon maple extract

1/3 cup Grape-Nuts cereal

1/3 cup walnuts, chopped

1. If preparing the crumb crust, prebake it at 400°F for about 5 minutes. Set aside. If making the pastry crust, partially prebake for 15 minutes at 425°F as directed (page 45). Remove the liner and set the shell aside.

2. In a bowl, whisk together the egg plus whites, salt, sugar, melted butter, corn syrup, maple syrup, and extract.

3. Pour the mixture into the prebaked pie shell. Sprinkle the Grape-Nuts over the pie and push them under the surface gently with a spatula. Sprinkle the chopped nuts on top.

4. Bake at 400°F for 10 minutes, then reduce the heat to 350°F and bake about 20 minutes longer, until a stainless-steel knife inserted 1 inch from the edge comes out clean. Cool on a wire rack.

Nutritional Analysis (per serving with crumb crust): 261 calories; 4 g protein; 7.8 g fat; 2.4 g satfat; 47 g carbohydrate; 200 mg sodium; 29 mg cholesterol

continued

Advance Preparation

Pie is best served the day it is made.

Special Equipment

9-inch pie plate

Temperature and Time

Prebake crumb shell: 400°F for 5 minutes. Prebake pie crust: 425°F for 15 minutes. Filled pie: 400°F for 10 minutes, then 350°F for 20 minutes

BUTTERMILK CHESS PIE

Yield: One 9-inch pie; 10 servings

Buttermilk Chess Pie is an old-fashioned Southern specialty, one of a family of traditionally rich pies laden with eggs and butter and heavily sweetened with sugar and, originally, molasses. I have always loved these classics, but have avoided them because of the fat and cholesterol. This one, made with naturally low-fat buttermilk, lends itself more easily than most to modification without loss of flavor.

Advance Preparation

Make the pie on the same day it is to be served; refrigerate after pie has cooled.

Special Equipment

9-inch pie plate, preferably Pyrex; pie weights or rice or beans; pastry brush; cookie sheet

Temperature and Time

Partially prebake pie shell: 425°F for 15 minutes. Filled pie: 350°F for 35 to 40 minutes

Pie Shell
> **1 recipe All-Purpose Pie Crust (page 45)**

Filling
> **2 tablespoons unsalted butter**
> **2 large eggs plus 1 large egg white**
> **1 cup granulated sugar**
> **2 tablespoons unsifted all-purpose flour**
> **Pinch of salt**
> **1/4 teaspoon ground cinnamon**
> **1 1/2 cups nonfat or low-fat buttermilk**
> **2 teaspoons vanilla extract**

1. Position a rack in the lower third of the oven and preheat the oven to 425°F. Prepare the pie crust, flute the edge, and chill until firm to minimize shrinkage. Then partially prebake as directed (page 45). Set pastry shell on wire rack to cool.

2. Melt the butter in a small saucepan over medium-low heat and cook until it turns golden brown and has a nutty aroma, about 4 minutes. Set aside to cool slightly but not solidify.

3. In a mixing bowl, whisk together the eggs and egg white. Use a pastry brush to brush a coating of this beaten egg over the still-warm pastry. (You will use the rest of the egg in the filling.) Return the shell to the oven (without the foil liner) to bake 3 to 5 minutes longer, just until the pastry is opaque but not browned. Remove from the oven and set aside to cool. Reduce the oven heat to 350°F and place a rack in the center of the oven.

4. Make the filling. Add the sugar to the previously beaten eggs and beat until the mixture is thick and light colored. Beat in the melted and cooled butter and all the other remaining ingredients. Pour the mixture into the pastry shell, set the pie on a sturdy cookie sheet for ease in handling, and place in the center of the oven.

5. Bake the pie for 35 to 40 minutes, until the top is a pale golden color, slightly puffed up, and a knife inserted in the center comes out clean. Cool on a wire rack. Serve at room temperature.

Nutritional Analysis (per serving): 239 calories; 4 g protein; 10 g fat; 2 g satfat; 32 g carbohydrate; 192 mg sodium; 49 mg cholesterol

---

Light Touch

My original recipe has 47% calories from fat; each serving contains 295 calories, 16 g fat, 8 g satfat, and 117 mg cholesterol. Without sacrificing taste and texture, I have shaved this just enough to make a difference (41% calories from fat, cutting 5 g fat and 6 g satfat per serving). The only dramatic change is the cut of 68 mg cholesterol per serving, done by replacing the classic butter crust with a reduced-fat pastry shell, dropping a yolk and 3 1/3 tablespoons butter, and using nonfat buttermilk. The majority of the fat left is in the crust. If you want to shave points (I don't think it is worth the trouble), you can reduce the butter in the filling by 1 tablespoon to reach 38%, or eliminate all the butter (35%). Serve this pie as a special treat and remember that it wouldn't be chess pie if it wasn't a little buttery.

SOUTHERN SWEET POTATO PIE

The sweet potato (Ipomoea batatas) *is native to tropical areas of the Western Hemisphere. An important food of the Aztecs, this curiosity was discovered by sixteenth-century Spanish explorers and imported to Europe, where it gained great popularity. According to Waverley Root* (Eating in America, *Ecco Press, 1976), it was endowed "quite gratuitously with the reputation of being an aphrodisiac," and probably for this reason became a favorite of Henry VIII, who preferred his potatoes baked into sweet, spicy pies. In North America, Native Americans in Southern areas ate sweet potatoes and introduced them to the European colonists. Over a hundred years later, African slaves found the sweet Southern tuber similar to the yams they knew in their homeland.*

There are two types of sweet potato grown in the United States: a pale yellow sweet potato with yellow flesh and a darker orange-skinned tuber with vivid coral-hued flesh. They can be cooked the same way. Canned sweet potatoes, or yams, can be substituted in this pie.

An enlightened version of a Southern classic, this recipe was developed by my baking assistant Ann Martin. It is moderately sweet with a creamy texture. Although the filling can be mixed in a bowl with a spoon, it is much better in this case to use a food processor or blender to purée the potato with the cream cheese; this is the only way to completely rid the mixture of tiny flecks of cream cheese.

Advance Preparation

The partially prebaked pie shell can be prepared 1 day ahead. Serve the pie the day it is baked.

Special Equipment

9-inch pie plate, preferably Pyrex; pastry brush

Temperature and Time

Partially prebake pie shell: 425°F for 15 minutes. Filled pie: 375°F for 35 minutes

Pie Shell

1 recipe All-Purpose Pie Crust (page 45)

Egg Glaze

1 large egg white beaten with 2 teaspoons water

Filling

2 medium-size sweet potatoes or yams (about 14 ounces total raw weight or 1¹/₂ cups canned)

¹/₄ cup light cream cheese

1 large egg

1 cup evaporated skim milk

¹/₂ cup packed light brown sugar

1¹/₂ teaspoons cornstarch

¹/₂ teaspoon salt

1¹/₂ teaspoons ground cinnamon

¹/₂ teaspoon ground nutmeg

¹/₄ teaspoon ground cloves

¹/₄ teaspoon ground ginger

1. Position a rack in the lower third of the oven and preheat the oven to 425°F.

2. Prepare the pie crust as directed, flute the edge, and chill until firm. Partially prebake as directed (page 45). Reduce the oven temperature to 375°F. While the pastry shell is still hot, brush it with the egg glaze, then set it aside.

3. If using raw sweet potatoes, peel them and cut into chunks. Cover with water and boil about 15 minutes, until fork-tender. Drain well. Mash with a fork or purée in a food processor or blender, then measure; you need 1½ cups.

4. Place the correct amount of sweet potato in the processor or blender and add the cream cheese. Purée until completely smooth. Add the egg and milk and pulse to blend. Turn off the machine and scrape down the bowl and blade. Pulse 2 or 3 times more.

5. In a small bowl, combine all the dry ingredients: sugar, cornstarch, salt, and spices. Whisk to blend, then add all at once to the mixture in the processor bowl and pulse 7 or 8 times just to combine. Turn the mixture out into the prepared pastry shell and bake for about 35 minutes, until the top is dry to the touch and the center is no longer jiggly when the pie plate is tapped. A knife inserted about 2 inches from the center should come out clean. Cool the pie on a wire rack.

Nutritional Analysis (per serving): 247 calories; 5 g protein; 9 g fat; 0.8 g satfat; 36 g carbohydrate; 292 mg sodium; 24 mg cholesterol

Light Touch

By dropping 1 egg and replacing heavy cream with evaporated skim milk, I have reduced calories from fat by 27% from the classic 45% (to 33%), dropping 40 calories, half the fat, and about one fourth the cholesterol per serving.

PUMPKIN CUSTARD PIE

Yield: One 9-inch pie; 10 servings

Classic pumpkin pie is traditionally made with heavy cream and lots of yolks baked in a buttery pastry crust. This enlightened version keeps the strong spicy flavor of the original and maintains the rich creamy texture with the addition of a little light cream cheese and evaporated skim milk. Choose the crust you prefer: the lowest in fat is the Graham–Grape-Nuts Crumb Crust, the next is the easy-to-make Phyllo Pie Shell, and the highest in fat is the traditional All-Purpose Pie Crust.

It is important to partially prebake the pie shell in order to prevent it from becoming soggy when the soft custard is placed it in. To further waterproof the pastry (or crumb) shell, brush it with egg glaze as soon as it has been prebaked, while still warm.

Pie Shell

1 recipe Graham–Grape-Nuts Crumb Crust (page 54), 9-inch Phyllo Pie Shell (page 48), or All-Purpose Pie Crust (page 45)

Egg Glaze

1 large egg white beaten with 2 teaspoons water

Filling

$^1/_4$ cup light cream cheese, at room temperature

$^1/_2$ cup packed dark brown sugar

1 tablespoon cornstarch

$1^1/_4$ cups canned plain pumpkin purée

1 large egg plus 1 large egg white

$1^1/_2$ cups evaporated skim milk

2 tablespoons unsalted butter, melted

1 teaspoon vanilla extract

$^1/_4$ teaspoon salt

$1^1/_2$ teaspoons ground cinnamon

1 teaspoon ground allspice

$^1/_2$ teaspoon ground nutmeg

$^1/_2$ teaspoon ground ginger

$^1/_4$ teaspoon ground cloves

1. Prepare and partially prebake the crust of your choice following the specific recipe. Set the crust aside. Position a rack in the center of the oven and preheat the oven to 425°F.

Advance Preparation

The partially prebaked pie shell can be prepared ahead. The filled pie should be served the day it is baked; the crust softens on standing.

Special Equipment

9-inch pie plate, preferably Pyrex; pastry brush

Temperature and Time

Partially prebake pie shell according to your choice of pastry recipe. Filled pie: 425°F for 10 minutes, then 350°F for 35 minutes

2. In a large bowl with an electric mixer, cream together the cream cheese, brown sugar, and cornstarch until smooth. (If the cream cheese is difficult to blend, use a food processor or blender, then transfer mixture to electric mixer.) Beat in the pumpkin, then the egg plus white, milk, melted butter, vanilla, salt, and all the spices. Pour the custard filling into the prepared pie shell and bake at 425°F for 10 minutes, then reduce the heat to 350°F and bake 35 minutes, until the top is golden brown and a knife inserted 1 inch from the edge comes out clean. Cool the pie on a wire rack.

Nutritional Analysis (per serving with crumb crust): 204 calories; 6 g protein; 6.6 g fat; 2 g satfat; 31 g carbohydrate; 268 mg sodium; 33 mg cholesterol

---

Light Touch

In my book *As Easy as Pie*, the classic pumpkin custard pie obtains 64% of its calories from fat. I have reduced that by 55% (to 29%) by switching to a low-fat crumb crust, cutting 2 yolks, and substituting evaporated skim milk for heavy cream.

PUMPKIN CHIFFON PIE

Yield: One 9-inch pie; 10 servings

Thanksgiving would not be the same in my family without my mother's creamy pumpkin chiffon pie, generously laced with rum and whipped cream. For this variation, I have replaced the whipped cream with cooked meringue (boiled icing), kept all the spices, and left the rum up to you. The texture is unctuous and silken, the flavor bright. You can even add a little cream without doing too much damage (see Light Touch on the next page).

The crumb crust is baked a few minutes to firm it up but this is a no-bake pie filling, set with gelatin. Note: You will need 2 double boilers (which can be improvised from deep metal bowls or saucepans set over larger pots), one to make the pumpkin custard, the other to make the meringue.

Advance Preparation

Crumb crust may be prepared a day ahead. Filled pie must be refrigerated for 3 hours minimum. The complete pie may be made 1 day ahead and refrigerated.

Special Equipment

9-inch pie plate; 2 double boilers (see introductory note); hand-held electric mixer

Temperature and Time

Bake crust: 350°F for 7 minutes

Pie Shell

1 recipe Gingersnap–Graham Cracker Crumb Crust (page 53)

Filling

4 teaspoons unflavored gelatin

$1/4$ cup fresh orange juice

2 large egg yolks

$1^1/2$ cups granulated sugar, divided

$1/2$ teaspoon salt

1 teaspoon ground cinnamon

$3/4$ teaspoon ground nutmeg

$3/4$ teaspoon ground ginger

$1/8$ teaspoon ground cloves

$1^1/4$ cups canned plain pumpkin purée

2 teaspoons vanilla extract

3 tablespoons dark rum (optional)

3 large egg whites

Scant $1/3$ cup water

2 teaspoons light corn syrup

1. Prepare the crust, bake as directed to firm it up, then set it aside to cool completely.

2. In a small saucepan, sprinkle the gelatin over the orange juice and allow to stand about 3 minutes to soften. Stir the mixture over low heat until the gelatin is dissolved; do not boil. Remove from the heat and set aside.

3. In the top of a double boiler, whisk together the egg yolks and $1/4$ cup of the sugar until thick and light lemon-colored. Add the salt, spices, and dissolved gelatin. Set over (not touching) gently boiling water and whisk constantly until the mixture thickens enough to generously coat a spoon.

4. Remove the double boiler from the heat and stir or whisk into the thickened custard the pumpkin, vanilla, and rum if used. Set the pan aside off the heat to cool the mixture while the meringue is prepared.

5. To make the meringue, set up the bottom of a double boiler, or a saucepan, with just enough water in it that the top part, or a metal bowl, can sit above it without getting wet. Bring this water to a simmer. In the top of this double boiler, combine the egg whites, the remaining 1¼ cups sugar, the water, and corn syrup.

6. When the water is simmering, set the top pan over it, and immediately begin whipping the whites with a hand-held electric mixer on medium speed. Whip about 3 minutes, then increase speed to high and whip 3 to 4 minutes longer, until the sugar is dissolved (it won't feel grainy) and the whites are satiny and hold stiff peaks. Remove the top from the heat and whip a minute longer to cool the whites.

7. Fold the pumpkin mixture into the whipped whites. Turn the mixture out into the prepared pie shell, smooth the top, and refrigerate. After about 2 hours the top should be set enough to cover with plastic wrap (to protect the flavor). Chill a total of 3 hours minimum.

Nutritional Analysis (per serving without rum): 285 calories; 5 g protein; 8 g fat; 2 g satfat; 50 g carbohydrate; 212 mg sodium; 49 mg cholesterol

Light Touch

You would never guess that this rich-tasting pie has only 26% calories from fat, a reduction of 51% from the original. By cutting yolks and heavy cream, I have removed over half the fat per serving, two thirds the satfat, and half the cholesterol. You could even add back ¼ cup heavy cream, whipped and folded in at the very end; this would push the calories from fat to 30% and add 20 calories, 2 g fat, 1.5 g satfat, and 8 mg cholesterol per serving.

LEMON MERINGUE PIE

Yield: One 9-inch pie; 10 servings

This is everyone's favorite. I have made some modifications but kept the same old-fashioned flavor and creamy texture. The use of orange juice mellows the sharpness of the lemon slightly but does not really alter the taste of the pie. For a change, you can make an orange meringue pie, substituting orange for all the lemon. Classic lemon pies are baked in a pastry shell, but for a change I use a prebaked Phyllo Pie Shell. Either one is fine.

Pie Shell

1 recipe 9-inch Phyllo Pie Shell (page 48) or All-Purpose Pie Crust (page 45), completely prebaked

Filling

1 cup plus 2 tablespoons granulated sugar

3 tablespoons cornstarch

1 tablespoon unsifted all-purpose flour

Pinch of salt

1 cup fresh orange juice or water

1 cup plain nonfat yogurt, top liquid poured off

2 tablespoons unsalted butter, melted

1 tablespoon grated lemon zest

$1/2$ cup plus 2 tablespoons fresh lemon juice

Meringue Topping

4 large egg whites

Pinch of salt

$1/4$ teaspoon cream of tartar

6 tablespoons granulated sugar

Advance Preparation

The completely baked pie shell can be prepared a day ahead. Filled pie must be refrigerated for 3 hours minimum. The finished pie is best served the day it is made; the crust will soften if it stands too long.

Special Equipment

9-inch pie plate

Temperature and Time

Completely prebake pastry shell according to your choice of pastry recipe. Brown meringue: 400°F for 10 to 12 minutes

1. Prepare the pie shell and set it aside.

2. Make the filling. In a heavy-bottomed nonreactive saucepan, whisk together the sugar, cornstarch, flour, and salt. Whisk in the orange juice or water and yogurt and set over medium heat. Whisk constantly until the mixture comes to a boil. Reduce the heat slightly and stir for about 5 minutes, until thickened enough to generously coat a spoon. Remove the pan from the heat and whisk in the melted butter, lemon zest, and lemon juice. Set the filling aside until cool, then refrigerate for at least 3 hours. The filling will thicken as it cools.

3. When the filling is thick, pour it into the prebaked pie shell.

4. Position a rack in the center of the oven and preheat the oven to 400°F.

5. To make the meringue, combine the egg whites, salt, and cream of tartar in a large grease-free mixing bowl. Whip with an electric mixer on medium speed until foamy. Gradually add the sugar while increasing the speed to high; whip until the whites are stiff but not dry. Pinch the meringue between your fingers to be sure no grains of sugar remain undissolved.

6. Spoon the meringue over the warm lemon filling in the pie shell and smooth it onto the edges of the crust all around, sealing it to prevent shrinking. Shape the meringue into low peaks or swirls with the back of a spoon. Bake the pie in the preheated oven 10 to 12 minutes, watching very carefully, until the meringue is golden brown; do not let it burn. Cool the pie on a wire rack, then refrigerate. Refrigerate leftovers.

Nutritional Analysis (per serving with Phyllo Pie Shell): 235 calories; 4 g protein; 6 g fat; 3.8 g satfat; 44 g carbohydrate; 86 mg sodium; 17 mg cholesterol

---

Light Touch

Although rich and flavorful, my enlightened Lemon Meringue Pie has only 23% calories from fat; this is 61 fewer calories, half the fat, and about one sixth the cholesterol of the classic version. If you prefer All-Purpose Pie Crust to the phyllo, you will add 50 calories, 4 g fat, and 10 mg cholesterol per serving, increasing the calories from fat to only 28%.

BANANA SPLIT PIE

Yield: One 9-inch pie; 10 servings

Simply outrageous, not to mention quick, easy, and irresistible. Your kids will love this old-fashioned treat and never guess that the fat content has been modified. For another old favorite, try the variation on the next page for Chocolate Cream Pie with Meringue Topping.

Pie Shell

1 recipe Low-Fat Graham Cracker Crumb Crust (page 51), unbaked or prebaked, as you wish

Filling

^{2}/$_3$ cup granulated sugar

^{1}/$_4$ cup cornstarch

^{1}/$_4$ teaspoon salt

2^1/$_2$ cups 2% milk

^{1}/$_4$ cup evaporated skim milk

2 large egg yolks

1 teaspoon vanilla extract

1 teaspoon banana extract (optional)

2 tablespoons sifted unsweetened cocoa, regular or Dutch-processed

1 to 2 bananas (enough slices to line pie plate)

Meringue Topping

4 large egg whites

Pinch of salt

^{1}/$_4$ teaspoon cream of tartar

6 tablespoons granulated sugar

Advance Preparation

The crumb crust can be made a day or two ahead. Filled pie must be refrigerated for 3 hours minimum. The pie is best served the day it is made but can be made and refrigerated 1 day ahead; bottom crust may soften slightly after 1 day.

Special Equipment

9-inch pie plate

Temperature and Time

Brown meringue: 400°F for 10 to 12 minutes

---

1. Prepare the pie shell and set it aside.

2. To make the filling, combine the sugar, cornstarch, and salt in a heavy-bottomed saucepan. In a bowl, whisk both types of milk into the yolks, then whisk this mixture into the dry ingredients in the saucepan. Whisk well to be sure all the cornstarch is picked up and dissolved. Set the pan over medium heat and cook, stirring occasionally, for about 5 minutes, then stir constantly for about 7 minutes longer, until the custard filling thickens and comes to a boil. Whisk continuously while the custard boils for 1 full minute. It should be thick enough to generously coat the back of a spoon. Stir in the vanilla.

3. Spoon about half the custard filling into a bowl and whisk in the cocoa. Whisk the banana extract if used into the filling remaining in the saucepan.

4. Peel and slice the banana(s), spreading the slices in an even layer over the pie shell. Spread the cocoa mixture over the slices, then spread the vanilla or banana-flavored custard on top. Set the pie aside while you prepare the meringue.

5. Position a rack in the center of the oven and preheat the oven to 400°F.

6. To make the meringue, in a large grease-free mixing bowl, combine the egg whites, salt, and cream of tartar. Whip with an electric mixer on medium speed until foamy. Gradually add the sugar while increasing the speed to high; whip until the whites are stiff but not dry. Pinch the meringue between your fingers to be sure no grains of sugar remain undissolved.

7. Spoon the meringue over the warm (or hot) filling in the pie shell and smooth it onto the edges of the crust all around, sealing it to prevent shrinking. Shape the meringue into low peaks or swirls with the back of a spoon. Bake the pie in the preheated oven 10 to 12 minutes, watching carefully, until the meringue is golden brown; do not let it burn. Cool the pie on a wire rack, then refrigerate covered with plastic wrap for at least 3 hours. Refrigerate leftovers.

Nutritional Analysis (per serving): 237 calories; 5 g protein; 6.5 g fat; 2 g satfat; 41 g carbohydrate; 214 mg sodium; 49 mg cholesterol

CHOCOLATE CREAM PIE WITH MERINGUE TOPPING

Prepare a 9-inch Chocolate Crumb Crust (page 55), baked or unbaked. Fill with Homemade Chocolate Pudding (page 178). Top with meringue made and browned as in the recipe above, steps 6 and 7.

Nutritional Analysis (per serving): 231 calories; 5 g protein; 7 g fat; 1.6 g satfat; 37 g carbohydrate; 107 mg sodium; 27 mg cholesterol

---

Light Touch

This rich pie will surprise anyone who hears it has only 24% calories from fat. That is a reduction of 56% from the classic version. By replacing the whipped cream with meringue and using low-fat milk, I was able to cut 117 calories per serving and more than two thirds the fat and cholesterol from the original. I kept in the 2 egg yolks because they give needed richness to the filling. The chocolate cream pie variation has 28% calories from fat.

COCONUT CREAM PIE

This is an old favorite: rich creamy coconut custard pudding decorated with toasted coconut. I like to bake it in a crisp phyllo shell, made by layering a few sheets of the store-bought phyllo dough. If you are a traditionalist, use my All-Purpose Pie Crust or any crumb crust. Toasted coconut is often mixed into the custard but since we don't use very much because it is high in fat, I prefer it sprinkled over the top where it can be seen. If you want to top the pie with meringue as in Banana Split Pie (page 86), sprinkle the coconut over the meringue before browning.

Pie Shell and Topping*

1 recipe 9-inch Phyllo Pie Shell (page 48), completely prebaked; or All-Purpose Pie Crust (page 45), completely prebaked; or your favorite crumb crust (see Index), baked at 350°F for 8 minutes

¹/₄ cup shredded sweetened coconut

Filling (makes 3¹/₄ cups)

²/₃ cup granulated sugar

¹/₄ cup cornstarch

¹/₄ teaspoon salt

2¹/₂ cups 2% milk

¹/₄ cup evaporated skim milk

2 large egg yolks

1 teaspoon vanilla extract

2 teaspoons coconut extract

1. Prepare the pie shell of your choice and set it aside. In a frying pan set over medium heat, toss the coconut for 4 to 5 minutes, until it is crisp and golden brown. Set it aside to cool.

2. To make the filling, combine the sugar, cornstarch, and salt in a heavy-bottomed saucepan. In a bowl, whisk the milk and skim milk into the yolks, then whisk this mixture into the dry ingredients in the saucepan. Whisk well to be sure all the cornstarch is picked up and dissolved. Set the pan over medium heat and cook, stirring occasionally, for about 5 minutes, then stir constantly for about 7 minutes longer, until the custard filling thickens and comes to a boil. Whisk to remove any lumps while the custard boils for 1 full minute. It should be thick enough to generously coat the back of a spoon. Stir in the flavoring extracts.

3. Spoon the hot custard filling into the prepared pie shell and sprinkle on the toasted coconut. Set aside to cool, then refrigerate. Alternatively, prepare meringue as on page 87, steps 6 and 7, sprinkle on the coconut, and brown as directed. Refrigerate for at least 3 hours. Bring chilled pie to room temperature before serving. Refrigerate leftovers.

Advance Preparation

Filled pie must be refrigerated for 3 hours minimum. This pie is best served the day it is made; if held longer, the bottom crust softens as the pudding begins to release liquid.

Special Equipment

9-inch pie plate

Temperature and Time

Completely prebake pie shell according to your choice of pastry recipe

Nutritional Analysis (per serving with phyllo crust and coconut but without meringue): 184 calories; 3 g protein; 7 g fat; 3 g satfat; 27 g carbohydrate; 118 g sodium; 55 mg cholesterol

Light Touch

By substituting 2% milk for regular milk, evaporated skim milk for heavy cream, and a low-fat phyllo crust for butter pastry, I have cut each serving by almost 100 calories and half the fat, and reduced the percentage of calories from fat by 24%, to 35%, as compared to the original.

When phyllo is replaced with low-fat All-Purpose Pie Crust plus coconut, the calories from fat climb a little, to 41%.

Coconut contains a high percentage of saturated fat; for this reason, I use a small amount, just to give flavor and texture. Dropping the coconut cuts 27 calories and 2 g fat per serving, down to 39%.

STRAWBERRY CREAM PIE

Yield: One 10-inch pie; 10 to 12 servings; or eight 4-inch tartlets

Make this no-bake pie at the height of berry season. The fresh ripe strawberries retain their sweetness because they are not cooked. Instead, they are blended with strawberry preserves, vanilla yogurt, and a little whipped cream if you feel indulgent, and are presented in a chocolate crumb crust. Garnish your pie with additional strawberry slices for a memorable, quick-and-easy summer dessert.

You can also forget about the crust entirely and serve strawberry cream in goblets garnished with a whole berry.

Pie Shell

1 recipe Chocolate Crumb Crust (page 55) or other crumb crust of your choice for a pie or 1½ recipes crumb crust for 8 tartlets

Filling *(makes 4 cups)*

1½ cups vanilla nonfat or low-fat yogurt

1 quart fresh ripe strawberries, rinsed, patted dry, and hulled

3 tablespoons light cream cheese or Neufchâtel cheese

⅓ cup granulated sugar

¼ cup strawberry preserves

2 tablespoons Chambord or crème de cassis (optional)

Pinch of salt

⅓ cup fresh orange juice or water

2 teaspoons fresh lemon juice

3½ teaspoons unflavored gelatin

Advance Preparation

The vanilla yogurt needs to drain about 30 minutes before being added to the filling; this can be done a day ahead. The pie contains gelatin and needs about 3 hours to set in the refrigerator. Make early in the day to be served, or 1 day ahead.

Special Equipment

Cheesecloth-lined strainer; 10-inch pie plate or eight 4-inch tartlet pans

1. Prepare crumb crust; to make it more firm when sliced, you can bake it a few minutes as indicated in the recipe, and set it aside to cool completely.

2. Measure the yogurt into a cheesecloth-lined strainer set over a bowl and drain for about 30 minutes; you should have about 1¼ cups of yogurt. Discard the liquid (or drink it; it is high in calcium).

3. Reserve 4 or 5 of the best strawberries for garnishing the pie. Halve the rest and set aside.

4. In a food processor or blender, mix together quickly the cream cheese and sugar. Add the drained yogurt, halved berries, preserves, Chambord or cassis if used, and salt; pulse to blend but do not purée completely—there should still be some pieces of berries.

5. In a small nonreactive saucepan, combine the orange juice and lemon juice. Sprinkle on the gelatin and let stand for about 3 minutes to soften. Stir the mixture over low heat just until the gelatin dissolves; do not boil.

Remove from the heat and stir in a few tablespoons of the strawberry cream to cool the gelatin. Then pour the gelatin mixture into the strawberry cream and pulse or stir to blend in.

6. Spread the strawberry cream into the prepared crumb shell(s) and refrigerate at least 3 hours to set. Before serving, garnish with slices of the reserved strawberries. Refrigerate leftovers.

Nutritional Analysis (per serving): 234 calories; 5 g protein; 7 g fat; 0.9 satfat; 37 g carbohydrate; 187 mg sodium; 6 mg cholesterol

---

Light Touch

This enlightened strawberry cream tastes rich and full of berries but has only 28% calories from fat, a dramatic 38% reduction compared to classic strawberry cream pie, which also has twice the fat, 8 times the satfat, and 10 times the cholesterol! For extra creaminess, at the end of step 5, you can fold in 1/4 cup heavy cream, whipped to stiff peaks; it pushes calories from fat to 33% and adds 20 calories, 2.3 g fat, and 14 mg cholesterol per serving.

MANDARIN MOUSSE PIE

Yield: One 10-inch pie; 10 to 12 servings; or about 12 small tartlets

This velvety mousse combines the tangy flavor of mandarin oranges or tangerines with the richness of yogurt blended with a little whipped cream. An easy-to-make cooked meringue replaces traditional raw meringue to enhance the creamy texture. You can substitute blood oranges or other citrus fruit for the tangerines. I like to make this in a prebaked Phyllo Pie Shell because of the delightful flakiness of the crust. However, since the filling is not baked, it can go in any crumb crust or even a meringue (angel) shell. Or you can use the mousse to fill individual crumb or pastry tartlet shells or Tulip Shells or Phyllo Cups, or serve it plain in long-stemmed goblets. Note: When fresh tangerines, mandarin oranges, or blood oranges are not in season, use frozen tangerine juice (available in the frozen juice section of the food market) or orange juice plus the grated zest of any type of orange. This recipe was developed by Lynnia Milliun, who prefers to use blood oranges when she can find them and recommends serving the pie with fresh blueberries and Blueberry-Honey Sauce (page 259). I like to garnish Mandarin Mousse tartlets with chopped green pistachio nuts.

Pie Shell

1 recipe 10-inch Phyllo Pie Shell (page 48), prebaked and cooled; or any crumb crust or meringue shell (see Index)

Filling *(makes 4 cups)*

1¹/₂ cups orange or plain nonfat yogurt

3 tablespoons frozen tangerine or orange juice concentrate, thawed but not diluted

¹/₃ cup fresh tangerine juice (or juice from mandarin or blood orange; or substitute frozen tangerine juice, diluted)

2¹/₂ teaspoons unflavored gelatin

2 teaspoons grated zest of tangerine or mandarin or other type of orange

2 tablespoons tangerine or orange liqueur (Mandarin or Grand Marnier, for example)

Meringue

2 large egg whites

³/₄ cup granulated sugar

3 tablespoons cold water

2 teaspoons light corn syrup

1 teaspoon vanilla extract

¹/₂ teaspoon orange extract

¹/₃ cup heavy cream

Advance Preparation

Drain yogurt 10 minutes before using in recipe. Chill the filled pie at least 4 hours or up to 1 day ahead.

Special Equipment

10-inch pie plate; hand-held electric mixer (for meringue); pastry brush

Temperature and Time

Prebake phyllo pastry shell: 400°F for 10 to 15 minutes

Garnish (optional)

1/3 cup orange marmalade, warmed and strained

Freshly cut segments from orange or tangerine or blood orange, or canned mandarin orange segments, well drained and blotted dry on paper towels

1. Prepare the pie shell and set it aside. Measure the yogurt into a strainer set over a bowl and let drain for at least 10 minutes to remove excess liquid.

2. In a small nonreactive saucepan, stir together the juice concentrate and regular juice, then sprinkle on the gelatin and allow to sit about 3 minutes to soften. Stir over low heat just until the gelatin is dissolved; do not boil. Remove from the heat and transfer to a medium-sized metal bowl. Whisk in the yogurt, zest, and liqueur. Place the bowl in the refrigerator to chill, 30 to 40 minutes.

3. Prepare the meringue: In the top of a double boiler, combine the egg whites, sugar, water, and corn syrup. Set over (not touching) a pan of simmering water and immediately begin whipping with a hand-held beater on medium speed. Whip about 3 minutes, then increase the speed to high and whip about 5 minutes longer, until the whites look satiny and hold stiff peaks. Remove the top of the double boiler from the heat, add vanilla and orange extracts, and beat 30 seconds longer. Set aside in a pan of cold water; stir occasionally until cool to the touch.

4. With a chilled bowl and chilled beaters, whip the cream until soft peaks form.

5. Remove the juice-gelatin mixture from the refrigerator; it should be slightly thickened and able to mound on a spoon like egg whites. Fold the meringue into the juice-gelatin mixture, then fold in the whipped cream. Spoon the mixture into the prepared pie shell and chill at least 4 hours or overnight.

6. To garnish the top, warm the marmalade in a small saucepan, then brush a little over the pie top. Arrange orange segments in a neat pattern on the top, then brush them with more marmalade. Refrigerate to set the marmalade glaze. Refrigerate leftover pie.

Nutritional Analysis (per serving): 183 calories; 4 g protein; 6.6 g fat; 4 g satfat; 28 g carbohydrate; 63 mg sodium; 21 mg cholesterol

---

Light Touch

This is really a Bavarian cream, blending gelatin, meringue, and whipped cream; in its classic form, however, the volume of the meringue would be reduced and the heavy cream increased, raising the calories from fat to about 40%. The rich, creamy mouth-feel of this light version belies the fact that it has only 32% calories from fat. If you drop all the whipped cream, you can cut the calories from fat to 21%, eliminating 27 calories per serving and about half the fat and cholesterol.

KEY LIME PIE

This reinterpretation of the classic is based on a relatively new product: reduced-fat sweetened condensed milk, which blends with light cream cheese to create a marvelously creamy texture with excellent flavor. Use Key limes if available; they are yellower in color and slightly different in acidity than the more common Persian limes, though the latter are a fine substitute.

Low-fat sweetened condensed milk is a mixture of whole and skim milk and 40% to 45% sugar, heated until 60% of the water evaporates. This product has the unique ability to set a mixture which contains a certain level of acidity, which is why this pie does not need gelatin. I like to make Key Lime Pie in a traditional crumb crust, though it is more original and equally delicious in a prebaked Phyllo Pie Shell.

Advance Preparation

This pie is best served the day it is made. The pie shell may be prepared a day ahead. Filled pie must be chilled for 3 hours minimum.

Special Equipment

9-inch pie plate

Temperature and Time

Completely prebake pie shell according to your choice of pastry recipe

Pie Shell

1 recipe Graham–Grape-Nuts Crumb Crust (page 54) or any other crumb crust of your choice (see Index), or completely prebaked 9-inch Phyllo Pie Shell (page 48)

Filling

One 14-ounce can low-fat sweetened condensed milk

8 ounces light cream cheese or Neufchâtel, at room temperature

2 teaspoons grated lime zest

7 tablespoons fresh lime juice

1. Prepare the pie shell, prebake, and set it aside.

2. In a blender, food processor, or electric mixer, combine all the filling ingredients and beat until absolutely smooth.

3. Pour the filling into the prepared shell and refrigerate at least 3 hours, until set. Refrigerate leftovers.

Nutritional Analysis (per serving): 291 calories; 8 g protein; 8 g fat; 1.8 g satfat; 46 g carbohydrate; 253 mg sodium; 16 mg cholesterol

Light Touch

When made in a Graham–Grape-Nuts Crumb Crust, the calories from fat are 26%, a 40% reduction compared to the classic version which has 5 g more fat and over 4 times the cholesterol per serving. When made in the phyllo crust, which is dabbed with a little butter, this enlightened pie contains 31% calories from fat, about 1 extra g fat per serving compared to the recipe as written.

PEACHES 'N' CREAM PIE

Yield: One 9-inch pie; 8 to 10 servings

This peach pie contains a delectably creamy custard yet is made with just 2 table-spoons of sugar; flavor and sweetness come from the ripeness of the fruit, so pick the best. Nectarines are a fine substitute for peaches; or try a blend of peaches and plums or nectarines and blueberries.

This recipe is my adaptation of a favorite from Nancy Mowbray of Wakefield, Rhode Island. A professional in the field of early childhood education, Nancy has had diabetes for twenty-five years. Her interest in this illness and its treatment led to her second career: facilitating diabetes support groups throughout the state of Rhode Island, working with parents, children, and schools. She enthusiastically shared this recipe because it is easy and quick to prepare, tastes good, and contains a minimal amount of sugar, so it is especially appealing to those who wish to restrict sugar or carbohydrates in their diets.

Note: Instead of sugar, you could add the equivalent amount of sugar substitute or 1 or 2 tablespoons of Steel's Vanilla Nature Sweet (page 323) or any sugar-free all-fruit peach preserves.

Advance Preparation

The pie is best served on the day it is baked; the custard tends to soften the pastry if it stands longer.

Special Equipment

9-inch pie plate; whisk

Temperature and Time

425°F for 15 minutes for fruit alone; 375°F for 30 minutes after adding custard

Pie Shell

    1 recipe All-Purpose Pie Crust (page 45), made *without* the sugar (if on sugar-restricted diet)

Fruit

    7 or 8 large ripe peaches or nectarines

    3 tablespoons unsifted all-purpose flour

    2 tablespoons granulated sugar (see Note, above), or to taste

    1 teaspoon ground cinnamon

Custard

    1 large egg

    3/4 cup vanilla low-fat or nonfat yogurt, top liquid poured off

    1 tablespoon cornstarch

1. Prepare the pastry, press it into place in a pie plate, and set it in the refrigerator while you prepare the filling. Position a rack in the lower third of the oven and preheat the oven to 425°F.

2. To peel the peaches (don't peel nectarines if using them), drop them into a large pot of boiling water, boil for about 2 minutes, then transfer them with a slotted spoon to a bowl of cold water. Drain when peaches are cool. The skins will slip off. Pit and slice the peaches or nectarines into a bowl and toss with the flour, sugar, and cinnamon. Spread the fruit in the prepared pie plate and place in the preheated oven to bake for 15 minutes.

continued

3. While the pie has its first baking, whisk together in a bowl the egg, yogurt, and cornstarch.

4. When the pie is removed from the oven after 15 minutes, lower the oven temperature to 375°F. Pour the custard over the pie and return it to the oven to bake an additional 30 minutes, until the fruit is tender when pierced with the tip of a knife and the pastry is golden brown. Cool on a wire rack.

Nutritional Analysis (per serving with sugar-free pie crust and 2 tablespoons sugar in filling): 181 calories; 4 g protein; 8 g fat; 1 g satfat; 24 g carbohydrate; 127 mg sodium; 21 mg cholesterol

---

Light Touch

You can also make this pie with a Low-Sugar Graham Cracker Crumb Crust (page 51), although it would add slightly more sugar than the homemade pie crust. The latter has enough fat in it to raise the pie to about 39% calories from fat; the per serving figures, however, are well within the limits for reduced-fat diets.

GINNIE HAGAN'S VERMONT BLUEBERRY PIE

Yield: One 9-inch pie; 10 servings

Ginnie Sweatt Hagan, our neighbor in northern Vermont, is not only a warm and caring friend, creative baker, amazing gardener, and nurse; she is first and foremost the best berry picker in the Northeast Kingdom. This pie is one Ginnie often makes for her family. It reminds me of one I tasted at an ice cream social labeled "Blueberry Boycatcher." When I asked about the title, I was told, "Well, this is the one that you catch your boy with!"

This recipe combines fresh and cooked berries. Ginnie usually places about a third of the fresh berries in the baked shell, then pours on a cooked mixture of berries, sugar, and cornstarch, which she tops with the remaining fresh berries. To bind the berries together when sliced, she tops the pie with whipped cream. I, alas, remove the cream and simply stir all the fresh berries into the portion that is cooked; there is just enough sauce to hold the berries together. For a Red-White-and-Blue Fourth of July Pie, see page 98.

Advance Preparation

The pastry shell can be baked a day in advance. Chill the filled pie for 3 hours minimum. Pie is best served the day it is made.

Special Equipment

9-inch pie plate

Temperature and Time

Prebake shell: 425°F about 10 minutes, then 350°F 10 to 15 minutes

Pie Shell

1 recipe All-Purpose Pie Crust (page 45), completely prebaked

Filling

6 cups fresh blueberries, picked over, rinsed, and patted dry

5 tablespoons fresh orange juice, divided

1/4 cup granulated sugar

1/2 teaspoon ground nutmeg

1 tablespoon cornstarch

1. Prepare the pastry shell, prebake, and set it aside.

2. In a 1½-quart saucepan, combine 2 cups of the berries with 3 tablespoons of the orange juice, the sugar, and nutmeg. Cook over medium-high heat, stirring occasionally, 4 to 5 minutes, until the berries begin to release their juice. With the side of the spoon, mash a few berries against the pan side. Remove the pan from the heat.

3. In a cup, dissolve the cornstarch in the remaining 2 tablespoons of orange juice. Add the mixture to the berries in the pan, return to medium-high heat, and stir until the mixture reaches a boil. Boil 1 full minute, until the sauce is no longer cloudy and is thick enough to generously coat a spoon. It will have the consistency of preserves.

4. Add the remaining 4 cups of fresh berries to the pan, stirring very gently just to coat them with the thickened juice. Turn the berry mixture into the pie shell. Chill for at least 3 hours.

Nutritional Analysis (per serving): 185 calories; 2 g protein; 7.7 g fat; 0.6 g satfat; 29 g carbohydrate; 113 mg sodium; 0 mg cholesterol

continued

RED-WHITE-AND-BLUE FOURTH OF JULY PIE

Prepare the recipe above, but use only 2 cups blueberries, putting them in the cooked mixture made in step 2. Substitute 4 cups fresh raspberries for the remaining berries stirred very gently into the cooked mixture. Top each serving of pie with a dollop of Vanilla Cream (page 247), topped by a few fresh berries. The nutritional analysis (minus the cream) is nearly the same as for the blueberry pie.

Light Touch

Although this pie has 36% calories from fat (all the fat is in the pie shell), there is zero cholesterol and the per-slice calorie and fat figures are definitely low enough to fit into a reduced-fat plan.

FRESH CHERRY CLAFOUTI

Yield: One 10-inch clafouti; 8 to 10 servings

This classic French country dessert originated in the Limousin region, where it is made with fresh cherries baked into a sweetened batter similar in texture to a Yorkshire pudding. Preparation is quick and easy. If using fresh cherries, it helps to have either a small child with a pointy finger, a cherry stoner, or a hair pin to remove the pits; lacking these, I do it with a small paring knife, cutting the cherries in half as I pit them. Fresh sweet cherries are delicious in season, but any type of berries or sliced fresh or (drained) canned or (thawed) frozen fruit can be substituted.

Although this is really just a sweet fruited pancake whipped up in a minute, it makes a splendid country dinner party presentation, especially when served warm from the oven with a sprinkling of confectioners' sugar on top.

Butter-flavor no-stick cooking spray

Fruit Mixture

1¹/₂ pounds fresh sweet cherries (such as Bing), stemmed, stoned, whole or halved (3 to 3¹/₂ cups total fruit) or one 16¹/₂-ounce can pitted dark sweet cherries in syrup, well drained

3 tablespoons dark rum or orange or peach liqueur (optional)

Batter

1 cup 1% milk

2 large eggs plus 1 large egg white

2 teaspoons vanilla extract

¹/₂ teaspoon ground nutmeg

¹/₂ cup granulated sugar

Pinch of salt

²/₃ cup unsifted all-purpose flour

Topping

1 tablespoon confectioners' sugar

1. Position a rack in the center of the oven and preheat the oven to 350°F. Lightly coat a pie plate with cooking spray.

2. Prepare the cherries and toss them in a bowl with the rum or liqueur.

3. In a food processor, blender, or bowl with a whisk, beat together the milk, eggs plus white, vanilla, nutmeg, sugar, and salt. Add the flour and pulse or beat only until mixed in; do not overwork.

continued

---

4. Spread the fruit mixture in the prepared plate, then pour the batter on top. Bake about 35 minutes, until the top is puffed up and golden brown. Allow to cool on a rack about 5 minutes, then sift on a little confectioners' sugar and serve warm. Or set aside at room temperature and reheat a few minutes before serving.

Nutritional Analysis (per serving): 199 calories; 5 g protein; 2.5 g fat; 0.8 g satfat; 38 g carbohydrate; 73 mg sodium; 55 mg cholesterol

Light Touch

A classic clafouti yields only 26% calories from fat, but has 93 mg cholesterol and 6 g fat (3 saturated) per serving. By dropping 1 yolk, omitting the cream, and using low-fat milk, the taste and texture are preserved, calories stay nearly the same, but calories from fat drop to just 11%, cutting out half the fat, two thirds the satfat, and 38 mg cholesterol per serving.

FOURTH OF JULY FIRECRACKER PIE

Yield: One 9-inch pie; 10 servings

A surprising pie that will bite you back! The mystery ingredient that causes a minor explosion in your mouth (tell your guests after they taste it): a dash of mild green Tabasco Jalapeño Sauce. Blended with sweetened cream cheese and sour cream, it creates a sweet-sour-spicy effect. The idea may be surprising but the taste is sensational, especially when combined with sweet berries. And don't forget the patriotic colors... the white cream filling is decorated with rings of red strawberry slices and fresh blueberries, with a berry star in the center. Red, white, blue, sweet, and hot!

Note: If you don't have Tabasco Jalapeño Sauce, substitute 2 to 3 tablespoons of orange liqueur or 1 teaspoon of vanilla or almond extract. You can use a plain fruit glaze without gelatin if planning to serve the pie within 2 to 3 hours of brushing on and chilling the glaze. To hold the glaze longer without its melting, use Firm Fruit Glaze with gelatin.

Pie Shell

1 recipe Low-Fat Graham Cracker Crumb Crust (page 51), prebaked

Filling

$^2/_3$ cup nonfat sour cream

$^1/_2$ cup light cream cheese or Neufchâtel cheese, at room temperature

3 tablespoons granulated sugar

$^1/_2$ teaspoon ground nutmeg

2 teaspoons Tabasco Jalapeño Sauce, or to taste

Fruit

1 pint fresh ripe strawberries, rinsed, patted dry, and hulled

$^1/_2$ pint fresh blueberries, picked over, rinsed, and patted dry

Glaze

1 recipe All-Purpose Fruit Glaze (page 270) or Firm Fruit Glaze (page 271), made with apricot preserves

1. Prepare the crumb crust, prebake, and set it aside to cool.

2. Make the filling. In food processor or blender, combine the sour cream, cream cheese, sugar, nutmeg, and Tabasco Jalapeño Sauce. Begin with 1 to 1$^1/_2$ teaspoons of the sauce and taste as you add more until you reach your comfort zone. Flavors intensify a little on standing.

continued

---

3. Spread the cream filling onto the crumb shell and smooth the top. Slice the strawberries vertically (through the stem ends) and arrange them in an overlapping ring around the outer edge of the pie. Next add a ring of blueberries 2 or 3 berries wide. In the center arrange 6 good strawberry slices into a star shape (wide ends to middle) and fill with a few blueberries.

4. Prepare the glaze and gently brush it over the pieces of fruit, taking care not to drizzle it onto the white cream filling. Chill the pie until ready to serve, at least 2 hours. Refrigerate leftovers.

Nutritional Analysis (per serving): 201 calories; 3 g protein; 6.7 g fat; 1 g satfat; 33 g carbohydrate; 176 mg sodium; 7 mg cholesterol

Light Touch

This pie has 29% calories from fat. If you prefer to use an All-Purpose Pie Crust (page 45), the total calories from fat are raised to 38%, adding 20 calories and 2 g fat per slice.

MISSISSIPPI MUD PIE

An inelegant name, perhaps, but a deeply satisfying creation for the most serious chocoholic. Beneath the dark crackled surface, as crusty as a mud puddle baked in the sun, lies a dense velvety-rich chocolate filling. When warm from the oven, it is soft and silken, a tender mousse on the tongue; when chilled, it is solid, a creamy fudge. You won't be able to resist this one, and no one will guess the fat has been seriously reduced. The original butter crust is replaced with a quick and easy graham cracker crumb crust; if you prefer an all-chocolate experience, substitute a Chocolate Crumb Crust (page 55).

Pie Shell

1 recipe Graham–Grape-Nuts Crumb Crust (page 54) or
   Low-Fat Graham Cracker Crumb Crust (page 51)

Filling

2 tablespoons unsalted butter

1 ounce unsweetened chocolate

1/2 ounce semisweet chocolate

1/2 cup unsifted unsweetened cocoa, preferably Dutch-processed

Pinch of salt

Pinch of ground nutmeg

1 tablespoon plus 1 teaspoon cornstarch

1/2 cup granulated sugar

1/2 cup packed dark brown sugar

1 tablespoon instant coffee or espresso powder

1/3 cup light cream cheese, at room temperature

1 large egg plus 2 large egg whites

1/4 cup nonfat sour cream

1/4 cup dark corn syrup

1 tablespoon vanilla extract

Garnish (optional)

10 candied coffee beans or regular coffee beans

Advance Preparation

The pie can be made a day or two ahead and refrigerated. Wrapped airtight, the pie can be frozen up to 1 week without flavor loss. Serve at room temperature or barely warm.

Special Equipment

Small double boiler or microwaveable bowl; 10-inch pie plate

Temperature and Time

325°F for 40 to 45 minutes

---

1. Prepare a crumb crust and press the crumbs into an even layer over the bottom of the pie plate and about two thirds of the way up the sides; don't bring crumbs up to the rim (or they may overbrown during baking). Freeze any excess crumbs for another use. Set aside; in warm weather, refrigerate. Position a rack in the center of the oven and preheat the oven to 325°F.

continued

2. In the top of a small double boiler, combine the butter with the unsweetened and semisweet solid chocolate and set over simmering water until melted. Or melt the butter and chocolate in the microwave on 50% power for about 1 minute; stir, then repeat if necessary until smooth. Stir the chocolate mixture together and set it aside to cool slightly.

3. In an electric mixer bowl or a food processor fitted with the steel blade, blend the dry ingredients: cocoa, salt, nutmeg, cornstarch, both sugars, and powdered coffee. Add the cream cheese and pulse or beat until completely blended into the dry mixture. Add the wet ingredients: egg plus whites, sour cream, cream cheese, corn syrup, and vanilla. Scrape in the melted butter and chocolate mixture. Blend just until smooth; don't overbeat.

4. Scrape the filling into the prepared pie shell. Bake the pie for 40 to 45 minutes, until the top puffs up slightly, appears shiny, and feels dry to the touch. The top may be crackled. It will sink down and flatten as it cools. If you wish to garnish the pie, arrange the coffee beans in a ring around the edge, so each bean will mark one of ten servings. Serve warm; or cool completely, then refrigerate, but bring to room temperature before serving.

Nutritional Analysis (per serving): 279 calories; 5 g protein; 10 g fat; 2.6 g satfat; 47 g carbohydrate; 220 mg sodium; 32 mg cholesterol

---

Light Touch

Classic Mississippi Mud Pie was always one of my favorite desserts, though my eyes were invariably bigger than my stomach; I never could do it justice because it was so rich. My new version has a 43% reduction in fat (29% calories from fat). This is achieved by substituting a crumb crust, replacing half the solid chocolate with cocoa, cutting three quarters of the butter (replacing it with some low-fat cream cheese), dropping 2 yolks, and adding nonfat sour cream. To put back some pizzazz, I have added nutmeg, extra vanilla, and coffee.

PEACH PIZZA

Yield: One 12-inch "pie"; 12 servings

A pie without a pie plate, this easy-to-make free-form pastry is also known as a French galette or Italian crostata. The pie crust is simply rolled out, topped with a layer of sugared sliced fruit, and baked on a cookie sheet. Simple and fun to make . . . let the kids help you.

Low-Sugar Note: For individuals with diabetes or those on other low-sugar diets, omit all sugar in the crust and fruit; for sweetening, substitute any sugar-free all-fruit preserves for the regular preserves in the recipe.

Pastry

1½ recipes Reduced-Fat Cream Cheese Pastry (page 47)

Fruit Filling

1¾ to 2 pounds (5 or 6 large) ripe peaches, peeled, pitted, and sliced, or nectarines, left unpeeled but pitted and sliced (about 4 cups)

1 tablespoon fresh lemon or lime juice

¼ cup granulated sugar, divided

½ teaspoon ground cinnamon

½ teaspoon ground nutmeg

1 tablespoon all-purpose flour

½ cup apricot or peach preserves

¼ cup crushed crisp rice or wheat flake cereal or graham cracker crumbs

Egg Glaze

1 large egg white

2 teaspoons water

Topping

1 tablespoon confectioners' sugar

Advance Preparation

This is best when baked fresh, but will stand 4 or 5 hours without softening.

Special Equipment

18-inch square of heavy-duty aluminum foil; cookie sheet with only 1 edge; pastry brush; pastry scraper or broad spatula

Temperature and Time

425°F for 15 minutes, then 350°F about 20 minutes longer

1. Prepare the pastry and chill it for about 30 minutes while peeling and pitting peaches: To peel peaches, drop them into a large pot of boiling water, boil for about 2 minutes, then transfer them with a slotted spoon to a bowl of cold water. Drain when peaches are cool. The skins will slip off.

2. Position a rack in the center of the oven and preheat the oven to 425°F.

3. Thinly slice the peeled peaches, or unpeeled nectarines, into a large bowl and toss with the lemon or lime juice, 3 tablespoons of the granulated sugar, the cinnamon, nutmeg, and flour.

continued

4. Measure an 18-inch square of heavy-duty foil, turn it shiny side down, and lightly sprinkle it with flour. With your fingernail or a toothpick, draw a rough 14-inch-diameter circle on the foil as a guide to rolling out the dough. Shape the dough into a flat disk and set it in the center of the marked foil circle. Top the dough with a sheet of plastic wrap, and roll it into a 14-inch disk fitting approximately into the marked circle. Alternatively, without the rolling pin, you can simply press the dough with your fingers (through the plastic wrap) into this circle (children love to do this). Slide the foil and dough onto a flat cookie sheet and peel off the plastic wrap. With your fingernail or a toothpick, measure and lightly mark a 12-inch-diameter circle on the rolled dough, leaving a 2-inch-wide border which will later be folded up over the fruit.

5. In a small bowl or cup, beat together the egg white and water for the glaze. Working inside the marked 12-inch dough circle, brush on some of the egg glaze, spread on the preserves, then sprinkle with the cereal or crumbs to absorb excess fruit juice.

6. Put the prepared fruit slices on top of the crumbs, either placing the slices in carefully arranged overlapping concentric circles or simply tossing them on at random and spreading to a fairly even layer.

7. Use a pastry scraper or a spatula dipped in flour to loosen the 2-inch dough border all around. Gently flip it up and over the fruit, allowing it to fold over itself like fabric. Brush any pastry cracks with a little egg glaze and pinch to seal. Brush egg glaze over the pastry border, then sprinkle the border with the remaining 1 tablespoon of granulated sugar.

8. Bake the pie at 425°F for 15 minutes, then reduce the heat to 350°F and bake an additional 20 minutes, until the dough border is golden brown and the fruit slices are tender when pierced with the tip of a knife. Cool on a wire rack. Before serving, sift a little confectioners' sugar over the top. Cut into wedges to serve.

Nutritional Analysis (per serving): 227 calories; 4 g protein; 8.5 g fat; 2 g satfat; 35 g carbohydrate; 206 mg sodium; 12 mg cholesterol

---
Light Touch

The cream cheese pastry is the easiest dough to handle for this purpose and also has the best flavor. Although there is no fat in the fruit filling, the pastry pushes the total calories from fat to 33%.

TORTILLA TARTS

Yield: One 8-inch tart; 2 to 3 servings

Slice ripe nectarines onto a toasted flour tortilla, sprinkle with a pinch of sugar, broil for a few minutes, and what do you have? An original and delightful fruit tart that is quick and easy to make (children love to prepare them).

The size of the tart depends upon the diameter of the tortilla. Some brands available in supermarkets are about 8 inches in diameter. If your flour tortillas are a different size, adjust the quantity of topping to fit. Watch broiling time because you are only heating the fruit through and caramelizing the top. If using apples, select soft, sweet McIntosh, for example, and slice them thinly. Individuals on sugar-free diets should substitute sugar-free all-fruit preserves for the sugar. For a special treat, top each tart with a spoonful of Margarita Sorbet (page 212) and sprinkle on a few grains of cayenne pepper.

One 8-inch flour tortilla

1¹/₂ tablespoons apricot or other fruit preserves

2 ripe nectarines, left unpeeled, pitted, and thinly sliced

1 teaspoon granulated sugar

Pinch of ground cinnamon or nutmeg

1. To toast the tortilla, preheat an ungreased skillet (best *not* to use a non-stick type). When the surface is hot, add the tortilla and warm 20 to 30 seconds on each side, until it becomes brown-spotted and crisp; it may begin to puff up in a few places. Set the tortilla on a cookie sheet or other flat baking pan. Preheat the broiler.

2. Top the toasted tortilla with the preserves, then arrange the nectarine slices in an attractive pattern of overlapping rows. Be sure to use enough fruit to cover the top completely. Sprinkle the fruit with sugar and cinnamon or nutmeg.

3. Place the tortilla tart about 4 inches below a preheated broiler and broil for 4 to 5 minutes, watching carefully, until the fruit edges are golden brown and the top is bubbling and caramelized.

Nutritional Analysis (per half a tart): 192 calories; 3 g protein; 2.6 g fat; 0.5 g satfat; 41 g carbohydrate; 167 mg sodium; 0 mg cholesterol

Advance Preparation

The flour tortillas can be toasted ahead, but the fruit should be added as close to serving time as possible so the tortilla stays crisp.

Special Equipment

Heavy-bottomed frying pan slightly larger in diameter than tortilla (10-inch, for example); pastry brush

Temperature and Time

Broil tart for 4 to 5 minutes

Light Touch

Flour tortillas make a perfect pie crust: only 12% calories from fat, zero cholesterol, and, best of all, no preparation (if you buy them ready-made).

BURRITO BLINTZES

Yield: 10 filled burrito blintzes; 10 servings

Roll a tortilla around sweetened cinnamon cottage cheese and a few blueberries and caramelize the package under a broiler to make this fabulous, if not exactly kosher, cross-cultural dessert. Eat it out of hand—crisp and sugary crust, warm creamy filling...the perfect snack or buffet treat. Quick, easy, and delectable, this was created by my daughter, Cassandra, who is a talented baker.

Use any fresh berries in season: raspberries, blackberries, sliced fresh strawberries, or frozen whole unsweetened berries, thawed. Finely chopped fresh apricots or peaches are also good mixed with fresh blueberries. Be creative; this dessert is casual and fun.

Ten 8-inch flour tortillas, thawed if frozen, but not toasted

Glaze
  ¹/₂ cup apricot preserves
  ¹/₄ cup honey

Cheese Filling
  2 cups nonfat cottage cheese
  3 tablespoons fresh lemon juice
  ¹/₄ cup granulated sugar, or to taste
  ¹/₂ teaspoon ground cinnamon, or to taste
  2 tablespoons vanilla extract

Fruit
  1 pint fresh blueberries, picked over, rinsed, and patted dry

Topping
  3 tablespoons granulated sugar, divided

Advance Preparation

Burrito blintzes are best made fresh.

Special Equipment

Jelly roll pan or cookie sheet with edges all around; baking parchment or aluminum foil

Temperature and Time

Broil about 4 minutes per side

1. If the tortillas were frozen, be sure they are room temperature so they will be flexible. Set out a jelly roll pan or other baking dish with an edge and line it with baking parchment or aluminum foil; set aside. Preheat the broiler.

2. In a small bowl, stir together the preserves and honey to make a glaze. Set aside.

3. Make the cheese filling. In a blender, food processor, or bowl, combine the cottage cheese, lemon juice, sugar, cinnamon, and vanilla. Pulse or beat until well mixed but not puréed; you should still see some of cottage cheese texture. Taste and adjust the flavor if needed.

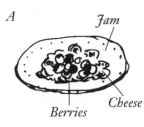

A

Jam

Berries   *Cheese*

B

C

D

4. To fill burritos, set one flour tortilla flat on a work surface. Spread about 2 teaspoons of the glaze over the top, then spoon about 3 level tablespoons of the cheese filling onto the center (*A*). Add a few fresh berries (the number depends upon their size). To fold like a blintz, bring the bottom edge up over the filling (*B*), then fold in each side flap (*C*). Holding the sides in place, roll the top edge down and tuck it under the bottom. Place the folded burrito on the prepared baking sheet with the tucked edge on the bottom (*D*), holding the filled "pillow" in place. Repeat, filling and folding all the tortillas.

5. Sprinkle the top of each burrito with about ½ teaspoon of the granulated sugar. Place the baking sheet 4 to 5 inches below the preheated broiler and broil about 4 minutes, just until the tops are golden brown and caramelized. Remove the pan from the broiler, turn over each burrito, sprinkle each with another ½ teaspoon of the sugar topping and broil the second side until browned. Cool slightly and serve warm, with additional fresh berries alongside.

Nutritional Analysis (per burrito): 310 calories; 9 g protein; 4 g fat; 1 g satfat; 61 g carbohydrate; 492 mg sodium; 4 mg cholesterol

Light Touch

Store-bought flour tortillas are low in fat and have no cholesterol, but they are very high in sodium. However, they are easier than making your own crepes or blintzes. Because of the sweetening, this dessert is high in calories but has only 12% calories from fat.

VALENTINE HEART TARTS

Yield: 8 to 9 individual tartlets

A chocolate crumb crust cradles strawberry cream in these easy-to-make heart-shaped tartlets. Tartlet molds in heart shapes are sold in gourmet and kitchen supply shops and by mail order (see pages 372–373). Be sure to garnish your tartlets with a whole strawberry or a fresh mint sprig.

1½ recipes Chocolate Crumb Crust (page 55)

1 recipe Strawberry Cream Pie, filling alone through step 5 (page 90)

8 fresh whole strawberries, rinsed and patted dry

Fresh mint sprigs

1. Prepare the crumb crust, pressing it into tartlet molds and prebake or refrigerate them to set while you prepare the filling.

2. Prepare the strawberry cream and fill the tartlet molds. Chill at least 3 hours, or overnight. Before serving, garnish each tartlet with a whole fresh strawberry or slices fanned out, or a mint sprig.

Nutritional Analysis (per tartlet with no garnish): 250 calories; 6 g protein; 7 g fat; 0.9 g satfat; 41 g carbohydrate; 81 mg sodium; 6 mg cholesterol

---

Advance Preparation

Chill filled tartlets for 3 hours minimum. Make tartlets 1 day ahead and refrigerate until ready to serve.

Special Equipment

Eight 3- to 4-inch heart-shaped tartlet molds, oven-proof Pyrex or metal

Temperature and Time

Prebake crust: 350°F for 8 minutes

Light Touch

The fact that this beautiful and tasty treat has a minimum of saturated fat and cholesterol and obtains only 25% of its calories from fat should make you especially glad to share it with someone you love.

CHOCOLATE-CARAMEL TURTLE TARTLETS

Yield: 8 to 10 individual tartlets; or one 9-inch pie; 10 servings

Remember turtle candies? I have always loved those gooey chocolate-covered caramels with little pecan feet, the taste inspiration for these individual chocolate mousse tartlets topped by caramel sauce and toasted pecans. Turtle heaven. Be sure to toast the pecans in advance, to heighten their flavor. This is an easy recipe for entertaining and can also be made in a single pie shell.

1½ recipes Chocolate Crumb Crust (page 55) for tartlets or 1 recipe for 9-inch pie

1 recipe Chocolate Mousse (page 186)

1 recipe Extra-Thick Caramel Sauce (page 264)

⅓ cup pecans, chopped and toasted (page 333)

1. Prepare the crumb crust, press it into the tartlet pans or a single pie plate, and prebake or refrigerate. Divide the prepared mousse evenly between the tartlet pans or spread it all into the pie shell. Refrigerate at least 3 hours to set the mousse.

2. Shortly before serving, remove the sauce from the refrigerator so it is not too stiff.

3. To serve, pour some caramel sauce over each tartlet and sprinkle a few chopped nuts on top. Or pour the sauce over the top of the filled pie and sprinkle with the chopped nuts.

Nutritional Analysis (per tartlet with 1 scant tablespoon extra-thick sauce and a sprinkling of nuts on top): 351 calories; 6 g protein; 13.6 g fat; 2.1 g satfat; 55 g carbohydrate; 72 mg sodium; 27 mg cholesterol

Advance Preparation

Chill filled tartlets for 3 hours minimum. Pecans can be toasted several days ahead. Caramel sauce can be made a week ahead, covered, and refrigerated.

Special Equipment

Eight to ten 4-inch tartlet pans or one 9-inch pie plate

Temperature and Time

Prebake crust: 350°F for 8 minutes

Light Touch

Our turtle confection with all the trimmings has just 33% calories from fat and very little saturated fat. If you cut the sauce to a scant 1 tablespoon and omit all the nuts, you come back to 30% calories from fat, 331 calories, and 12 g fat per serving. I say go for the nuts.

Cakes,
PLAIN AND FANCY

Carry Baker baked a cake
Bobby Baker stayed awake
All the night with stomach-ache.
Profite brides, by this mistake!
—Pots, Pans, & Pie Plates &
How to Use Them. *1905. Lord
Baltimore Press, Friedenwald Co.,
Baltimore, Maryland*

From this little pamphlet published in Baltimore at the turn of the century, it is clear that Carry Baker needed a better recipe. Another of her dessert introductions: "T'was a snowy day in winter/ The thermometer said zero/ 'We have ice cream, dear, for dinner,'/ Thus she welcomed home her hero." On second thought, she needed a lot more than a good recipe.

You won't be serving your hero ice cream on a snowy day with this large selection of cakes to choose from.

Coffee cakes invite sharing, not only of good talk, but of the recipes themselves. Claire's Fruit Pudding Cake is typical, a cake shared by friends, then passed along to me.

Banana-Apricot Cake, on the other hand, is a serendipitous discovery, made by combining ingredients on hand. There are more than twenty-seven cakes in this chapter. Besides the coffee cakes, there are so-called plain, or conventional, old-fashioned favorites such as all-purpose berry shortcake, layer, Bundt, and pound cakes, and Steve Keneipp's Coffee-Spice Angel Food Cake, a new take on an old favorite.

To lead off the fancy cakes category, I have a group of four break-their-hearts chocolate cakes—Chocolate–Sour Cream Cake, Midnight Chocolate Cake, Cocoa Cake, and Drop-Dead Chocolate-Espresso Mousse Cake—plus two extra-rich cheesecakes for party galas. To guarantee festive holidays, try glamorous ruby-red Cranberry Upside-down Cake, New Year's Honey Cake, or an unusual Belgian Honey Cake, fall harvest Pumpkin Cream Bombe, Father's Day "Tie" Cake, spring Almond or Chocolate Sponge Roll, and a Double Chocolate Passover Sponge Cake. Need more drama? Try our finale, a Fresh Orange Wedding Cake, complete with three tiers covered with Orange Buttercream decorated with Sugared Rose Petals.

SOUR CREAM COFFEE CAKE WITH CHOCOLATE-ALMOND STREUSEL

Yield: One 9-inch cake; 12 servings

This moist, flavorful coffee cake is rippled with chocolate-almond crumbs. The basic cake is flavored with vanilla extract and vanilla yogurt, but you can vary this to your taste by adding different flavor extracts or a variety of flavored yogurts (apricot or orange yogurt for orange extract, coffee yogurt for coffee extract).

If you prefer the streusel plain vanilla, omit the cocoa, use $^1/_2$ cup flour in the streusel, and replace the almond extract with vanilla.

Butter-flavor no-stick cooking spray

Advance Preparation

Cake can be made a day or two ahead and stored airtight at room temperature, or it can be double wrapped and frozen up to 2 weeks. Serve warm or at room temperature.

Special Equipment

8- or 9-inch square baking pan

Temperature and Time

350°F for 45 to 55 minutes

Streusel Crumbs

$^1/_3$ cup packed dark brown sugar

3 tablespoons granulated sugar

$^1/_3$ cup Grape-Nuts cereal

3 tablespoons walnuts or pecans

$1^1/_2$ teaspoons ground cinnamon

$^1/_2$ cup minus 2 tablespoons unsifted cake flour

2 tablespoons unsweetened cocoa

2 tablespoons unsalted butter, at room temperature

2 tablespoons light cream cheese, at room temperature

$^1/_2$ teaspoon almond extract

Batter

2 cups sifted cake flour

1 cup granulated sugar

$^1/_2$ teaspoon baking powder

$^3/_4$ teaspoon baking soda

$^1/_4$ teaspoon salt

2 large egg yolks

$^1/_2$ cup vanilla or plain nonfat or low-fat yogurt, top liquid poured off

$^2/_3$ cup nonfat or low-fat sour cream

$^1/_4$ cup ($^1/_2$ stick) unsalted butter, softened but not melted

2 teaspoons vanilla extract

1. Position a rack in the center of the oven and preheat the oven to 350°F. Lightly coat a baking pan with cooking spray.

continued

2. Make the streusel. In the workbowl of a food processor fitted with the steel blade, combine the brown and white sugars, Grape-Nuts, walnuts, and cinnamon. Pulse a few times, just until the nuts are coarsely chopped. Add the flour, cocoa, butter, cream cheese, and extract and pulse just until large crumbs form. If the mixture is too powdery, add 2 or 3 drops of water and pulse 4 or 5 more times. Turn the crumbs out into a bowl and set aside. Wipe out the workbowl with a paper towel.

3. Make the cake. Combine and whisk together in a medium-sized mixing bowl the cake flour, sugar, baking powder, baking soda, and salt. Set aside.

4. In the processor workbowl combine the egg yolks, yogurt, sour cream, butter, and vanilla. Blend until smooth. Add the flour mixture all at once and pulse about 10 to 12 times, just to combine; do *not* overwork or try to blend it completely smooth or the cake will be tough. The batter should be very thick.

5. Spread about two thirds of the batter into the prepared pan and sprinkle on a scant ³/₄ cup of the streusel. Spread on the remaining batter, then sprinkle on the rest of the streusel.

6. Bake for 45 to 55 minutes, until the top is golden brown and springy to the touch and a cake tester inserted in the center comes out dry. Cool the cake in the pan on a wire rack about 10 minutes, then cut into squares and serve from the pan.

Nutritional Analysis (per serving): 284 calories; 5 g protein; 9 g fat; 4 g satfat; 47 g carbohydrate; 165 mg sodium; 53 mg cholesterol

---

Light Touch

One of my favorite classic sour cream coffee cakes is so rich and fat-laden that it contains 56% calories from fat per serving. This version has half the fat (28% calories from fat), yet the flavor and texture leave nothing to be desired.

Most of this moist richness comes from the 6 tablespoons of butter in the recipe (more than any other cake in this book). If you are feeling expansive, you can raise the ante (to 33% calories from fat) by adding to the streusel crumbs an extra 3 tablespoons Grape-Nuts and ¹/₃ cup chopped nuts and increasing the butter in the batter from ¹/₄ to ¹/₃ cup. Note: This is one of the rare reduced-fat recipes in which you can use up egg yolks; no whites are needed.

CLAIRE'S FRUIT PUDDING CAKE

Yield: 5 cups batter; one 9-inch cake; 9 servings

This recipe, given to me by my good friend Claire Rosenberg, is a winner. It has a soft texture somewhere between a pudding and a cake. It is sweet, tender, filled with fruit, and quick and easy to prepare. Use whatever fruit is in season and serve it warm for breakfast or brunch.

Butter-flavor no-stick cooking spray

1 cup nonfat or low-fat sour cream or plain yogurt, top liquid poured off

2 large egg whites

³/₄ cup granulated sugar (use 1 cup if made with rhubarb)

1 teaspoon vanilla extract

1¹/₂ cups sifted all-purpose flour, or 1 cup all-purpose and ¹/₂ cup whole wheat flour

¹/₂ teaspoon salt

¹/₂ teaspoon baking powder

1 teaspoon baking soda

3 cups seasonal fruit of your choice—try 2 cups fresh blueberries plus 1 cup fresh or frozen nectarine or peach slices; or 3 cups blueberries and/or raspberries; or cut-up rhubarb

Advance Preparation

The cake can be made a day ahead but is best served warm from the oven.

Special Equipment

8- or 9-inch square baking dish

Temperature and Time

350°F for 40 to 45 minutes

1. Position a rack in the center of the oven and preheat the oven to 350°F. Lightly coat a baking pan with cooking spray; set aside.

2. In a large mixing bowl, beat or whisk together the sour cream, egg whites, sugar, and vanilla.

3. On top of the wet ingredients, toss in the flour, salt, baking powder, and baking soda. Whisk to blend well. Stir in the fruit.

4. Turn the batter out into the prepared pan and bake 40 to 45 minutes, until golden brown on top. A cake tester should come out clean or with just a few moist crumbs clinging to it. Cool the cake in the pan on a wire rack about 10 minutes, then cut it into squares and serve warm from the pan.

Nutritional Analysis (per serving): 190 calories; 5 g protein; 0.3 g fat; 0 g satfat; 42 g carbohydrate; 260 mg sodium; 0 mg cholesterol

Light Touch

In its original form, this recipe contained only 24% calories from fat and was perfectly acceptable as a reduced-fat cake. By eliminating an egg yolk, substituting another white, and using nonfat sour cream, I removed all the cholesterol and nearly all the fat, dropping to 2% the calories from fat—a dramatic change. Try either version, depending upon your own dietary needs; both taste great.

BERRY SHORTCAKE

Yield: 12 servings

Can you improve upon a classic? It is not something I would undertake on a whim, but when I came up with these lemon-and-nutmeg–scented biscuits, I knew they would be delicious topped with sweet berries and vanilla cream. Strawberries are traditional, but all berries are eligible, especially mixed (blueberries and raspberries, for example, or blackberries and wineberries).

The cream is up to you. Low-fat frozen vanilla yogurt is first choice when someone is looking over your shoulder; for an indulgence, try a double recipe (4 cups) of Vanilla Cream, page 247, divine plain or with honey but still down-to-earth compared with whipped cream.

Butter-flavor no-stick cooking spray

Lemon-Nutmeg Biscuits

2 cups unsifted cake flour

2 teaspoons baking powder

$^1/_2$ teaspoon baking soda

$^1/_2$ teaspoon salt

3 tablespoons granulated sugar

1 tablespoon grated lemon zest

$^1/_2$ teaspoon ground nutmeg

$^1/_4$ cup canola oil

$^3/_4$ cup buttermilk

Biscuit Glaze

$^1/_3$ cup buttermilk

2 tablespoons granulated sugar

Fruit

6 cups (1$^1/_2$ quarts) fresh blueberries or mixed berries, picked over, rinsed, patted dry, and hulled if necessary

3 tablespoons water

$^1/_4$ to $^1/_2$ cup granulated sugar, or to taste

Cream

1$^1/_2$ quarts vanilla low-fat or nonfat frozen yogurt

1. Position a rack in the center of the oven and preheat the oven to 400°F. Lightly coat a baking sheet with cooking spray.

2. First prepare the biscuits. In a large mixing bowl, whisk together the flour, baking powder, baking soda, salt, sugar, lemon zest, and nutmeg. Add the oil and buttermilk and whisk just until blended. Don't overwork the batter or it will toughen.

Advance Preparation

Biscuits can be prepared ahead, wrapped airtight, and frozen up to 1 month, but they are much better when prepared fresh. Fruit can be sugared and refrigerated several hours in advance. Vanilla Cream can be prepared a day ahead, covered, and refrigerated. Assemble the shortcakes just before serving.

Special Equipment

Baking parchment (optional); round cookie cutter, approximately 2 inches in diameter; pastry brush

Temperature and Time

Biscuits: 400°F for 12 to 15 minutes

3. Form the dough into a ball; if it is very sticky, stir in 1 to 2 tablespoons more flour. Transfer the dough to a lightly floured surface and pat it into a rectangle about 1/2 inch thick. Using a 2-inch round cookie cutter, cut out 12 biscuits (a 2 1/2-inch cutter makes 10; a 3-inch makes 6). Place the biscuits on the prepared baking sheet.

4. To glaze the biscuits, brush the tops with buttermilk and sprinkle on a little sugar. Bake for 12 to 15 minutes, until well risen and golden on top. Transfer to a wire rack to cool.

5. Prepare the fruit. Set aside about 1 cup of berries for garnish. Combine 2 cups of the berries with water and 2 tablespoons of the sugar in a nonreactive saucepan. Cook 4 to 5 minutes on medium heat to release the berry juices. Add the remaining berries and stir in sugar to taste. Refrigerate until needed.

6. To assemble the shortcakes, slice each biscuit in half horizontally with a serrated knife. Set the bottom half of each on a dessert plate; cover with about 1/3 cup of the frozen yogurt, then with 1/2 cup of the berries. Cover with the top half of the biscuit and add 2 generous tablespoons of yogurt and a few berries. Repeat with the remaining biscuits and filling. Serve the shortcakes garnished with some of the reserved berries alongside.

Nutritional Analysis (per serving with 1/2 cup low-fat frozen yogurt): 330 calories; 7 g protein; 7.6 g fat; 1.9 g satfat; 59 g carbohydrate; 265 mg sodium; 10 mg cholesterol

Light Touch

With only 20% calories from fat, low-fat frozen yogurt makes this affordable in terms of fat content; nonfat frozen yogurt, which is slightly less creamy, cuts the numbers a little more. If you can allow yourself 32% calories from fat, 4 g more fat, and 3 mg more cholesterol, try the Vanilla Cream. Whatever your choice, you can feel smug comparing it to the old-fashioned biscuits with whipped cream—with twice the fat at 65% calories from fat and 24 g fat (12 g satfat) per serving.

BANANA-APRICOT CAKE

Yield: 4 cups batter; 12 servings (2¹/₄ × 3-inch slices)

Affectionately known as banapricot cake, this is my new best friend. Like many happy culinary discoveries, this arose when necessity tripped over serendipity on the way to the oven. I was snacking on some lovely moist dried apricots while trying to decide what to do with some seriously brown bananas when it became perfectly clear that they should be combined. I have always found plain banana bread to be slightly cloying, but this blend with apricots is a perfect balance between sweet and richly tangy fruits. The cake itself is not too sweet, very moist, and it keeps well. Using the food processor to coarsely chop the fruit as well as to mix this cake makes preparation a snap; however, the chopping and mixing can also be done with an electric mixer or by hand.

This is the perfect coffee cake for a brunch party, but my breakfast treat is to cut a slice in half and toast it.

Advance Preparation

Cake can be baked ahead, double-wrapped, and frozen up to 2 weeks.

Special Equipment

8 - or 9-inch square baking pan

Temperature and Time

350°F for 35 to 45 minutes

Butter-flavor no-stick cooking spray

All-purpose flour for dusting the pan

Batter

4 ounces (¹/₂ cup firmly packed) dried apricot halves (preferably moist style, or see step 2)

¹/₂ cup plus 2 tablespoons granulated sugar

1 cup ripe bananas (about 2 medium or 3 small)

¹/₄ cup canola oil

1 large egg plus 2 large egg whites

¹/₂ cup low-fat sour cream

¹/₃ cup fresh orange juice

2 teaspoons vanilla extract

³/₄ cup unsifted all-purpose flour

³/₄ cup unsifted whole wheat pastry flour (or use a total of 1¹/₂ cups all-purpose flour)

1 teaspoon baking powder

¹/₂ teaspoon baking soda

¹/₂ teaspoon salt

1 teaspoon ground cinnamon

¹/₂ teaspoon ground nutmeg

¹/₄ teaspoon ground ginger

Topping (optional)

1 tablespoon confectioners' sugar

1. Position a rack in the center of the oven and preheat the oven to 350°F. Coat a baking pan with cooking spray. Dust the pan with flour, then tap out excess flour.

2. For best results, the apricots should be flexible and moist. If yours are hard, cover them with about ¼ cup of water or orange juice and microwave on high for 5-second spurts until soft; or soak them in liquid about 30 minutes at room temperature, then drain. In a food processor fitted with the steel blade, combine the apricots and sugar. Pulse to chop the fruit roughly into ¼-inch bits. Remove the mixture to a bowl and set aside.

3. Add the bananas, to the workbowl and pulse to mash. Add the oil, egg and whites, sour cream, orange juice, and vanilla and pulse to blend well. Add back the apricot-sugar mixture and pulse just to combine.

4. In a mixing bowl, combine the flours, baking powder, baking soda, salt, cinnamon, nutmeg, and ginger. Whisk them together, then add them all at once to the wet ingredients in the processor and pulse just until blended in. Do not overwork or gluten will build up in the batter and the cake will not be tender.

5. Spoon the batter into the prepared pan, smooth the top, and bake 35 to 45 minutes, until the top is golden brown, springy to the touch, and a cake tester inserted in the center comes out nearly clean (some of the sticky fruit may show). Cool in the pan on a wire rack. Before serving, sift on a light topping of confectioners' sugar. Cut into 12 pieces and serve directly from the pan.

Nutritional Analysis (per serving): 199 calories; 4 g protein; 6 g fat; 0.5 g satfat; 34 g carbohydrate; 174 mg sodium; 18 mg cholesterol

Light Touch

My old-fashioned banana cake has 47% of its calories from fat. This lightened version has all the flavor and moist texture but contains less than half the sugar and fat; cholesterol drops with the elimination of 2 yolks. The result: a reduction of 45% calories from fat (to 26%). I add flavor with extra vanilla and spices and enhance moisture with fat-reduced sour cream. Whole wheat flour is a boost to nutritional value, but texture and taste are just as good with all white flour. The fruit gives nearly 3 g dietary fiber per serving.

Note: If you prefer to cut 9 large slices to serve this for dessert, the numbers rise only slightly: 276 calories, 8 g fat, 0.7 g satfat, and 24 mg cholesterol per serving.

HOLIDAY CRANBERRY UPSIDE-DOWN CAKE

Yield: One 10-inch cake; 10 to 12 servings

Old-fashioned upside-down cake never looked so glamorous! Glowing ruby-red cranberries trimmed with tiny white stars top an apple and spice cake.

This is easy to prepare once you know three tricks; you can whip it up at the last minute or make it ahead to freeze until needed. Secret number one: Small aspic or cookie cutters are used to stamp stars (or hearts or Christmas trees) from apple slices that are set in the cranberry topping. If you don't have cutters, use a paring knife and invent your own shapes. Secret number two: A solid layer of sweet, quick-cooking apple slices (Delicious or McIntosh, for example) must be carefully positioned between the cranberries and the cake batter; without this barrier, the batter mingles with the berries as they bake so that the unmolded cake top is disappointingly plain. Secret number 3: Use solidly frozen cranberries to retain the bright red color; thawed or fresh berries darken as they bake. Note: Substituting dark corn syrup in the topping will dull and darken the color of the cake top; it is best avoided. Granny Smith apples work but should be sliced extra thin. Serve the cake plain or with Brandied Cranberry-Maple Sauce (page 261), Vanilla Cream (page 247), or vanilla frozen yogurt.

Butter-flavor no-stick cooking spray

Topping

$^1/_2$ **cup granulated sugar**

$^1/_3$ **cup light corn syrup**

1 teaspoon unsalted butter

1 tablespoon grated orange zest

$^1/_2$ **teaspoon ground cinnamon**

2 to 2$^1/_2$ apples (such as Red or Golden Delicious or McIntosh), peeled, cored, and thinly sliced, preferably crosswise: cut 3 slices $^1/_4$ inch thick, the rest $^1/_8$ inch thick

2 cups frozen whole cranberries

Batter

3 tablespoons fresh orange or apple juice

$^1/_3$ **cup canola oil**

1 large egg plus 1 egg white

1 teaspoon vanilla extract

1 teaspoon orange or maple extract (optional)

$^2/_3$ **cup granulated sugar**

1$^1/_2$ cups sifted cake flour

1 teaspoon baking powder

$^1/_4$ **teaspoon salt**

Advance Preparation

Cake is best served freshly baked or warm, but may be prepared ahead, wrapped airtight, and frozen up to 2 weeks.

Special Equipment

10-inch deep-dish metal or flameproof pie plate, casserole, or skillet; small ($^1/_2$- to $^3/_4$-inch) aspic or cookie cutters or sharp paring knife; flat serving platter about 12 inches in diameter (slightly larger than baking pan); pastry brush

Temperature and Time

325°F for 35 to 40 minutes

1 teaspoon ground cinnamon

1 teaspoon ground nutmeg

1 teaspoon ground ginger

¹/₄ teaspoon ground allspice (optional)

Glaze

¹/₂ cup seedless raspberry jam or red currant preserves

1. Position a rack in the center of the oven and preheat the oven to 325°F.

2. To prepare the topping, lightly coat a 10-inch flameproof pie plate or skillet with cooking spray and add the sugar, corn syrup, butter, orange zest, and cinnamon. Set the plate on the stovetop over low heat and stir 3 to 4 minutes, until the mixture begins to liquefy. Remove the pan from the heat.

3. Use canapé cutters or a sharp paring knife to cut out 5 or 6 small decorative stars or other shapes in the ¹/₄-inch-thick apple slices. Keeping in mind that the bottom of the plate will later be the top of the cake, carefully position the decorative apple shapes on the bottom of the plate (it is okay if sugar syrup covers them), then place the frozen cranberries around them, completely surrounding the decorations, forming an even layer in the plate bottom.

4. Arrange the remaining sliced apples in 2 even layers completely covering the cranberries and apple designs. Use small pieces to fill in any holes. This barrier is essential to keep the berries in place and separated from the cake batter during baking.

5. To prepare the cake batter, whisk together in a large mixing bowl the orange juice, oil, egg plus white, vanilla, and orange extract, if using. Beat in the sugar. Add all the dry ingredients: flour, baking powder, salt, and spices. Whisk or stir until completely blended and smooth.

6. Taking care not to disturb the arrangement of apple slices, spoon the cake batter over the fruit and smooth the top gently. Place the pan in the preheated oven and bake 35 to 40 minutes, until the cake top is golden brown and dry to the touch and a cake tester inserted about 2 inches from the edge comes out clean. The center may still be slightly softer.

7. Cool the cake on a wire rack 3 to 4 minutes. Run a knife blade around the pan edge, then cover with a platter, hold both containers together with potholders, and invert. Lift off the baking pan. If necessary, use the tip of a knife to reposition any fruit that sticks to the baking pan.

8. To make the glaze, stir the preserves or jam in a small saucepan over medium heat until liquefied. Use a pastry brush to brush the glaze over the cranberries, keeping the glaze off the decorative apple slices. Serve the cake warm or at room temperature, with sauce if desired.

Nutritional Analysis (per serving): 327 calories; 3 g protein; 8 g fat; 1 g satfat; 62 g carbohydrate; 108 mg sodium; 22 mg cholesterol

continued

Classic upside-down cake is usually made with 2 eggs and about $^{1}/_{3}$ cup butter, giving it about 34% calories from fat. Not extravagant, but high in saturated fat. Compare this to my enlightened version with just 23% calories from fat, achieved by dropping 1 egg yolk and replacing all but 1 teaspoon of butter with heart-healthy canola oil.

ALMOND SPONGE ROLL

─────────────────────────────*Yield: One 10-inch roll; 12 servings*

This is a light, almond-flavored sponge cake baked in a jelly roll pan. It has a fine, tender crumb and is flexible enough to be rolled without cracking. Fill it with anything that comes to mind, from fruit preserves to a generous cup of Apricot Mousse (page 188) or Vanilla Cream (page 247) sprinkled with fresh raspberries and toasted sliced almonds. Be sure to top the cake with a sifting of confectioners' sugar and a few toasted almond slices for an elegant finish. For fall holidays, make the spiced sponge variation that follows, filled with Pumpkin 'n' Spice Cream (page 247).

Instead of being rolled around a filling, this cake may be cut with a large cookie cutter into petits fours or individual shaped cakes (see Mother's Day Peach Melba, page 208). Or the cake can be sliced crosswise into quarters, then each quarter split horizontally, making eight layers to be filled and stacked into a tall oblong cake.

Butter-flavor no-stick cooking spray
All-purpose flour for dusting pan

Batter
$^{1}/_{2}$ cup sifted cake flour
$^{1}/_{4}$ cup sifted cornstarch
1 teaspoon baking powder
2 large eggs, separated, plus 2 large egg whites
Pinch of salt
$^{1}/_{2}$ cup plus 2 tablespoons granulated sugar, divided
1 tablespoon canola or safflower oil
1 teaspoon vanilla extract
1 teaspoon almond extract

Unmolding and Topping Cake
$^{1}/_{4}$ cup plus 2 tablespoons confectioners' sugar, divided
$^{1}/_{4}$ cup almond slices (optional), toasted (page 333)

Advance Preparation

Cake can be baked ahead, rolled in a towel, and left to cool several hours or overnight. Or, left in the towel, it can be enveloped in a plastic bag and frozen up to 1 week. Thaw, still wrapped, overnight in the refrigerator.

Special Equipment

$15^{1}/_{2} \times 10^{1}/_{2}$-inch jelly roll pan; baking parchment or wax paper; tea towel at least 10×18 inches; serrated knife

Temperature and Time

350°F for 11 to 13 minutes

1. Position a rack in the center of the oven and preheat the oven to 350°F. Dot a jelly roll pan in a few spots with cooking spray, then line the bottom with baking parchment or wax paper; the spray will hold down the paper. Lightly coat the paper with cooking spray, dust it with flour, and tap out excess flour.

2. Sift together the flour, cornstarch, and baking powder. Set aside.

3. In a grease-free medium-sized bowl, combine the egg whites and salt. With an electric mixer on medium speed, whip until the whites are foamy. Gradually add $1/4$ cup plus 2 tablespoons of the granulated sugar, whipping until the whites are stiff but not dry. Set the whipped whites aside. Shake off the beaters and, without washing them, return them to the mixer.

4. In a medium-sized bowl, combine the 2 egg yolks, the oil, extracts, and remaining $1/4$ cup of granulated sugar. With the electric mixer, whip until thick and light colored. Scrape down the bowl and beaters. Whip on high speed 3 to 4 minutes, until the batter forms a ribbon falling back on itself when the machine is turned off and the beater is lifted.

5. Fold about one third of the beaten whites into the batter, then fold in a few tablespoons of the flour mixture. Gently fold in the remaining whites and flour, alternating, in several additions. The batter should remain light, airy, and smooth.

    Turn the batter out into the prepared pan, smoothing the top and spreading it to the edges of the pan with a spatula. Bake for 11 to 13 minutes, until the top of the cake is golden, feels springy to the touch, and the edges begin to pull away from the pan sides. Do not overbake or the cake will dry out and be difficult to roll or handle.

6. While the cake bakes, spread out a tea towel on a work surface and sift over it $1/4$ cup of the confectioners' sugar, covering an area roughly 10×15 inches.

7. As soon as the cake is baked, invert the pan over the sugared area of the towel. Lift off the pan and peel off the paper. Use a serrated knife to trim a scant $1/8$-inch edge all around the cake. If you plan to roll the cake up over a filling, roll it into a towel now to cool. To do this, fold one end of the towel over a short end of the cake and roll them up together. Set the roll seam side down on a wire rack to cool. If you are using the cake in flat layers, let it cool completely while flat on a wire rack.

8. Fill and finish the cake per your individual recipe (see the introduction, above). Sift the remaining 2 tablespoons confectioners' sugar over the top and sprinkle on a few toasted almond slices. Slice the cake with a serrated knife.

Nutritional Analysis (per serving without filling): 103 calories; 2 g protein; 2 g fat; trace satfat; 19 g carbohydrate; 70 mg sodium; 36 mg cholesterol

continued

SPICED SPONGE ROLL

Prepare the sponge roll recipe above but omit the almond extract. Along with the dry ingredients, add 1 teaspoon ground cinnamon, 1¹/₂ teaspoons ground nutmeg, and ¹/₄ teaspoon each ground cloves and ground ginger.

ORANGE OR LEMON SPONGE ROLL

Prepare the sponge roll recipe above, substituting orange or lemon extract for the almond extract and adding the grated zest of 1 orange or lemon.

Light Touch

A classic jelly roll is made with 4 whole eggs and contains 15% calories from fat. By dropping 2 yolks and substituting 1 tablespoon of oil, I actually raise the number of calories from fat to 18% but cut approximately half the cholesterol, altering the total fat distribution slightly. Baking powder bolsters the leavening power of the yolk-reduced egg foam.

CHOCOLATE SPONGE ROLL

Yield: One 10-inch roll; 12 servings

This light chocolate cake is the basic black dress of my baking repertoire . . . it goes everywhere, pairs with every other flavor, and is always in good taste. Best of all, it is easy to make and rolls without cracking. Use it with any filling you like, from Honey-Vanilla Cream (page 247) with fresh raspberries to Apricot-Orange Cake Filling (page 254). Make an extra one to freeze for unexpected company.

Advance Preparation

The cake can be baked up to 1 month in advance, rolled up in a tea towel, wrapped airtight in a heavy-duty plastic bag and foil, and frozen. Thaw, still wrapped, overnight in the refrigerator. Wrapped in plastic wrap, the cake will hold about 2 days at room temperature without drying out.

Special Equipment

10¹/₂ × 15¹/₂-inch jelly roll pan; baking parchment or wax paper; tea towel at least 10 × 18 inches; serrated knife

Temperature and Time

350°F for 15 minutes

Butter-flavor no-stick cooking spray

²/₃ cup sifted unsweetened Dutch-processed cocoa, divided, plus extra for dusting the pan

5 tablespoons sifted cake flour

2 tablespoons sifted cornstarch

¹/₂ teaspoon baking powder

¹/₄ teaspoon baking soda

¹/₄ teaspoon salt

¹/₈ teaspoon ground cinnamon

2 large eggs, separated, plus 3 large egg whites, at room temperature

³/₄ cup granulated sugar, divided

1 teaspoon vanilla extract

1. Position a rack in the center of the oven and preheat the oven to 350°F. Dot a jelly roll pan with a few spots of cooking spray, then line the bottom with baking parchment or wax paper. Lightly coat the paper with cooking spray. Dust the paper with sifted cocoa and tap out the excess cocoa.

2. Sift together ¹/₃ cup of the cocoa, the flour, cornstarch, baking powder, baking soda, salt, and cinnamon into a medium-sized bowl.

3. In a large grease-free bowl, using an electric mixer, whip all the egg whites until foamy. Gradually add ¹/₂ cup of the sugar, whipping until the whites are stiff but not dry. Shake off the beaters and, without washing them, return them to the mixer. Set the whites aside.

4. In another large bowl, combine the egg yolks and vanilla. With the electric mixer on medium speed, whip the mixture until it turns pale yellow, about 1 minute. Add the remaining ¹/₄ cup of sugar and whip 3 to 4 minutes longer, until the batter forms a ribbon falling back on itself when the mixer is turned off and the beaters are lifted.

5. Fold about one third of the beaten whites into the batter, then fold in one third of the flour-cocoa mixture. Alternately fold the remaining whites and cocoa mixture into the batter in several additions. Turn the batter into the prepared pan, spreading it to the edges and smoothing the top. Bake for about 15 minutes, just until the top of the cake feels springy to the touch and the sides begin to shrink from the pan. Do not overbake.

continued

6. Meanwhile, spread out a tea towel on a work surface and sift the remaining ⅓ cup of cocoa over it, covering an area roughly 10 × 15 inches.

7. As soon as the cake is baked, invert it over the towel so the cake falls from the pan onto the cocoa. Lift off the pan and peel off the paper. With a serrated knife, trim away a scant ⅛-inch edge all around the cake. Fold one end of the towel over a short end of the cake and roll them up together. Set the roll seam side down on a rack to cool.

8. When completely cold, the cake can be double wrapped and stored in the refrigerator up to 2 days, or frozen. Or it can be filled (see the introduction, above). To fill the cake, unroll it on a work surface. Spread your choice of filling over the cake and reroll. Place the cake seam side down on a serving platter. Decorate according to specific recipe directions, or sift a little cocoa or confectioners' sugar over the top.

Nutritional Analysis (per serving without filling): 91 calories; 3 g protein; 1.7 g fat; 0.8 g satfat; 18 g carbohydrate; 134 mg sodium; 36 mg cholesterol

Light Touch

This delicious cake gets only 16% of its calories from fat. When fruit or another low-fat filling is added, the numbers are even lower.

FATHER'S DAY "TIE" CAKE

Yield: One 10-inch sponge roll; 12 servings

Advance Preparation

The filling can be made a couple of days ahead, covered, and refrigerated. The sponge roll can be made up to 2 days ahead, wrapped in a tea towel and plastic wrap, and refrigerated. Fill the cake the day it is to be served, and add the stenciled design no more than about 4 hours ahead.

Special Equipment

Craft paper or medium-stiff bond or typing paper at least 6 × 11 inches; scissors or X-Acto knife; cardboard or old magazine (to put under paper while cutting); small (3- to 5-inch diameter) medium-mesh sifter

This is as much fun to make as it is to receive: an easy-to-prepare Chocolate Sponge Roll filled with not-too-sweet Apricot-Orange Cake Filling, topped with a sifted confectioners' sugar and cinnamon design in the shape of a striped tie. Be sure to let the kids help you put the simple stencil design on top; it is easy to do when following the diagrams. The best part is that the cake can be made in advance, then brought out to surprise Dad when you are ready to celebrate.

1 recipe Chocolate Sponge Roll (page 129)
1 recipe Apricot-Orange Cake Filling (page 254)

Topping

¹/₂ cup unsifted unsweetened cocoa
¹/₄ cup confectioners' sugar
1 tablespoon ground cinnamon

1. Prepare the cake, roll it in the tea towel, and set to cool. Unroll, spread the cake with filling, and reroll.

2. On a large piece of wax paper set on a large tray (to contain the mess), sift a generous layer of cocoa slightly wider than the cake. Roll the cake in the cocoa, completely coating it. With a broad spatula, lift the cake off the wax paper and set it on another, clean, sheet of paper.

3. To make the tie stencil, sketch a tie shape (*A*) on a piece of paper about 6 × 14 inches; keep the tie area in the center of the paper. Set the paper on cardboard and use an X-Acto knife to cut out the shape, leaving the border intact. Or poke a hole through the center of the tie area and cut out the shape with scissors. Also cut 5 strips of paper about 2 × 6 inches.

4. Place the stencil lengthwise on top of the cocoa-covered cake. Using a small sifter, sift confectioners' sugar over the stenciled area (*B*). Lift the paper straight up and away from the cake, shake it off on scrap paper, and wipe the surface of the stencil with paper towels. Now set the strips on a

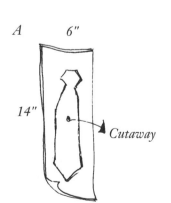

A   6"

14"

Cutaway

B   *Stenciled sugar tie*

diagonal over the sugared tie (*C*) and cover it with the tie stencil (*D*). Sift cinnamon over the holes between the paper strips. Carefully lift the stencil and strips straight up and off the cake, shaking them clean over scrap paper.

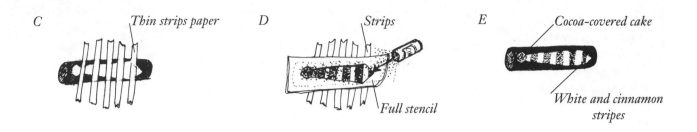

C   *Thin strips paper*   *D*   *Strips*   *E*   *Cocoa-covered cake*

Full stencil   *White and cinnamon stripes*

You should now have a white tie with brown stripes (*E*). Do not touch the cake surface before serving.

Nutritional Analysis (per serving): 210 calories; 4 g protein; 3 g fat; 1.6 g satfat; 47 g carbohydrate; 162 mg sodium; 37 mg cholesterol

Light Touch

The fact that this cake obtains a mere 12% calories from fat is an additional gift to father.

DOUBLE CHOCOLATE PASSOVER SPONGE CAKE

Yield: 7 cups batter; one 9-inch tube cake; 14 to 16 servings

This cake is surprising: light of crumb but very moist and richly chocolate in flavor. A perfect finale for a seder or any special occasion, and especially good accompanied by fresh strawberries and/or Raspberry Sauce (page 258). Because regular wheat flour is proscribed on this holiday, the cake is made with a combination of matzoh meal and potato flour (also called potato starch); both are available in large supermarkets, many gourmet shops, and natural food stores. Note: Don't be tempted to make this in a decorative Bundt pan; because the pan is not greased, it would not unmold properly.

Advance Preparation

Cake keeps several days at room temperature if wrapped in plastic wrap or airtight plastic bag. Double-wrapped, it can be frozen about 1 week.

Special Equipment

9 × 3- or 4-inch plain tube pan or medium-sized angel food pan with removable bottom panel

Temperature and Time

350°F for 50 to 55 minutes

Batter

- 1/2 cup plus 2 tablespoons matzoh meal
- 1/2 cup potato flour (potato starch)
- 1/4 cup unsifted unsweetened Dutch-processed cocoa
- 1 cup granulated sugar, divided
- 1/2 teaspoon salt
- 1/4 teaspoon ground cinnamon
- 1/3 cup canola or other light vegetable oil
- 2 large egg yolks
- 3/4 cup skim milk
- 3 tablespoons vanilla or plain nonfat yogurt, top liquid poured off
- 2 teaspoons vanilla extract
- 1 teaspoon instant espresso or regular coffee powder
- 6 large egg whites
- Pinch of cream of tartar
- 1 ounce semisweet or unsweetened chocolate, grated

Topping

- 2 tablespoons confectioners' sugar, sifted

1. Position a rack in the center of the oven and preheat the oven to 350°F. (Do not grease the tube pan.)

2. In a large mixing bowl, sift together the matzoh meal, potato flour, cocoa, 1/2 cup of the sugar, the salt, and cinnamon. Dump in any granules of matzoh meal caught in the sifter. Make a well in the center of the dry ingredients and add the oil, yolks, milk, yogurt, vanilla extract, and espresso powder. Do not mix.

continued

3. In a large grease-free bowl, whip the egg whites and cream of tartar until foamy. Gradually add the remaining ½ cup of sugar and whip until the whites are satiny and just beginning to feel stiff but are not dry; do not overbeat. Shake off the beaters into the bowl and, without washing them, return them to the mixer. With the mixer on low speed, blend together the dry and liquid ingredients in the first bowl. Gradually—and very gently without beating—fold in the whipped whites along with the grated chocolate. Don't worry if some streaks of white remain.

4. Turn the batter out into the ungreased pan. Bake for 50 to 55 minutes, until the top is springy to the touch and a cake tester inserted in the center comes out clean. Invert the pan so it stands upside down on its own feet, or hang it upside down over the neck of a bottle or large funnel. Let cool completely.

5. To remove the cake from the pan, slide the blade of a long thin knife between the cake and the sides of the pan to loosen it. Run the knife around the center tube. Remove the sides first, then slide the knife between the pan bottom and the cake to release it. To serve, sprinkle with confectioners' sugar and cut with a serrated knife.

Nutritional Analysis (per serving): 184 calories; 4 g protein, 7 g fat; 0.7 g satfat, 28 g carbohydrate; 125 mg sodium; 31 mg cholesterol

Light Touch

This cake traditionally includes 6 whole eggs and ½ cup vegetable oil; it has 44% calories from fat, 245 calories, 12 g fat, and 107 mg cholesterol per serving. I have played with the recipe in many ways; by using only 1 yolk and cutting back the oil to ¼ cup, you can reach a mere 28% calories from fat. However, my final preference, and the way the recipe is written, gives the richest result and the moistest crumb by using 2 yolks and ⅓ cup of oil to get 33% calories from fat. Trust me, the difference is worth it and per slice the change in fat is negligible. The use of 1 ounce of solid chocolate along with the cocoa enhances the complexity of the chocolate flavor, as does the pinch of cinnamon.

Gluten-Free Orange Biscotti, Chocolate Chip Cookies,
Peanut Butter Cookies, Oatmeal-Raisin-Walnut Cookies

Old-fashioned Deep-Dish Blueberry–Honey Cobbler; Apple–Golden Raisin–Honey Pie

Glazed Ginger Tartlets, Cream Cheese Marbleized Brownies,
Luscious Lemon Squares, Berry Bars with Streusel Topping

Lemon Meringue Pie, Chocolate Cream Pie with Meringue Topping, Coconut Cream Pie

Fourth of July Firecracker Pie

Peach Pizza, Plum Tortilla Tart

Chocolate-Caramel Turtle Tartlets, Valentine Heart Tarts

Berry Shortcake

Holiday Cranberry Upside-down Cake

Orange Cheesecake with Amber Sugar Beads and Cracked Caramel

Fresh Orange Wedding Cake

Upside-down Apple Bread Pudding, Apricot Mousse, Raspberry-Rhubarb Fool

Trifle

Tropical Dreams, Burgundy Poached Pears in Meringue Shells

Mother's Day Peach Melba

Pineapple-Apricot Crown, Favorite Christmas Bread,
Santa Lucia Braids and Buns, Sticky Honey Buns

STEVE KENEIPP'S COFFEE-SPICE ANGEL FOOD CAKE

Yield: 11 cups batter; one 10-inch tube cake with 12 to 14 servings; or two 8- or 9-inch tubes, each serving 10 to 12

Advance Preparation

Angel food cake can be baked ahead, wrapped airtight, and kept fresh at room temperature for several days, or double-wrapped and frozen for 2 weeks. After this, flavor begins to deteriorate in the freezer.

Special Equipment

One 10 × 4-inch angel food cake or tube pan or two 8- or 9 × 3¹⁄₄-inch angel food cake or tube pans (with removable bottoms if possible); triple sifter (optional); large (11- to 14-inch-diameter) mixing bowl; long narrow wooden skewer or cake tester; serrated knife or pronged angel food cake cutter

Temperature and Time

350°F for 45 to 50 minutes for 10-inch tube cake; 35 to 40 minutes for 8- or 9-inch tube cakes

Consider this a treasure hunt. Travel twenty miles northwest of Indianapolis to the town of Noblesville, Indiana, and you will find a jewel called The Classic Kitchen. This intimate, elegant restaurant, run by chef/proprietor Steve Keneipp, takes pride in serving high-flavor, reduced-fat foods that "satisfy all the senses, not just the palate." Beauty and bright tastes are Steve's hallmark. You will find both in this recipe, which I have adapted from one he generously shared with me.

In this recipe, the egg whites produce about 11 cups of foam; if the largest bowl of your electric mixer is not this big, whip the whites in two batches, then fold them together with the dry ingredients in another larger bowl.

Note: For success with angel food cakes, follow these four tips: (1) Do not grease the pan; the rising batter must cling to the pan sides in order to hold itself up. (2) Put the cake in the preheated oven as soon as the batter is ready. The cake is risen entirely by the egg foam, which will begin to deflate if the cake stands too long before baking. (3) Use an accurate oven thermometer; egg whites are protein, which will shrink if overheated. Between 325° and 350°F seems ideal; overheated means dried out. (4) The cake must hang upside down in its pan until completely cool; if cooled upright, its own weight will cause it to sink and be very dense.

Batter

- 1¹⁄₄ **cups sifted cake flour**
- ¹⁄₂ **teaspoon each: ground cinnamon, nutmeg, cloves, ginger, cardamom, and allspice**
- 1³⁄₄ **cups granulated sugar, divided**
- 2 **tablespoons instant coffee powder or 1 tablespoon instant espresso powder**
- 1 **tablespoon vanilla extract**
- 1⁷⁄₈ **cups large egg whites (about 14), at room temperature**
- ¹⁄₂ **teaspoon salt**
- 1¹⁄₂ **teaspoons cream of tartar**

Topping

1 **tablespoon unsweetened cocoa or confectioners' sugar**

1. Position a rack in the center of the oven and preheat the oven to 350°F. (Do not grease the cake pan.)

2. Combine the sifted flour with the spices and ³⁄₄ cup of the granulated sugar and put through a triple sifter, or put 3 times through a plain sifter; set the mixture aside.

continued

3. In a cup, stir together the coffee powder and vanilla and set aside.

4. In the largest (grease-free) bowl of your electric mixer, combine the egg whites, salt, and cream of tartar. With the mixer on medium speed, whip the whites until foamy, then gradually add the remaining 1 cup of sugar and increase the mixer speed while whipping until soft peaks form. With this large volume of foam, it is sometimes difficult to judge the stiffness, so turn off the mixer and lift some foam on the end of a spatula to look at it. With a rubber spatula, scrape the coffee-vanilla mixture into the whites. Continue whipping until the whites are stiff but not dry.

5. Unless your mixer bowl is extra large, it will now be filled to the brim. Scrape the whipped whites into an even larger bowl. With a spatula, gradually fold in the flour mixture a few tablespoons at a time, taking care not to deflate the foam. Spoon the batter into the baking pan(s); if using 2 pans, fill each about two thirds full (5½ cups of batter).

6. Bake the cake(s) in the preheated oven 45 to 50 minutes for the 10-inch pan, or 35 to 40 minutes for the 8- or 9-inch pans, until the cake top is golden brown, springy to the touch, and a cake tester inserted in the center comes out clean. Leaving the cake in its pan, turn it upside down and balance it on its elongated tube or side legs, or hang the tube upside down over the neck of a tall bottle. Allow to hang upside down for several hours, until completely cold.

7. To remove the cake from the pan, slide the blade of a long thin knife up and down between the cake and pan sides to loosen. Repeat around the center tube. Top the cake with a flat plate, invert, and lift off the pan. If your pan has a removable bottom, slide the knife between pan bottom and cake to release it; if using a plain tube pan, give a sharp downward rap with the pan to dislodge the cake and it will fall out. Before serving, sift a little cocoa or confectioners' sugar over the cake top. Cut into slices with a serrated knife or pronged angel food cake cutter.

Nutritional Analysis (per serving): 175 calories; 5 g protein; trace fat; 0 mg satfat; 39 g carbohydrate; 183 mg sodium; 0 mg cholesterol

— *Light Touch* —

With only 1% calories from fat, this is a pretty pure angel: no fat, no cholesterol.

ORANGE LAYER CAKE

Yield: 5²/₃ to 6 cups batter (variation depends upon volume of whipped egg whites); one 2-layer 8- or 9-inch cake; or one 10-inch cake; 12 servings if plain, 20 if filled and frosted

This is a fine-grained, flavorful orange cake, perfect for any festive occasion, from a birthday to an anniversary party or wedding. It is especially good filled with Apricot-Orange Cake Filling (page 254) and frosted with Orange Buttercream (page 275). You can leave this a two-layer cake, or slice each layer in half with a serrated knife, making a four-layer cake.

Butter-flavor no-stick cooking spray
All-purpose flour for dusting the pan(s)
2¹/₂ cups sifted cake flour
2¹/₄ teaspoons baking powder
¹/₄ teaspoon salt
4 large egg whites, at room temperature
1¹/₂ cups granulated sugar, divided
³/₄ cup 2% milk
1 large egg yolk
¹/₄ cup plain nonfat yogurt
¹/₄ cup canola oil
2 teaspoons vanilla extract
2 teaspoons orange extract
2 tablespoons grated orange zest

Advance Preparation

The cake can be baked ahead, double-wrapped, and refrigerated up to 2 days or frozen up to 2 weeks. To thaw, place wrapped cake in refrigerator overnight.

Special Equipment

Two 8- or 9-inch round layer cake pans or one 10-inch layer cake pan; baking parchment or wax paper; instant-read thermometer (optional)

Baking Temperature and Time

350°F for 25 to 30 minutes for 8- or 9-inch layers; 35 to 38 minutes for 10-inch layer

1. Position a rack in the center of the oven or divide the oven in thirds, depending upon the number of layers to be baked. Preheat the oven to 350°F. Coat each pan with cooking spray. Line the bottom of each pan with baking parchment or wax paper, coat the paper liners with cooking spray, and dust with flour; tap out excess flour. Set the pans aside.

2. In a bowl, sift together the flour, baking powder, and salt; set aside.

3. Place the egg whites in a large grease-free mixing bowl. With a clean beater, whip the whites until foamy, then gradually add ¹/₂ cup of the sugar while beating on medium-high speed until almost stiff (don't overbeat); the whites should be satiny, glossy, and perfectly smooth. Remove the bowl from the mixer stand and set it aside; shake the beaters into the bowl, then return the beaters to the mixer without washing them.

4. In a small saucepan, place the milk over low heat until just lukewarm to the touch (95° to 100°F on an instant-read thermometer). Set the milk aside.

continued

5. In another large mixing bowl, combine the egg yolk, yogurt, oil, both extracts, and the grated zest. Beat to blend, then add the remaining 1 cup of sugar. With the mixer on low speed, slowly pour in the lukewarm milk while beating constantly for 2 to 3 minutes, until the mixture is light colored and the sugar is dissolved. Stop and scrape down the mixer bowl and beater.

6. With the mixer on low speed, gradually blend the flour mixture into the yolk batter. Beat until smooth. Remove the bowl from the mixer stand and fold in the whipped whites, adding about 1 cup at a time until no large clumps are visible.

7. Spoon the batter into the prepared pan(s) and smooth the top with a spatula. Tap the pan once sharply on the counter to remove any large air bubbles.

8. Bake the 8- or 9-inch layers in the oven for 25 to 30 minutes (10-inch cake bakes 35 to 38 minutes), until the top is golden and springy to the touch and a cake tester inserted in the center comes out clean or with just a crumb or two attached. Cool the cake in the pan(s) on a wire rack about 10 minutes. Top with another rack or a wax paper–covered cardboard disk and invert; remove the pan(s) and peel off the paper liners. Cool the cake completely.

9. To fill the cake with Apricot-Orange Cake Filling, use a serrated knife to slice each layer in half horizontally. Place one layer, cut side up, on a serving plate and top with about ⅔ cup of filling. Repeat, adding layers and filling, ending with a layer cut side down. Frost the sides and top of the cake with Orange Buttercream.

Nutritional Analysis (per serving unfilled 2-layer cake): 239 calories; 4 g protein; 5 g fat; 0.7 g satfat; 44 g carbohydrate; 137 mg sodium; 19 mg cholesterol

Nutritional Analysis (per serving filled with Apricot-Orange Cake Filling and frosted with Orange Buttercream: 324 calories; 3 g protein; 7.2 g fat; 2.6 g satfat; 63.9 g carbohydrate; 99 mg sodium; 22 mg cholesterol

---

Light Touch

This delicious cake by itself has only 20% calories from fat, a reduction of 47% compared to my classic version with ½ cup butter. When divided into four layers, filled with Apricot-Orange Cake Filling (which has only 7% calories from fat) and frosted with Orange Buttercream (which, by itself, has 25%), it still has 20% calories from fat but it becomes a very rich, very big cake. For this reason, I cut 20 servings, and base the analysis on that number instead of on 12 as for the plain cake.

ORANGE BUNDT CAKE

Yield: About 6¹/₂ cups batter; one 9-inch Bundt, serving 16; or 2 medium-sized loaves, each serving 10

This is a crowd-pleaser... easy and reliable to make, a fine-grained cake with a light but moist texture and a strong orange flavor. Serve it with a little confectioners' sugar on top or dress it up with Orange Icing Glaze (page 272) and Brandied Cranberry-Maple Sauce (page 261) or some fresh berries. The recipe is large enough to make one large Bundt cake or two loaves (one for the freezer). You can change the flavor, substituting lemon for the orange, or omit the orange and add 1 teaspoon of almond extract along with the vanilla.

Butter-flavor no-stick cooking spray

All-purpose flour for dusting the pan(s)

Batter

2¹/₄ cups sifted cake flour

1¹/₈ teaspoons baking powder

¹/₄ teaspoon baking soda

³/₄ teaspoon salt

3 large egg whites, at room temperature

1¹/₄ cups granulated sugar, divided

¹/₃ cup canola oil

1 large egg

¹/₃ cup nonfat sour cream

¹/₃ cup unsweetened applesauce

1 tablespoon vanilla extract

1 teaspoon orange extract

2 tablespoons packed grated orange zest

¹/₂ cup fresh orange juice

Topping

1 or 2 tablespoons confectioners' sugar

1. Position a rack in the center of the oven and preheat the oven to 350°F. Generously coat one Bundt pan or two loaf pans with cooking spray, then dust with flour; tap out excess flour.

2. In a medium-sized bowl, whisk together the flour, baking powder, baking soda, and salt; set aside.

continued

3. In a large grease-free bowl with the electric mixer on medium speed, whip the egg whites until foamy. Gradually add ¼ cup of the sugar, whipping until the whites are stiff but not dry. Remove the bowl from the mixer, shake the beaters into the bowl, then return the beaters to mixer without washing them. Set the whites aside.

4. Using the same beaters with another bowl, combine and beat together the oil, the remaining 1 cup of sugar, the whole egg, sour cream, applesauce, vanilla and orange extracts, grated orange zest, and orange juice. Gradually beat in the flour mixture in several additions. Scrape down the bowl and beaters. Fold in the whipped whites.

5. Turn the batter into the prepared pan(s). Bake the Bundt for 40 to 45 minutes, the loaf pans for 30 to 35 minutes, until the cake is golden brown and springy to the touch; there will be a shallow crack down the middle and a cake tester inserted in the center will come out dry. Cool the cake(s) in the pan(s) on a wire rack for about 10 minutes, then remove cake(s) from pan(s) and cool completely on the rack. Before serving, dust lightly with confectioners' sugar.

Nutritional Analysis (per Bundt-pan serving): 173 calories; 3 g protein; 5 g fat; 0.4 g satfat; 30 g carbohydrate; 123 mg sodium; 13 mg cholesterol

Nutritional Analysis (per loaf-pan serving): 138 calories; 2 g protein; 4 g fat; 0.3 g satfat; 24 g carbohydrate; 98 mg sodium; 11 mg cholesterol

Light Touch

My favorite classic sour cream pound cake has 39% calories from fat. This reformed version reduces the calories from fat by 34%, to 26%, cutting out almost half the calories and one third the fat per serving by dropping 2 yolks and adding a third white, substituting nonfat sour cream, and replacing the butter with oil plus applesauce. The changes required alteration of the dry ingredients and substitution of cake flour for all-purpose, to achieve a more tender crumb.

LEMON POUND CAKE

Yield: 5 cups batter; one 9- to 9¹/₂-inch Bundt cake;
14 to 16 servings

Richly flavored, tender of crumb, fully satisfying, and utterly delectable, this cake will quickly endear itself. If you don't mention it, guests will never suspect this has less than half the fat of a classic pound cake.

This cake may inspire your creativity; the recipe can take it. I like to add the grated zest of an orange to the lemon-flavored cake, but you can also make an orange version by substituting grated orange zest and intensely flavored orange juice (2 tablespoons undiluted frozen juice concentrate plus 2 tablespoons water). The flavor and color of the cake will change very slightly, depending on the type of sugar you use.

Advance Preparation

Drain yogurt 30 minutes before beginning recipe. Wrapped airtight, pound cake will keep a week at room temperature, or it can be double-wrapped and frozen up to 3 weeks without loss of flavor.

Special Equipment

9- to 9¹/₂-inch (10- to 12-cup-capacity) Bundt or tube pan; fine-mesh strainer or colander lined with cheesecloth

Temperature and Time

350°F for 55 to 60 minutes

³/₄ cup plain or lemon nonfat or low-fat yogurt, preferably without gums or gelatin added

Butter-flavor no-stick cooking spray

All-purpose flour for dusting the pan

¹/₄ cup (¹/₂ stick) unsalted butter

3¹/₂ cups sifted cake flour

1¹/₂ teaspoons baking powder

¹/₄ teaspoon baking soda

¹/₂ teaspoon salt

¹/₄ cup light cream cheese, at room temperature

1 cup granulated sugar

1 cup packed light or dark brown sugar or substitute granulated sugar

2 tablespoons canola oil

2 large eggs plus 3 large egg whites

¹/₄ cup fresh lemon juice

Grated zest of 1 lemon

1 teaspoon lemon extract (optional)

2 teaspoons vanilla extract

Topping

2 tablespoons confectioners' sugar

1. Measure the yogurt into a fine-mesh strainer or cheesecloth-lined colander set over a bowl and drain for about 30 minutes to remove excess liquid whey if possible. If your yogurt won't drain, use it anyway.

2. Position a rack in the center of the oven and preheat the oven to 350°F. Generously coat a Bundt or tube pan with cooking spray, then dust with flour; tap out excess flour.

continued

3. Melt the butter in a small saucepan set over medium heat. Cook until the butter begins to turn golden brown and have a nutty fragrance, about 4 minutes. Watch carefully so the butter does not burn. Set aside to cool.

4. In a medium-sized mixing bowl, whisk together the flour, baking powder, baking soda, and salt. Set aside.

5. In a large mixing bowl, beat together until well blended the cream cheese, both sugars, and the oil. Beat in the melted and cooled butter (with all its browned bits), the eggs and whites, drained yogurt, lemon juice and zest, lemon extract if used, and vanilla. With the mixer on the lowest speed, slowly add all the dry ingredients and beat just until completely smooth. The batter will be quite thick.

6. Spoon the batter into the prepared pan and bake for 55 to 60 minutes, until the top is golden brown with a few cracks, is springy to the touch, and a cake tester inserted in the center comes out with just a few crumbs clinging to it. Cool in the pan on a wire rack for about 10 minutes. Run the tip of a paring knife between the cake and the center tube and check to see that the cake edges are not stuck to the pan sides. Top the cake with a flat plate or another rack and invert. Tap sharply, then lift off the pan. Sift on a light dusting of confectioners' sugar before serving. Cut with a serrated knife.

Nutritional Analysis (per serving): 294 calories; 5 g protein; 7 g fat; 2.6 g satfat; 53 g carbohydrate; 173 mg sodium; 41 mg cholesterol

Light Touch

A classic pound cake of this size weighs in with a not-surprising 51% calories from fat. I was able to save the texture and taste but pare calories from fat down to 22%; per serving I have cut 115 calories, 107 mg cholesterol, 16 g fat, and 11.5 g satfat. To do this, I cut eggs and butter in half, and retained only 1/4 cup butter (browned to increase its flavor). For additional (but less saturated) fat, I added some light cream cheese and canola oil. For extra flavor, I replaced granulated sugar with brown sugar and increased the lemon and vanilla.

Pumpkin Pound Cake with Maple Glaze

*Yield: 5 cups batter; one 9-inch Bundt cake;
14 to 16 servings*

*A moist spiced cake with a fine crumb topped with maple icing glaze, this keeps
well and serves a crowd—the perfect addition to a fall holiday buffet. For added
glamour, serve with Praline Sauce (page 263) or warm Bourbon Cream Sauce
(page 262). Note: Regular whole wheat flour or whole wheat pastry flour (sold in
natural food stores) may be substituted for part of the cake flour.*

Butter-flavor no-stick cooking spray

All-purpose flour for dusting the pan

Batter

**3¹/₂ cups sifted cake flour (or 2 cups whole wheat flour plus
1¹/₂ cups sifted cake flour)**

1¹/₂ teaspoons baking powder

¹/₄ teaspoon baking soda

³/₄ teaspoon salt

¹/₄ cup (¹/₂ stick) unsalted butter

**¹/₄ cup light cream cheese or Neufchâtel cheese, at room
temperature**

1 cup packed dark brown sugar

1 cup granulated sugar

2 large eggs plus 1 large egg white

3 tablespoons canola oil

3 tablespoons dark corn syrup

2 teaspoons vanilla extract

2 teaspoons ground cinnamon

1¹/₂ teaspoons ground nutmeg

³/₄ teaspoon ground ginger

¹/₂ teaspoon ground mace or allspice

¹/₈ teaspoon ground cloves

1 cup canned plain pumpkin purée

¹/₂ cup fresh orange juice or skim milk

Maple Glaze

1 cup sifted confectioners' sugar

3 tablespoons pure maple syrup, or as needed

1 or 2 drops vanilla or maple extract (optional)

10 walnut halves or ¹/₄ cup walnut pieces (optional)

continued

Advance Preparation

*The cake can be baked
several days ahead and
kept covered at room
temperature. Or it can
be double-wrapped and
frozen for up to 2 weeks.*

Special Equipment

*9-inch (10-cup-capacity)
Bundt or tube pan*

Temperature and
Time

*350°F for 65 to 70
minutes*

---

1.   Position a rack in the center of the oven and preheat the oven to 350°F. Generously coat a Bundt or tube pan with cooking spray, then dust with flour; tap out excess flour.

2.   In a medium-sized bowl, combine the flour, baking powder, baking soda, and salt. Whisk to blend and set aside.

3.   In a small saucepan, place the butter over medium heat for several minutes, until it begins to turn golden brown and have a nutty fragrance. Watch carefully so butter does not burn. Set aside to cool.

4.   In a large mixing bowl, beat together until smooth the cream cheese and both sugars. Add the eggs plus white, the oil, corn syrup, vanilla, spices, pumpkin, and juice. Beat well.

5.   With the mixer on the lowest speed, slowly add all the dry ingredients and beat only until completely smooth; don't overwork. The batter will be quite thick.

6.   Spoon the batter into the prepared baking pan and bake 65 to 70 minutes, until well risen, a rich golden brown, and the top is springy to the touch and slightly cracked; a cake tester inserted in the center should come out with just a few crumbs clinging to it. Cool the cake on a wire rack about 10 minutes. Run the tip of a paring knife between the cake and center tube and check to see that cake edges are not stuck to pan sides. Top the cake with a flat plate or another rack and invert. Tap sharply, then lift off the pan.

7.   To make Maple Glaze, stir together the confectioners' sugar and just enough syrup to make a thick, runny icing glaze that drips like syrup from the spoon. Add flavoring if desired. Drizzle the glaze over the top of the cold cake and position the nuts, if using on top. The glaze will harden as it air-dries.

Nutritional Analysis (per serving with nuts and glaze): 366 calories; 4 g protein; 9 g fat; 2.7 g satfat; 68 g carbohydrate; 215 mg sodium; 41 mg cholesterol

Light Touch

The pumpkin purée in this batter contributes flavor, viscosity, and moisture to the cake, replacing some of the fat. While a classic pound cake can contain as much as 51% calories from fat, we have removed some eggs and butter as well as adding the pumpkin, to reach a low 23%. The nuts on top contribute texture and visual appeal, but also add 14 calories and 1 g fat per serving. Without nuts, the calories from fat drop to 20%. You can freeze any leftover pumpkin purée.

CHOCOLATE–SOUR CREAM CAKE

Yield: 5 cups batter; two 8-inch layers or one 8½- to 9-inch tube cake; 14 to 16 servings

This moderately sweet, moist chocolate cake makes a perfect birthday layer cake. For easy entertaining, it can be made in advance and keeps well. I like to use orange flavoring with the chocolate, but if you prefer, you can substitute coffee extract and cold brewed coffee for the orange extract and orange juice. The quick-fix procedure is designed for the food processor, though with some simple changes in mixing order as noted, you can also use an electric mixer.

Butter-flavor no-stick cooking spray
Unsweetened Dutch-processed cocoa for dusting the pan(s)

Batter

1 ounce unsweetened chocolate, chopped
½ cup unsifted unsweetened Dutch-processed cocoa
2¼ cups sifted all-purpose flour
1 teaspoon baking powder
¾ teaspoon baking soda
¾ teaspoon salt
Pinch of ground cinnamon
¼ cup Neufchâtel or light cream cheese, at room temperature
1 cup low-fat sour cream or vanilla or plain low-fat yogurt, top liquid poured off
2 large eggs
1⅓ cups packed dark brown sugar
1 cup fresh orange juice, strong black coffee, or water
⅓ cup canola oil
2 teaspoons vanilla extract
½ teaspoon orange or coffee extract
1½ teaspoons grated orange zest (only for orange-chocolate cake)

Filling (only for layer cake)

¾ cup orange marmalade or apricot preserves

Frosting (optional)

⅓ cup sifted unsweetened cocoa or confectioners' sugar or 1 recipe Orange-Chocolate Frosting (page 276)

1. Position a rack in the center of the oven and preheat the oven to 350°F. Coat the baking pan(s) with cooking spray, line the pan bottom(s) with baking parchment or wax paper, spray again, then dust with sifted cocoa. Prepare a plain tube pan the same way. Set aside.

continued

Advance Preparation

The cake can be wrapped airtight and kept at room temperature about 1 week or frozen up to 3 weeks.

Special Equipment

Two 8 × 1½-inch round layer cake pans or one 8½- or 9-inch plain tube pan (10-cup capacity); baking parchment or wax paper

Temperature and Time

350°F for 32 to 35 minutes for layers; 45 to 50 minutes for tube pan

2. Melt the solid chocolate in the top of a small double boiler set over barely simmering water. Or melt in the microwave at 50% power for about 1 minute; stir, then repeat if necessary until smooth. Set the chocolate aside.

3. Measure the cocoa, flour, baking powder, baking soda, salt, and cinnamon into a mixing bowl, whisk together to blend, then set aside.

4. In the workbowl of a food processor fitted with the steel blade, combine and blend together the Neufchâtel cheese and sour cream for about 15 seconds, until absolutely smooth. Add the eggs, brown sugar, orange juice, oil, and flavorings and process until very smooth.

5. Add and mix in the melted chocolate. Add the dry ingredients all at once and pulse 10 to 15 seconds only, just until the flour is blended in. (Note: If you are using an electric mixer instead of a processor, blending order must be changed. First, cream together until smooth the cream cheese and brown sugar, then beat in the eggs, sour cream, oil, both extracts, grated zest, and melted chocolate. Finally, alternately add and blend together the dry ingredients and the orange juice or other liquid.)

6. Pour the batter into the prepared pan(s) and bake for 32 to 35 minutes for layers, or 45 to 50 minutes for a tube pan, until the cake top feels springy to the touch and a cake tester inserted in the center comes out with only a few crumbs attached. Cool the cake in the pan(s) on a wire rack about 10 minutes, then top with another rack or cardboard cake disk and invert; lift off the pan(s) and peel off the paper or foil; cool completely.

7. Filling and frosting: If making a layer cake, spread preserves on one layer, add the top layer, and finish with sifted cocoa or confectioners' sugar or spread with Orange-Chocolate Frosting.

Nutritional Analysis (per serving for 2 layers filled but not frosted): 313 calories; 5 g protein; 9 g fat; 1 g satfat; 54 g carbohydrate; 257 mg sodium; 32 mg cholesterol

Light Touch

The moist crumb of this cake is like an old-fashioned sour cream–chocolate cake, but the classic cup of dairy sour cream and 3/4 cup butter are replaced by a small amount of canola oil, light cream cheese, and low-fat sour cream. Brown sugar (which holds moisture and adds flavor) is used instead of traditional white sugar. The presence of an ounce of solid chocolate in addition to the cocoa gives depth to the chocolate flavor. Omitting all the butter and eliminating 1 egg reduces the cholesterol content. Compare the enlightened result—27% calories from fat (including preserves filling but no frosting)—to the classic sour cream layer cake (without frosting) at 49%. If you bake this version in a tube pan (omitting the filling), you drop 48 calories per serving but the fat stays the same.

MIDNIGHT CHOCOLATE CAKE

Yield: 5 cups batter; one 9-inch Bundt cake with 12 servings; or 9-inch 2-layer cake with 14 to 16 servings; or 10 × 15-inch sheet cake with 28 servings (2 × 2¹/₂ inches)

Why midnight? First, because the color is so deep and dark, and second, because I quickly discovered this cake is an irresistible midnight snack. It was developed as a brownie by my friend Philadelphia food maven and culinary consultant Aliza Green; I have taken the liberty of adapting it into a full-fledged cake. Moist and dense, with a fine tender grain and a deep chocolate, not-too-sweet taste, it is a wonderful Bundt or layer cake and of course can always be a sheet cake/brownie cut into squares and served from the pan.

Butter-flavor no-stick cooking spray
Unsweetened Dutch-processed cocoa for dusting the pan(s)

Batter
2 ounces semisweet chocolate
1 cup sifted cake flour
³/₄ cup unsifted unsweetened Dutch-processed cocoa
1/4 teaspoon salt
1/2 teaspoon baking powder
1/4 teaspoon baking soda
Pinch of nutmeg
2 large eggs plus 3 large egg whites
2 tablespoons vanilla or plain nonfat yogurt
1¹/4 cups granulated sugar
³/₄ cup dark corn syrup
³/₄ cup unsweetened applesauce
1/4 cup canola oil
1 tablespoon vanilla extract

Topping (optional)
1 to 2 tablespoons unsweetened cocoa

1. Position a rack in the center of the oven and preheat the oven to 325°F. Lightly coat a pan with cooking spray and sift on cocoa; tap out excess cocoa. For a Bundt pan, generously coat the depressions of the design with spray, then sift on cocoa.

2. Melt the chocolate in the top of a small double boiler set over simmering water. Set it aside to cool.

continued

3. In a medium-sized bowl, whisk together the flour, cocoa, salt, baking powder, baking soda, and nutmeg; set aside.

4. In a larger bowl, combine and beat together the eggs plus whites, yogurt, sugar, corn syrup, applesauce, oil, and vanilla. Stir or slowly beat in the dry ingredients, blending just until smooth. Scrape in the melted chocolate and beat well. The batter will be quite runny.

5. Pour the batter into the prepared pan, smooth the top, and bake it for 55 to 60 minutes for a Bundt cake, 25 to 30 minutes for layers, or 25 to 28 minutes for a sheet cake. Bake until the cake is springy to the touch and a cake tester inserted in the center comes out clean or with just a few crumbs attached; don't overbake or the cake will be dry.

6. Cool the cake in the pan(s) about 5 minutes on a wire rack, then invert and remove the pan(s). Cool completely. If making a sheet cake, cut into squares and serve from the pan. If you wish, sift some unsweetened cocoa on top just before serving.

Nutritional Analysis : 271 calories; 4 g protein; 8 g fat; 1 g satfat; 50 g carbohydrate; 142 mg sodium; 36 mg cholesterol

---

Light Touch

In taste and texture, this recipe recalls a dense version of classic chocolate buttermilk cake; my favorite contains 50% calories from fat and each serving packs 23 g fat, 11 of which are saturated. You would never guess that this reformed version has about half the fat (26% calories from fat). Applesauce and corn syrup replace some of the fat of the original; both these ingredients replicate some of the properties of solid fat, adding moisture and viscosity which hold air beaten into the batter. Cake flour replaces all-purpose because it requires less fat to make a tender crumb.

COCOA CAKE

Yield: About 3¹/₈ cups batter; one 9 × 1¹/₂-inch layer cake; 10 servings

This is a quick, easy chocolate cake with an exceptionally fine, tender crumb. I like to slice the single layer in half horizontally and fill it with apricot preserves or sweetened crushed fresh raspberries before topping with sifted confectioners' sugar, but you can simply leave it as one layer and serve slices with Raspberry Sauce (page 258).

Butter-flavor no-stick cooking spray

Unsweetened Dutch-processed cocoa or cake flour for dusting the pan

Batter

¹/₄ cup (¹/₂ stick) unsalted butter, cut up

1 ounce semisweet chocolate, chopped

1 cup sifted cake flour

¹/₂ cup plus 2 tablespoons unsifted unsweetened Dutch-processed cocoa

¹/₂ teaspoon baking powder

¹/₄ teaspoon salt

Pinch of ground nutmeg

1¹/₄ cups packed light brown sugar

¹/₃ cup unsweetened applesauce

1 large egg plus 2 large egg whites

2 teaspoons vanilla extract

Topping

1¹/₂ tablespoons sifted confectioners' sugar

Advance Preparation

Wrapped airtight, the cake keeps several days at room temperature. Double-wrapped, it can be frozen up to 2 weeks.

Special Equipment

9 × 1¹/₂-inch round (or square) cake pan

Temperature and Time

350°F for 27 minutes

---

1. Position a rack in the center of the oven and preheat the oven to 350°F. Lightly coat a baking pan with cooking spray; dust with sifted cocoa or flour and tap out the excess.

2. In a small saucepan, combine the butter and chopped chocolate; set over medium-low heat until melted. Stir, and set aside to cool.

3. In a bowl, combine the flour, cocoa, baking powder, salt, and nutmeg and whisk to blend.

4. In the large bowl of an electric mixer, crumble in the brown sugar and beat together with the applesauce, egg plus whites, and vanilla. Beat in the melted butter-chocolate mixture. Add the dry ingredients all at once and beat only to blend well; do not overwork. The batter will be quite thick.

continued

5. Spoon the batter into the prepared pan, smooth the top, and bake about 27 minutes, just until the top is springy to the touch and a cake tester inserted in the center has only a crumb or two sticking to it. Don't overbake or the cake will be dry.

6. Cool on a wire rack about 10 minutes, cover with a platter or another rack, and invert. Lift off the baking pan and cool completely. Sift on confectioners' sugar before serving or slice in half crosswise with a serrated knife and fill with preserves before adding the sugar topping.

Nutritional Analysis (per serving): 237 calories; 4 g protein; 8 g fat; 3.8 g satfat; 41 g carbohydrate; 127 mg sodium; 35 mg cholesterol

Light Touch

Compared with a traditional devil's food cake (without icing), which can have up to 46% calories from fat, 270 calories, and 14 g fat per serving, this cake has only 29% calories from fat and cuts the fat nearly in half. I developed this recipe accidentally when I was trying to find a formula for fudgy brownies; the addition of applesauce, which I expected to add moisture to the brownies, instead created a tender crumb more suitable for a cake.

DROP-DEAD CHOCOLATE-ESPRESSO MOUSSE CAKE

Yield: 3³/4 cups batter; one 8-inch cake; 12 servings

With a texture between that of a pudding (while warm) and tender fudge (chilled overnight), this moist chocolate confection is really to die for. Believe it or not, it is also one of the quickest and easiest cakes you will ever make; some of the ingredients are melted together in a pan, then the batter is whisked together by hand, without any mixer. Instead of coffee, you can substitute almond, orange, or hazelnut extract. The creamy texture results from baking in the water bath, a simple process that assures even heat and a moist oven. To die and go to heaven, serve this with Vanilla Custard Sauce (page 255) or Raspberry Sauce (page 258).

Advance Preparation

The cake can be served warm, about 1 hour afer baking, or can be baked up to 3 days in advance and refrigerated, covered. Bring to room temperature before serving if chilled.

Special Equipment

8 × 2-inch springform pan; heavy-duty aluminum foil; roasting pan large enough to hold cake pan for water bath; large (about 2-quart) saucepan

Temperature and Time

325°F for 50 to 55 minutes

Batter

1 cup whole milk (not low-fat)

1¹/4 cups granulated sugar

2 tablespoons plus 1 teaspoon espresso coffee powder or regular instant coffee

2 tablespoons unsalted butter, cut up

3 ounces semisweet chocolate, coarsely chopped

2 large eggs plus 1 large egg white

2 teaspoons vanilla extract

¹/2 cup unsifted unsweetened Dutch-processed cocoa (such as Droste) or regular unsweetened cocoa plus ¹/8 teaspoon baking soda

1¹/3 cups unsifted all-purpose flour, spooned into measuring cup and leveled off

¹/2 teaspoon baking powder

¹/2 teaspoon salt

Crumb Crust

Butter-flavor no-stick cooking spray

¹/4 cup chocolate wafer or chocolate graham cracker crumbs

Topping (optional)

1 to 2 tablespoons unsweetened cocoa

1. Position a rack in the center of the oven and preheat the oven to 325°F.

2. In a large saucepan, combine the milk, sugar, coffee powder, butter, and chocolate. Set over very low heat and stir on and off until the sugar dissolves and the solids melt; stir to blend. Do not boil. Remove from the heat and set aside to cool until no longer hot to the touch.

3. In a large mixing bowl, lightly whisk together the eggs, egg white, and vanilla; set aside. Place a sifter over a second bowl and measure into it the

cocoa, flour, baking powder, and salt. Stir/sift the dry ingredients into the bowl and set aside.

4. To prepare the crumb crust, coat the inside of a springform pan with cooking spray, add the crumbs, and rotate and tilt the pan until the entire inside is covered. Spread any excess crumbs over the pan bottom. Cut a piece of heavy-duty aluminum foil (or two layers of regular foil) about 15 inches square, set the pan in the center of the foil, and pleat and crimp the foil tightly against the pan sides. This will prevent water from seeping into the pan during baking in the water bath.

5. Test the temperature of the chocolate liquid; if comfortable to touch, whisk a little chocolate into the egg mixture to warm it slightly, then whisk all the eggs into all the chocolate and blend very well. Whisk this mixture into the dry ingredients. When thoroughly blended (no flour mixture should be visible), pour the batter into the prepared pan.

6. Set the pan (in its foil jacket) in the center of a roasting pan and add hot water until it reaches about one third of the way up the pan sides. Set the pans in the oven and bake for 50 to 55 minutes, until the cake top is raised, shiny, and slightly springy when pressed with your finger. A cake tester inserted about 1 inch in from the edge will come out with a few moist crumbs attached. Remove the pan from the water bath, cool on a wire rack for about 15 minutes, then peel away the foil jacket. Allow to cool for at least 45 minutes longer before serving, or refrigerate overnight. To serve, remove the side of the springform pan, leaving the cake on the pan bottom. The top requires no decoration, but you can sift on a light dusting of cocoa just before serving if you wish.

Nutritional Analysis (per serving): 225 calories; 5 g protein; 7 g fat; 2 g satfat; 40 g carbohydrate; 169 mg sodium; 44 mg cholesterol

---

Light Touch

Classic chocolate mousse cake is one of my all-time favorites; the recipe in my book *A Piece of Cake* is so rich it packs 60% calories from fat. My new version cuts more than half the calories from fat (a 58% reduction), reaching 25%, without loss of flavor or texture. To do this, I have retained 3 ounces of solid chocolate (from the 16 ounces used originally) and added cocoa (Dutch-processed cocoa gives a richer taste), cut out 4 egg yolks, and substituted whole milk for an equal amount of heavy cream. Resist the temptation to alter the basic recipe; extensive testing proves this is best made with whole milk instead of low-fat (which has a tendency to curdle when heated) and all-purpose flour.

CHOCOLATE MARBLEIZED SEMOLINA CAKE

Yield: 1 loaf cake; sixteen ¹/₂-inch-thick slices;
8 servings

The texture of this unusual, elegantly marbleized chocolate-orange cake may surprise you at first. It is almost as moist as a pudding and was originally made with semolina, a coarsely ground granule milled from durum wheat. (Don't confuse this with ground semolina flour, used, for example, to make pasta.) Ground semolina is available in natural food stores and Italian markets. I have substituted farina, commonly sold as Cream of Wheat cereal, which gives a similar texture.

In Italy, pastry chefs have long favored semolina as the base for a variety of delightful puddings, called budini. *I first fell in love with the texture of baked semolina cake when, during a trip to Italy a few years ago, I tasted* budino all'arancio *(orange pudding) in a small Venetian pastry shop. The moist, sweet wedges served on gilded paper plates became my family's daily afternoon treat.*

While budini *are made in many regions of Italy and vary in flavor, the semolina is always cooked in an aromatic liquid that infuses it with richness, and the final batter is always baked in a water bath (bain-marie), as a custard is, to maintain the smooth, puddinglike texture.*

I have followed this pattern, cooking the farina in sweetened orange juice and using the bain-marie, but the recipe is my own re-creation of our first Venetian budino. *This cake is not difficult to make and can be prepared well in advance. The slices are attractively marbled with orange and chocolate batters.*

Advance Preparation

Make the cake at least 1 day ahead, as it needs to chill overnight. It can be made up to a week ahead and kept covered in the refrigerator.

Special Equipment

Aluminum foil; 1 average loaf pan, about 8¹/₂ × 4¹/₂ × 2³/₄ inches; small roasting pan large enough to hold loaf pan for water bath; instant-read thermometer (optional)

Temperature and Time

350°F for 60 to 65 minutes

Butter-flavor no-stick cooking spray

Batter

    1 ounce semisweet chocolate, chopped

    2 cups fresh orange juice

    ¹/₂ cup packed light brown sugar

    ¹/₈ teaspoon salt

    ³/₄ cup Cream of Wheat cereal (quick-cooking type)

    2 tablespoons unsalted butter

    2 large eggs

    1 teaspoon vanilla extract

    ¹/₂ teaspoon orange extract (optional)

    2 tablespoons unsweetened cocoa

To serve

    1 recipe Chocolate Sauce (page 265)

    1 whole orange, cut into extra-thin slices (optional)

    Fresh mint sprigs (optional)

continued

1. To prepare the loaf pan for baking, line it completely (bottom and sides) with 2 strips of foil that extend about 1 inch beyond both the ends and sides of the pan. Press both strips flat into place. Lightly coat the lined pan with cooking spray. Set aside with roasting pan.

2. Melt the chocolate in the top of a double boiler set over barely simmering water. Or, in a microwaveable bowl, melt it in microwave at 50% power for about 1 minute; stir, then repeat if necessary until smooth.

3. In a large nonreactive saucepan, bring to a boil the orange juice, brown sugar, and salt. Sprinkle on the Cream of Wheat and whisk constantly. Lower the heat to a simmer and continue to whisk for $2\frac{1}{2}$ to 3 minutes, until a thick paste forms and the pan bottom is visible as you stir. You will have about $2\frac{1}{2}$ cups of cooked farina. Transfer the farina to the large bowl of an electric mixer and beat until cool, about 3 minutes.

4. In a small saucepan, heat the butter over medium heat for several minutes, until it begins to turn golden brown and has a nutty aroma. Watch carefully so the butter does not burn. Set it aside to cool slightly.

5. Position a rack in the center of the oven and preheat the oven to 350°F. Add to the farina in the mixing bowl the eggs, cooled melted butter (with all its browned bits), vanilla, and orange extract if used and stir to blend. Remove half of the batter (about $1\frac{3}{4}$ cups) to a clean bowl and beat in the cocoa and the melted chocolate, blending until the batter is an even color.

6. Alternately spoon chocolate and orange batters into the lined loaf pan. Pull a table knife blade through the batter (without touching the lining on the bottom) once or twice to create a marbleized pattern.

7. Cut another piece of foil and crimp it tightly over the top of the loaf pan, sealing it. Set the loaf pan in the roasting pan and pour hot water into the roasting pan about halfway up the pan sides. Bake for 60 to 65 minutes. Remove the top foil carefully, then test with an instant-read thermometer: 1 inch from the edge the temperature should be 175° to 180°F. A cake tester inserted in the center of the loaf should come out nearly clean, with just a few gooey crumbs stuck to it. Cool the cake on a wire rack about 2 hours, then re-cover with the top foil and refrigerate overnight to firm up the texture and mellow the flavors.

8. To serve, uncover the cold cake, top with a serving platter, and invert. Lift off the pan and peel off the foil. Slice with a damp knife into $\frac{1}{2}$-inch-thick slices. On each plate, set 2 slices, slightly overlapping, in a scant pool of chocolate sauce. If you wish, garnish with fresh orange and mint.

Nutritional Analysis (per 2 slices without sauce or garnish): 203 calories; 4 g protein; 6 g fat; 2 g satfat; 34 g carbohydrate; 66 mg sodium; 62 mg cholesterol

Light Touch

My analysis of a Venetian *budino* recipe weighs in at about 44% calories from fat. By cutting out a yolk, dropping 2 ounces of chocolate and half the butter, I have cut the calories from fat to 26% but kept the rich flavor and unique texture.

Madly Moka Cheesecake

Yield: 6 cups batter; one 8-inch cake; 12 servings

Chocolate and espresso flavor this rich cheesecake topped with elegant-but-easy chocolate curls to create a dinner party prizewinner. The hidden bonus for the hostess: The cake is best when made a day or two in advance so the flavors can blend, or it can be frozen. If you prefer an all-chocolate cake, simply omit the coffee from the recipe. This cake is baked in a water bath to add moisture and provide even heat to the delicate batter, guaranteeing that your cake will be smooth on top without any cracks. For an unusual variation, try Chocolate-Flecked Cheesecake (page 157), in which grated solid chocolate added to vanilla batter gives it an appealing flecked appearance.

Crumb Crust

Butter-flavor no-stick cooking spray

3 tablespoons chocolate wafer crumbs

1 tablespoon granulated sugar

Batter

1 ounce unsweetened chocolate

2 ounces semisweet chocolate

1/4 cup unsifted cake flour

1 tablespoon cornstarch

Generous pinch of baking soda

Scant 1/8 teaspoon salt

1/3 cup plus 1 tablespoon unsifted unsweetened Dutch-processed cocoa (regular Hershey unsweetened cocoa plus a pinch of baking soda can be substituted)

3 cups (24 ounces) nonfat cottage cheese

1 1/2 cups (12 ounces) light cream cheese, at room temperature

1 tablespoon vanilla extract

1 tablespoon plus 1 teaspoon instant espresso or regular coffee powder

1 1/4 cups granulated sugar

1 large egg plus 2 large egg whites

Chocolate Curls or Shavings (page 289)

1 bar or block semisweet chocolate

1 teaspoon confectioners' sugar

continued

Advance Preparation

After baking, the cake needs 1 hour in the oven with the heat off and the door closed. Then place the cake on a rack to cool before chilling it at least 4 hours, preferably overnight, in the refrigerator. For best results, bake 1 day in advance. The chilled cake can also be double-wrapped and frozen up to 2 weeks.

Special Equipment

8 × 2-inch springform pan; heavy-duty aluminum foil; roasting pan large enough to contain springform for water bath; vegetable peeler (for chocolate curls)

Temperature and Time

325°F for 1 hour

1.   Position a rack in the center of the oven and preheat the oven to 325°F. Cut a sheet of heavy-duty aluminum foil and mold it (loosely for the time being) completely around the outside of the springform pan; this will prevent leaks during baking in the water bath. Remove the pan from the foil and set it aside.

2.   Coat the inside of the springform pan with cooking spray. In a cup, blend together the chocolate wafer crumbs and sugar, then dust the inside of the baking pan with this mixture. Spread excess crumbs evenly over the bottom of the pan and set it aside.

3.   Coarsely chop the chocolates and set them to melt in the top of a double boiler over low heat; remove from the heat and set it aside to cool.

4.   Place a sifter over a medium-sized bowl and measure into it the flour, cornstarch, baking soda, salt, and cocoa. Stir/sift the ingredients into the bowl and set aside.

5.   Place the nonfat cottage cheese in a strainer set over a bowl, cover the cheese with a piece of plastic wrap or wax paper, and press on it with your hand to force out any excess liquid (some brands will not drain). In a blender or food processor, process the cottage cheese 2 to 3 full minutes, until absolutely smooth, without any graininess. Scrape down the bowl and blade once or twice. Add the cream cheese and process until smooth.

Stir the vanilla and coffee powder together in a cup, then add it to the cheese mixture with the sugar, egg and egg whites, and melted and cooled chocolate. Pulse to blend. Add the dry ingredients all at once and pulse only to combine; do not overwork the mixture.

6.   Pour the batter into the prepared pan. Set the pan inside the molded foil and press the foil tight around the pan sides so no water can penetrate. Place the foil-wrapped pan into the roasting pan and add hot water to reach about one third of the way up the pan sides. Bake for 1 hour, until the top is dry and glossy and you can touch the surface lightly without leaving a mark. Turn off the heat, and leave the cake inside with the door closed for another hour.

Remove the cake from the water bath and foil wrapper and cool completely on a rack in a draft-free location. Refrigerate, covered with foil or plastic wrap, at least 4 hours or overnight, until completely chilled.

7.   Follow the directions to make chocolate curls or grated shavings and pile them on the cake top. Sift a tiny bit of confectioners' sugar over the chocolate curls just before serving.

Nutritional Analysis (per serving, without a chocolate curl): 254 calories; 12 g protein; 9 g fat; 0.5 g satfat; 37 g carbohydrate; 438 mg sodium; 33 mg cholesterol

CHOCOLATE-FLECKED CHEESECAKE

This is a vanilla cheesecake with flecks of grated chocolate that remain visible after baking. Prepare the recipe above with the following changes: Omit the unsweetened chocolate and 1 ounce of semisweet; grate the remaining 1 ounce of semisweet chocolate on the medium holes of a box grater over wax paper. Add the grated chocolate to the dry ingredients after they are sifted together in step 4. Omit the espresso or coffee powder. Along with the vanilla, if you wish, add 3 to 4 tablespoons dark rum or white crème de cacao.

Nutritional Analysis (per serving with a chocolate curl): 236 calories; 11 g protein; 6 g fat; trace g satfat; 35 g carbohydrate; 408 mg sodium; 33 mg cholesterol

Light Touch

This divine creation contains only 29% calories from fat, a 57% reduction from a classic New York cheesecake (68%) with 615 calories, 48 g fat, and 200 mg cholesterol per serving. The abundant dairy products provide 57 mg calcium, and practically no saturated fat, although the cottage cheese adds a lot of sodium. The Chocolate-Flecked Cheesecake contains only 23% calories from fat.

BLACK-AND-WHITE MARBLE CHEESECAKE

Yield: One 8-inch cake; 12 servings

This quick and easy cheesecake has a marbleized design baked right onto the top. The cake itself is baked in a water bath to guarantee a creamy texture by modifying the heat; the water also provides extra oven moisture to help prevent the cake top from cracking. If it cracks in spite of your best efforts, add an unbaked Marbleized Sour Cream Topping (page 281). For totally different flavors and presentations, try Nectarine Cheesecake and Orange Cheesecake with Amber Sugar Beads on pages 159 and 160.

You can mix this batter in an electric mixer or a food processor; the latter does a somewhat better job of smoothing this type of cream cheese, which has a tendency to leave small white bits throughout the batter.

Crumb Crust

Butter-flavor no-stick cooking spray

3 tablespoons chocolate wafer, amaretti, or graham cracker crumbs

1 tablespoon granulated sugar

Batter

1 ounce semisweet chocolate

2 cups (16 ounces) fat-free-for-baking cream cheese

1¹/₂ cups (12 ounces) light cream cheese

One 14-ounce can low-fat sweetened condensed milk (*not* evaporated milk)

1 large egg plus 3 large whites

¹/₄ cup unsifted all-purpose or cake flour

1 tablespoon vanilla extract

3 tablespoons dark rum (optional)

Advance Preparation

After baking, the cake needs 30 minutes longer in the oven with the heat off and the door propped open. Cool completely, then the cake needs to chill and firm in the refrigerator at least 4 hours, or preferably overnight.

Special Equipment

8-inch springform pan; heavy-duty aluminum foil; roasting pan large enough to contain the springform for a water bath

Temperature and Time

325°F for 50 minutes, then 30 minutes longer in oven with heat off and door propped open

1. Position a rack in the center of the oven and preheat the oven to 325°F. Cut a sheet of heavy-duty foil and mold it (loosely for the time being) around the outside of a springform pan to prevent leaks during baking in the water bath. Remove the pan from the foil and set it aside.

2. Make the crumb crust. Coat the inside of the springform pan with cooking spray. In a cup, blend together the cookie crumbs and sugar, then dust the inside of the baking pan with this mixture. Spread the excess crumbs evenly over the bottom of the pan and set it aside.

3. Make the cake batter. Melt the solid chocolate in the top of a double boiler set over barely simmering water. Or melt it in the microwave at 50% power for about 1 minute; then stir and repeat until smooth.

4. In a food processor fitted with the steel blade or electric mixer, beat the two types of cream cheese together until completely smooth. (Be careful not to overbeat or the fat-free cream cheese may liquefy; if that happens, use it anyway.) Scrape down the bowl and blade or beaters. Add the condensed milk, egg and egg whites, flour, and flavorings. Blend until smooth.

5. Pour all but $1/2$ cup of the batter into the prepared pan. Stir the melted chocolate into the batter remaining in the container. Swirl/drizzle the chocolate mixture over the top of the batter in the pan, then use a knife tip to draw lines through the batter, creating a marbleized pattern. Alternatively, you can stir the chocolate into $1/4$ cup of the batter and put it into a pint-size, heavy-duty plastic bag with a tiny hole cut in one corner. Draw a design or spiral pattern or write a message over the white cake top.

6. Set the pan inside the molded foil and press the foil tightly around the pan sides so no water can penetrate. Place the cake pan into a roasting pan and add hot water to come about halfway up the cake pan sides. Bake about 50 minutes, until the top is dry and puffed up and the center is still slightly soft but no longer jiggles when the pan is tapped. Turn off the heat, prop the oven door open slightly, and leave the cake inside in the water bath for about 30 minutes. Then cool the cake completely on a rack in a draft-free location. Refrigerate, covered with foil or plastic wrap, at least 4 hours or overnight until completely chilled. Remove the sides of the springform pan and leave the cake on the pan bottom to serve.

Nutritional Analysis (per serving): 286 calories; 14 g protein; 8.9 g fat; 1.7 g satfat; 36 g carbohydrate; 436 mg sodium; 41 mg cholesterol

NECTARINE CHEESECAKE

Prepare recipe above as directed with the following changes: Substitute peach schnapps for the dark rum. Omit the chocolate completely. For topping, warm about $2/3$ cup peach preserves mixed with 2 teaspoons fresh lemon juice. Spread all but 2 tablespoons of the preserves over the chilled cake top. Thinly slice 2 unpeeled, ripe nectarines (or peeled peaches) and arrange the slices in a decorative pattern covering the cake top. Brush the remaining preserves over the fruit slices. Add a sprig of mint in the center. Chill until ready to serve.

Nutritional Analysis (per serving): 335 calories; 14 g protein; 8.3 g fat; 1.7 g satfat; 50 g carbohydrate; 437 mg sodium; 41 mg cholesterol

continued

ORANGE CHEESECAKE WITH AMBER SUGAR BEADS

Prepare Black-and-White Marble Cheesecake with the following changes: Use amaretti crumbs for the crust. Omit the chocolate completely. Substitute 1 teaspoon orange extract, grated zest of 1 large orange, and 3 tablespoons orange liqueur such as Grand Marnier for the dark rum. Prepare Amber Sugar Beads and Cracked Caramel (page 292). Before serving, arrange them on top of and around the chilled cake, serving some beads with each portion of cake.

Nutritional Analysis (per serving): 305 calories; 14 g protein; 8.2 g fat; 1.7 g satfat; 42 g carbohydrate; 436 mg sodium; 41 mg cholesterol

---

Light Touch

The marble cheesecake is made with two special products: fat-free-for-baking cream cheese, not to be confused with "free" or fat-free cream cheese that is *not* meant to be baked or heated (read the label carefully), and low-fat sweetened condensed milk, which has half the fat of the regular version and is available in most supermarkets.

This contains only 28% calories from fat, a reduction of 54% from one of my favorite classic cheesecakes, lightened with whipped egg whites. At 61%, it had 100 more calories and three times the fat per serving. Nectarine Cheesecake has 22% calories from fat and Orange Cheesecake, 24%.

The large number of dairy products gives each serving a bonus of 60 mg calcium.

PUMPKIN CREAM BOMBE

Glazed, garnished, and glamorous, this is the perfect do-ahead finale for your Thanksgiving or Christmas dinner. It has all the drama of a molded frozen dessert, and it really tastes wonderful. An orange sponge cake (use store-bought sponge or pound cake if you are in a hurry) envelopes the easy-to-prepare pumpkin pie "ice cream" in a rounded mold. For an even easier alternative, simply spread the yogurt over the Orange Sponge Roll and roll like a jelly roll before wrapping and freezing. Brush with glaze before serving.

Cake

1 recipe Orange Sponge Roll (page 128), or two 8-inch layers store-bought sponge or pound cake in plain flavor that complements pumpkin

Filling

Double recipe (1 quart total) Pumpkin Frozen Yogurt (page 215)

Glaze

²/₃ cup orange marmalade or apricot preserves

Garnish

¹/₄ cup pecans or walnuts, chopped and toasted (page 333), or chopped pistachio nuts

1. Bake and cool the sponge cake. Using a serrated knife, cut the rectangular cake in half crosswise, then cut each piece in half horizontally, making 4 thin layers. If you have a store-bought layer cake, slice each layer in half horizontally. Cover the layers with plastic wrap until ready to assemble the cake.

2. Prepare the pumpkin frozen yogurt mixture. If it has been made ahead and frozen, soften it, or warm it a few seconds in the microwave, before assembling the cake.

3. Line the round bowl with 1 or 2 large pieces of plastic wrap, allowing the wrap to overhang the bowl by at least 2 inches all around.

4. Cut wedge-shaped sections of the cake and fit them into the bowl, placing the points toward the bottom center. Cover the entire surface, using slivers and scraps to fill in any gaps if necessary.

5. Fill the cake-lined bowl with the pumpkin yogurt, packing it firmly. Cover the top with more thin slices of cake. Pull the overhanging plastic wrap over the top of the cake, then cover with another piece of wrap and a layer of foil, pressed tight. Freeze the cake for at least 4 hours.

continued

Advance Preparation

The yogurt can be made 2 weeks ahead. The cake can be baked no more than 2 weeks ahead, wrapped airtight, and frozen. Thaw and slice before assembling the bombe. The assembled bombe must be wrapped and frozen at least 4 hours, or up to 5 days ahead.

Special Equipment

1¹/₂-quart hemispherical bowl (metal or Pyrex is best); pastry brush

Temperature and Time

Bake cake: 350°F for 11 to 13 minutes

6. Several hours before it is to be served, remove the cake from the freezer, peel off the wrappings, top with a flat serving plate, and invert. Lift off the bowl and peel off the plastic wrap.

7. In a small saucepan, warm the marmalade or preserves, strain to remove fruit pieces, then brush it over the cake. Sprinkle the chopped toasted nuts over the glaze. Return the cake to the freezer uncovered, or lightly covered with plastic wrap. Remove from the freezer about 30 minutes before serving; in very hot weather serve directly from the freezer. Cut into wedges to serve. Freeze leftovers.

Nutritional Analysis (per serving): 319 calories; 6 g protein; 6 g fat; 1.7 g satfat; 61 g carbohydrate; 147 mg sodium; 51 mg cholesterol

---

Light Touch

This surprising dessert looks and tastes like much more than it is... only 17% calories from fat. Compare this to a classic version, from my book *A Piece of Cake*, made with extra-rich ice cream and 1/2 cup nuts, which packs 45% calories from fat.

PEAR-PRUNE-BRANDY CAKE

*Yield: 5 cups batter; one 8- to 8½-inch cake;
10 servings*

This unusual cake was inspired by a moist, homey dessert I first tasted in a bistro in Gascony, France, where dried prunes are traditionally macerated in Armagnac, the local brandy, before being used in a variety of confections. Cognac, a slightly more refined French brandy, or Calvados, a brandy made from apples, may be substituted. Cornmeal lends texture and flavor; applesauce and pears mellow the brandy and add richness. This is a very special treat, to be shared with a good friend on a late fall afternoon beside a fire with a glass of fine brandy.

Advance Preparation

Cake keeps well about a week if wrapped airtight. Or wrap and refrigerate up to 3 days. Serve at room temperature or warmed.

Special Equipment

8- to 8½-inch spring-form pan; small microwaveable bowl; baking parchment or wax paper

Temperature and Time

350°F for 45 to 50 minutes

1 cup packed, pitted dried prunes (preferably "moist" style),
    cut into quarters with an oiled knife

⅓ cup Armagnac, Cognac, or Calvados

Butter-flavor no-stick cooking spray

¾ cup yellow cornmeal plus 3 tablespoons for pan preparation

2 tablespoons unsalted butter

2 tablespoons canola oil

⅓ cup unsweetened applesauce

2 teaspoons grated lemon zest

½ cup granulated sugar

¼ cup nonfat sour cream

2 teaspoons vanilla extract

1 large egg plus 1 large egg white

1 cup sifted all-purpose flour

1 teaspoon baking powder

¼ teaspoon baking soda

¼ teaspoon salt

2 large, ripe Bartlett, Bosc, or Anjou pears, peeled, cored, and
    cut into ½-inch dice (about 2¼ cups)

Topping
3 tablespoons granulated sugar

1. Combine the cut-up prunes with the brandy in a microwaveable bowl, partially cover with plastic wrap, and microwave on full power for 30 to 45 seconds, until plumped; or macerate about 1 hour at room temperature. Drain and reserve liquid as well as fruit.

2. Position a rack in the center of the oven and preheat the oven to 350°F. Coat a baking pan with cooking spray, line the bottom with baking parchment or wax paper, and spray the paper with oil. Dust the inside of the pan with about 3 tablespoons of the cornmeal, then tap out the excess.

continued

3. In a small saucepan, melt the butter over medium heat for several minutes, until it begins to turn golden brown and have a nutty aroma. Watch carefully so the butter does not burn.

4. In the large bowl of an electric mixer, beat together the melted butter, oil, applesauce, lemon zest, sugar, sour cream, and vanilla. Beat in the egg and egg white, and 3 tablespoons of the liquid drained from the soaked prunes (if you don't have enough, use any fruit juice).

5. Set a large strainer over the bowl of batter, add the flour, baking powder and soda, and salt. Stir and sift these dry ingredients onto the mixture below. With the mixer on low speed, blend all together. Stir in the chopped pears and soaked prunes.

6. Turn the batter out into the prepared pan and top with a generous sprinkling of granulated sugar. Bake the cake 45 to 50 minutes, until the top is golden, the edges are slightly browned and beginning to pull away from the pan sides, and a tester in the center comes out with just a few crumbs sticking to it. Cool the cake about 15 minutes on a wire rack, then remove the sides of the pan and cool completely.

Nutritional Analysis (per serving): 269 calories; 4 g protein; 6 g fat; 2 g satfat; 46 g carbohydrate; 125 mg sodium; 28 mg cholesterol

Light Touch

Although this cake is seriously rich in taste and texture, it contains only 20% calories from fat. These considerations were clearly neither in the mind nor the recipe of the Gascon baker who started my journey of re-creation, but I have kept egg yolks and butter to a minimum without sacrificing anything from my taste memory.

NEW YEAR'S HONEY CAKE

Yield: 3 cups batter; 1 loaf; 12 servings

This traditional Jewish New Year honey cake expresses the wish for a sweet year. It is a moist, rather dense cake with a fine grain, and it keeps well. Strong coffee is blended with the batter to offset the sweetness of the honey.

Butter-flavor no-stick cooking spray

All-purpose flour for dusting the pan

Batter

$^3/_4$ **cup honey**

$^1/_2$ **cup strong black coffee (or $^1/_2$ cup boiling water stirred into 1 teaspoon instant regular or decaffeinated coffee powder)**

$1^3/_4$ **cups sifted all-purpose flour**

1 teaspoon baking powder

$^1/_2$ **teaspoon baking soda**

Pinch of salt

2 large eggs

2 tablespoons light (extra-virgin) olive oil or canola oil

$^1/_2$ **cup granulated sugar**

$^1/_2$ **teaspoon ground cinnamon**

$^1/_2$ **teaspoon ground nutmeg**

$^1/_8$ **teaspoon ground ginger**

$^1/_8$ **teaspoon ground cloves**

1. Position a rack in the center of the oven and preheat the oven to 350°F. Coat a loaf pan with cooking spray, then dust with flour; tap out excess.

2. Lightly coat a measuring cup with cooking spray (to prevent sticking), then measure the honey into a heatproof bowl or 2-cup Pyrex measure. Stir in the hot coffee and mix until the honey is dissolved. Set aside.

3. Combine in a bowl the flour, baking powder, baking soda, and salt, whisk to blend, and set aside.

4. In the large bowl of an electric mixer, combine and beat together the eggs, oil, sugar, and spices. With the mixer on low speed, alternately add the honey-coffee mixture and dry ingredients in several additions. The batter will be quite liquid.

5. Pour the batter into the prepared pan and bake the cake for 50 to 55 minutes, until it turns a rich golden brown color and a cake tester inserted in the center comes out clean. Cool the cake in the pan on a wire rack about 10 minutes, then tip out and cool completely. Slice with a serrated knife.

Nutritional Analysis (per serving): 190 calories; 3 g protein; 3 g fat; 0.6 g satfat; 38 g carbohydrate; 97 mg sodium; 36 mg cholesterol

continued

Advance Preparation

Cake keeps 1 week, wrapped airtight. Or it can be double-wrapped and frozen up to 2 weeks.

Special Equipment

Medium-sized loaf pan ($8^1/_4 \times 4^1/_2$ inches)

Temperature and Time

350°F for 50 to 55 minutes

Surprisingly, when I analyzed this classic recipe I discovered it contained only 15% calories from fat; there was no need to make modifications in ingredients.

BELGIAN HONEY CAKE

Yield: 9 cups batter; one 9- or 10-inch tube cake; 16 servings

This dense, moist tube cake is studded with golden raisins and perfumed with orange, lemon, and ground fennel seeds. A thin wedge served with a glass of port is just the thing to soothe your spirit on a cold winter afternoon. Topped with icing glaze and almonds, it makes a perfect holiday cake for your Christmas or New Year's buffet. Note: There is $1/4$ cup of baking powder in the recipe; this is not a typographical error. Fennel seeds give this cake a unique flavor but may be omitted if you cannot locate them.

Advance Preparation

The cake can be made ahead and kept at least 1 week at room temperature, 2 weeks refrigerated. Wrapped airtight, it can be frozen up to 3 weeks.

Special Equipment

9- or 10-inch plain tube pan (such as angel food pan, 10-cup capacity) or 9-inch tube-shaped springform pan; baking parchment or wax paper

Temperature and Time

400°F for 30 minutes; then 350°F for 7 to 10 minutes

Butter-flavor no-stick cooking spray

All-purpose flour for dusting the pan

Batter

$1^1/3$ cups honey

$1^1/3$ cups granulated sugar

5 tablespoons unsalted butter, cut up

$1^3/4$ cups water

Zest of 1 lemon and 1 orange, removed in strips with a vegetable peeler

4 cups sifted all-purpose flour

1 tablespoon ground fennel seeds

$1/2$ cup golden raisins

$1/4$ cup baking powder

$1/4$ teaspoon salt

Topping (optional)

$1/2$ cup sifted confectioners' sugar

1 to $1^1/2$ tablespoons skim milk or fresh orange or lemon juice

$1/4$ teaspoon vanilla extract

16 whole or halved blanched almonds or halved pecans or walnuts

1.   Position a rack in the center of the oven and preheat the oven to 400°F. Cut a piece of baking parchment or wax paper to fit the bottom of a tube pan. Lightly coat the entire inside of the pan with cooking spray. Position the paper in the pan bottom and press down. Coat the paper with cooking spray, then dust the inside of the pan with flour; tap out excess flour.

2.   In a medium-sized saucepan, combine the honey, sugar, butter, and water and set over medium-low heat, stirring occasionally, until the butter is melted and all the sugar is dissolved. Remove from the heat and set aside to cool until comfortable to touch.

3.   In a blender or the workbowl of a food processor fitted with the steel blade, combine the lemon and orange zests (just the brightly colored part of the peel) and the flour and fennel. Process until the zest is finely minced. Add the raisins and give just about 4 quick pulses, only to coarsely chop the raisins and coat them with the flour mixture. Turn out the mixture into a large bowl. (Alternatively, grate the citrus zest and hand-chop the raisins before adding the flour and fennel in a bowl.)

4.   Add the baking powder (¼ cup *is* correct) and salt to the flour-spice mixture in the bowl; with the beaters on lowest speed, gradually add the melted honey mixture and beat until smooth. The batter will foam up. Pour the batter into the prepared pan.

5.   Bake at 400°F for 30 minutes, then reduce the heat to 350°F, cover the cake lightly with a piece of aluminum foil to prevent overbrowning, and bake for 7 to 10 minutes longer, until a cake tester inserted in the center comes out clean and the cake top is golden and firm; it will not, however, be springy to the touch. Cool the cake in its pan on a wire rack for about 20 minutes, then invert and lift off the pan. The flavor of the cake is best if it stands overnight to mellow.

6.   To make the topping glaze, combine the sugar, milk or juice, and vanilla in a small bowl and whisk until completely smooth and soft enough to drip from a spoon. Drizzle the glaze over the cake top in a lacy pattern or spread evenly on top, allowing some to run down the sides. Arrange the nuts in a ring around the top. The glaze hardens as it cools.

Nutritional Analysis (per serving with topping): 340 calories; 4 g protein; 5 g fat; 2.5 g sat-fat; 73 g carbohydrate; 285 mg sodium; 10 mg cholesterol

Light Touch

Created by my baking assistant Lynnia Milliun, this is a naturally low-fat cake, with just 13% of its calories from fat. Calories from carbohydrates, however, are relatively high: 83%.

FRESH ORANGE WEDDING CAKE

"In all the wedding cake, hope is the sweetest of the plums."—*Douglas Jerrold*

Yield: Seven times the basic cake recipe makes one 3-tier cake; each 4-inch-high tier is made up of 2 layers (each split, making 4 layers): 6, 10, and 14 inches in diameter. Serves 75 to 125 (average serving size about 4 inches high, 2 inches deep, ³/₄ to 1 inch wide).

This is a fine-grained orange-flavored cake. It is light in texture and low in fat, but has enough body to support three thick tiers filled with a delectable Apricot Mousse and frosted with Orange Buttercream. Making a wedding cake at home may seem a daunting task, but this recipe allows you to do the work in stages far in advance. The cake layers can be frozen up to two weeks ahead, the filling and icing made three or four days in advance. And you don't have to be a decorating wizard; just use fresh rosebuds or Sugared Rose Petals (page 288). The cake can also be baked in a smaller size for other festive occasions.

I developed this recipe as a cover story for Cooking Light *magazine (April 1995); it was their idea, based on many requests from readers. With its great taste and moderately indulgent buttercream icing, this is indeed a celebration recipe, not a sacrificial one.*

GENERAL NOTES BEFORE BEGINNING TO BAKE

- Plan ahead. Read through the entire recipe, advance preparation, and equipment checklist before beginning.
- Be sure you have enough extra refrigerator and/or freezer space. Note that the largest cake layer is 14 inches in diameter, sits on a cardboard disk 16 inches in diameter, and when three layers are stacked and decorated they can measure 14 to 16 inches tall. If you lack refrigerator or freezer height, remove a shelf.
- Although the full recipe will serve 125, if the top layer is saved (for the first anniversary), the remaining two layers will serve about 75 to 100; smaller slices will serve 125 or more. If you need an additional 36 to 40 servings, make 1¹/₂ times the basic recipe, bake and frost it in a 9 × 13-inch sheet pan, and arrange slices on plates in the kitchen so it is not on view.
- When the basic cake recipe is doubled, the larger quantity of batter may be too much for some electric mixer bowls or some hand-held mixers; if this is the case, divide the mixture and beat one portion at a time. The double quantity will fit into a 4¹/₂-quart KitchenAid bowl but it is tight. Folding the meringue into the batter is simplified if you use a 5- or 6-quart (extra-large) mixing bowl. Also, for mixing and folding large quantities, it helps to use an extra-large spatula such as a KitchenAid spoonula, with a 13¹/₂-inch-long handle.

Advance Preparation

Many steps can be done ahead. Allow an entire afternoon to bake, cool, wrap, and refrigerate or freeze the cake layers. Double-wrapped in plastic wrap plus heavy-duty aluminum foil, the cakes can be refrigerated up to 2 days or frozen up to 2 weeks. To thaw, place the wrapped cakes in the refrigerator overnight. To prevent drying out, freeze cakes before slicing into layers. Allow at least a couple of hours to prepare the Apricot Mousse filling, and chill it about 3 hours, or up to 4 days, before using. The frosting is best made 1 day before the wedding, then covered and refrigerated. On the day before the wedding, allow several hours to fill, frost, and stack the layers. (I like to fill, frost—with a first coating—and freeze each tier separately a couple of days before the wedding, then thaw overnight in the refrigerator, and assemble and frost with a finishing coat on the day before or the morning of the wedding.)

1 round cake pan 14 × 2 inches; 1 or 2 round cake pans 10 × 2 inches; 2 round cake pans 6 × 2 inches (all with straight sides); 2 large bowls for electric mixer (optional but useful); baking parchment, wax paper, or aluminum foil; extra-large rubber spatula (optional); instant-read thermometer (optional); 1 or 2 large wire racks to support cooling layers; 3 cardboard cake rounds (6-inch, 10-inch, 14-inch, and 16-inch); serrated knife with blade 12 to 14 inches long; dental floss; broad long spatula or cookie sheet without edging (for lifting cake layers); double boiler or large metal bowl that will fit over large saucepan; one 24-inch-long wooden dowel, ¼ inch in diameter, plus coping saw or strong shears to cut dowel; 11 plastic drinking straws; scissors; icing spatulas, large and small; 16- to 18-inch nylon pastry bag fitted with ½-inch star tip for piping border decorations; rotating cake stand or lazy Susan (optional); ceremonial cake-cutting knife tied with white ribbon

- When separating large numbers of eggs, it is safer to do them one at a time, putting the yolks in one bowl and the whites in a custard cup before adding them to the big mixing bowl. This prevents a spilled bit of yolk (which would inhibit whipping of meringue) from dropping into the whites. Remember that eggs separate most easily when cold but beat to the fullest volume when at room temperature. Cold whites can be quickly warmed by setting the bowl of whites into another bowl of hot water. Stir the whites until warm or comfortable to the touch (of a very clean finger).

- To prevent the top crust of each cake layer from sticking to the plastic wrap during storage, lightly dust the plastic wrap with flour before using.

Ingredients

CAKE: **7 times recipe Orange Layer Cake (page 137)**

FILLING: **1 recipe Apricot Mousse (page 188)**

FROSTING: **5 times recipe Orange Buttercream Frosting (page 275)**

Specific Directions for Baking Layers

1. Two 14-inch cake layers require making the basic recipe four times. To do this, double the basic recipe and bake it in one 14-inch pan as directed. Repeat to make a second 14-inch cake. Bake the cake 35 to 38 minutes, until a cake tester inserted in the center comes out clean.

2. Two 10-inch cake layers require making the basic recipe twice. To do this, make one batch of the basic recipe and bake it in one 10-inch pan. Repeat to make a second 10-inch cake. (Obviously, if you have two 10-inch pans, you can just double the recipe and split it evenly between the two pans, baking them at the same time.) Bake cake(s) 35 to 38 minutes, until a cake tester inserted in the center comes out clean.

3. One 6-inch cake layer requires making the basic recipe just once. To do this, make one batch of the basic recipe and divide the batter evenly between two 6-inch pans. Bake about 35 minutes, until a cake tester inserted in the center comes out clean.

Baking Order for Layers

The baking order of the cakes is important to make sure the pans have enough time to be cooled, washed, and greased before being used again. Assuming that you have one 14-inch, one 10-inch, and two 6-inch pans, bake the cakes in this order: one 14-inch, one 10-inch, two 6-inch, one 14-inch, one 10-inch.

continued

Preparing and Icing the Layers

1. Bake and completely cool all the cake layers; defrost, still wrapped, overnight in the refrigerator, if frozen. Then unwrap. Prepare and chill the Apricot Mousse filling. Prepare the buttercream frosting.

2. Cover each cardboard cake round with aluminum foil, then poke dowel holes in the rounds: Center the 6-inch round over the 10-inch round and, using the tip of a knife or a pair of scissors, poke a hole through both. Push the 1/4-inch dowel through both rounds to widen the holes. Set rounds aside.

3. With a serrated knife, slice the domed top off each cake layer, making it perfectly flat. Slice each layer in half horizontally; lift up the top half with a broad spatula or an edgeless cookie sheet and slide it onto a piece of aluminum foil or wax paper. Brush off any crumbs. Stack the layers in groups of four of the same size, with paper or foil between each layer.

4. Place nearby the foil-covered cake rounds, straws and scissors, sliced layers, apricot filling, buttercream (remove this from the refrigerator one batch at a time and beat with a little milk until smooth if stiff from chilling), and icing spatulas.

5. Each tier is filled, frosted, and chilled separately before being stacked. To make the 14-inch tier, put a dab of buttercream in the center of the foil-covered 14-inch cardboard round. Place one 14-inch cake layer on top and spread the surface with about 1 1/3 cups of the filling, spreading it to within 1/4 inch of the edge. Top with a second cake layer, pressed flat. Level the top and align the sides. Fill and stack the remaining two 14-inch layers but do *not* coat the top with filling. Check to be sure the top of the tier is level and the sides are aligned.

6. Center the 10-inch cardboard round on top of the 14-inch tier and draw around it with the tip of a knife, slightly marking the cake's surface (*A*); remove the round.

Cut 6 plastic straws the height of this 14-inch tier. Insert the straws, evenly spaced, just inside the marked circle to support the weight of the next layer (*B*). Be sure no straws protrude above the surface.

A

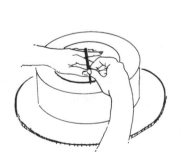

B

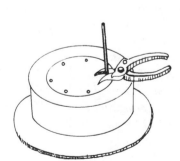

7. With an icing spatula, spread about 1½ cups of the buttercream around the sides and about 1⅓ cups buttercream on the top of this tier. This amount of icing makes a thin coating, just enough to seal in the crumbs so the second coating can be spread smoothly. Place this tier in the refrigerator to chill.

8. To assemble the 10-inch tier, place a dab of buttercream in the center of the 10-inch cardboard round, top with one 10-inch cake layer, and spread with a scant 1 cup of the filling spread to within ¼ inch of the edge. Repeat, stacking the remaining 10-inch layers following the procedure for the 14-inch tier but using a scant 1 cup filling between the layers. Do not coat the top layer.

Following the procedure in step 6, mark the top of this tier with the 6-inch cardboard round, then insert 5 plastic straw dowels as before, cut to the height of this tier. Be sure no straws protrude above the surface.

Spread about 1⅓ cups of the buttercream around the sides of the tier and a scant 1 cup on top. Place this tier in the refrigerator to chill.

9. To make the 6-inch tier, place a dab of buttercream in the center of the 6-inch cardboard round, top with one 6-inch cake layer, and spread with ⅓ cup of the filling to within ¼ inch of the edge. Repeat, filling and stacking only as many of the remaining 6-inch layers as you need to reach 4 inches in height (the same as the other tiers). Freeze whatever cake remains for another use. Check to be sure the top of the tier is level and the sides are aligned.

Spread about ¾ to 1 cup of the buttercream around the sides and ⅓ cup on top of the tier and place in the refrigerator to chill. Cover and refrigerate any remaining buttercream for later use.

Assembling the Cake

1. On the morning of the wedding or one day in advance, stack the layers, centering them one on top of the other. Stand the wooden dowel on the table next to the cake and measure its height, marking it off on the dowel. With shears or a coping saw, cut the dowel at this mark; use a knife to sharpen one end to a point. Carefully insert the pointed end of the dowel through the center of the cake, passing it down through the previously made holes in the cake rounds. The dowel will keep the layers from sliding sideways (*C*).

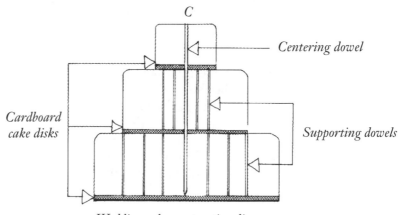

Wedding cake construction diagram

continued

2. Set the cake on the 16-inch cardboard-covered cake pan for ease in handling and decorating. Decorate the cake. Place at least 1 cup of buttercream in a pastry bag fitted with a ¹/₂-inch star tip and set it aside. With an icing spatula, spread the remaining buttercream over the cake to make an even coating. With the pastry bag, pipe a border around the base of each layer (*D*).

3. If you wish to decorate the cake with rosebuds, be sure they have been rinsed free of possible spray, then gently blot dry with tissues (this can be done a day in advance and the uncut roses refrigerated standing in water).

Add fresh rosebuds on the top and around the edges of each tier to complete the design. Remove the flowers just before serving.

4. To serve the cake: The bride and groom make the first cut in the cake using a beribboned ceremonial knife.

To cut the cake for serving: Use a long serrated knife to cut completely around the base of the middle tier down through the bottom tier. Cut 1-inch wedge-shaped slices around the outer edge of bottom tier (*E*). Plate these slices. Lift off the top tier (*F*); set it aside to cut and serve or save. Cut a ring around the base mark left by the top tier (*G*), then cut wedge-shaped slices from middle tier (*H*). Pull the centering dowel out of the cake and discard. Pull out the straw dowels from the middle layer. Cut the middle core cake into serving wedges (*I*). Lift off the middle cardboard disk and remove the remaining straws. Cut the bottom tier into serving slices.

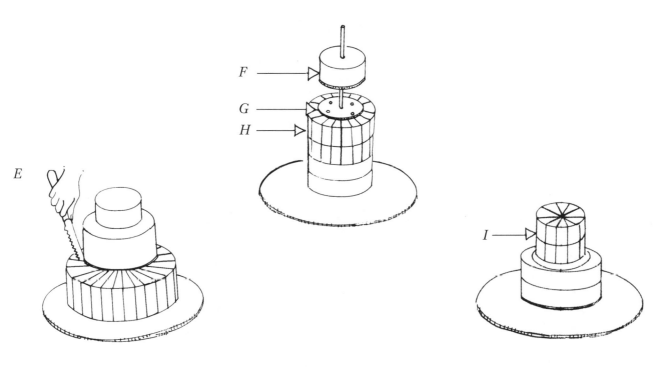

Nutritional Analysis (per slice, filled and frosted): 289 calories; 3 g protein; 6 g fat; 2 g sat-fat; 56 g carbohydrate; 106 mg sodium; 20 mg cholesterol

Light Touch

My favorite classic wedding cake recipe is a rich butter cake filled and frosted with French egg-yolk buttercream. It obtains 57% of its calories from fat. When cut into 125 slices, each one has 331 calories, 21 g fat (13 saturated), and 122 mg cholesterol. My "enlightened luxury cake" (including cake, filling, and frosting) reduces calories from fat by 65%, to just 20%, cutting over two thirds the fat and 100 mg cholesterol per serving.

To do this, I substituted cake flour for all-purpose because it requires less fat to tenderize it. I replaced the butter with a reduced quantity of canola oil (eliminating more saturated fat) and nonfat yogurt (which contributes moisture and tenderizing power). I dropped half the yolks (keeping some to contribute richness and add some fat) doubled the number of egg whites, and replaced whole milk with low-fat. Since the cake now needed more flavor, I increased the vanilla, added orange extract plus grated orange zest, and chose a vibrant sweet/tart Apricot Mousse for the filling. Since this is, after all, a wedding cake, I insisted on using some butter, saving it for the buttercream frosting, which has its creamy texture further enhanced by the presence of a little light cream cheese.

Puddings

Is there anything more soothing than a bowl of homemade chocolate pudding? I mean besides actually eating it warm right from the pot, licking the wooden spoon. If you can imagine yourself, curled up beside a fire on an icy evening nestled between a good novel and a big bowl of pecan-apple pudding, you begin to get the idea.

Pudding is the perfect comfort food. But it needn't be saved just for stressed-out bathrobe-clutching moments. In fact, at a tuxedo occasion, it can set the stiffest guest at ease. Try serving a homey pudding, mousse, or casual easy-to-make trifle at a fancy dinner party and see how much it is appreciated. Its homelike familiarity disarms, like asking your dinner table partner about his or her children instead of trying to wheedle a hot stock tip. Even globally chic tiramisù is just an Italian designer pudding with a pedigree.

The eleven recipes in this chapter include something for everyone, from Homemade Chocolate Pudding to Trifle.

HOMEMADE CHOCOLATE PUDDING

*Yield: About 2¹/₂ cups; enough to fill one 9-inch pie or
8 mini-tartlets or tulip shells; eight ¹/₃-cup servings*

*This dark, silky pudding is just as easy to make as, and far better tasting than, a
packaged pudding. Use this as a filling for Chocolate Tulip Shells (page 30), individual tartlets made with Chocolate Crumb Crust (page 55), or as the basis for
Chocolate Cream Pie topped with meringue (page 87). Or, serve the pudding by
itself in stemmed glasses garnished with Chocolate Curls (page 289).*

¹/₃ **cup granulated sugar**

¹/₄ **cup plus 2 tablespoons unsifted unsweetened regular cocoa**

¹/₄ **cup cornstarch**

Pinch of salt

2 cups 1% milk

¹/₄ **cup dark corn syrup**

1 large egg

2 teaspoons vanilla extract

Advance Preparation

*Pudding needs about
2 hours to set. It can be
made a day ahead and
refrigerated.*

Special Equipment

*1¹/₂-quart heavy-
bottomed saucepan*

1. In a heavy-bottomed medium-sized saucepan, whisk together the sugar,
cocoa, cornstarch, and salt. Whisk in the milk and corn syrup. Set the pan
over medium-high heat and whisk constantly until the mixture comes to a
full rolling boil. Whisk for 1 full minute longer, then remove from the heat.

2. In a small bowl, beat the egg lightly. Whisk in a few tablespoons of the
hot pudding to warm the egg without scrambling it. Add the warm egg
mixture to the pudding in the pan and whisk well to blend.

3. Return the pan to medium-low heat and cook, whisking continuously,
for 45 to 60 seconds. Remove the pan from the heat and stir in the vanilla.
Cover with plastic wrap to prevent a skin from forming as it cools. Allow to
cool, then refrigerate until thoroughly chilled, at least 2 hours.

Nutritional Analysis (per serving): 121 calories; 4 g protein; 2 g fat; 0.6 g satfat; 25 g carbohydrate; 84 mg sodium; 29 mg cholesterol

Light Touch

A packaged pudding mix gets about 17% of its calories from fat while this recipe gets only 12%
and contains no unfamiliar additives. To reduce the fat, I have used low-fat milk and cocoa
rather than melted solid chocolate.

LUCY'S PECAN-APPLE PUDDING

Yield: 3 cups batter; 4 servings (recipe can be doubled)

My mother-in-law, Lucy Purdy, loves this recipe because it meets her requirement for absolutely effortless baking. The only time spent is preparing one apple, and you don't even have to peel it before grating unless you want to (I don't); you can mix the batter by hand in just a minute. The result is a moist, richly flavored pudding with just a hint of cakey texture, filled with sweetly spiced apples and nuts.

Advance Preparation

Best on day it is made; serve warm from the oven or at room temperature.

Special Equipment

1- or 1^1/$_2$-quart oven-proof baking dish

Temperature and Time

350°F for 40 to 45 minutes

Butter-flavor no-stick cooking spray

2 large eggs

1 teaspoon vanilla extract

^{1}/$_2$ cup granulated sugar

^{1}/$_4$ cup unsifted cake flour

2 teaspoons baking powder

^{1}/$_2$ teaspoon salt

^{1}/$_2$ teaspoon ground nutmeg

^{1}/$_8$ teaspoon ground ginger

^{1}/$_4$ cup chopped pecans

1 or 2 large apples, peeled, cored, and grated (1 cup grated)

1. Position a rack in the center of the oven and preheat the oven to 350°F. Lightly coat a baking pan with cooking spray.

2. In a mixing bowl, whisk together the eggs, vanilla, and sugar. Whisk together and add the dry ingredients. Stir in the nuts and grated apple.

3. Turn the batter out into the prepared pan and bake for 40 to 45 minutes, until the top is golden brown and springy to the touch and a knife inserted in the center comes out clean. Serve warm, spooned from the baking pan.

Nutritional Analysis (per serving): 228 calories; 4 g protein; 7 g fat; 1 g satfat; 38 g carbohydrate; 463 mg sodium; 107 mg cholesterol

Light Touch

For nearly thirty years, my family enjoyed this recipe in its classic form: 1 whole cup of chopped nuts in the cake topped with a cup of whipped heavy cream. Did we care (or know) that the calories from fat came to 66%, or that each serving contained 569 calories, 43 g fat, 16 g satfat, and 188 mg cholesterol? We do now, hence the removal of most of the nuts and all the whipped cream. Although there is no butter or oil in the cake, the fat comes from egg yolks and pecans. The taste is just as great as the original, but with an added pleasure: a 58% drop in calories from fat, to 28%!

GRANDMA'S NOODLE PUDDING

Yield: Twelve 1-cup servings

When I was growing up, this was one of my grandmother Clara's culinary highlights. My mother carried on the tradition, serving this warm, fragrant fruit-studded pudding (kugel, in Yiddish) for both sweet and savory occasions—an accompaniment to roasted meat or poultry, for a brunch or breakfast, or as a comforting snack.

It is now my turn to pass on the tradition, and I do so with pleasure, having removed the guilt. Resist the temptation to cut out any more fat, however, or the kugel will lose its creamy texture and dry out.

12 ounces broad noodles, preferably labeled "yolk- and cholesterol-free" or "yolk-free"

Butter-flavor no-stick cooking spray

1¹/₂ large apples (such as Golden Delicious), peeled, cored, and thinly sliced (about 1¹/₂ cups)

¹/₂ cup (3 ounces) dried apricot halves, coarsely cut

¹/₂ cup golden or dark raisins

3 large eggs plus 1 large egg white

1¹/₂ cups 2% milk

2 cups vanilla low-fat yogurt, top liquid poured off

¹/₂ cup granulated sugar

1¹/₄ cups 2% cottage cheese

1 teaspoon vanilla extract

1 teaspoon ground cinnamon

¹/₂ teaspoon ground nutmeg

¹/₄ teaspoon salt

Topping

¹/₄ cup toasted wheat germ

¹/₄ cup graham cracker or other cracker crumbs

¹/₂ teaspoon ground nutmeg

Advance Preparation

The noodle pudding may be made a day or two ahead and refrigerated. Before serving, top with foil and warm at 325°F for 20 to 30 minutes; if it starts to dry out, pour on a little 2% or skim milk and return to the oven.

Special Equipment

Large pot; colander; 9 × 13-inch baking dish

Temperature and Time

350°F for 35 minutes

1. Cook the noodles: In a large pot, bring about 4 quarts of water to a rapid boil, add the noodles, stir a few times, and cook, uncovered, for 5 to 7 minutes, until just barely tender when bitten through; don't overcook, as they will later be baked. Drain in a colander and rinse with cold water. Set aside.

2. Position a rack in the center of the oven and preheat the oven to 350°F. Lightly coat a baking dish with no-stick spray, then add and toss together the drained noodles, apple slices, cut-up apricots, and raisins.

3. In a large mixing bowl, whisk together the whole eggs plus egg white, milk, yogurt, and sugar. Add cottage cheese, vanilla, spices, and salt and whisk again. Pour over the noodles and fruit in the baking dish and stir gently just to blend.

4. Combine topping ingredients in a small cup and sprinkle evenly over the pudding. Bake about 35 minutes, until a knife inserted in the center comes out clean and the pudding top is golden brown. Serve warm or at room temperature.

Nutritional Analysis (per serving): 287 calories; 13 g protein; 3.6 g fat; 1.2 g satfat; 60 g carbohydrate; 211 mg sodium; 57 mg cholesterol

---

Light Touch

Today, new products make it easier to cut the fat and cholesterol from classic *kugel* without losing taste. Select cholesterol-and-egg-yolk-free wide noodles (available in the supermarket) and low-fat sour cream or yogurt (better than fat-free) instead of dairy sour cream. After many less-than-delicious trials, I have reduced the calories from fat by 72%, to just 11%. To keep the creamy richness, the recipe needs the 2% cottage cheese and 2% milk. It's good for you, too, with 70 mg calcium and 3 g dietary fiber per serving. Depending upon your own tolerance for cholesterol, you could cut back to 2 whole eggs, eliminating 18 mg cholesterol. If you take a devil-may-care attitude, toss in my grandma's original 6 whole eggs; total fat only climbs to 14% calories from fat, with 305 calories and 5 g fat; but watch out for the cholesterol—it soars to 111 mg.

UPSIDE-DOWN APPLE BREAD PUDDING WITH BOURBON CREAM SAUCE

Yield: 8 servings

This idea is adapted from a recipe suggested by the Washington (State) Apple Commission. To make an old-fashioned Raisin Bread Pudding without apples, see the variation on page 183.

Bread Custard

8 slices store-bought or homemade raisin bread torn up (about 4 cups pieces)

1¼ cups 1% milk

1 large egg plus 2 large whites

¼ cup packed dark brown sugar

1 teaspoon vanilla extract

Pinch of salt

Apples

1 tablespoon unsalted butter

3 Golden Delicious or Granny Smith apples, peeled, cored, and thinly sliced (about 3 cups)

¼ cup packed dark brown sugar

2 tablespoons dark corn syrup

½ teaspoon ground nutmeg

Pinch of ground ginger

Butter-flavor no-stick cooking spray

To Top and Serve

½ cup apricot preserves

1 recipe Bourbon Cream Sauce (page 262)

Advance Preparation

The pudding can be made ahead and rewarmed before serving but it is best served the day it is prepared. The bread can be soaked in custard up to 2 hours before making the pudding. The apples in syrup can be prepared separately a day in advance.

Special Equipment

Large (10- to 12-inch) frying pan; slotted spoon; 9-inch cake pan; pastry brush

Temperature and Time

350°F for 30 to 35 minutes

1. Make the bread custard: Arrange the torn bread pieces in a shallow casserole. In a bowl, whisk together the milk, egg and whites, brown sugar, vanilla, and salt. Pour over the bread and press the bread pieces down under the liquid. Cover with plastic wrap and refrigerate for at least 15 minutes while you prepare the fruit. This step can be done up to 2 hours ahead.

2. Prepare the apples: In a large frying pan, melt the butter over medium heat, then add the apple slices and cook 2 to 3 minutes. Add the brown sugar, corn syrup, and spices and cook, stirring occasionally, for about 8 minutes, until the apples are just tender when pierced with a knife but still hold their shape.

3. Lightly coat a 9-inch cake pan with cooking spray. With a slotted spoon, transfer the apple slices from the frying pan to the cake pan. You may arrange the slices in neat concentric circles, or rows, or scatter them at random. Leave the apple juice in the frying pan; set the cake pan aside.

4. Position a rack in the center of the oven and preheat the oven to 350°F. Return the frying pan to the heat and rapidly boil the pan juices 2 to 3 minutes, until reduced to a thick syrup. Pour this syrup over the apples in the cake pan.

5. Remove the bread custard from the refrigerator. With a slotted spoon, arrange the soaked bread pieces over the apple slices, covering the apples completely. Pour on any liquid custard. Gently pat the bread to flatten the top. Bake the pudding in the preheated oven for 30 to 35 minutes, until the top is golden brown and slightly puffed up. It will be firm to the touch and a knife inserted in the center will come out clean. Cool the pudding on a rack about 10 minutes. Cut around the edge of the pudding to release it, then top with a large flat platter and invert. Lift off the cake pan; the apples will be facing up.

6. In a small saucepan, warm the apricot preserves and pour or brush them over the top. Serve warm with Bourbon Cream Sauce.

Nutritional Analysis (per serving without sauce): 263 calories; 5 g protein; 4 g fat; 1.6 g satfat; 54 g carbohydrate; 161 mg sodium; 32 mg cholesterol

RAISIN BREAD PUDDING

Position a rack in the center of the oven and preheat the oven to 350°F. Place in a 1¹/₂-quart baking dish 4 cups cut-up lightly toasted raisin bread. In a bowl, whisk together 2 cups of 2% milk, 2 tablespoons packed brown sugar, and a pinch of salt; pour over the bread and allow to soak at least 15 minutes. Whisk together an additional 1 cup milk with 1 large egg plus 2 whites, 1 teaspoon vanilla extract, and ¹/₂ cup granulated sugar; add ¹/₂ teaspoon ground cinnamon or nutmeg if the bread does not have cinnamon in it. Pour this mixture over the soaked bread and bake about 45 minutes, until golden brown on top. For a slightly creamier texture, set the baking dish in a larger pan and pour enough hot water in the pan to come about a third of the way up the side of the pudding dish. Bake for 50 to 55 minutes, until a knife inserted 1 inch from the edge comes out clean but the center is still creamy.

Nutritional Analysis (per serving): 173 calories; 6 g protein; 3 g fat; 1 g satfat; 32 g carbohydrate; 163 mg sodium; 31 mg cholesterol

Light Touch

My favorite classic bread pudding had 10 g fat (5 saturated), and 127 mg cholesterol and 30% calories from fat per serving. I have reduced fat by 57%, to 13% calories from fat (15% for the variation), by cutting out egg yolks and butter and using low-fat milk.

RASPBERRY-RHUBARB FOOL

Yield: Eight 1-cup servings

Fruit fools are an old-fashioned favorite: a quick, easy blend of choice summer fruit with a foamy cloud of rich whipped cream. This version, which I adapted with permission from a basic formula by Lisa Cherkasky in Eating Well *magazine (June 1994) is a delightful compromise using some whipped cream and vanilla yogurt.*

Rhubarb and raspberries complement each other well, but the recipe is infinitely variable depending upon the fruit at hand. In spring, use strawberries with rhubarb. When rhubarb is in season, I like to cut up fresh stalks and freeze them in 2-cup bags so I have a supply on hand. You will need to adjust the quantity of sugar depending upon the sweetness of the berries used. Two special ingredients enhance the flavor: sweet red vermouth with a flowery herbal taste, and ground ginger, for a slight kick. For a special presentation, serve your fool in long-stemmed glass goblets, or use as a filling for Chocolate Tulip Shells (page 30), served with Raspberry Sauce (page 258).

2 cups vanilla nonfat or low-fat yogurt without added gums

1¹⁄₈ pounds rhubarb stalks, washed, trimmed, and cut into ¹⁄₂-inch pieces (4 cups cut up)

1 quart whole fresh raspberries or strawberries (rinsed, hulled, and halved) or 4 cups frozen unsweetened whole berries, thawed

¹⁄₄ cup sweet red vermouth or red or white wine or fruit juice

1 cup packed light brown sugar, or to taste

One 2- or 3-inch piece stick cinnamon

¹⁄₄ teaspoon ground ginger

Two 2-inch-long strips lemon zest

¹⁄₂ cup heavy cream

Advance Preparation

The yogurt needs to drain at least 1 hour before it is used in this recipe; can be done 1 day ahead. Fruit mixture can be made a day or two ahead and chilled. Allow assembled recipe to chill at least 2 hours before serving.

Special Equipment

Large (3-quart) saucepan; strainer set over bowl; long-handled fork (optional); chilled bowl and beater for whipping cream

1. Measure the yogurt into a strainer set over a medium-sized mixing bowl and allow to drain in the refrigerator for at least 1 hour, until the volume is reduced to 1¹⁄₂ cups. At this point, discard the liquid and transfer the yogurt to the bowl until needed.

2. In a 3-quart saucepan, combine the rhubarb, berries, wine, brown sugar, cinnamon stick, ginger, and lemon zest. Stir together, set over medium-high heat, and bring to a boil. Reduce the heat to medium, cover the pan, and cook, stirring occasionally, for 8 to 10 minutes, until the rhubarb is soft. Uncover the pan, raise the heat, and stir while cooking another 5 to 8 minutes, until somewhat thickened. You will have about 1 quart of fruit. With a long-handled fork, pick out and discard the cinnamon stick and lemon strips. Taste and adjust sugar if necessary. Turn the mixture into a bowl, cover, and chill thoroughly. You can make this a day or two ahead.

3. Fold the cold fruit mixture into the drained yogurt. With a chilled bowl and beater, whip the cream until stiff peaks form, then fold it into the fruit/yogurt, leaving it slightly streaked looking. Cover and chill at least 2 hours (or up to 8) before serving. Garnish each serving with a few fresh berries or a mint sprig.

Nutritional Analysis (per serving): 278 calories; 4 g protein; 6 g fat; 3 g satfat; 54 g carbohydrate; 54 mg sodium; 22 mg cholesterol

---

Light Touch

With only 19% calories from fat, this is a welcome summer treat. Of course you could omit the whipped cream, but I think the texture is best with it. While you are feeling virtuous, gloat over the fact that you have only one third the fat per serving of the classic recipe. The original fool, who made this with 1½ cups heavy cream (and no yogurt), had 40% calories from fat, and twice the satfat and cholesterol per serving.

CHOCOLATE MOUSSE

Yield: 4 cups; ten ¹/₄-cup servings

Classic chocolate mousse, an ethereal blend of dark chocolate, whipped cream, egg yolks, and whipped egg whites, presents us with several dilemmas. How to resist it at all is the first. The quantity of fat and the fact that the egg whites are uncooked (raising the possibility of health hazard) are the others. The truth is that I need to have chocolate mousse in my life, so the other, technical, problems must—and can—be solved. Instead of whipped cream, this recipe uses a cooked meringue (actually an easy-to-make seven-minute icing). You can vary the flavor if you wish by adding ¹/₂ teaspoon peppermint extract (Peppermint-Chocolate Mousse) or 1 teaspoon orange extract (Orange-Chocolate Mousse) or 1 teaspoon coffee extract (Mocha Mousse). Make Chocolate Mousse Tartlets using this recipe to fill small tartlet shells lined with Chocolate Crumb Crust (page 55).

1 cup skim milk, divided

1 large egg

¹/₄ cup plus 2 teaspoons light corn syrup, divided

¹/₂ cup unsifted unsweetened cocoa, preferably Dutch-processed

2 teaspoons unflavored gelatin

¹/₂ cup plus 1 tablespoon water, divided

2 ounces semisweet chocolate, finely chopped

¹/₄ cup light cream cheese, slightly softened and cut up

1 teaspoon vanilla extract

2 large egg whites

³/₄ cup granulated sugar

Advance Preparation

The mousse must be refrigerated at least 3 hours, to set. It can be made 1 day ahead, covered, and refrigerated.

Special Equipment

Double boiler; hand-held electric mixer

1. In a medium-sized bowl, combine ¹/₄ cup of milk, the whole egg, ¹/₄ cup of the corn syrup, and the cocoa. Whisk together until smooth.

2. In a heavy-bottomed saucepan, heat the remaining ³/₄ cup of milk until it just begins to simmer and bubbles appear around the edges; remove it from the heat at once.

3. Whisk some of the hot milk into the cocoa mixture to warm it, then whisk the cocoa mixture into the remaining hot milk in the saucepan. Cook over medium heat, whisking constantly, for about 5 minutes, until slightly thickened. Remove from the heat.

4. In a small saucepan, sprinkle the gelatin over ¹/₄ cup of the water and allow to stand for about 3 minutes to soften. Stir the mixture over low heat just until the gelatin is dissolved; do not boil. Remove from the heat.

5. Add the chopped chocolate and cream cheese to the hot cocoa mixture and whisk very hard until melted and absolutely smooth. Beat in the vanilla and any other flavoring extract along with the dissolved gelatin. Set aside to cool.

6. To prepare the meringue, set up the bottom of a double boiler with just enough water in it that the top part can sit above it without getting wet. Bring the water to a simmer. In the top of the double boiler, combine the egg whites, sugar, remaining 5 tablespoons of water, and remaining 2 teaspoons of corn syrup. Place over the simmering water and immediately begin beating with a hand-held electric mixer on medium speed. Whip about 3 minutes, then increase to high and whip about 3 minutes longer, until the whites make a satiny foam that holds soft peaks and mounds on the beater. Immediately remove the meringue from the heat and transfer it to a cool bowl to stop the cooking process.

7. Whisk about 1 cup of the meringue into the chocolate mixture to lighten it, then fold in the remaining meringue. Turn it into a bowl or into prepared tartlet shells or a pie shell. Let cool. To prevent absorption of flavors, you can cover the mousse with plastic wrap, holding it off the surface with several toothpicks. Refrigerate at least 3 hours, or overnight, to set.

Nutritional Analysis (per serving): 152 calories; 4.6 g protein; 3.7 g fat; 0.2 g satfat; 20 g carbohydrate; 73 mg sodium; 24 mg cholesterol

Light Touch

With just 20% calories from fat, this is a very friendly mousse. In fact, it is reduced 67% from a classic recipe made with 4 eggs, 1/2 cup butter, 12 ounces solid chocolate, and 1/2 cup heavy cream plus another 1/2 cup cream in the topping. By dropping most of the solid chocolate and replacing it with low-fat cocoa, cutting 3 yolks and all the butter, and replacing whipped cream with fat-free meringue, we shave most of the fat but save the creamy mouth-feel. This texture is further enhanced by the addition of some light cream cheese.

APRICOT MOUSSE

Yield: About 10 cups. Approximately 8½ to 9 cups are needed to fill a 3-tier Fresh Orange Wedding Cake (page 168). Recipe can be cut in half.

This mousse is an intensely flavored sweet-tart filling good for a wedding cake or any other layer cake or roulade. The recipe is designed to be large enough to fill a three-tier wedding cake. It can be cut in half to fill one prebaked 9-inch meringue or pastry shell, or to make eight 4-inch tartlets lined with a double recipe of Gingersnap–Graham Cracker Crumb Crust (page 53) and garnished with chopped pistachio nuts. If you have some extra mousse left over after filling a cake, serve it in stemmed glasses with a dab of vanilla yogurt on top.

Note: The meringue in this filling is actually a seven-minute boiled icing. The full quantity is quite large, best whipped in a 4½- to 5-quart metal bowl set over a large pot of simmering water. If you don't have this equipment, simply cut the recipe in half and make two easily manageable batches. When first made, the mousse is cream colored but it darkens to a pale apricot tone after several hours.

Advance Preparation

The filling may be made in stages. The apricot purée alone may be prepared up to 5 days ahead, covered, and refrigerated. The completed mousse takes about 3 hours to set before it can be spread on a cake; it can be covered and refrigerated up to 4 days ahead.

Special Equipment

2½- to 3-quart nonreactive pot with lid; small (2- to 3-cup) nonreactive saucepan; rubber-tipped spatula; 4½- to 5-quart metal bowl and large saucepan to hold it, making an improvised double boiler; large pot or pan to hold 4½-quart bowl in ice water bath; hand-held electric mixer

4 cups packed (24 ounces) dried apricot halves

4½ cups fresh orange juice, divided

3 tablespoons plus 1 teaspoon unflavored gelatin

4 large egg whites, at room temperature

3 cups granulated sugar

½ cup plus 2 tablespoons water

4 teaspoons light corn syrup

2 teaspoons vanilla extract

1. In a 2½- to 3-quart nonreactive pot, combine the dried apricots with 2½ cups of the orange juice. Cover, bring to a boil, reduce the heat, and simmer 20 to 25 minutes, until the apricots are fork-tender.

2. In a blender or food processor, combine half the apricot mixture with ¼ cup of the orange juice and pulse until smooth. Transfer this purée to a 4½- to 5-quart metal bowl. Repeat, making a purée with the remaining apricots plus another ¼ cup of orange juice; this time, leave the apricot purée in the blender or processor bowl.

3. Measure the remaining 1½ cups of orange juice into a small nonreactive saucepan and sprinkle on the gelatin. Allow to soften for about 3 minutes, then set over low heat and stir until the gelatin is dissolved. Test by pinching the mixture between your fingers to be sure no graininess remains; do not boil. Remove from the heat and add to the purée remaining in the blender or processor. Blend until smooth, then stir it into the apricot purée in the large bowl.

4. Place the bowl of apricot purée in a larger bowl filled with ice water. Let stand, stirring occasionally, about 30 minutes, until the purée is cool to the touch and thick enough to mound on the spoon like pudding. Check the mixture and remove from the ice water bath if it begins to set hard.

5. While the purée cools, prepare the meringue. Place the egg whites, sugar, water, and corn syrup in the top of a large double boiler or a 4- to 5-quart metal bowl. Stir the mixture, then place it over (not touching) a pot of simmering water. Whip the mixture with a hand-held electric beater on medium speed for about 7 minutes. Increase the speed to high and whip for another 10 minutes, or longer, until the whites are smooth, satiny, and nearly hold stiff peaks. Remove the bowl of meringue from the heat, add the vanilla, and whip to blend. Note: Depending upon the size of your electric beaters, it may take a total of 25 minutes to whip this volume of whites. If you have smaller equipment and want to do half the amount at one time, it will take about 7 minutes for each batch.

6. When the apricot purée is cooled and thickened, stir or whip it well. (If it has become rubbery, stir it over a bowl of warm water until it has returned to a smooth, thick consistency.) Fold the meringue into the apricot purée using a large spatula and an over/under motion; don't stir or the whites will lose volume. Don't worry if it looks streaked. Cool the mousse completely, cover with plastic wrap, and refrigerate at least 3 hours, or up to 4 days.

Nutritional Analysis (per heaping ¹/₂-cup serving): 251 calories; 4 g protein; 0.2 g fat; 0 g satfat; 62 g carbohydrate; 21 mg sodium; 0 mg cholesterol

Light Touch

With only 1% calories from fat, this is as light as you could wish; there are, however, 93% calories from carbohydrates, hence the 251 calories. The fruit supplies 3 g dietary fiber per serving. Compare this to a conventional mousse enriched with whipped cream: 45% calories from fat, 320 calories, 17 g fat, and 61 mg cholesterol per serving.

TIRAMISÙ

Yield: 12 servings

An incredibly rich, internationally loved Italian dessert, tiramisù *(meaning "pick-me-up") is made of coffee- and brandy-soaked ladyfingers layered with a heavenly custard of eggs, triple-cream mascarpone cheese, sometimes also heavy cream, topped with shaved chocolate and sifted cocoa. The presentation is informal, somewhere between a pudding and a soft cake; it is usually assembled in a deep platter or shallow bowl and served with a spoon. In its homeland, variations abound, depending upon the chef and the region of Italy in which it is prepared. For example, panettone or sponge cake sometimes substitutes for ladyfingers; spirits vary from the classic brandy, rum, or coffee liqueur to Sambuca Romana or amaretto. This creative latitude is good news for us, because mascarpone (a thick rich cheese that gives this dessert its unique character) contains astronomical amounts of fat. To bring this ethereal confection into our realm of reality, use a small portion of mascarpone for its unique flavor but replace the rest with a blend of light cream cheese and seven-minute icing (easy-to-make cooked meringue).*

Mascarpone is available in gourmet and cheese shops, Italian markets, and many large supermarkets. Homemade ladyfingers are good, and benefit from being lightly toasted to give more texture. Store-bought ladyfingers are even softer and should always be toasted. If using ladyfingers or sponge cake, sprinkle or brush on the coffee-liqueur mixture instead of dipping the cake into it. The crisp savoiardi, *such as Bisconova, available in Italian food shops are best; they are firm enough to dip into liquid and still hold their shape. If I cannot find them, I substitute crisp Stella d'Oro Egg Jumbo Cookies sold in supermarkets; they are larger than ladyfingers (2 by 4 inches). You will need about 30, or most of two packages.*

Advance Preparation

Assemble the tiramisù at least 6 hours or up to a day ahead, so flavors can blend. Keep refrigerated.

Special Equipment

Double boiler or saucepan with round-bottomed metal bowl set comfortably into it (for icing); hand-held electric mixer or hand rotary beater; instant-read thermometer (optional); oval or rectangular serving platter with deep edge (approximately 2 quarts) or 2$^{1}/_{2}$- to 3-quart trifle or soufflé dish or 10-cup casserole

Cake

50 to 60 store-bought ladyfingers (depending upon size), or Italian *savoiardi* biscuits, or 30 Stella d'Oro Egg Jumbo Cookies (2 packages)

Seven-Minute Icing

2 large egg whites

1$^{1}/_{3}$ cups granulated sugar

$^{1}/_{4}$ cup water

2 teaspoons light corn syrup

Filling

$^{3}/_{4}$ cup nonfat cottage cheese

$^{1}/_{2}$ cup (4 ounces) mascarpone cheese

$^{1}/_{2}$ cup (4 ounces) light cream cheese

1 tablespoon brandy or dark rum

2 teaspoons vanilla extract

Soaking Liquid

3 tablespoons brandy or dark rum

**³/₄ cup strong black French roast or espresso coffee or
1 tablespoon Medaglia d'Oro instant espresso powder dissolved
in ³/₄ cup hot water**

Topping

1 tablespoon unsweetened Dutch-processed cocoa

¹/₄ to ¹/₃ ounce semisweet chocolate, grated or shaved

1. If using ladyfingers, place them flat side up and toast lightly; set them aside. Add just enough water to the bottom of a double boiler so that the top part can sit above it without getting wet. Bring the water to a simmer.

2. Prepare the Seven-Minute Icing: In the top part of the double boiler, combine the egg whites, sugar, water, and corn syrup. Set over the simmering water and immediately begin to whip with a hand-held electric or rotary mixer. Whip on medium speed for about 3 minutes, then increase speed and whip on high until soft peaks form, about 4 minutes longer with an electric mixer, up to 10 minutes with a rotary beater (about 140°F on an instant-read thermometer). Remove the bowl from the heat and beat until stiff peaks form, about 2 minutes longer. Set the egg whites aside to cool (they won't deflate).

3. Make the filling: Place the cottage cheese in a strainer over a bowl and press gently but firmly on top to remove any excess liquid; some brands will not drain and that is fine. Put the cottage cheese in the workbowl of a food processor or blender and process about 3 minutes, until absolutely smooth without a hint of graininess. Add the mascarpone, cream cheese, brandy, and vanilla. Pulse until creamy and smooth.

4. Check the temperature of the egg whites; they should be cool to the touch, about 85°F on the instant-read thermometer. (If they're still too hot, spread them on a flat platter and refrigerate for a few minutes.) Turn the whites out into a large mixing bowl. Fold in about 1 cup of the cheese mixture, then little by little fold in the rest.

5. Make the coffee liquid: In a widemouthed bowl, combine the brandy or other liqueur with the brewed coffee or instant coffee powder dissolved in the hot water. Note: Make about 1¹/₂ times the soaking-liquid recipe if using *savoiardi* or Stella d'Oro Egg Jumbo Cookies, which are dipped into the liquid and soak it up.

6. To assemble the tiramisù, place the ladyfingers, cheese mixture, and coffee liquid near your serving platter. If using regular ladyfingers, brush or sprinkle them with coffee liquid and arrange a layer on the bottom of the serving platter. Top with about a quarter of the creamy filling, cover with another layer of coffee-soaked ladyfingers, and top with another quarter of the creamy filling. Repeat once or twice more (depending upon the size of your platter), ending with cream on top, smoothed evenly.

continued

Alternatively, if using the larger-sized Egg Jumbo Cookies, dip 10 cookies in the soaking liquid and arrange on a large (approximately 11- × 15-inch) platter. Top with a generous 1½ cups of the cream filling. Top with another 10 dipped cookies and another 1½ cups of cream. Add a third layer of dipped cookies and top with all the remaining cream (nearly 2 cups), spread evenly over the top.

7.   To finish, sift the cocoa over the cream, then garnish with grated or shaved semisweet chocolate scattered over the top. Or, to be fancy, top with Chocolate Curls (page 289).

8.   Stick several toothpicks into the top of the tiramisù, then cover the platter with plastic wrap; the toothpicks hold the wrap above the topping. Refrigerate 6 hours or overnight. Refrigerate leftovers.

Nutritional Analysis (per serving): 341 calories; 8 g protein; 7.8 g fat; 0.5 g satfat; 59 g carbohydrate; 194 mg sodium; 92 mg cholesterol

---

Light Touch

My favorite classic tiramisù recipe contains a sinfully creamy 54% calories from fat; not surprisingly, each serving contains nearly 600 calories, 37 g fat, and a whopping 243 mg cholesterol. I have cut almost half the calories, three quarters of the fat, and two thirds the cholesterol per serving! This was done by cutting all the cream and yolks, keeping only one sixth of the mascarpone (just enough to lend flavor), and substituting a blend of low-fat cream cheese and nonfat cottage cheese which still gives a very creamy mouth-feel. Total fat is cut by 61% to 21% calories from fat. My enlightened tiramisù is still the number-one hit at parties, and that is the only number that really matters!

TRIFLE

Yield: 6 servings

A classic English trifle layers wine-soaked cake with fruit preserves, fresh berries or sliced fruit, vanilla pastry cream, and whipped cream. Serve this in your prettiest glass dish, preferably a footed trifle bowl, to display the colorful layers. Trifle is a very personal dish, with as many variations as there are chefs. Make it your own by using the ripest berries or sliced fruit in season, and whatever leftover cake you happen to have.

3 ounces store-bought ladyfingers (about 12) or one 9-inch layer of any cake

$^1/_4$ to $^1/_2$ cup sweet or cream sherry or dark rum

$^3/_4$ cup fruit preserves, Brandied Cranberry-Maple Sauce (page 261), or Blueberry-Honey Sauce (page 259)

2 cups sliced fresh fruit (peeled peaches, nectarines, plums, pears, bananas, for example) or 2 cups fresh berries, picked over and hulled (sliced if strawberries) or whole frozen berries or sliced peaches, thawed

1 recipe Shortcut Vanilla Pastry Cream (page 248), Ricotta Cream (page 250), or Vanilla Custard Sauce (page 255)

$^3/_4$ cup coarsely crushed amaretti (12 cookies) or honey-cinnamon or chocolate graham crackers

Topping (optional)

$^1/_2$ recipe Seven-Minute Icing (page 277) or honey variation (page 278) or $^1/_3$ cup heavy cream, whipped (see Light Touch)

1. Line the bottom of the serving bowl completely with the ladyfingers or pieces of cake cut to fit. Sprinkle the cake with some of the sherry or rum and spread with the preserves. Top the cake with some of the prepared fruit.

2. Cover the fruit with some of the pastry cream and about half the crushed amaretti or crackers. Add another layer of fruit and cream, topped with the remaining crumbs. If you wish, top with the icing or whipped cream. Chill at least 3 hours before serving.

Nutritional Analysis (per serving made with raspberries, graham cracker crumbs, and without topping): 337 calories; 5 g protein; 2.8 g fat; 1.2 g satfat; 72 g carbohydrate; 186 mg sodium; 42 mg cholesterol

---

Advance Preparation

For the flavors to blend and mellow, trifle needs 3 hours or overnight to chill. The cake and pastry cream can be prepared a couple of days in advance of assembly.

Special Equipment

1$^1/_2$- to 2-quart glass bowl or trifle dish or soufflé dish

---

Light Touch

The recipe as written has just 7% calories from fat. If you top it with the half recipe of fat-free Seven-Minute Icing, you add 75 calories and 20 g carbohydrates. If you want to have your whipped cream and eat it, too, add $^1/_3$ cup heavy cream, whipped; this adds about 50 calories, 5 g fat, and almost 20 mg cholesterol per serving (total calories from fat only rises to 18%).

STEAMED FIG-DATE-APRICOT PUDDING

Yield: 5 cups batter; 2-quart pudding; 12 to 14 servings

Rich and spicy, filled with fruit, and moist enough to stay fresh at least a week, this is the ideal holiday cake. The secret ingredients are grated carrot and potato, both of which lend moisture and texture yet are essentially invisible. The steaming is easy to do in improvised equipment if you don't have a pudding mold.

For Christmas, New Year's Eve, or any special occasion, serve this pudding with Cinnamon-Apple Custard Sauce (page 256) or Bourbon Cream Sauce (page 262).

Advance Preparation

Pudding will need to steam for 2 hours. Can be made 3 to 4 days ahead, wrapped airtight, and stored in refrigerator. Before serving, reheat in 325°F oven at least 30 minutes.

Special Equipment

2-quart pudding mold with tight-fitting lid or 2-quart heatproof bowl plus heavy-duty aluminum foil and a heavy-duty rubber band or string; large steaming kettle such as Dutch oven or other large covered pot to hold mold; bain marie rack or trivet or several canning jar rings wired together in a ring to hold the steaming mold; flat serving platter

Temperature and Time

Steam pudding: 2 hours

¹/₂ cup (3 ounces) seedless raisins

³/₄ cup (5 ounces) dried apricot halves, cut up

Grated zest of 1 lemon or orange

¹/₂ cup dry red vermouth or red or white wine or apple juice

¹/₂ pound (about 1¹/₂ cups) dried figs, diced

¹/₂ pound (about 1¹/₄ cups) pitted dates, diced

1 cup sifted all-purpose flour

1¹/₂ teaspoons baking powder

1 teaspoon baking soda

1 teaspoon salt

³/₄ teaspoon ground nutmeg

¹/₂ teaspoon ground allspice

¹/₂ teaspoon ground cloves

¹/₄ teaspoon ground ginger

1 teaspoon almond extract or 1 tablespoon almond oil

2 tablespoons unsalted butter, at room temperature

1 cup packed dark brown sugar or ¹/₂ cup packed light plus ¹/₂ cup dark brown sugar

2 large eggs

1 large carrot, peeled and grated (³/₄ cup)

1 large white potato, peeled and grated (³/₄ cup)

¹/₄ cup skim milk

Butter-flavor no-stick cooking spray

1. In a small microwaveable bowl, combine the raisins, apricot pieces, and citrus zest with the wine or juice. Partially cover with plastic wrap and microwave on high for 30 seconds. Or combine the ingredients in a small saucepan over low heat and simmer for about 5 minutes. Set aside to soak; when the fruit is moist, strain and discard (or drink) the excess liquid. Add the diced figs and dates.

2. In a mixing bowl, whisk together to blend the flour, baking powder, soda, salt, and spices. Set the dry ingredients aside.

3. In the large bowl of an electric mixer, cream together the almond extract, butter, and brown sugar until blended. Beat in the eggs, grated carrot and potato, and milk.

4. Add the dry ingredients and blend the mixture on low speed. Fold in the soaked and drained fruit mixture.

5. Generously coat the inside of a mold or baking dish with cooking spray, dust with flour, then tap out excess flour. Turn the batter into the mold or dish. Oil the mold lid and fasten it in place, or oil a piece of heavy-duty foil large enough to generously cover the bowl and place it oiled side down over the top. Pinch the foil edges tightly around the rim, then fasten in place with a rubber band or string.

6. Place the steamer rack or trivet in the bottom of a steamer pot, set the pudding mold in place, and add hot water to reach about halfway up the mold sides. Cover the pot, set it over high heat, and bring the water to a boil. Reduce the heat to medium and boil slowly for about 2 hours. Add more boiling water if needed to keep the water level constant.

7. Lift the mold from the steamer pot and carefully remove the mold lid or foil. The pudding should be well risen and springy to the touch, and a knife inserted in the center should come out clean. Cool on a wire rack, uncovered, about 10 minutes. Run the tip of a paring knife around the rim of the mold to loosen it, then top with a flat platter and invert. Lift off the mold. Serve the pudding warm, with sauce alongside.

Nutritional Analysis (per serving): 287 calories; 4 g protein; 3 g fat; 1.6 g satfat; 65 g carbohydrate; 314 mg sodium, 41 mg cholesterol

---

Light Touch

The classic version British figgy pudding usually includes a cup of chopped nuts, about 1/3 cup butter, 2 eggs, and some whole milk or cream. Compared to many puddings, it is relatively low in fat (approximately 29% calories from fat), with 382 calories, 13 g fat, 4 g satfat, and 51 mg cholesterol per serving. By dropping the nuts, cutting all but 2 tablespoons of butter, and substituting skim milk, I have cut almost two thirds the fat, down to only 10% calories from fat, eliminating 10 g fat per serving. The presence of all the fruit adds 553 mg potassium, 81 mg calcium, and 5 g dietary fiber per serving, making this a very healthful holiday treat.

Fruit
DESSERTS AND SORBETS

While many of the desserts in this book contain fruit, they are the primary focus of the recipes in this chapter. There is a lot of room for individual creativity here. For example, you can serve Chilled Blueberry-Raspberry Soup with May Wine or Chilled Cantaloupe Soup as an appetizer or dessert, or either can be frozen and served as a sorbet. The four "real" fruit sorbets I include here are each made in minutes simply by blending frozen fruit juice concentrate with vanilla yogurt and flavoring, then freezing (without a special machine).

Pears are presented two ways: First, poached in spiced Burgundy wine and served with sauce on crisp Meringue Shells and, second, poached in a nonalcoholic but flavorful blend of herbal teas. Tropical fruits sparkling with candied ginger form the centerpiece of Tropical Dreams, a dazzling compote served in Chocolate Tulip Shells from the Caribbean island of Saint Martin.

CHILLED BLUEBERRY-RASPBERRY SOUP WITH MAY WINE

Yield: Six 1-cup servings

Chilled fruit soup is sometimes a surprise but always a delight. My neighbor and friend Ann Swift, a talented young actress, recently served this recipe to a group of friends at a taste-testing party for some of my works in progress. I asked Ann to mention that the soup was suitable either as an appetizer or dessert. Next morning she returned with a full report and an empty bowl. None of the guests was familiar with fruit soups, but all had loved the taste. Serving time, however, was problematic: one felt it was too sweet for a first course, another liked the surprise value of serving a sweet before dinner. One suggested replacing wine with grape juice and making kids' frozen popsicles. On their scale of poor to excellent it rated "excellent" across the board!

The fruit is cooked just long enough to release its juice, then strained, thickened slightly with cornstarch, and blended with wine to enhance the flavor. You can be creative with this recipe. For the fruit, substitute 1 1/2 quarts of strawberries. The honey or sugar can be omitted or replaced with sugar-free all-fruit preserves, making this suitable for low-sugar or sugar-free diets. Use your favorite wine or experiment with different juice flavors.

Serve this for dessert after a heavy meal or make it the centerpiece of a summer brunch. For a bonus, freeze it into a sorbet. You don't need an ice cream maker, simply freeze it in a plastic container and chop up the ice crystals two or three times during the freezing process.

Advance Preparation

The fruit soup can be made up to 2 days in ahead, covered, and refrigerated. It can be frozen up to 2 weeks. Needs to chill a minimum of 3 hours.

Special Equipment

2-quart saucepan; medium-coarse strainer; food processor or blender

4 cups fresh blueberries, picked over and rinsed, or frozen whole unsweetened berries

2 cups fresh raspberries, picked over and rinsed, or frozen whole unsweetened berries

1 cup fresh orange juice

1/2 cup honey, granulated sugar, or raspberry or blueberry preserves, or to taste

3/4 teaspoon ground nutmeg

2 1/2 tablespoons cornstarch

1 1/3 cups May wine or other slightly sweet or fruity white wine, or fruit juice (such as orange, apple, white grape), divided

Garnish

1 cup fresh whole raspberries or blueberries or sliced strawberries (don't use frozen berries for the garnish)

1 cup vanilla low-fat yogurt

Fresh mint sprigs (optional)

1. In a large saucepan, combine the berries and set over medium-high heat. Cook, stirring, for 4 to 5 minutes, until the berries release some of their juices. Transfer the berries to a food processor or blender (in small batches if necessary) and purée.

2. Turn the fruit out into a strainer set over a bowl and strain to remove the seeds and berry skins. (Straining is optional and removes $1/2$ to $3/4$ cup of the total volume.)

3. You will have about 5 cups of purée after straining. Stir in the orange juice, sweetener (honey or sugar or preserves), and nutmeg. In a cup, dissolve the cornstarch in $1/3$ cup of the wine or fruit juice, then add to the fruit soup. Return the mixture to the pan, place over medium heat, and cook, stirring constantly, until it comes to a boil for a full 60 seconds to cook the cornstarch. Stir until the soup is smooth, thickened, and no longer cloudy.

4. Remove from the heat and stir in the remaining 1 cup of May wine or fruit juice. Taste and adjust sweetener if needed. Chill 3 hours, or overnight.

5. To serve, you can add a few fresh berries, a small dollop of vanilla yogurt, and a mint sprig to each bowl of chilled soup.

Nutritional Analysis (per serving): 273 calories; 4 g protein; 1 g fat; trace satfat; 57 g carbohydrate; 38 mg sodium; 0 mg cholesterol

---

Light Touch

This is almost pure light…full flavor, 1 g fat, and no cholesterol; the calories are primarily from carbohydrates. If you use extremely ripe sweet berries and omit the sweetener entirely, you can cut 87 calories and 34 g carbohydrate per serving.

CHILLED CANTALOUPE SOUP

Yield: 5¹/₂ to 6 cups; 6 to 8 servings

When cantaloupes reach their peak of ripeness, make this quick and easy soup to serve at your midsummer backyard barbecue, or pack it in a thermos and take it on a picnic. Chilled fruit soups are popular in Scandinavia, but are just beginning to catch on here. They are a great way to start, or to finish, a meal. I serve this as a first course, and even those guests who find it unusual are won over by the taste, which is richly fruity, refreshing, and not too sweet. The surprise ingredient is tea; lemon or peppermint (brewed from tea bags) goes well with the melon, but you will enjoy experimenting with other herbal blends (caffeine-free or regular) brewed from tea bags, loose leaves, or bottled, such as peach or raspberry ice tea. If extra guests drop in, here's a foolproof tip: "Water" the soup with a cup or two of chilled Champagne or white wine, or make the Cantaloupe-Champagne variation on page 203.

You can whip this up in a blender in several batches, or in a food processor. The flavor is best after mellowing several hours, or overnight (up to 2 days, in fact) in the refrigerator, a great do-ahead for entertaining.

Advance Preparation

To chill thoroughly and mellow flavor, prepare at least 3 hours in advance, or overnight. The tea can be prepared a day ahead.

Special Equipment

Blender or food processor

1 cup water, rapidly boiling

2 tea bags lemon-flavored herbal tea

1 tea bag peppermint tea or 2 generous teaspoons loose tea

1 tea bag regular black tea or 2 generous teaspoons loose tea

2 average-sized very ripe cantaloupes (each about 2¹/₄ pounds), peeled, seeded, and cut into chunks (about 6 cups cut up)

¹/₄ cup frozen unsweetened apple juice concentrate, thawed but not diluted

2 tablespoons honey

1 cup (8 ounces) low-fat yogurt (lemon, peach, plain, or vanilla), top liquid poured off

2 tablespoons fresh lemon juice, or to taste, depending on flavor of tea and melon (optional)

Garnish

Fresh mint leaves

1. In a 2-cup measure, pour the cup of boiling water over all the tea bags and brew at least 3 to 5 minutes (or prepare a day ahead). When the tea reaches maximum strength, discard the bags.

2. In a blender (in batches) or in a food processor fitted with the steel blade, purée the cut-up melon with the tea and apple juice concentrate. Process until as smooth as possible; the melon will retain a slight granular texture, which is fine. Add the honey, yogurt, and, depending upon the flavor of tea used and ripeness of the melon, lemon juice if desired; taste and adjust sweetness if needed. Blend until smooth.

3. Chill for at least 3 hours. Garnish each serving with 2 or 3 fresh mint leaves.

Nutritional Analysis (per serving): 132 calories; 3 g protein; 0.8 g fat; 0 satfat; 30 mg carbohydrate; 46 mg sodium; 0 mg cholesterol

CHILLED CANTALOUPE-CHAMPAGNE SOUP

Prepare the recipe above but omit the tea, substituting 1 cup dry Champagne or white wine (or $^1/_2$ cup wine plus $^1/_2$ cup fresh orange juice) to the cubed melon before blending.

Light Touch

With only 5% calories from fat, less than 1 g fat, and no cholesterol per serving, this guilt-free recipe delivers flavor and satisfaction. Individuals with diabetes can omit honey if they wish; there is sufficient sweetness from the apple juice concentrate and ripe fruit.

BURGUNDY POACHED PEARS IN MERINGUE SHELLS

Yield: 6 servings

Crisp ivory meringue shells cradle ruby-red, wine-soaked pears in this elegant dessert. A perfect light finish to a hearty winter feast, this is easy to prepare and can be made well in advance. For a bonus, the pears are stuffed with apples and golden raisins, and sauced with a glorious syrupy reduction of the sweetened poaching liquid sparked with pear brandy. For a different flavor, try Poached Pears in Herbal Tea (page 206).

Note: For graceful eating, serve with knife and fork; when poached correctly, the pears are tender but with some body rather than mushy; they may tend to slip on the meringue base. If you are in a hurry, omit the meringue shells and serve the pears and syrup in stemmed glasses with a crisp cookie such as Chocolate Tulip Shells (page 30) baked flat instead of formed into cups.

Meringue Shells

Six 3-inch meringue shells (page 50)

Poached Pears

3½ cups (750 ml bottle) dry red wine such as Burgundy or Bordeaux

½ cup water

1¼ cups granulated sugar

2 tablespoons fresh lemon juice

2 strips lemon zest, about ½ by 2 inches

1 stick cinnamon or ½ teaspoon ground

6 firm pears such as Bosc (about 3 pounds)

1 Greening or Granny Smith apple, peeled, cored, and quartered

¼ cup packed golden raisins

2 to 3 tablespoons pear brandy (optional)

1 tablespoon packed dark brown sugar

1. Prepare the meringue shells (preferably a day or two in advance); place in an airtight box or freeze. If you have leftover meringue batter, make extra shells in case one breaks, or shape meringue into cookies.

2. Prepare the pear-poaching liquid: In a nonreactive pan large enough to contain the 6 pears, combine the red wine, water, sugar, lemon juice, lemon zest, and cinnamon. Set over medium heat, stirring a few times until the sugar dissolves, and cook for about 5 minutes.

3. While the syrup cooks, peel the pears with a vegetable peeler, leaving the stems intact. Use a melon baller or grapefruit knife to scoop out most of the core from the bottom end of each pear. Cut a thin slice off the bottom

Advance Preparation

The meringue shells can be made several days ahead and stored in an airtight container or frozen. After poaching, the pears must cool in the syrup at least 3 hours, and preferably overnight to absorb flavor and color; after this, the syrup can be reduced. Or pears can stay refrigerated in the syrup (before it is reduced) for up to 3 days. Assemble and add the sauce immediately before serving to keep the meringues crisp.

Special Equipment

For meringues, see page 50; for pears: 3- to 3½-quart nonreactive saucepan with lid; slotted spoon; melon baller or grapefruit knife; baking parchment (optional)

Temperature and Time

Bake meringues: 275°F for 1½ hours minimum. Poach pears: 30 minutes plus 3 hours minimum to cool of each pear so it will stand upright. As each pear is finished, gently set it into the poaching liquid so it will not discolor.

4. Add the quartered apple and the raisins to the pears in the wine mixture. If possible, stand the pears upright; however, it is all right if they are upside down or on their sides—just turn them over every now and then during cooking, so they will color and cook evenly in the syrup. The wine mixture should cover the fruit; if it doesn't, set a piece of baking parchment in the pan on top of the pears and liquid to hold in the moisture. Cover the pan and cook over low heat for 20 minutes. Test the apples at the base with a knife tip—if they are tender, use a slotted spoon to remove them from the syrup and place them in a small bowl. Cover the pan again and continue cooking the pears for another 15 to 20 minutes, until the thick pear bottoms are tender when pierced with a skewer or the tip of a knife. Total cooking time depends upon the variety and ripeness of the pears, averaging 35 to 45 minutes; hard pears can take longer. When properly done, pears should be tender but not soft or mushy.

5. With a slotted spoon, remove the pears from the syrup; strain the syrup into a bowl. Remove and discard the lemon zest and cinnamon stick. Transfer the wine-soaked raisins to the bowl with the apples, cover, and refrigerate. Pour the syrup back over the pears and refrigerate, covered, for at least 3 hours or up to 3 days. Turn the pears occasionally so they color evenly in the syrup.

6. To prepare the wine sauce, remove the pears from the syrup and set them upright in a bowl, taking care not to knock off the stems. You will have about 3½ cups of syrup; place it in a nonreactive pan and boil rapidly over high heat for 30 to 35 minutes (watching carefully during the last 10 minutes), until it is thick, syrupy, and able to coat a spoon; it will have reduced to about 1¼ cups. Remove this syrup from the heat, taste and add sugar or lemon juice if needed, and stir in the brandy if desired. Set the sauce aside while you stuff the pears.

7. Chop the apples, mix with the raisins and brown sugar, and stuff some into the hollow core of each pear. Stand the stuffed pears upright in a bowl and pour some of the reduced sauce over them. Cover with plastic wrap and refrigerate until about 1 hour before serving time. Note: The sauce thickens as it chills; if you think it is too stiff, stir it over a pan of hot water for about 30 seconds, until it softens.

8. Just before serving, stand each stuffed pear in a meringue shell and glaze with a generous spoonful of reduced wine syrup. Pass any additional syrup in a pitcher.

Nutritional Analysis (per serving with meringue shell but no brandy): 409 calories; 3 g protein; 0.7 g fat; 0 g satfat; 99 g carbohydrate; 89 mg sodium; 0 mg cholesterol

Nutritional Analysis (per serving without meringue shell or brandy): 309 calories; 1 g protein; 0.7 g fat; 0 g satfat; 75 g carbohydrate; 15 mg sodium; 0 mg cholesterol

continued

POACHED PEARS IN HERBAL TEA

I like to use cinnamon-spice tea, but you may wish to experiment with other flavor combinations. Prepare the recipe above, but replace the wine with water. To make the poaching liquid in step 2, use 4 cups water. Bring the water, lemon juice, lemon zest, cinnamon, and 3/4 cup sugar to a full boil. Add 6 tea bags (4 apple-cinnamon spice and 2 Darjeeling or Earl Grey or black tea) and remove the pan from the heat. Allow the tea to steep for about 5 minutes. Stir to be sure the sugar is dissolved.

In step 6, you will have about 3 cups syrup after you remove the pears. Boil it about 25 minutes, to a scant 1 cup, when it will be quite syrupy but will not coat a spoon. Remove from the heat and stir in about 3 teaspoons fresh lemon juice, or to taste. Add pear brandy if you wish; however, it tends to mask the tea flavor.

Light Touch

Although it contains a lot of calories from the meringue and wine, this classic dessert is cholesterol and fat free (1% calories from fat). The use of tea in the variation does not change the fat or cholesterol content.

TROPICAL DREAMS

A fitting name for a dessert created in one of the most paradisiacal locations on the globe: Orient Bay on the French side of the Caribbean island of Saint Martin. Nestled in a palmetto grove hugging a ribbon of sand beside the deep turquoise bay, the elegant five-star Esmeralda Resort is known for its exceptional restaurant, l'Astrolabe, presided over by a fast-rising star from the south of France, Chef Michel Royer. Royer's creativity at l'Astrolabe is evident in his tropical desserts such as bananas flamed with rum on a crêpe napped with crème anglaise decorated with chocolate and apricots. The dessert of my tropical dreams, loosely adapted from memory, is inspired by Royer's tropical fruit compote featuring fresh pineapple segments caramelized in a light syrup, topped with candied ginger, and served on a sugar wafer. My crisp Chocolate Tulip Shells resemble his gaufrette wafers in taste and texture. The touch of grated fresh gingerroot added to the fruit at the last minute wakes up your senses and gives an unforgettable sparkle to the dish.

Note: The gingerroot can be minced fine instead of grated, or omitted altogether. Other tropical fruits such as orange or papaya can be substituted for those listed.

6 to 8 (allow extra for breakage) Chocolate Tulip Shells (page 30) or Phyllo Cups (page 49)

Fruit

1 kiwi, peeled, quartered, and sliced
2 cups fresh pineapple chunks
1 ripe mango, peeled, pitted, and thinly sliced
1/3 cup packed light brown sugar
1/4 cup fresh orange juice
1 tablespoon fresh lime or lemon juice
2 tablespoons dark rum or peach schnapps (optional)
2 tablespoons finely chopped candied ginger

Topping

1/2 teaspoon peeled and grated fresh gingerroot, or to taste
1 tablespoon confectioners' sugar

1. Prepare the shells or cups and set them aside until ready to serve. In a large mixing bowl, combine all the fruit ingredients. Toss the fruit, cover, and refrigerate, at least 2 hours, until shortly before serving.

2. To serve, place 1 shell or cup on each serving dish. With a slotted spoon, scoop a scant 1/2 cup of the fruit mixture (with a minimum of liquid) into each cup. Sprinkle a pinch of fresh gingerroot over the fruit.

continued

Advance Preparation

The tulip shells can be prepared early on the day they are to be served. Be sure they are crisp before filling with fruit. The fruit must be prepared ahead, covered, and chilled for at least 2 hours.

Special Equipment

Muffin tins or juice glasses for forming tulip cookies

3. Just before serving, sift a very fine dusting of confectioners' sugar over each pastry cup.

Nutritional Analysis (per serving): 216 calories; 2 g protein; 5.5 g fat; 1.7 g satfat; 40 g carbohydrate; 45 mg sodium; 7 mg cholesterol

---

Light Touch

This recipe contains 22% calories from fat, all of it in the pastry shells. If you want fat-free perfection, forget the pastry and serve the fruit in a glass dish.

MOTHER'S DAY PEACH MELBA

Yield: 4 servings

Why not make Mom the star of the show and give her a special dessert? This one is simple enough for a child to make, especially if a canned peach half is used with store-bought cake. The only trick is to cut out the cake with a heart-shaped cookie cutter; the raspberry sauce can, in a pinch, be a handful of raspberries mashed with a little sugar. If Dad wants to get into the act, he can grill the peach half over coals to give extra flavor. Or you can bake the peaches in the oven. Adjust the quantities below to fit your own family: 1 cake heart and 1 peach half plus 2 to 3 tablespoons of frozen yogurt and about 3 tablespoons of sauce per serving. Keep it simple, and keep it a surprise.

The original Peach Melba (neither as delicious nor as dramatic) was created at the turn of the century by the great French chef Escoffier in honor of Australian opera singer Dame Nellie Melba. The peach halves were poached in syrup, covered with vanilla ice cream and raspberry sauce Melba, sprinkled with almonds, and topped with whipped cream.

Advance Preparation

Assemble dessert just before serving.

Special Equipment

Oven-proof dish for baking peaches or grill to broil over coals

Temperature and Time

Bake sponge roll: 350°F for 11 to 13 minutes. Bake peaches: 350°F for 25 minutes; or grill: 15 minutes

Sauce

¹/₂ **recipe Raspberry Sauce (page 258)**

Cake

¹/₂ **recipe Almond Sponge Roll (page 126), or any unfrosted vanilla or orange sponge or pound cake**

Peaches

2 medium-sized peaches, or 4 canned peach halves, well drained

2 tablespoons fresh lemon juice (optional)

1 tablespoon packed dark brown sugar

¹/₂ **teaspoon ground cinnamon**

¹/₂ **teaspoon butter or margarine**

Filling and Garnish

¹/₂ pint vanilla low-fat or nonfat frozen yogurt

Fresh mint sprigs

1. Prepare the sauce and refrigerate until ready to serve. Prepare the cake and let it cool completely. A homemade sponge roll will be about ³/₄ to 1 inch thick. If using a store-bought cake, use a serrated knife to slice it; you will need 4 slices about 4 × 4 × ³/₄ inch. Use a large heart-shaped cookie cutter (or a paring knife and a template made of cardboard) to cut out cake hearts about 4 inches across and 4 inches high. Make one heart per serving. Double-wrap leftover cake and freeze it. Cover the hearts with plastic wrap and set aside.

2. Fresh peaches must be peeled. To peel: Put them into a large pot of boiling water for about 2 minutes, then transfer them with a slotted spoon to a bowl of cold water. Drain when cool. The skins will slip off. Cut each peach in half and discard the pits. If not using them immediately, brush the peach halves with lemon juice to prevent discoloration. Canned peach halves must be well drained and blotted with a paper towel. Set on a plate, sprinkle with a few drops of lemon juice, cover with plastic wrap, and refrigerate until ready to use.

3. To bake the peaches: Place the halves, cut side up, in an ovenproof baking dish and fill the cavities with a little of the brown sugar, cinnamon, and a tiny pinch of the butter. Bake for 25 minutes.

  To grill the peaches: Place peach halves, cut side up, on a 20 × 20-inch sheet of heavy-duty aluminum foil. Sprinkle some brown sugar, cinnamon, and butter into the cavity of each peach. Fold the foil in half and pinch the fold closed, enveloping the peaches. Place the envelope over medium-hot coals for about 15 minutes, until the peaches are heated through.

4. To serve, set one heart-shaped cake on each plate, top with a peach half, sugar-filled center up, and add a small scoop of frozen yogurt. Top with a drizzle of raspberry sauce. Garnish with a mint sprig and a handmade Mother's Day card.

Nutritional Analysis (per serving): 297 calories; 6 g protein; 5 g fat; 1.6 g satfat; 57 g carbohydrate; 104 mg sodium; 60 mg cholesterol

Light Touch

Part of the gift to Mother is the fact that this recipe contains only 15% calories from fat, a 50% reduction from the classic version.

JACK-O'-LANTERN CUPS

Yield: 10 to 12 servings

Chocolate Tulip Shell cookies hold scoops of pumpkin "ice cream" topped with jack-o'-lantern faces drawn with chocolate syrup or quickly fashioned with chocolate chips. Prepare and freeze them in advance for a Halloween party. Be sure to let the kids help. Tulip Shells are fun to make but fragile; a sturdier alternative is to use Chocolate Crumb Crust pressed into tartlet molds.

1 recipe Chocolate Tulip Shells (page 30) or Chocolate Crumb Crust (page 55) pressed into tartlet molds

Double recipe (1 quart) Pumpkin Frozen Yogurt (page 215)

1 recipe Steve's Spa Chocolate Sauce (page 266) or Chocolate Sauce (page 265) or mini-chocolate chips

1. Prepare the tulip shells or chocolate crumb tartlet molds. If making tartlets, bake as directed then unmold before filling. Be sure shells or tartlets are completely cold before proceeding.

2. Shortly before serving, scoop about $1/3$ cup of the yogurt into each cup and round the top.

3. Put about $1/2$ cup of the chocolate sauce into a plastic bag, seal, and cut a very tiny hole ($1/8$ inch maximum size) in one corner. Squeeze the chocolate lines of a jack-o'-lantern face over the filling in each cup. Alternatively, arrange chocolate chips on the filling to make the face.

Nutritional Analysis (per serving tulip filled with frozen yogurt topped with Steve's Spa Chocolate Sauce): 278 calories; 5 g protein; 8 g fat; 3 g satfat; 50 g carbohydrate; 157 mg sodium; 11 mg cholesterol

Advance Preparation

Yogurt can be prepared up to 1 week ahead and frozen. Chocolate crumb crust tartlet shells can be prepared 1 or 2 days ahead and refrigerated. Tulips should be made the day they are to be served (try not to make them in humid weather, as they soften). If the weather disappoints you, forget the tulips and put a scoop of the yogurt on top of a homemade or store-bought cookie. You can prepare and decorate the tulip shells in advance, set them on a cookie sheet, and freeze until about 10 minutes before serving time. Note: If not frozen in advance, fill and decorate the tulip shells just before serving; they may soften if left standing too long.

Special Equipment

Pint-sized self-sealing plastic bag; scissors

Light Touch

With just 24% calories from fat, these are not too scary for Halloween.

PIÑA COLADA SORBET

Yield: About 1 1/3 cups; four 1/3-cup servings

Pineapple and coconut flavors blend in this mellow tropical dessert. Piña colada mix is a frozen concentrate sold with juices in the supermarket. Coconut and pineapple extracts help to strengthen the flavor; they are available in many supermarkets or by mail order from the King Arthur catalogue and other suppliers (see pages 372–373). This is a great recipe for entertaining. Prepare it in advance without any special ice cream making equipment; just pour the mixture into a carton and pop it in the freezer. Double or triple the recipe to serve a crowd but adjust extracts and sugar carefully, to taste. Serve the sorbet in a glass by itself or use to fill Chocolate Tulip Shells (page 30) or Phyllo Cups (page 49).

Advance Preparation

Make the sorbet at least 6 hours or up to 1 day ahead.

Special Equipment

Freezer container or plastic carton with lid

1 cup vanilla low-fat yogurt, top liquid poured off

1 tablespoon light corn syrup

1/3 cup frozen piña colada mix concentrate, thawed but not diluted

1/4 teaspoon vanilla extract

1/4 teaspoon coconut extract

1/4 teaspoon pineapple extract

1 to 2 tablespoons granulated sugar, to taste (optional)

1. In a mixing bowl with a spoon or whisk, combine the yogurt, corn syrup, piña colada concentrate, and flavorings. Blend until completely smooth. Taste and stir in the sugar if needed.

2. Turn out into a freezer container, cover, and freeze. After about 1 1/2 to 2 hours, stir well with a fork to break up large ice crystals; cover and return to the freezer for another 4 to 4 1/2 hours. If frozen very hard, allow to stand at room temperature for about 20 minutes before serving.

Nutritional Analysis (per serving with 2 tablespoons sugar): 90 calories; 3 g protein; 2.5 g fat; 1.7 g satfat; 30 g carbohydrate; 55 mg sodium; 0 mg cholesterol

Light Touch

This delicious cholesterol-free sorbet gets about 25% of its calories from fat; it has about 50 fewer calories per serving than a commercial sherbet.

MARGARITA SORBET

Yield: About 1 1/2 cups; four generous 1/3-cup servings

The refreshing sweet-sour flavor makes this quick and easy dessert a perfect ending to a spicy Mexican meal. If you are feeling adventurous, pour a splash of tequila over the top just before serving or put a scoop on top of a Tortilla Tart (page 107) and sprinkle with a few grains of cayenne pepper for a touch of the Yucatan. This recipe is great for entertaining. Prepare it in advance without any special ice cream making equipment; just pour the mixture into a carton and pop it in the freezer. Double or triple the recipe to serve a crowd. Frozen margarita mix is sold with frozen juices in the supermarket.

1 cup vanilla low-fat yogurt, top liquid poured off

1/2 cup frozen margarita mix concentrate, thawed but not diluted

1 tablespoon light corn syrup

1. In a mixing bowl with a spoon or whisk, combine all the ingredients and blend until completely smooth.

2. Turn out into a freezer container, cover, and freeze. After 1 1/2 to 2 hours, stir well with a fork to break up large ice crystals; cover and return to the freezer for another 4 to 4 1/2 hours. If frozen very hard, allow to stand at room temperature for about 20 minutes before serving.

Nutritional Analysis (per serving): 65 calories; 3 g protein; 0.5 g fat; 0 g satfat; 25 g carbohydrate; 46 mg sodium; 0 mg cholesterol

> ### Advance Preparation
>
> Make the sorbet at least 6 hours or up to 1 day ahead.
>
> ### Special Equipment
>
> Freezer container or plastic carton with lid

Light Touch

High taste but only 4% calories from fat. Enjoy your dessert even more knowing it contains neither saturated fat nor cholesterol and has only about half the calories of a commercial sherbet.

STRAWBERRY DAIQUIRI SORBET

Yield: About 1 1/2 cups; four generous 1/3-cup servings

Serve this for dessert on a balmy tropical night, or feature it as first course for a Sunday brunch, topped with a splash of rum. The color is bright pink, with a strong clean strawberry flavor enhanced by a touch of lemon juice. Serve the sorbet in a glass by itself or use it to fill Chocolate Tulip Shells (page 30) or Phyllo Cups (page 49). Garnish with fresh strawberry slices. This recipe is great for entertaining. Make it in advance without any special ice cream making equipment; just pour the mixture into a carton and pop it in the freezer. Double or triple the recipe to serve a crowd, but adjust the lemon juice to taste if making a large quantity.

Advance Preparation

Make the sorbet at least 6 hours or up to 1 day ahead.

Special Equipment

Freezer container or plastic carton with lid

1 cup vanilla low-fat yogurt, top liquid poured off

1/2 cup frozen strawberry daiquiri mix concentrate, thawed but not diluted

1 tablespoon light corn syrup

1/2 teaspoon fresh lemon juice (omit if yogurt is very tangy)

1. In a mixing bowl using a spoon or whisk, combine all the ingredients and blend until completely smooth. Taste and adjust flavoring if needed.

2. Turn out into a freezer container, cover, and freeze. After about 1 1/2 to 2 hours, stir well with a fork to break up large ice crystals; cover and return to the freezer for another 4 to 4 1/2 hours. If frozen very hard, allow to stand at room temperature for about 20 minutes before serving.

Nutritional Analysis (per serving): 65 calories; 3 g protein; 0.5 g fat; 0 g satfat; 30 g carbohydrate; 46 mg sodium; 0 mg cholesterol

Light Touch

Here's something you can enjoy with nary a gram of guilt. At only 3% calories from fat, this dessert has no saturated fat, no cholesterol, and just a 1/2 g fat per serving. A classic orange sherbet weighs in at about twice the calories and fat per serving.

SPICED CRANBERRY SORBET

Yield: About 1 1/3 cups; four 1/3-cup servings

I serve this as a between-courses palate refresher or as a side dish at Thanksgiving. The dark rose color is especially appealing and the clean spiced taste is welcome after rich foods. It is a great recipe for entertaining. Prepare it in advance without any special ice cream making equipment; just pour the mixture into a carton and pop it in the freezer. Double or triple the recipe to serve a crowd. Frozen cranberry juice concentrate is sold with other frozen juices in the supermarket.

1/3 cup plain low-fat yogurt, top liquid poured off

8 ounces frozen unsweetened cranberry juice concentrate, thawed but not diluted

1 tablespoon light corn syrup

1/8 teaspoon each ground nutmeg, cinnamon, and ginger

1. In a mixing bowl with a spoon or whisk, combine all the ingredients and blend until completely smooth. Taste and adjust flavoring if needed.

2. Turn out into a freezer container, cover, and freeze. After 1 1/2 to 2 hours, stir well with a fork to break up large ice crystals; cover and return to the freezer for another 4 to 4 1/2 hours. If frozen very hard, allow to stand at room temperature for about 20 minutes before serving.

Nutritional Analysis (per serving): 32 calories; 1 g protein; 0.1 g fat; 0 g satfat; 42 g carbohydrate; 18 mg sodium; 0 mg cholesterol

Advance Preparation

Make the sorbet at least 6 hours or up to 1 day ahead.

Special Equipment

Freezer container or plastic carton with lid

Light Touch

With just 1% calories from fat, this cholesterol-free and saturated-fat-free recipe has about one quarter the number of calories of a commercial fruit sherbet.

PUMPKIN FROZEN YOGURT

Yield: 1 pint; four ¹/₂-cup servings

Close your eyes and focus on the taste of a lightly spiced pumpkin pie with rich cream on top; now imagine that whipped and frozen. Now make this recipe.

It couldn't be easier—just blend canned pumpkin with vanilla frozen yogurt and add a few spices. A delectable confection made well in advance, ready to fill Chocolate Tulip Shells (page 30) for Halloween (kids love these with jack-o'-lantern faces added with chocolate sauce). For Thanksgiving, make sophisticated individual servings in Phyllo Cups (page 49) topped by a few toasted pecans or walnuts. Or use it as a filling for a Pumpkin Cream Bombe (page 161).

Note: If you increase the volume of the recipe, adjust the spices to taste. Leftover canned pumpkin can be placed in an airtight container and frozen for later use.

For a party Pumpkin Pizza, bake one recipe Fudge or Blond Brownies in a 9- or 10-inch round pan, then turn it out onto a pizza tin or cardboard round. Spread with Pumpkin Frozen Yogurt, drizzle on Chocolate Sauce (page 265) and Extra-Thick Caramel Sauce (page 264), and sprinkle on a few chopped pecans, walnuts, or toasted pumpkin seeds. Keep frozen; serve cut into wedges.

1 pint best-quality frozen vanilla yogurt, softened
¹/₂ cup canned plain pumpkin purée
2 teaspoons granulated sugar
¹/₄ teaspoon each ground cinnamon, nutmeg, and ginger
¹/₈ teaspoon ground cloves
Pinch of salt

1. In a large mixing bowl, combine the softened frozen yogurt with all the remaining ingredients and beat until thoroughly mixed.

2. Repack in the yogurt container (or another freezer container with a lid) and place in the freezer until solid, several hours or overnight.

Nutritional Analysis (per serving): 149 calories; 4 g protein; 2.5 g fat; 1.5 g satfat; 28 g carbohydrate; 94 mg sodium; 10 mg cholesterol

---

Advance Preparation

Mixture can be prepared up to 2 weeks ahead. Must be frozen for served hours minimum before serving.

Special Equipment

Freezer container with lid

Light Touch

This creamy dessert has a very rich taste and mouth-feel although it has only 15% calories from fat and very little fat or cholesterol.

Quick-Rising
SWEET YEAST BREADS

These delectable breads rise and shine in half the time of classic yeast breads. The secret is in the relatively new quick-rise active dry yeast sold in premeasured envelopes from Red Star as "Quick-Rise" and from Fleischmann's as "RapidRise," to name a few brands available in supermarkets. There is one important difference between "quick" and "classic" types of yeast. In my experience, the quickly rising type gives wonderful results with slightly sweet breads, especially those with fruit fillings. For old-fashioned peasant breads with yeasty dough perfumed with robust earthy fragrance, the long slow fermentation required with classic yeast is essential.

Quick-rising yeast can be used in your old recipes simply by cutting rising times in half; however, best results come from redesigned procedures that capitalize on this yeast's unique properties. In this technique, the dry quick yeast is first combined with a portion of the flour, sugar, and salt. Then a hot liquid is blended into the dry ingredients, and the mixture is beaten for a few minutes to start the development of the gluten in the flour before additional flour is added. The liquid used is hot: I specify 115° to 120°F in these recipes for a margin of safety. In actual fact, you are safe if the temperature rises up to (but no higher than) 130°F, so aiming for 115°F gives a built-in safety factor. This is much hotter than the 105° to 115°F for traditional yeast recipes.

The first rising time will be about half that of a traditional yeast bread. The dough will not quite double in bulk; this is normal with quick yeast. However, it should feel soft and slightly spongy to the touch. The second rise is also relatively short, about 20 minutes, and will result in slightly less than double the dough bulk. In the heat of the oven (temperature 350° to 375°F) the baking rise will be exceptional.

Breads are completely baked when they have turned a rich golden brown in color and sound hollow when tapped on the bottom with your knuckle. Turn them out of the pan at once and cool them on a wire rack. Note: If the bottom surface of a bread overbrowns, simply let it cool completely, then rub the blackened surface against the small holes of a box grater held over the sink and shake off crumbs.

Holiday yeast breads are traditionally rich, although the proportion of eggs, butter, and sugar has been reduced in the following recipes. They range from Sticky Honey Buns to a fruit-filled orange dough shaped into Christmas trees, and make multiple loaves for gift-giving; all can be double-wrapped airtight and stored in the freezer for 3 to 4 weeks. Be aware that reduced-fat breads do not survive freezer storage as long as higher-fat classic recipes.

To rewarm yeast buns, place on a baking sheet in a 350°F oven for about 10 minutes.

DRIED CHERRY–RAISIN BREAD

Low-fat ricotta cheese adds richness while tenderizing this wholesome lemon-scented dough rolled around a filling of apricot preserves, dried cherries, and golden raisins. The real flavor secret is in softening the fruit by soaking it in sweet red vermouth. Baker's bonus: Drink the drained soaking vermouth while the bread bakes! Read about quick-rising yeast on pages 324–325.

Dough

- $1/2$ cup dried cherries (1.2 ounces; other dried fruit can be substituted)
- $1/2$ cup golden raisins
- $1/3$ cup sweet vermouth, brandy, or wine
- $2^1/2$ to 3 cups all-purpose or bread flour
- $1/3$ cup granulated sugar
- 2 packages quick-rising active dry yeast
- 1 teaspoon salt
- $1^1/2$ cups 1% milk
- 2 tablespoons canola oil
- 2 tablespoons pure maple syrup or honey
- $1/2$ cup part-skim or nonfat ricotta, fine curd or pressed through a strainer
- 2 teaspoons lemon extract
- 2 teaspoons packed grated lemon zest
- 1 teaspoon ground nutmeg
- $3/4$ cup whole wheat flour
- Butter-flavor no-stick cooking spray

Filling

- $1/2$ cup apricot preserves

Glaze

- 1 large egg
- 2 teaspoons water

Advance Preparation

Dried fruits must be soaked in liquid about 30 minutes before adding to filling. Breads can be double-wrapped airtight and frozen up to 1 month.

Special Equipment

Electric mixer fitted with paddle attachment, if available, or dough hook; instant-read thermometer; pastry brush; 2 cookie sheets or 5 mini-loaf pans ($3 \times 5^1/2$ inches; 2-cup capacity)

Temperature and Time

First rise: 20 to 30 minutes. Second rise: 20 minutes. Bake: 375°F for 25 to 30 minutes

1. In a small bowl, combine the dried cherries, raisins, and sweet vermouth or brandy. Let stand at room temperature for about 30 minutes, or place in a microwaveable bowl and microwave on high power for 30 seconds.

2. In a large mixing bowl, whisk together 2 cups of the flour, the sugar, yeast, and salt. Set aside.

continued

3. In a medium-sized saucepan, combine the milk, oil, and syrup or honey. Stir gently over medium heat until the mixture reaches 115° to 120°F on an instant-read thermometer (it will feel hot to the touch).

4. Add the warm liquid to the dry ingredients and stir with a sturdy spoon until smooth. Add the ricotta, lemon extract, lemon zest, and nutmeg. Beat with a wooden spoon or electric mixer (fitted with a paddle attachment, if available) on medium speed until blended. Stir or slowly beat in the whole wheat flour, then gradually add more white flour until the dough becomes too stiff to stir by hand, or until it comes away from the sides of the mixer bowl.

5. Turn the dough out onto a lightly floured board and knead for about 10 minutes, until the dough feels smooth and elastic, gradually incorporating a little more white flour as necessary, just to prevent sticking (excess flour will make bread tough). (Alternatively, the dough can be kneaded with an electric mixer fitted with a dough hook; beat at low speed for about 5 minutes.)

6. Form the dough into a ball and place in a lightly oiled large bowl, turning the ball once to coat the top. Cover with plastic wrap or wax paper and set in a warm location to rise until spongy, 20 to 30 minutes. Reserve the oiled plastic wrap or paper.

7. Drain the soaking fruit through a strainer. Set the fruit aside (reserve the liquid for another use). Lightly coat baking pan(s) with cooking spray and set aside.

8. Punch down the dough and turn it out onto a lightly floured surface; knead 4 or 5 times. Divide the dough into 6 equal portions; reserve 1 for decorating tops of logs. Press or pat each of the 5 remaining portions into a 6-inch square. Spread with a generous tablespoon of the apricot preserves, leaving about 1/2 inch of clean border around dough. Sprinkle a generous tablespoon of drained fruit on top, then tightly roll up each piece into a log and place seam side down on the prepared cookie sheet, spacing them 3-inches apart, or in oiled mini-loaf pans.

9. In a small bowl, beat the egg with the water for a glaze. Brush a little glaze over the top of each loaf. (Don't let it drip or it will stick to the pan.) To decorate the top, pull bits of dough off the reserved dough portion. Roll pencil-thin lengths about 7 inches long, then form them into two S shapes atop each loaf, end to end (*A*). Or form vines and leaves (*B*) if you wish. After adding decorations to each loaf, brush again with egg glaze. Form a roll from any leftover dough and add to baking sheet.

A   *B*

10. Cover the decorated loaves with reserved oiled paper and set them to rise in a warm location until nearly doubled in bulk, about 20 minutes. Meanwhile, preheat the oven to 375°F.

11. Uncover the loaves and brush them once more with egg glaze. Bake for 25 to 30 minutes, until golden brown. Remove the loaves from the pans and cool on wire racks.

Nutritional Analysis (per slice): 94 calories; 2 g protein; 1.2 g fat; 0.2 g satfat; 18 g carbohydrate; 64 mg sodium; 6 mg cholesterol

---

Light Touch

My original form of this recipe contains 27% calories from fat. I have cut this by 56% using low-fat milk, 2 tablespoons oil instead of butter, and low- or nonfat ricotta, to reach 12%, a saving of two thirds the fat and cholesterol and 19 calories per slice.

STICKY HONEY BUNS

In less than two hours from start to finish, you can serve these cinnamon-raisin rolls dripping with honey-nut-caramel glaze. Gooey and comforting, they make breakfast or brunch a festive occasion. Sticky buns are considered by some culinary historians to be a Pennsylvania specialty, derived from German schnecken, *or cinnamon buns. This sticky bun version has been popular with natives of Philadelphia and neighboring Germantown since the 1600s; in the nineteenth century, Philadelphia sticky buns were a well-known local specialty. Read about quick-rising yeast on pages 324–325.*

Dough

3¹⁄₂ to 4 cups all-purpose or bread flour

1 package quick-rising active dry yeast

1 teaspoon salt

³⁄₄ cup water

¹⁄₂ cup 1% milk

2 tablespoons honey

2 tablespoons plus ¹⁄₂ teaspoon canola oil, divided

1 large egg white

Filling

¹⁄₄ cup granulated sugar

2 teaspoons ground cinnamon

¹⁄₂ cup golden or seedless raisins

Topping

Butter-flavor no-stick cooking spray

¹⁄₂ cup packed dark brown sugar

2 teaspoons butter

3 tablespoons honey

¹⁄₄ cup chopped walnuts or blanched almonds

Advance Preparation

These are best when made no more than a day ahead and served warm.

Special Equipment

13 × 9-inch baking pan; electric mixer fitted with paddle attachment, if available, and/or dough hook; instant-read thermometer (optional); wax paper; pastry brush

Temperature and Time

First rise: 20 to 30 minutes. Second rise: 20 minutes. Bake: 375°F for 25 to 30 minutes

1. Make the dough: In a large mixing bowl, combine 2 cups of the flour, the yeast, and salt; set aside.

2. In a small saucepan, combine the water, milk, honey, and 2 tablespoons of the oil. Set over low heat until warm to the touch, 115° to 120°F on an instant-read thermometer. Add the warm liquid to the flour mixture and stir with a sturdy spoon or beat in an electric mixer (with the paddle attachment, if available) on medium speed until blended. Beat in the egg white, then continue to beat about 3 minutes to start the gluten development. Once the mixture is very smooth, gradually add another 1¹⁄₂ cups of the flour, beating until a soft dough is formed. Change to the dough hook and continue to beat at low speed for 5 minutes. Or, if you prefer to knead by hand, turn the dough out onto a lightly floured work surface and knead for about 10 minutes, gradually incorporating more flour as necessary to prevent sticking (excess flour will make the buns tough).

3. When the dough feels smooth and elastic, form it into a ball and place in a lightly oiled bowl. Turn the ball of dough to oil the top, cover the bowl with wax paper, and set it in a warm location to rise until spongy, 20 to 30 minutes.

4. In a small bowl, combine the sugar and cinnamon for the filling and set aside.

5. Prepare the topping in a 13 × 9-inch baking pan: Spray the pan with cooking spray, then sprinkle on an even coating of brown sugar. Add small pinches of butter, drizzle on the honey, and scatter the nuts on top.

6. Punch down the dough and turn it out onto a lightly floured surface. Pat or roll (don't stretch) the dough into a rectangle about 12 × 15 inches. Brush the dough with the remaining ¹/₂ teaspoon of oil, then evenly sprinkle on the cinnamon-sugar filling and top with the raisins. Beginning at one short end, roll the dough up tightly into a log. Pinch the long edge to seal. With a sharp knife, cut crosswise into 12 even slices. Set the slices flat on the topping mixture in the baking pan, in rows of three. Cover with oiled wax paper or plastic wrap and put in a warm place to rise until nearly doubled, about 20 minutes.

7. Position a rack in the center of the oven and preheat the oven to 375°F. Bake the rolls for 25 to 30 minutes, until golden brown. Cool in the pan about 30 seconds, then top with a slightly larger flat pan or tray. Holding both pans together, invert. Allow the upper pan to stay in place for a minute or two while the topping drips down, then carefully lift it off. Cool a few minutes before serving.

Nutritional Analysis (per bun): 301 calories; 6 g protein; 5 g fat; 0.8 g satfat; 59 g carbohydrate; 193 mg sodium; 2 mg cholesterol

---

Light Touch

I have reduced the original 36% calories from fat to 15%, eliminating 240 calories and 15 g fat per bun by substituting a small amount of canola oil for a large amount of butter and using 1 egg white instead of 3 eggs in the dough. The new coating syrup is still rich but contains much less butter and just ¹/₄ cup nuts. All the sweeteners push calories up, but the fat content is low.

SANTA LUCIA SAFFRON BUNS AND BRAID

In Sweden, the Christmas season begins with the celebration of Santa Lucia Day, the Festival of Light, on December 13. Traditionally, on this morning the eldest daughter of the family dresses up as Lucia, wearing a white gown with a red sash and with an evergreen wreath topped by candles on her head. Her younger sisters wear the same costume, without the crown. Together they sing the melody "Santa Lucia" as they parade through the house carrying a tray of Lucia sweet yellow saffron buns to serve to the family.

The sunny color and unique fragrance of this bread come from the saffron, dried stigmas of a special crocus flower (Crocus sativus); the stigmas are removed from approximately seventy-five thousand hand-picked blossoms to produce one pound of saffron. Although this is one of the world's most expensive spices, you fortunately need only a couple of pinches in this recipe. Read about quick-rising yeast on pages 324–325.

Dough

1 cup seedless raisins, plus extra for decoration

³/4 cup warm water (optional)

4 to 4¹/2 cups all-purpose or bread flour

¹/2 cup granulated sugar

2 packages quick-rising active dry yeast

1 teaspoon salt

1¹/4 cups 1% milk

2 tablespoons canola oil

2 tablespoons unsalted butter

¹/2 teaspoon (2 generous pinches) saffron threads

1 large egg plus 1 large yolk

Butter-flavor no-stick cooking spray

Glaze

1 large egg

2 teaspoons water

Topping

¹/4 cup coarse-grain or pearl sugar

¹/3 cup blanched almonds, finely chopped

1. If the raisins are moist, set them aside. If they are very dry, combine the raisins with the water and set aside in a bowl to soak for about 30 minutes (or microwave on high for 45 seconds); drain the liquid and reserve the raisins. In a large mixing bowl, whisk together 2 cups of the flour, the sugar, yeast, and salt. Set aside.

Advance Preparation

Soak raisins in liquid about 30 minutes before adding to recipe. The baked bread can be double-wrapped airtight and frozen up to 1 month.

Special Equipment

Electric mixer fitted with paddle attachment, if available, or dough hook; pastry brush; cookie sheets; wax paper; kitchen shears (optional)

Temperature and Time

First rise: 40 minutes. Second rise: 20 minutes. Bake: 350°F for 25 minutes for rolls, up to 35 minutes for large rings

2. In a medium-sized saucepan, combine the milk, oil, butter, and saffron. Set over medium heat and warm to 115° to 120°F on an instant-read thermometer (it will feel hot to the touch).

3. Add the warmed liquid to the flour mixture and stir once or twice. Then add the whole egg and yolk and beat with a sturdy spoon or an electric mixer (using the paddle attachment, if available) on medium speed, until blended. Stir or slowly beat in more flour, ½ cup at a time, until the dough becomes too stiff to stir. Fit the mixer with the dough hook and beat at low speed for 5 minutes more. Or turn the dough out onto a lightly floured board and knead about 10 minutes, until the dough feels smooth and elastic, gradually incorporating a little more flour as necessary just to prevent sticking (excess flour will make bread tough).

4. Flatten the dough into a rectangle and sprinkle evenly with the well-drained raisins. Fold over and knead 4 or 5 times to distribute the raisins.

5. Form the dough into a ball and place it in a lightly oiled large bowl, turning the ball once to coat the top. Cover with plastic wrap or wax paper and set in a warm location to rise until spongy, 40 minutes or slightly longer.

6. Meanwhile, in a small bowl, beat together the egg and water to make a glaze.

7. Lightly coat the baking sheets with cooking spray; set them aside. Punch down the dough and turn it out onto a lightly floured board.

8. To shape Lucia Buns (see diagrams), divide the dough into twelve equal portions.

To make a sun face, roll one portion into a ball (reserving a small piece for decoration), then flatten slightly into a domed shape about 3 inches across. With kitchen shears or a sharp knife, snip six or seven ½-inch-deep "rays" evenly spaced around the edges. Place each sun on the prepared baking sheet, spacing them 3 inches apart. Arrange the rays evenly and brush the top of the face and rays with egg glaze. Shape bits of the reserved dough to form eyes, nose, mouth, cheek, and chin spots and apply to the face. Glaze again.

Santa Lucia sun face

continued

To form a Lucia crown, shape one portion of dough into a rectangle about 4 inches long and 2 inches wide; then flatten the piece slightly and use kitchen shears or a sharp knife to snip four or five ½-inch long cuts in the top long edge. Curve the base downward so the top segments open and spread like the top of a crown.

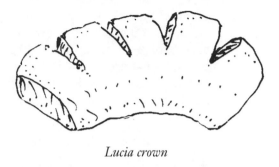

Lucia crown

To make S shapes, roll one portion of dough into a 9 × 1-inch rope and coil the ends in opposite directions, forming an S. Brush with egg glaze and push a raisin down into the center of each coil.

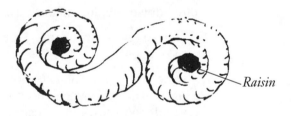

Raisin

To make two large braided rings, divide the entire dough mass in half; each will make one ring. To make a ring, divide one portion of the dough into thirds and roll each third into a rope about 1 × 20 inches. Pinch together the ends of the three ropes, then braid them. Pinch the ends of the braid together to fasten, then pull the ends around and pinch them together to form a circle. Set on a prepared baking sheet. Put your fingers inside the circle and push out gently to widen it into an even ring about 8 inches across (measuring to the outside edge). Repeat with the remaining dough; set on a separate baking sheet.

Lucia braided ring

9. Cover the shaped pieces with oiled wax paper or plastic wrap and set in a warm location to rise about 20 minutes, until nearly doubled in bulk. Position 2 racks to divide the oven in thirds and preheat the oven to 350°F.

10. When risen, brush the shapes (again if already done) with egg glaze and (except for the sun face) sprinkle with the coarse or pearl sugar and chopped almonds. Bake 20 to 35 minutes (the final baking time will depend on the size and shape of what you're baking; a large braid can take up to 10 minutes longer), until well risen and a rich golden brown. Cool on a wire rack. Serve warm or split and toasted.

Nutritional Analysis (per bun): 322 calories; 8 g protein; 6.3 g fat; 2 g satfat; 59 g carbohydrate; 205 mg sodium; 60 mg cholesterol

Light Touch

In its classic form, this sweet rich dough is not extravagant, 33% calories from fat, but I have cut it by 45%, to 18% by removing over half the fat, adding 2 tablespoons canola oil, dropping 1 egg yolk, and cutting back on the almonds.

PINEAPPLE-APRICOT CROWN

Yield: One 15-inch-wide crown; 24 slices; or two 12-inch-wide crowns; 12 to 14 slices each

Flavored with pineapple juice, this quick-rising dough is rolled out, spread with dried apricots and crushed pineapple, then formed into a decorative crown. For a dramatic as well as delectable presentation for a holiday buffet, make one giant crown for a party or two medium-sized crowns—one to serve and one for a gift. Note: If you don't have dried apricots and crystallized ginger, substitute ³/₄ cup apricot preserves mixed with the drained crushed pineapple. Read about quick-rising yeast on pages 324–325.

Dough

1 cup (6 ounces) dried apricots, packed (be sure color is bright, not dark brown)

3 tablespoons chopped crystallized ginger (optional)

¹/₄ cup dark rum or pineapple (or other fruit) juice or water

4 to 4¹/₂ cups all-purpose or bread flour

¹/₃ cup granulated sugar

2 packages quick-rising active dry yeast

1¹/₂ teaspoons salt

One 20-ounce can unsweetened crushed pineapple

2 tablespoons canola oil

1 large egg plus 1 large egg white

Butter-flavor no-stick cooking spray

Glaze

1 large egg

2 teaspoons water

1 to 2 tablespoons granulated or pearl sugar

Icing

¹/₃ cup sifted confectioners' sugar

1. In a small bowl, toss together the apricots, ginger, and rum. Let stand in a warm place until plump, about 15 minutes.

2. In a large mixing bowl, whisk together 2 cups of the flour, the sugar, yeast, and salt; set aside.

3. Set a strainer over a bowl and empty the can of pineapple into it. Press hard to extract the juice; you should have about 1¹/₃ cups of juice and about 1 cup of fruit. Set the fruit aside.

continued

4. In a small nonreactive saucepan, combine 1 cup plus 2 tablespoons of the drained pineapple juice (reserve whatever remains) with the oil. Set on medium heat and warm to 115° to 120°F on an instant-read thermometer (it will feel hot to the touch).

5. Add the warmed liquid to the flour mixture and stir once or twice. Stir in the whole egg and egg white. Beat with a sturdy spoon or an electric mixer (use the paddle attachment, if available) on medium speed until blended. Stir or slowly beat in the remaining flour, ¹/₂ cup at a time, until the dough becomes too stiff to stir.

6. Turn the dough out onto a lightly floured board and knead, gradually incorporating a little more flour as necessary just to prevent sticking (excess flour will make the bread tough) until the dough feels smooth and elastic, about 10 minutes. (Alternatively, the dough can be kneaded for about 5 minutes in an electric mixer fitted with a dough hook.)

7. Form the dough into a ball and place in a lightly oiled large bowl, turning the ball once to coat the top. Cover the bowl with plastic wrap or wax paper and set it in a warm location to rise until spongy, 20 to 30 minutes.

8. Drain and discard the liquid from the apricots and ginger. Put the fruit in a food processor or blender and chop it coarsely (do not purée). Or you can chop on a cutting board. Add the reserved drained pineapple and chop it together with the apricot mixture. Set aside.

9. Lightly coat one or two baking sheets with cooking spray; set aside. Punch down the dough to remove excess gas. Turn the dough out onto a lightly floured surface and pat or roll it (don't stretch) into a 14 × 18-inch rectangle for one large crown or divide the dough in half and press into a 9 × 12-inch rectangle for each smaller crown.

10. In either case, the finishing procedure is the same. Spread the chopped fruit mixture evenly over the dough, using it all for one large crown or half (1 cup each) on each smaller portion of dough. Lift one 14-inch edge of the dough and fold it over, covering the filling in a strip 3¹/₂ to 4 inches wide (*A*). Roll the dough over 2 more times, keeping the width even and ending with the seam on the bottom.

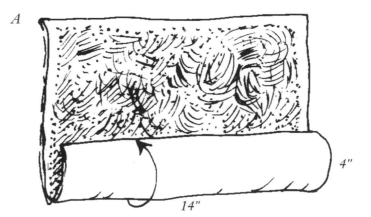

continued

11. Slide or gently ease the dough roll, seam side down, onto the prepared baking pan. Gently press on the dough roll to even the shape and flatten to a 4-inch width. Using kitchen shears or a sharp knife, make cuts along the top (long) edge of the roll about two thirds of the way through the roll and about 1¹/₂ inches apart (*B*). Bend the uncut base of the roll into a downward-facing curve so the cut segments on top fan out slightly, making the crown. Lift each cut strip and twist it sideways, so the spiral lies flat on the pan, exposing the filling (*C*).

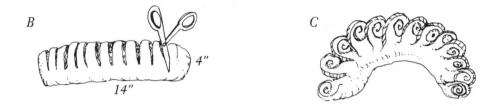

12. Cover each crown with lightly oiled wax paper or plastic wrap and set it in a warm location to rise until nearly doubled in bulk, about 20 minutes. Meanwhile, preheat the oven to 375°F.

13. In a small bowl, beat together the egg and water to make a glaze. Brush the top of the risen crown with the egg glaze and sprinkle on some sugar. Place in the oven and bake for 20 to 25 minutes, until golden brown. With a wide spatula, carefully transfer the crown to a wire rack set over a piece of wax paper. Set aside until completely cool.

14. Make the icing. In a small bowl, beat together the confectioners' sugar and 2 tablespoons of the remaining pineapple juice. Drizzle the icing over the crown.

Nutritional Analysis (per slice with pineapple juice instead of rum): 144 calories; 4 g protein; 1.8 g fat; 0.2 g satfat; 28 g carbohydrate; 142 mg sodium; 18 mg cholesterol

Light Touch

Although my classic recipe was not extremely high fat (20% calories from fat), I have substituted pineapple juice for the milk, dropped 1 yolk, and replaced the butter with oil to achieve a 45% reduction (to 11%).

SWEDISH CARDAMOM BRAIDS

Yield: 3 braided loaves; 8 slices each

Cardamom, traditionally used in Scandinavian baking, contributes a mild sweet/spicy flavor that is enhanced when the spice is soaked in warm milk before being added to the dough. Cinnamon, honey, and golden raisins add color, sweetness, and texture to this moderately sweet holiday bread glazed and decorated with chopped almonds and pearl sugar. Read about quick-rising yeast on pages 324–325.

Dough

3¹/₂ to 4 cups all-purpose or bread flour

¹/₄ cup granulated sugar

2 packages quick-rising active dry yeast

1 teaspoon salt

1¹/₄ cups plus 1 tablespoon 1% milk

2 tablespoons canola oil

2 tablespoons honey

1 teaspoon ground cardamom or ¹/₂ teaspoon crushed cardamom seeds

1 large egg white

1 cup golden raisins

Butter-flavor no-stick cooking spray

Filling

¹/₄ cup granulated sugar

¹/₂ teaspoon ground cinnamon

Glaze

1 large egg

1 tablespoon 1% milk

Topping

¹/₄ cup finely chopped slivered or sliced almonds

2 tablespoons coarse-grain or pearl sugar

Advance Preparation

Braids may be double-wrapped airtight and frozen for up to 1 month.

Special Equipment

Electric mixer fitted with paddle attachment, if available, or dough hook; instant-read thermometer; 2 cookie sheets; pastry brush

Temperature and Time

First rise: 20 to 25 minutes. Second rise: 20 minutes. Bake: 375°F for 20 to 22 minutes

1. In a large mixing bowl, whisk together 2 cups of the flour, the sugar, yeast, and salt.

2. In a medium-sized saucepan, combine the milk, oil, honey, and cardamom. Stir gently over medium heat until the mixture reaches 115° to 120°F on an instant-read thermometer (it will feel hot to the touch).

3. Add the warm liquid to the dry ingredients and stir a few times. Add the egg white and beat with a sturdy spoon or an electric mixer (use a paddle attachment, if available) on medium speed until blended. Stir or beat in the additional flour, ¹/₂ cup at a time, until the dough becomes too stiff to stir.

continued

4. Turn the dough out onto a lightly floured surface and knead for about 10 minutes, until the dough feels smooth and elastic, gradually incorporating a little more flour as necessary, just to prevent sticking (excess flour will make the bread tough). (Alternatively, the dough can be kneaded for about 5 minutes in an electric mixer fitted with a dough hook.)

5. Pat the dough into a large rectangle, sprinkle with the raisins, roll up the dough, and knead a few times to distribute the raisins.

6. Form the dough into a ball and place it in a lightly oiled large bowl, turning the dough ball once to coat the top. Cover the bowl with oiled plastic wrap or wax paper and set it in a warm location to rise until soft and spongy, 20 to 25 minutes. Reserve the oiled covering paper.

7. Lightly coat baking sheets with cooking spray and set aside. To make the filling, in a small bowl or cup, stir together the sugar and cinnamon.

8. Punch down the dough to remove excess gas. Place the dough on a lightly floured surface and divide it into thirds. Pat each piece into an 8 × 12-inch rectangle and sprinkle on about a third of the cinnamon-sugar mixture. Bring the long sides together, folding the dough in half, then cut the dough lengthwise into 3 long strips. Roll these into ropes 12 to 14 inches long, then braid them, pinching the ends together to hold. Repeat with the remaining 2 pieces of dough.

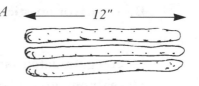

A ← — 12" — →

B

C

9. Set the braids several inches apart on prepared baking sheets. Top with the reserved plastic wrap or wax paper, oiled side down. Return the dough to a warm location to rise until nearly doubled, about 20 minutes. Preheat the oven to 375°F.

10. In a small bowl, beat the egg with the milk to make a glaze. After the braids have risen, brush the tops with glaze and sprinkle with chopped almonds and coarse or pearl sugar. Bake for 20 to 22 minutes, until golden brown. Cool on wire racks.

Nutritional Analysis (per slice): 147 calories; 4 g protein; 2 g fat; 0.2 g satfat; 29 g carbohydrate; 102 mg sodium; 0.5 mg cholesterol

---

Light Touch

Swedish baking is noted for its richness; the classical form of this recipe contains 1 cup whole milk, 4 eggs, and ½ cup butter and has 29% calories from fat. I have reduced this by 55%, to just 13%, by using low-fat milk, replacing the butter with just 2 tablespoons of oil, and replacing all the eggs in the dough with 1 egg white. This is a drop of 20 calories, 4 g fat, and (most dramatically) 44.5 mg cholesterol per slice.

PANETTONE

This egg-rich sweet Italian holiday bread is filled with sultanas and candied fruit peel and traditionally shaped into a tall cylindrical form with a domed top.

Classical panettone is said to have originated in Milan, but today the ubiquitous forms, a symbol of the Christmas season, are available around the world. According to Carol Field, in her book The Italian Baker *(Harper & Row, 1985), panettone is so intimately identified with the Italian spirit that during the uprisings for unification of Italy in 1821, candied red cherries and green citron were added to symbolize the new tricolor Italian flag.*

Instead of using store-bought candied fruits, I prefer to substitute dried cranberries or cherries soaked in brandy or fruit juice. Other good replacements are dried peaches, dried apples, and dried pears (found in gourmet shops or supermarkets), cut up. To bake panettone in the traditional cylindrical form, you will need two clean 28-ounce aluminum cans with the tops removed, such as those used for plum tomatoes. Read about quick-rising yeast on pages 324–325.

Dough

2 cups total mixed fruits, about ¹/₂ cup each, such as golden raisins, sultanas, or seedless raisins, candied orange peel, cut-up dried apricots, dried cranberries or dried cherries, or candied mixed fruits

³/₄ cup fruit juice or wine, or ¹/₄ cup brandy plus ¹/₂ cup water

¹/₂ cup (2 ounces) nuts, such as pine nuts and/or chopped blanched almonds

3¹/₂ to 4¹/₂ cups all-purpose or bread flour

³/₄ cup granulated sugar

1 teaspoon salt

2 packages quick-rising active dry yeast

1 cup 1% milk

2 tablespoons unsalted butter

2 large eggs

³/₄ teaspoon anise extract or 2 teaspoons anise seeds or 2 teaspoons vanilla or orange extract

Oil or butter-flavor no-stick cooking spray

Egg Glaze

1 large egg

2 teaspoons water

Advance Preparation

Dried fruits must soak for 30 minutes. Breads can be baked ahead, wrapped airtight, and frozen up to 4 weeks.

Special Equipment

Instant-read thermometer; electric mixer fitted with paddle attachment, if available, or dough hook; pastry brush; wax paper or baking parchment (optional)

Temperature and Time

First rise: 20 to 30 minutes. Second rise: 45 minutes. Bake: 350°F for 60 minutes

Icing

¹/₂ cup sifted confectioners' sugar

2 teaspoons 1% milk or water

Garnish (optional)

Candied red cherries or pine nuts

1. In a medium-sized bowl, combine the dried fruits (not candied fruits or peel) with the fruit juice or brandy and water and soak for 30 minutes (or place in a microwaveable bowl and microwave on high for 30 seconds). Drain the fruit, reserving the liquid for another purpose, and add the nuts. Set aside.

2. In a large mixing bowl, whisk together 2 cups of the flour, the sugar, salt, and yeast. Set aside.

3. In a medium-sized saucepan, combine the milk and butter and heat over medium to 115° to 120°F on an instant-read thermometer (it will feel hot.)

4. Add the warm liquid to the flour mixture and stir a few times with a sturdy spoon or beat with an electric mixer (use a paddle attachment, if available) on medium speed. Add the eggs and anise extract or other flavoring and beat until blended. Gradually stir or beat in the remaining flour, ¹/₂ cup at a time, until the dough becomes too stiff to stir.

5. Turn the dough out onto a lightly floured surface and knead for about 10 minutes, until the dough feels smooth and elastic, gradually incorporating a little more flour as necessary, just to prevent the dough from sticking (excess flour can make the dough tough). (Alternatively, the dough can be kneaded for 5 minutes with an electric mixer fitted with a dough hook.) Form the dough into a ball and place it in a large lightly oiled bowl. Turn the dough ball once to coat the top, cover the bowl with oiled plastic wrap or wax paper, and set it in a warm location to rise for 20 to 30 minutes, until soft and spongy. Reserve the oiled paper.

6. Generously oil the inside of two clean 28-ounce aluminum cans or coat them with cooking spray; line the bottom of each can with wax paper or baking parchment. Set the cans aside.

7. Punch down the dough and turn it out onto a lightly floured work surface. Press the dough into a 10 × 14-inch rectangle about ¹/₂ inch thick. Spread with the fruit-nut mixture. Roll the dough up and knead 5 or 6 times to distribute the fruit evenly.

8. Divide the dough in half and shape each half into a ball. Place one ball in each prepared can and, with a razor or sharp knife, slash an X into the top of each bread. Cover the top of each can with a piece of the oiled paper and return them to a warm place to rise until the dough nearly reaches the top of the cans, about 45 minutes. Note: Alternatively, you can shape the dough into two large or four small round balls, four 8-inch-long braids, or two large Christmas trees (see Favorite Christmas Bread diagrams, page 240); adjust baking times to suit different size breads.

continued

9. While the dough is rising, preheat the oven to 350°F. In a small bowl beat the egg and water to make a glaze. Brush the tops of the risen loaves with the egg wash (be careful not to let it drip down the sides or it will stick) and bake for about 60 minutes, until well browned and a skewer inserted into the center of a bread comes out clean. If the bread appears to be browning too quickly, cover loosely with foil. Cool the loaves in their cans on wire racks for about 10 minutes, then tip out of the cans, peel off the paper, and place the panettones on their sides on the rack, propped up with a jar, to completely cool.

10. In a small bowl, stir together the sugar and milk or water to make icing the consistency of heavy cream; adjust ingredients if needed. When the breads are cold, drizzle the icing over the domed top and stick on halved cherries or a few pine nuts for decoration if desired.

Nutritional Analysis (per slice): 187 calories; 5 g protein; 3 g fat; 1 g satfat; 37 g carbohydrate; 104 mg sodium; 30 mg cholesterol

Light Touch

A classical Milanese panettone has about 41% calories from fat. By cutting back, but not cutting out, my version is less rich but no less delicious. I cut all but 2 tablespoons of the butter, dropped 1 egg plus all the extra yolks, and used low-fat milk to get 15% calories from fat, a reduction of 72%, and a cut of 104 calories and 11 g fat per slice.

FAVORITE CHRISTMAS BREAD

*Yield: Four 8-inch-long braided loaves or four
9-inch-tall Christmas trees; about 10 slices per loaf*

This fruit-filled, orange-scented sweet bread has been a holiday favorite in my family for years. I like to form it into braids, angels, wreaths, and Christmas trees decorated with icing glaze and bright red candied cherries. Quick-rising yeast cuts preparation time in half (see pages 324–325), so you can make this in less than an hour and a half. This bread freezes well; make it early, and when the holidays arrive, shop in your own freezer—one recipe makes four gift breads.

Advance Preparation

Dried fruits must be soaked in liquid about 30 minutes before adding to the recipe. Baked breads can be wrapped airtight and frozen no more than 1 month ahead.

Special Equipment

Instant-read thermometer (optional); electric mixer fitted with paddle attachment, if available, or dough hook; 2 cookie sheets or flat baking sheets; kitchen shears (optional) or paring knife; pastry brush

Temperature and Time

First rise: 30 minutes. Second rise: 15 to 20 minutes. Bake: 350°F for 25 to 30 minutes

Dough

1 cup dried cranberries, dried cherries, or dark raisins

1 cup packed golden raisins

1¹/₂ cups warm water or orange juice

¹/₂ cup (2 ounces) pine nuts or slivered almonds

¹/₂ cup (2 ounces) chopped walnuts

5 to 6 cups all-purpose or bread flour

2 packages quick-rising active dry yeast

³/₄ cup granulated sugar

1¹/₂ teaspoons salt

1¹/₂ teaspoons ground cinnamon

1 teaspoon ground nutmeg

1¹/₂ cups plus 1 tablespoon 1% milk, divided

3 tablespoons canola oil

2 tablespoons unsulfured molasses

2 teaspoons grated orange zest

1 large egg

¹/₂ cup fresh orange juice

Butter-flavor no-stick cooking spray

Egg Glaze

1 large egg

2 teaspoons water

Icing and Decoration

¹/₂ cup sifted confectioners' sugar

1 tablespoon 1% milk

¹/₂ teaspoon vanilla extract

Candied red or green cherries, halved, or blanched almonds (optional)

continued

1. In a small bowl, combine the dried cranberries or cherries and raisins, cover with the warm water or juice, and let stand about 30 minutes to soften. Drain well. Combine with all the nuts. Set aside.

2. In a large mixing bowl, whisk together 2 cups of the flour, the yeast, sugar, salt, cinnamon, and nutmeg. Set aside.

3. In a medium-sized saucepan, combine 1½ cups of the milk, the oil, molasses, and grated orange zest. Heat over medium, stirring, to 115° to 120°F on an instant-read thermometer (it will feel hot to the touch). In a small bowl, stir the egg into the orange juice. Set aside. Add the warm milk mixture to the dry ingredients and stir once or twice. Then stir in the egg and orange juice. Beat with a sturdy spoon or an electric mixer (use the paddle attachment, if available) on medium speed until blended. Stir or slowly beat in the remaining flour, ½ cup at a time, until the dough becomes too stiff to stir.

4. Turn the dough out onto a lightly floured board and knead about 10 minutes, until it feels smooth and elastic, gradually incorporating a little more flour as necessary, just to prevent sticking (excess flour will make the bread tough). (Alternatively, the dough can be kneaded for 4 to 5 minutes with an electric mixer fitted with a dough hook.) On a very lightly floured board, pat the dough out into a flat rectangle, sprinkle on some of the fruits and nuts, fold over the dough, and knead it. Repeat, working in all the fruit and nuts.

5. Form the dough into a ball and place it in a lightly oiled large bowl, turning the ball once to coat the top. Cover the bowl with oiled plastic wrap or wax paper and set it in a warm location to rise until spongy, about 30 minutes.

6. Lightly coat two baking sheets with cooking spray; set them aside. Punch down the dough to remove excess gas. Turn the dough out onto a lightly floured work surface, divide it into quarters, and roll each quarter into a ball.

7. To shape one tree, press a dough ball into a triangle shape as shown, about 8 inches across at the base and 9 inches tall (*A*). Use kitchen shears or a sharp knife to cut 4 slices into each side for branches as shown; cut away a portion of the bottom edge to form the trunk (*B*). Repeat with remaining

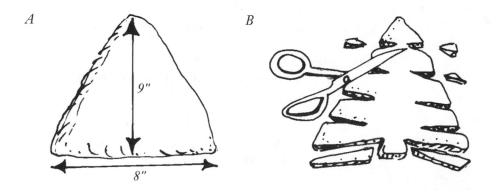

A

9"

8"

B

dough to make four trees. (Save dough scraps to add to remaining dough balls or form small rolls to bake with the breads.)

8. To shape one braid, divide one dough ball into thirds and roll each piece into a rope about $1^1/_2 \times 12$ inches. Braid the three ropes (see page 234) and pinch the ends together. Repeat with the remaining dough to make four braids.

9. Set the shaped breads a few inches apart on the prepared baking sheets. Cover the dough with oiled plastic wrap or wax paper and return it to a warm location to rise 15 to 20 minutes, until nearly doubled in bulk. Meanwhile, preheat the oven to 350°F.

10. In a small bowl, beat the egg with the water to make a glaze. After the breads have risen, gently brush the tops with the egg wash and bake 25 to 30 minutes, until golden brown; the bread should sound hollow when tapped. Cool on a wire rack.

11. To make the icing, stir together the confectioners' sugar, milk, and vanilla in a small bowl. Drizzle the icing over the cooled breads and add halved cherries or nuts for decoration. The icing hardens as it sets.

Nutritional Analysis (per slice): 131 calories; 4 g protein; 4 g fat; 0.6 g satfat; 25 g carbohydrate; 90 mg sodium; 11 mg cholesterol

---

Light Touch

My original form of this recipe has only 27% calories from fat, containing $1^3/_4$ cups whole milk, 2 eggs, and $^1/_3$ cup melted butter. I have cut this to 24%, dropping 10 calories and 1 g fat per slice, by using low-fat milk, 1 egg, and less fat, replacing butter with a little heart-healthy canola oil.

Pastry Creams,
CAKE FILLINGS,
AND SAUCES

The creams and fillings in this section have many functions. Vanilla Cream, for example, can be spread on pastry to form the base of a fruit tart or pie, set beneath fresh berries in a Chocolate Tulip Shell, or used as filling topped by raspberries in an Almond Sponge Roll. Fromage Blanc, Ricotta Cream, and Lemon Curd have similar uses, and Homemade Yogurt Cheese can be eaten plain, blended with fruit or spices, or baked into cheesecake. Marshmallow Fluff is a homemade version of the old childhood favorite; use it atop frozen yogurt sundaes or sandwich it between Chocolate Cookies to delight the kids.

Apricot-Orange Cake Filling was developed for the Orange Layer Cake but tastes good with nearly any layer or rolled cake; Apricot Mousse (page 188) can be substituted. For additional ideas, consider using the filling from one of the pies (Key Lime or Mandarin Mousse, for example) to fill a cake or Chocolate Tulip Shell. The choice is yours.

I developed the twelve sauces that follow to accompany or embellish a variety of desserts or cakes, although each is flavorful and enticing enough to be eaten alone with a spoon. The Vanilla Custard Sauce is an elegant accompaniment to Pear-Prune-Brandy Cake or Chocolate Marbleized Semolina Cake, sublime with Drop-Dead Chocolate-Espresso Mousse Cake, and perfection spooned over fresh raspberries in a Chocolate Tulip Shell. Cinnamon-Apple Custard Sauce, perfumed with herbal tea, is as good with Apple Pie or Tortilla Tarts as it is spooned over Steve Keneippe's Coffee-Spice Angel Food Cake. Fruit sauces include Berry (all-purpose), Raspberry, Blueberry-Honey, Plum, and Brandied Cranberry-Maple; all are excellent over plain cake or frozen yogurt or gilding a homemade pudding with a compatible flavor. Bourbon Cream Sauce goes with warm Steamed Fig-Date-Apricot Pudding or Raisin Bread Pudding. Praline Sauce enhances any pumpkin-flavored dessert or plain cake. Both chocolate sauces are divine on plain cake or yogurt sundaes.

For a bonus, all the sauces make excellent gifts from the kitchen, bottled in attractive jars with handwritten labels and recipes attached.

VANILLA CREAM

Yield: 2 cups; sixteen 2-tablespoon servings

This rich creamy mixture can be used as a sauce or a filling between layers of a cake, or under fruit in a tart shell. The cream cheese gives just enough body to hold when sliced, so extra gelatin is not needed. To fill a sponge roll, cut the recipe in half but use 1 full teaspoon of vanilla or other flavoring extract. The honey and pumpkin-spice variations that follow can be used to fill sponge rolls or Chocolate Tulip Shells (page 30).

1 cup vanilla low-fat yogurt (with no added gums)
1 cup (8 ounces) light cream cheese, at room temperature
2 tablespoons granulated sugar, or to taste
1 teaspoon vanilla extract

1. Measure the yogurt into a strainer set over a bowl and drain about 15 minutes. Discard liquid.

2. Combine in a mixing bowl the drained yogurt and the remaining ingredients. Whip with an electric mixer until smooth. Adjust flavoring if needed. Refrigerate until ready to use, at least an hour if you wish to thicken it.

Nutritional Analysis (per serving): 49 calories; 2 g protein; 3 g fat; 0 g satfat; 5 g carbohydrate; 90 mg sodium; 5 mg cholesterol

> ### Advance Preparation
>
> *Yogurt must drain for 15 minutes before use in recipe. The cream can be prepared up to 2 days ahead and stored, covered, in the refrigerator. If you want to thicken it, it will need to chill at least 1 hour.*
>
> ### Special Equipment
>
> *Strainer set over a bowl*

HONEY-VANILLA CREAM

Yield: 2 cups; sixteen 2-tablespoon servings

Prepare recipe above but replace 2 tablespoons of the yogurt with 2 tablespoons honey. Use only 1 tablespoon granulated sugar, or to taste.

Nutritional Analysis (per serving): 50 calories; 2 g protein; 2 g fat; 0 g satfat; 6 g carbohydrate; 81 mg sodium; 4 mg cholesterol

PUMPKIN 'N' SPICE CREAM

Yield: 3 cups; twelve 1/4-cup servings

Prepare Vanilla Cream above adding 1 cup canned unsweetened pumpkin purée; 1 1/2 teaspoons ground cinnamon, 3/4 teaspoon ground nutmeg, 1/4 teaspoon ground ginger, pinch of ground cloves, and brown or granulated sugar to taste. Make half the recipe to fill one sponge roll.

Nutritional Analysis (per serving): 78 calories; 3 g protein; 4 g fat; 0 g satfat; 9 g carbohydrate; 122 mg sodium; 7 mg cholesterol

continued

You can use either Neufchâtel or light cream cheese to make this thick creamy spread. With about 46% calories from fat in the plain version (40% in both variations), it may appear to be high in fat. However, it is not eaten alone, but rather with fruit and other low-fat elements in a dessert. Compared to a cream filling made with a blend of regular cream cheese and whipped cream, I have reduced the fat about 32%, so this easily fits into a low-fat plan.

SHORTCUT VANILLA PASTRY CREAM

Yield: 2 cups; sixteen 2-tablespoon servings

Packaged mix for vanilla cooked-style "pudding and pie filling" is sweeter than I would wish, but is an acceptable low-fat pastry filling if you are in a hurry. This cream is thick enough to fill a layer or rolled cake.

To make coffee flavor, dissolve 1 to 2 tablespoons instant coffee powder in the milk before adding. To make chocolate, whisk 2 tablespoons unsweetened cocoa into the dry powdered mix before adding the milk or use packaged chocolate pudding and pie filling with 1 tablespoon cocoa added.

Advance Preparation

Prepare cream up to 2 days in advance, cover, and refrigerate.

Special Equipment

1 1/2-quart saucepan

One 3 1/4-ounce package vanilla pudding and pie filling (cooked style)

2 cups 2% milk (use 1 3/4 cups for a thicker cream)

2 teaspoons vanilla extract or 1 teaspoon almond or maple extract

Prepare the filling according to directions on the package, whisking the powdered mix into the milk over medium heat and stirring continuously until it comes to a full bubbling boil. Remove from the heat, stir in the extract, cover with plastic wrap laid directly on the pudding (to prevent a skin from forming), and set aside to cool. Refrigerate. The filling thickens as it cools.

Nutritional Analysis (per serving): 35 calories per serving; 1 g protein; 0.6 g fat; 0.3 g satfat; 7 g carbohydrate; 56 mg sodium; 2 mg cholesterol

When made with 2% milk, this pastry cream has only 15% calories from fat; made with whole milk it has 24% calories from fat. The powdered mix alone contains just a trace of fat and no cholesterol.

FROMAGE BLANC

Yield: 1 cup; eight 2-tablespoon servings

This easy-to-make recipe includes a touch of whipped heavy cream. Serve it plain over fresh fruit or add gelatin so it will set into a stiffer filling for a roulade or layer cake.

1 cup 1% cottage cheese

¹/₃ cup sifted confectioners' sugar

2 teaspoons vanilla extract

¹/₄ cup heavy cream, chilled

For Cake Filling

³/₄ teaspoon unflavored gelatin

1 tablespoon cold water

Advance Preparation

You will need to chill it for 45 to 60 minutes before spreading, and then chill the frosted cake for 2 to 3 hours to set the fromage blanc. The plain cream can be prepared 2 days ahead and stored, covered, in the refrigerator.

Special Equipment

Strainer set over a bowl; food processor or blender

1. To remove excess liquid from the cottage cheese, place it in a strainer set over a bowl. Cover the cheese with a layer of plastic wrap or wax paper, and press on it with your hand, forcing out as much whey as possible. Some brands will not drain and will still work well.

2. Transfer the drained curds to a food processor or blender and add the sugar and vanilla. Purée until absolutely smooth; it can take 3 minutes for any trace of graininess to disappear.

3. In a small chilled bowl, whip the cream until medium-soft peaks form. Fold the cheese mixture into the whipped cream. *If the fromage blanc is to be used as a sauce*, cover and refrigerate.

4. *If using the fromage blanc as a cake filling*, add the gelatin: Sprinkle the gelatin over the water in a small pan. Allow it to stand for 3 minutes to soften, then stir over low heat just until the gelatin is completely dissolved; do not boil. Cool the gelatin to lukewarm, then gently but thoroughly, without losing volume, whisk the gelatin into the cheese-cream mixture. Chill for 45 to 60 minutes, until thickened enough to spread without running. Refrigerate the cake for at least 2 to 3 hours to completely set the fromage blanc.

Nutritional Analysis (per serving): 68 calories; 4 g protein; 3 g fat; 1.8 g satfat; 5 g carbohydrate; 119 mg sodium; 11 mg cholesterol

Light Touch

A classic form of this recipe obtains 68% of its calories from fat. Replacing the cream cheese with low-fat cottage cheese but keeping the whipped cream for its good flavor, I have cut 40% of the total calories from fat and three quarters of the fat and saturated fat per serving. This recipe still obtains nearly 41% calories from fat because of the heavy cream; it is meant to be eaten with fruit and other low-fat ingredients, to further diminish the total percentage of calories from fat.

RICOTTA CREAM

Yield: About 2 cups; eight ¼-cup servings

Serve this light creamy blend of ricotta and yogurt with sliced fresh fruit or mounded in a tart shell topped with berries. It has the consistency of sour cream and can also be served as a sauce with steamed pudding or Drop-Dead Chocolate-Espresso Mousse Cake (page 151). Note: A blender gives a much smoother product here than a food processor. To make Orange Cream, add 1 teaspoon grated orange zest, ½ teaspoon orange extract, and 2 tablespoons orange liqueur.

Advance Preparation

This can be made up to 2 days ahead; it benefits from at least 12 hours' refrigeration to blend flavors.

Special Equipment

Blender

16 ounces part-skim or nonfat ricotta cheese (or one 15-ounce container)

⅓ cup plain nonfat yogurt, top liquid poured off

Scant ¼ teaspoon salt

1½ teaspoons vanilla extract, or to taste

3 tablespoons granulated sugar, or to taste

Fresh lemon juice (optional)

1. In a blender, combine all the ingredients except the lemon juice. Purée for 2 to 3 minutes, until absolutely smooth, without a trace of graininess. Stop once to scrape down the sides of the blender container.

2. Remove the mixture from the blender and refrigerate, covered, for about 12 hours for the flavors to blend. Taste and adjust flavoring if desired. Add a drop or two of lemon juice if the flavor seems flat.

Nutritional Analysis (per serving): 98 calories; 7 g protein; 4 g fat; 2.6 g satfat; 8 g carbohydrate; 140 mg sodium; 17 mg cholesterol

Light Touch

This recipe contains 39% calories from fat, but that is significantly less than for an equal quantity of whipped heavy cream (96% calories from fat). Note that the per-serving figures are low, and, in fact, the cream will be served with other low-fat ingredients to further reduce the total fat of the dessert.

HOMEMADE YOGURT CHEESE

Yield: About 1¹⁄₄ cups; ten 2-tablespoon servings

This is nothing more than plain yogurt drained of its liquid. In texture and taste, it resembles the French soft cheese Boursin; it is delicious on its own, or blended with herbs or pepper or spices for a cracker spread. In baking cheesecakes as well as many other baked goods, yogurt cheese can be used as a substitute for cream cheese or even sour cream. This low-fat, low-calorie, low-cholesterol cheese is known in the Middle East as labna *and in India as* dehin.

Different brands of yogurt contain different additives. To make yogurt cheese, select a yogurt that does not contain modified food starch, vegetable food gums, or gelatin, all of which inhibit the draining of the whey, which contains valuable vitamins and minerals and may be saved for use in muffins and breads, or soups and gravies.

Yogurts also differ in the amount of liquid they contain. Therefore, it is impossible to be absolutely specific about the proportion of yogurt that will remain after draining. As a general rule, plan on ending up with slightly over one third of the original volume. In other words, start with 3 cups of yogurt to make a little more than 1 cup yogurt cheese; 6 cups yogurt yield 2¹⁄₄ cups of cheese.

3 cups plain nonfat yogurt

Here are 2 different easy methods to make the cheese:

Method 1: Set a colander or strainer over a deep bowl and line it with a triple thickness of cheesecloth. Add the yogurt, cover with plastic wrap, refrigerate, and let drain 24 hours.

Method 2: Cut or fold a triple thickness of cheesecloth about 14 inches square. Spoon the yogurt into the center of the cheesecloth, gather up the edges, and tie them together with a rubber band. Insert a chopstick through the knot and balance the chopstick over the edges of a deep bowl, so the cheesecloth bag hangs suspended inside; refrigerate the bowl for 24 hours to drain.

Whatever method you choose, drain the yogurt until it completely stops dripping. Squeeze the cheesecloth together gently to extract any remaining drops of whey. Turn out the cheese into a clean container, cover, and refrigerate.

Nutritional Analysis (per serving): 38 calories; 4 g protein; 0.1 g fat; 0 g satfat; 5 g carbohydrate; 52 mg sodium; 1 mg cholesterol

---

Advance Preparation

Yogurt cheese takes 24 hours to prepare; it keeps, refrigerated, up to 1 week.

Special Equipment

Cheesecloth; colander or strainer set over a deep bowl; chopstick

---

Light Touch

This versatile cheese has a scant 3% of its calories from fat.

MARSHMALLOW FLUFF

Yield: *About 5 cups*

This is the stuff childhood dreams are made of...fluffernutter sandwiches, gooey moon pies (chocolate cookies glued together with gobs of fluff)—and it's easy.

¾ cup plus 2 tablespoons water, divided
1 cup plus 2 tablespoons granulated sugar, divided
1 cup plus 2 tablespoons light corn syrup
1 envelope unflavored gelatin
4 large egg whites
Pinch of salt
1 teaspoon vanilla extract

Advance Preparation

Fluff keeps, covered in the refrigerator, at least 2 months.

Special Equipment

1½- to 2-quart heavy-bottomed saucepan; pastry brush; candy thermometer or glass of ice water

1. In a saucepan, combine ¾ cup of the water, 1 cup of the granulated sugar, and the corn syrup. Stir to mix, then set on medium-high heat. Clip a candy thermometer to the pan side. Bring the mixture to a boil and cook without stirring for 15 to 16 minutes, until the candy thermometer reads 239° to 240°F (a drop of syrup added to a glass of ice water will form a soft ball). During the boiling, wash down the inside of the pan several times with a pastry brush dipped in cold water to prevent sugar crystallization.

2. While the syrup cooks, sprinkle the gelatin over the remaining 2 tablespoons of water in a small saucepan. Set aside to soften.

3. When the syrup is almost cooked (after 10 minutes cooking time), begin to beat the egg whites with the salt in a large grease-free bowl using an electric mixer on medium speed. Whip the whites until foamy, then add the remaining 2 tablespoons of sugar and beat until the whites are nearly stiff but not dry. Turn off the mixer but leave the bowl of whites in place.

4. When the syrup reaches the correct temperature, remove from the heat and stir in the softened gelatin. The syrup will foam up, then subside. Stir for about 2 minutes, until the gelatin dissolves and no granules are visible.

5. Turn the mixer on low speed and gradually pour the hot gelatin-syrup over the whites while whipping. Pour the syrup in a steady stream between the side of the bowl and the beaters; do not scrape in any hardened bits of syrup. Add the vanilla, then continue whipping on high speed for about 5 minutes, until soft peaks form (if you want to use fluff for cake icing) or beat until stiff peaks form (to use for cookie or cake filling). Spoon the fluff into a container, cover, and refrigerate.

Nutritional Analysis (per serving): 50 calories; 1 g protein; 0 g fat; 0 g satfat; 12 g carbohydrate; 16 mg sodium; 0 mg cholesterol

Light Touch

This is as light as it gets—zero fat, zero cholesterol.

LEMON CURD

Yield: 1 cup; enough to cover 1 cake layer or 1 jelly roll; twelve 1 1/3-tablespoon servings

The flavor of this all-purpose pastry filling is excellent, but the color will be pale unless it is brightened with orange juice, which also cuts the sharpness of the lemon.

Advance Preparation

The curd can be prepared ahead, covered, and refrigerated 1 or 2 days. If too thick after chilling, warm for a few seconds in the microwave, then stir well before serving.

Special Equipment

Medium-sized heavy-bottomed nonreactive saucepan

1/2 cup granulated sugar

1 1/2 tablespoons cornstarch

1 teaspoon all-purpose flour

Pinch of salt

1/2 cup plus 1 tablespoon fresh orange juice

1 teaspoon grated lemon zest

1/4 cup fresh lemon juice

2 tablespoons heavy cream

1. In a medium-sized heavy-bottomed nonreactive saucepan, whisk together the sugar, cornstarch, flour, and salt.

2. In a cup, combine the orange juice, lemon zest, and lemon juice. Whisk into the dry ingredients. Place the pan over medium heat and whisk until the mixture comes to a boil. Boil, whisking constantly, for 1 full minute, until thickened and clear. Remove from the heat. Whisk in the cream. Set the curd aside until cool, then refrigerate; it thickens as it cools.

Nutritional Analysis (per serving): 46 calories; 0 g protein; 1 g fat; 0.5 g satfat; 10 g carbohydrate; 25 mg sodium; 3 mg cholesterol

Light Touch

A yolk- and butter-rich traditional lemon curd has about 30% calories from fat, but each serving packs 23 g fat, 13 of them saturated. To cut the fat nearly in half, and eliminate almost all the saturated fat, I have dropped the yolks and butter. Even though I add 2 tablespoons heavy cream for richness, there are only 17% calories from fat.

APRICOT-ORANGE CAKE FILLING

Yield: 2 cups; enough to fill one 2- to 4-layer cake or one sponge roll; twelve 2²/₃-tablespoon servings

This recipe is adapted from one I developed with Cooking Light *magazine for the Orange Layer Cake on page 137. It is also good with Orange or Chocolate Sponge Roll (pages 128 and 129), or to fill Phyllo Cups (page 49) or Chocolate Tulip Shells (page 30).*

Advance Preparation

The filling needs to chill about 4 hours before being spread on a cake. It can be cooled, covered, and refrigerated up to 4 days ahead.

Special Equipment

Medium-sized nonreactive saucepan; blender or food processor; small nonreactive saucepan

1½ cups fresh orange juice, divided

Grated zest of 1 orange

¾ cup (about 5 ounces) whole dried apricots

¾ cup granulated sugar

2½ tablespoons cornstarch

2 teaspoons unsalted butter

2½ tablespoons fresh lemon juice

1. In a medium-sized nonreactive saucepan, combine ¾ cup of the orange juice, the orange zest, and apricots. Bring to a boil, cover, reduce the heat, and simmer for about 20 minutes, until the apricots are fork-tender. Transfer the mixture to a blender or food processor and purée until nearly smooth.

2. In a small nonreactive saucepan, whisk together the sugar and cornstarch, then whisk in the remaining ¾ cup of orange juice and bring to a boil over medium heat. Boil, whisking constantly, for 60 seconds, until thickened and no longer cloudy.

3. Remove from the heat and stir in the butter, apricot purée, and lemon juice. Beat well, then set aside to cool. Cover and refrigerate at least 4 hours before using as cake filling.

Nutritional Analysis (per serving): 100 calories; 1 g protein; 1 g fat; 0.4 g satfat; 25 g carbohydrate; 2 mg sodium; 2 mg cholesterol

Light Touch

With only 7% calories from fat, this is definitely light. However, it gets 91% of its calories from carbohydrates, hence the 100 calories. The fruit provides 1.2 g dietary fiber per serving.

VANILLA CUSTARD SAUCE

Yield: About 1¹/₄ cups

This is a light custard sauce, not to be confused with a pastry cream, which is thicker. I developed this recipe in conjunction with Eating Well *magazine, to be served with a rich chocolate dessert, such as Drop-Dead Chocolate-Espresso Mousse Cake on page 151, or with fresh berries.*

1 cup plus 1 tablespoon skim milk, divided

1 large egg plus 1 large yolk

2 tablespoons granulated sugar

1¹/₂ teaspoons cornstarch

1¹/₂ teaspoons vanilla extract

1. In a medium-sized saucepan, whisk together 1 cup of the milk, the egg and egg yolk, and the sugar. Dissolve the cornstarch in the remaining 1 tablespoon of milk, then whisk it in.

2. Set the saucepan over medium heat and cook, stirring off and on with a wooden spoon, for 4 to 5 minutes. Then whisk continuously for the next 2 minutes, until the custard is thick enough to coat a spoon. Turn the spoon over and draw a line down its back; if the line does not close up, the custard is done. Do not allow the custard to come to a boil. Remove from the heat, stir in the vanilla, then strain into a bowl. Let cool. Refrigerate until served.

Nutritional Analysis (per 2¹/₂-tablespoon serving): 44 calories; 2 g protein; 1 g fat; 0.4 g satfat; 5 g carbohydrate; 26 mg sodium; 54 mg cholesterol

Advance Preparation

Sauce can be made a day ahead, covered, and refrigerated.

Special Equipment

Medium-sized saucepan; strainer set over a bowl

Light Touch

Although this recipe gets 27% of its calories from fat, most traditional egg custard sauces, made with several yolks, heavy cream, and butter, are at least half fat. There is some fat and cholesterol in this recipe because it has 2 yolks, but the servings are small, and the dessert it accompanies will also be low in fat. The addition of a little cornstarch stabilizes the custard and ensures reliability; nevertheless, do not let the custard boil or (as often happens with cooked skim milk) it may curdle.

CINNAMON-APPLE CUSTARD SAUCE

Yield: About 1¹/₄ cups

This rich creamy dessert sauce (not to be confused with thick pastry cream used as a filling) has a flavor redolent of cinnamon and apple—"cozy tasting," say my taste-testers. The magic ingredient: cinnamon-apple herbal tea steeped in hot milk used for the custard. Experiment with other herbal blends to vary the flavor and serve over spice cake, chocolate cake, chocolate soufflé, or apricot tarts.

1 cup plus 1 tablespoon 1% milk, divided

3 tea bags herbal cinnamon-apple tea

1¹/₂ teaspoons cornstarch

¹/₂ teaspoon all-purpose flour

1 large egg plus 1 large yolk

2¹/₂ tablespoons granulated sugar

¹/₂ teaspoon vanilla extract

Advance Preparation

Sauce can be made 1 day ahead, covered and refrigerated.

Special Equipment

1¹/₂-quart nonreactive saucepan; instant-read thermometer (optional); strainer set over a bowl

1. In a small nonreactive saucepan, scald 1 cup of the milk over medium heat until bubbles appear around the edges (140° to 145°F on an instant-read thermometer). Remove from the heat and immediately add the tea bags. Cover the pan. Allow the tea to steep for about 5 minutes, then press the tea bags against the pan side with the back of a spoon to extract the flavor and moisture; discard bags.

2. In a medium-sized mixing bowl, stir the cornstarch into the remaining 1 tablespoon of milk until dissolved, then whisk in the flour, egg and egg yolk, and sugar. Whisk this into the warm milk tea, set over medium heat, and continue whisking 4 to 5 minutes, until thickened enough to coat the back of a spoon so a line drawn through it with your finger will not close up immediately.

3. Remove the sauce from the heat, stir in the vanilla, and pour through a strainer into a bowl. Serve warm, at room temperature, or refrigerate and serve chilled.

Nutritional Analysis (per 2¹/₂-tablespoon serving): 47 calories; 2 g protein; 1.6 g fat; 0.6 g satfat; 6 g carbohydrate; 25 mg sodium; 55 mg cholesterol

Light Touch

Traditional custard sauce is made with several egg yolks, heavy cream, and butter; it is about half fat. This recipe reduces calories from fat to just 30% by cutting back yolks, replacing cream with low-fat milk, and eliminating butter. The addition of cornstarch plus flour stabilizes the sauce to prevent separation; nevertheless, do not let the mixture boil or it may tend to curdle because of the low fat content of the milk.

BERRY SAUCE

Yield: About 1¹/₃ cups; 10 generous 2-tablespoon servings

Use this master recipe to make a sauce with any type of berries to serve with plain sponge or pound cake. It is also a dramatic and flavorful topping for Ricotta Cream (page 250) served in Phyllo Cups (page 49).

2 cups fresh berries, rinsed, hulled, and sliced (if strawberries), or frozen whole unsweetened berries

¹/₃ to ¹/₂ cup granulated sugar, depending upon sweetness of berries

1¹/₂ to 2 tablespoons fresh lemon juice

Grated zest of ¹/₂ lemon or orange

¹/₂ cup plus 2 tablespoons water, divided

1 teaspoon cornstarch

3 tablespoons fruit liqueur, such as Chambord, Grand Marnier, or crème de cassis (optional)

Advance Preparation

The sauce can be prepared a day or two ahead and kept covered in the refrigerator.

Special Equipment

Medium-sized heavy-bottomed nonreactive saucepan

---

1. In a medium-sized heavy-bottomed nonreactive saucepan, combine the berries, ¹/₃ cup of the sugar, 1¹/₂ tablespoons of the lemon juice, the lemon or orange zest, and ¹/₂ cup of the water. Set over medium-high heat and cook, stirring and mashing the berries with the back of a large spoon, for 2 to 3 minutes to release the juices and dissolve the sugar.

2. In a cup, dissolve the cornstarch in the remaining 2 tablespoons of water. Stir it into the berries. Turn the heat to high, bring to a boil, and cook, stirring constantly, 45 to 60 seconds, until the mixture thickens and is no longer cloudy. Remove from the heat.

3. Stir in the liqueur if using it. Taste and adjust flavoring, adding more sugar or lemon juice if needed. Let cool. Serve at room temperature or chilled.

Nutritional Analysis (per serving with liqueur): 51 calories; 0 g protein; 0.1 g fat; 0 g satfat; 12 g carbohydrate; 2 mg sodium; 0 mg cholesterol

---

Light Touch

This sauce contains no cholesterol and gets only 2% calories from fat.

RASPBERRY SAUCE

Yield: About 1¹/₈ cups if completely strained; 1¹/₂ cups with some seeds

This sauce is good whether made with fresh or frozen berries. Serve it with Lemon Pound Cake (page 141) or Drop-Dead Chocolate-Espresso Mousse Cake (page 151).

The recipe uses three cups of berries, but nearly half a cup of volume is lost when all the seeds are strained out; the straining is optional. I prefer to strain just half the seeds, to keep a little texture.

3 cups fresh raspberries or one 12-ounce bag frozen unsweetened whole raspberries

3 tablespoons granulated sugar, or to taste

3 tablespoons water or orange juice, divided

1 scant tablespoon cornstarch

3 tablespoons raspberry liqueur (like Chambord), eau de vie (framboise), or crème de cassis (optional)

Advance Preparation

The sauce can be prepared ahead, covered, and refrigerated 2 or 3 days.

Special Equipment

Medium-sized nonreactive saucepan; strainer set over a bowl

1. In a medium-sized nonreactive saucepan, combine the raspberries, sugar, and 2 tablespoons of the water or juice. Set over medium heat and cook, stirring and mashing the berries with the back of a large spoon, for 2 to 3 minutes, until the berries release their juice and the sugar dissolves.

2. To remove the seeds, transfer the mixture to a strainer set over a small bowl. Stir and press on the berries with a spoon, then scrape any purée from the underside of the strainer into the bowl. Return the purée to the saucepan.

3. In a cup, dissolve the cornstarch in the remaining 1 tablespoon of water or juice. Add it to the purée and set the pan over high heat. Bring to a boil, stirring constantly; boil 45 to 60 seconds, until thickened and no longer cloudy. Remove from the heat and stir in the liqueur if using. Taste and adjust sugar if necessary. Let the sauce cool.

Nutritional Analysis (per 2-tablespoon serving): 58 calories; 0.4 g protein; 0.3 g fat; 0 g sat-fat; 12 g carbohydrate; 0 mg sodium; 0 mg cholesterol

Light Touch

This sauce gets only 4% of its calories from fat although it is very rich in flavor.

BLUEBERRY-HONEY SAUCE

Yield: About 1¹/₃ cups; 10 generous 2-tablespoon servings

This delectable sauce has a mellow honey overtone spiked with a little orange and lemon juice. A subtle pinch of nutmeg brings out the full berry flavor.

2 cups fresh blueberries, picked over and rinsed, or frozen unsweetened whole berries

¹/₂ cup plus 2 tablespoons fresh orange juice, divided

¹/₄ to ¹/₃ cup honey, to taste

Grated zest of ¹/₂ lemon

1 tablespoon fresh lemon juice

Pinch of ground nutmeg

1 tablespoon cornstarch

1. In a medium-sized heavy-bottomed nonreactive saucepan, combine the berries, ¹/₂ cup of the orange juice, ¹/₄ cup of the honey, the lemon zest and juice, and nutmeg. Set over medium-high heat and cook about 3 minutes, stirring and mashing some of the berries with the back of a wooden spoon, until the berries release their juice. Remove from the heat.

2. In a cup, dissolve the cornstarch in the remaining 2 tablespoons of juice and stir it into the blueberry mixture. Return the pan to high heat and stir, bringing to a full boil for 1 minute, until the sauce is thickened and no longer cloudy. Taste and adjust sweetening if needed. Serve warm or at room temperature.

Nutritional Analysis (per serving): 48 calories; 0.2 g protein; 0.1 g fat; 0 g satfat; 12 g carbohydrate; 2 mg sodium; 0 mg cholesterol

Advance Preparation

Sauce can be prepared ahead and kept covered in the refrigerator for up to 1 week.

Special Equipment:

Medium-sized nonreactive saucepan

Light Touch

With just 2% calories from fat, this sauce contains nothing but great taste.

PLUM SAUCE

Yield: About 1¹/₂ cups; twelve 2-tablespoon servings

This sauce was inspired by the incomparable British culinary writer Jane Grigson. Her Danish plum sauce is one of my favorites, "made with yellow-skinned red plums to go with boiled ham, salt pork and gammon" (Jane Grigson's Fruit Book, Atheneum, 1982). My adaptation is designed for desserts, but it does enhance the odd pork chop. Blending the plums with wine and honey mellows and enriches the flavor. Grigson adds about a tablespoon of tarragon vinegar; I prefer balsamic or raspberry vinegar or a dash of lemon juice to brighten the taste unless the plums are very tart. I like to use Empress, Santa Rosa, or Italian prune plums, but any variety will do.

¹/₂ **pound (about 3 large) plums, pitted and coarsely chopped**
¹/₃ **cup white wine or sweet red vermouth**
2 teaspoons balsamic or raspberry vinegar or fresh lemon juice
¹/₄ **cup honey**
2 tablespoons granulated sugar, only if needed

1. In a 2-quart heavy-bottomed nonreactive saucepan, combine the plums, wine, vinegar, and honey. Cover and simmer over medium heat for 10 to 15 minutes, stirring occasionally, until the plums are very soft.

2. Put the fruit mixture into a food processor or blender and pulse until puréed. Taste and adjust flavoring; if it is too tart, add more honey or a tablespoon or two of sugar. Serve at room temperature.

Nutritional Analysis (per serving): 45 calories; 0 g protein; 0 g fat; 0 g satfat; 10 g carbohydrate; 1 mg sodium; 0 mg cholesterol

Advance Preparation

Sauce may be prepared a day or two ahead, covered, and refrigerated.

Special Equipment

2-quart heavy-bottomed nonreactive saucepan; food processor or blender

Light Touch

The rich taste of this sauce fools you; it has only 4% calories from fat.

BRANDIED CRANBERRY-MAPLE SAUCE

—Yield: About 1¹/₂ cups; twelve 2-tablespoon servings

Bright red and bursting with bold flavor, this sauce has many uses: over plain cake or frozen yogurt, on pancakes or a soufflé, in a trifle or spread on a fruit tart beneath a layer of berries. It has even been known to grace a slice of roast pork or turkey. I like to make big batches of the recipe packed in 1-cup jars to give as house gifts for holiday presents.

2 cups fresh or frozen whole cranberries

¹/₂ cup fresh orange juice

¹/₂ cup granulated or packed light brown sugar

¹/₃ cup pure maple syrup

Pinch of ground cinnamon

Grated zest of ¹/₂ orange

2 to 3 tablespoons brandy, or to taste

1. In a medium-sized heavy-bottomed nonreactive saucepan, combine the berries and orange juice, cover, and bring to a boil. Reduce the heat slightly and cook for 5 to 8 minutes, until the berries pop and release their juice.

2. Remove the pan from the heat and stir in the sugar, maple syrup, cinnamon, orange zest, and brandy. Taste and adjust the flavoring if needed.

Nutritional Analysis (per serving): 74 calories; 0 g protein; 0 g fat; 0 g satfat; 18 g carbohydrate; 0 mg sodium; 0 mg cholesterol

Advance Preparation

Sauce can be made in advance and stored covered in the refrigerator up to 1 month.

Special Equipment

Medium-sized heavy-bottomed nonreactive saucepan

Light Touch

This is as light as it gets: 1% calories from fat.

BOURBON CREAM SAUCE

Yield: Scant 1¹/₂ cups; 10 scant 2¹/₂-tablespoon servings

The perfect sauce to serve warm over Steamed Fig-Date-Apricot Pudding (page 194) or Upside-down Apple Bread Pudding (page 182). For a change, you can omit the milk and bourbon, making a plain spiced cider sauce that is equally good, or go for broke and use a little heavy cream.

1 cup apple cider or apple juice, divided

¹/₄ cup packed dark brown sugar

1 teaspoon lightly salted butter

¹/₈ teaspoon ground ginger

¹/₈ teaspoon ground cinnamon

¹/₄ teaspoon ground nutmeg

1 tablespoon plus ¹/₂ teaspoon cornstarch

¹/₄ cup bourbon, applejack, or Calvados, or to taste

¹/₄ cup evaporated skim milk or 1% milk or heavy cream

Advance Preparation

Sauce can be prepared 1 day ahead, covered, and refrigerated. Warm before serving.

Special Equipment

1¹/₂-quart saucepan

---

1. In a small saucepan, combine ³/₄ cup of the cider or apple juice, the brown sugar, butter, and spices. Stir over medium heat for about 3 minutes, until the sugar dissolves.

2. In a cup, dissolve the cornstarch in the remaining ¹/₄ cup of cider or juice; add it to the hot cider mixture. Increase the heat and bring the mixture to a boil, stirring for 45 to 60 seconds, until thickened and no longer cloudy. Remove from the heat and stir in the bourbon and evaporated milk. Serve warm.

Nutritional Analysis (per serving with evaporated skim milk and bourbon): 58 calories; 0.5 g protein; 0.4 g fat; 0 g satfat; 10 g carbohydrate; 13 mg sodium; 1 mg cholesterol

Light Touch

With the evaporated skim milk and bourbon, this sauce contains 6% calories from fat. If you eliminate the milk and bourbon, you have fewer ingredients, so the percentage climbs to 9%. Heavy cream gives a richer taste but also adds 32% calories from fat plus 15 calories, 2 g fat, and 8 mg cholestereol per serving.

PRALINE SAUCE

Try this sweet sauce warm over Upside-down Apple Bread Pudding (page 182) or frozen vanilla yogurt or sponge cake. In New Orleans, praline sauce is a staple, served plain or fancy with a dash of bourbon or rum and a little heavy cream.

I have adapted this recipe from one developed in the test kitchen of Eating Well *magazine; it is used with their kind permission.*

2 teaspoons unsalted butter

1/4 cup pecans, chopped

1 tablespoon cornstarch

Pinch of salt

1/3 cup 2% milk

1 cup packed dark brown sugar

1 teaspoon vanilla extract

1 tablespoon bourbon or dark rum (optional)

2 tablespoons heavy cream (optional)

Advance Preparation

Sauce can be prepared ahead, covered, and refrigerated for up to 1 week.

Special Equipment

1 1/2-quart saucepan

---

1. In a small saucepan, stir together the butter and chopped pecans over medium heat. Cook, stirring, 1 to 2 minutes, until the nuts are toasted and aromatic. Remove the pan from the heat.

2. In a small cup, dissolve the cornstarch and salt in the milk, then add to the nuts. Crumble in the brown sugar and stir to mix.

3. Return the pan to medium heat and stir or whisk until the sauce reaches a boil. Boil about 45 seconds, until thickened and no longer cloudy. Remove from the heat. Stir in the vanilla and the bourbon or dark rum and cream, if used.

Nutritional Analysis (per serving without bourbon or cream): 72 calories; 0 g protein; 1.7 g fat; 0 g satfat; 14 g carbohydrate; 15 mg sodium; 2 mg cholesterol

Light Touch

In its plain form, this sauce contains 21% calories from fat. If you add a tablespoon of bourbon, the damage is imperceptible (2 extra calories). If you also add 2 tablespoons heavy cream, you raise the original numbers by 9 calories, nearly 1 g fat, and 2 mg cholesterol; calories from fat rises to 26%. Still not fatal, and worth it if you put the sauce on something that is extremely low in fat.

CARAMEL SAUCE

Yield: 1 cup; 12 scant 1/2-tablespoon servings

This is a sweet caramel-flavored sauce. Evaporated skim milk is used because it is concentrated and so provides greater richness than regular low-fat milk. Note: For Extra-Thick Caramel Sauce, use only 1/3 cup plus 1 tablespoon evaporated skim milk; makes 3/4 cup, 10 to 12 servings.

1 cup granulated sugar

1/3 cup water

1 tablespoon unsalted butter

3/4 cup evaporated skim milk

1 teaspoon dark corn syrup

1 teaspoon vanilla extract

1. In a 2-quart heavy-bottomed saucepan, combine the sugar and water. Stir once or twice, then use a pastry brush dipped into cold water to wash down the sides of the pan to prevent sugar crystallization. Clip a candy thermometer to the pan if using. Bring to a boil over medium-high heat, swirling the pan gently once or twice at first but not stirring. Boil for about 15 minutes, until the syrup turns a medium amber color (300°F on the candy thermometer). Remove the pan at once from the heat, as it can burn quickly at this point.

2. Let cool for about 1 minute, then stir in the butter. Slowly add the milk, stirring constantly. (The cool milk will bubble up and cause the caramel to solidify somewhat.) Return the pan to low heat and stir constantly for 2 or 3 minutes, until the caramel dissolves and the sauce is smooth.

3. Remove from the heat and stir in the corn syrup and vanilla. Cool completely before serving. The sauce thickens as it cools.

Nutritional Analysis (per serving): 84 calories; 1 g protein; 1 g fat; 0.6 g satfat; 18 g carbohydrate; 19 mg sodium; 3 mg cholesterol

Nutritional Analysis Extra-Thick Caramel Sauce (per serving): 94 calories; 1 g protein; 1 g fat; 0.7 g satfat; 21 g carbohydrate; 12 mg sodium; 4 mg cholesterol

Advance Preparation

Sauce can be prepared ahead, covered, and refrigerated for up to 1 week.

Special Equipment

2-quart heavy-bottomed saucepan; pastry brush; candy thermometer (optional)

Light Touch

With a deeply satisfying caramel flavor, this recipe gets only 11% of its calories from fat. When made the traditional way, using 1 cup heavy cream instead of evaporated milk and adding 3 tablespoons of butter, the figure leaps to 57%.

CHOCOLATE SAUCE

Yield: About ³/₄ cup; six 2-tablespoon servings

This all-purpose intensely chocolate sauce is most successful when made with a Dutch-processed (alkalized) unsweetened cocoa such as Droste, Fedora, or another imported brand; these taste slightly less bitter than regular cocoa. You can vary the flavor by adding 2 tablespoons of coffee liqueur, orange liqueur, raspberry brandy, or hazelnut liqueur.

Advance Preparation

Sauce can be made ahead, covered, and refrigerated about 1 week.

Special Equipment

1¹/₂-quart saucepan

¹/₃ cup unsifted unsweetened Dutch-processed cocoa

1 tablespoon cornstarch

¹/₄ cup plus 2 tablespoons packed dark brown sugar

¹/₃ cup skim milk

¹/₄ cup dark or light corn syrup

1 teaspoon vanilla extract or 2 tablespoons flavored liqueur

1. In a small saucepan, whisk together the cocoa, cornstarch, and brown sugar. Add the milk and whisk well, then add the corn syrup.

2. Set the pan over medium heat and stir while bringing it to a full boil. Lower the heat slightly and cook, whisking constantly, about 1 minute longer, until the sauce thickens and will generously coat a spoon. Remove it from the heat and stir in the vanilla or other flavoring if used. Cool, then refrigerate in a covered jar.

Nutritional Analysis (per serving): 115 calories; 1 g protein; 1 g fat; 0.5 g satfat; 28 g carbohydrate; 55 mg sodium; 0 mg cholesterol

Light Touch

This rich chocolatey sauce gets only 7% of its calories from fat.

STEVE'S SPA CHOCOLATE SAUCE

Yield: About 1½ cups; twelve 2-tablespoon servings

This is my adaptation of a creation by Steve Keneipp, chef/proprietor of the Classic Kitchen restaurant in Noblesville, Indiana. Dark, chocolatey, and very low in sugar; it is an unusual blend of cocoa, honey, and unsweetened grape juice concentrate. The taste is intense and a little different at first because it is not as sweet as a classic chocolate syrup. To gild the lily, you can jazz it up with a few tablespoons of your favorite liqueur.

To make a quick and easy server for the sauce, Steve likes to use a squeezable plastic "perm" bottle (sold at beauty supply shops). To make his famous Spa Sundae, drizzle about 1 generous tablespoon of the sauce over ½ cup of the best-quality nonfat frozen yogurt topped with fresh berries or cut-up fruit. Garnish with a mint sprig.

Advance Preparation

The sauce can be made 3 or 4 days ahead, covered, and refrigerated. Bring to room temperature before serving.

Special Equipment

Medium-sized saucepan

½ cup frozen unsweetened white grape juice concentrate, thawed but not diluted

½ cup honey

6 tablespoons water

1 cup unsifted unsweetened Dutch-processed cocoa

¼ teaspoon ground nutmeg

2 teaspoons vanilla extract

2 to 3 tablespoons flavored liqueur, such as Grand Marnier or Frangelico (hazelnut) (optional)

1. In a medium-sized saucepan, combine and bring to a simmer the juice concentrate, honey, and water. Whisk in the cocoa and nutmeg, beating until completely smooth and just beginning to boil. The mixture will be thick enough to coat a spoon.

2. Remove it from the heat. Whisk in the vanilla and any liqueur if using it. Pour into a bowl and chill. The sauce thickens as it cools.

Nutritional Analysis (per serving with 2 tablespoons liqueur): 88 calories; 1 g protein; 1 g fat; 0.8 g satfat; 20 g carbohydrate; 56 mg sodium; 0 mg cholesterol

Light Touch

Cocoa powder has almost all its saturated fat removed, so it gives a rich chocolate taste without the fat of solid chocolate. This recipe is useful for individuals with diabetes or on other special diets because it is sweetened with juice concentrate and honey instead of sugar; it contains a mere 12% calories from fat.

Glazes,
FROSTINGS, TOPPINGS,
AND FINISHING TOUCHES

All the recipes in this section are designed to top or garnish a dessert, either as an integral part of the recipe or as a finishing touch. Fruit glazes contain no fat, but add flavor, color, and an attractive appearance to fruit desserts, pies, and tarts. Oat Streusel (crumb) Topping adds texture to any baked fruit mixture. Icing glazes are used to drizzle or spread over baked goods. When a glamorous (but not buttery) icing is called for on a cake, use Seven-Minute Icing or Boiled Icing, a type of Italian meringue.

For a wedding cake or other lavish occasion when a little extravagance is called for, try the fat-reduced but delicious Orange Buttercream Frosting or Orange-Chocolate Frosting.

ALL-PURPOSE FRUIT GLAZE

Yield: 1 cup; enough to glaze two 9- to 11-inch tarts or one 2-layer 8- or 9-inch cake

This is a fruit glaze to use on top of fruit tarts, as a moisture-proof undercoating beneath fruit tart filling, or to coat cakes before icing them. Use apricot preserves or red currant jelly, whichever flavor and color best complement your fruit tart or cake.

1 cup best-quality apricot preserves or red currant jelly

2 tablespoons kirsch or other fruit liqueur (optional)

Special Equipment

1¹/₂-quart saucepan; sieve; pastry brush

1. In a small saucepan, stir the preserves or jelly over medium heat until melted.

2. Strain the preserves through a sieve (return fruit pieces to the preserves jar). Return the liquefied preserves to the saucepan, add liqueur if using it, and bring the mixture to a boil over medium heat. Let it cook a minute or two, until the glaze begins to thicken. Cool slightly.

3. Use a pastry brush to coat the dry fruit on top of a tart, or to coat a cake. Chill the pastry to set the glaze.

Nutritional Analysis (per 1¹/₂ tablespoons with liqueur): 96 calories; 0 g protein; 0 g fat; 0 g satfat; 23 g carbohydrate; 3 mg sodium; 0 mg cholesterol

Light Touch

You can't get lighter than this. It's free of everything except some fruit.

FIRM FRUIT GLAZE

Yield: About 1/2 cup; enough to glaze one 9- to 11-inch tart or one 8- or 9-inch cake

Use this glaze to top a fruit tart that must be held several hours before serving. The preserves are mixed with a little gelatin to keep the glaze from melting.

1/2 cup best-quality apricot preserves or red currant jelly
1 1/2 teaspoons unflavored gelatin
2 tablespoons kirsch or other fruit liqueur or fruit juice

> **Special Equipment**
>
> *1 1/2-quart saucepan; sieve*

1. In a small saucepan over medium heat, stir the preserves until melted. Then strain through a sieve, spoon any fruit segments into the preserves jar, and return the liquid preserves to the saucepan.

2. In a cup, stir together the gelatin and liqueur or fruit juice. Add to the preserves in the saucepan and stir over medium-low heat until the gelatin is completely dissolved. To test, pinch a drop between your fingers; if it is dissolved, you will not feel any graininess. Simmer the mixture about 30 seconds, then cool until warm to the touch before brushing it over the top of a fruit tart or cake. Chill to set the glaze.

Nutritional Analysis (per 1 1/2 teaspoons): 33 calories; 0 g protein; 0 g fat; 0 g satfat; 8 carbohydrate; 1 mg sodium; 0 mg cholesterol

Light Touch

Totally fat and cholesterol free, this has minimal calories and is as light as they come.

VANILLA ICING GLAZE

*Yield: 1/3 cup glaze; enough to glaze one
9-inch pie or cake*

*Spread this glaze over Bundt, tube, or layer cakes and cookies. The glaze hardens
as it dries. Variations follow for Orange, Lemon, or Cocoa Icing Glaze.*

1 cup sifted confectioners' sugar

**1½ to 2 tablespoons skim milk, fresh orange or lemon juice,
or strong black coffee (depending upon flavor desired)**

¼ teaspoon vanilla, almond, or maple extract

Advance Preparation

*The glaze can be made
several hours in advance
but must be kept sealed
with plastic wrap or it
will develop a crust on
top and dry out.*

1. Whisk together the sugar, 1½ tablespoons of the milk or other liquid, and the extract. Add a few more drops of milk or other liquid if needed to make the glaze soft enough to drip from a spoon.

2. Drizzle lacy-looking lines of icing over pastry, or spread it in a single, thin layer with the back of a spoon, letting it drip down the sides of the pastry or cake.

Nutritional Analysis (per scant tablespoon): 67 calories; 0 g protein; 0 g fat; 0 g satfat; 17 g carbohydrate; 4 mg sodium; 0 mg cholesterol

ORANGE OR LEMON ICING GLAZE

*Yield: 1 scant cup, enough to glaze an 8- or 9-inch
tube cake; double the recipe for a 10-inch tube cake*

*Use this to glaze an angel food cake or any sponge cake. Whisk together 1½ cups
sifted confectioners' sugar, 1 teaspoon grated orange or lemon zest, 3 tablespoons
fresh orange or lemon juice, and 2 teaspoons fresh lemon juice (whichever flavor
you use). Adjust for consistency and flavor, adding more liquid or sugar as needed.
Glaze should be runny, like heavy cream.*

COCOA ICING GLAZE

Yield: 1/2 cup

*Sift together 1 cup confectioners' sugar and 3 tablespoons unsweetened cocoa.
Whisk in 1/2 teaspoon vanilla extract, and 3 tablespoons water or skim milk, as
needed. Use as described above.*

Light Touch

Vanilla Icing Glaze is fat and cholesterol free. Orange or Lemon Icing Glaze has 50 calories and 13 g carbohydrate, but no fat or cholesterol. The trace amounts of fat in the Cocoa Icing Glaze give it a scant 6% calories from fat.

COOKIE FROSTING

*Yield: About 3/4 cup; enough to decorate about
4 dozen cookies*

Use this frosting to decorate festive cookies. Color it with liquid, paste, or powdered vegetable colors or, if you wish to avoid vegetable dyes, use seedless raspberry jam for pink and frozen orange juice concentrate (undiluted) for yellow-orange, substituting it for liquid in the recipe. Note: To make an easy decorating bag, cut a tiny hole in one corner of a heavy-duty pint-size plastic bag; add frosting, close the bag, and squeeze. Or drop a decorative metal icing tip into the hole in the plastic bag, so the icing will be forced out through the tip.

2 cups sifted confectioners' sugar

1 teaspoon vanilla extract or fresh lemon juice, strained

3 to 5 tablespoons skim milk or water or fruit juice, or as needed

> **Special Equipment**
>
> *Electric mixer; clean new paintbrush (optional)*

1. Measure the sugar into a bowl and use an electric mixer on low to beat in the extract plus 3 tablespoons of liquid. Slowly add additional liquid until the frosting is the correct consistency. It should spread easily and be perfectly smooth—about the consistency of soft cream cheese if you are spreading it with a butter knife or piping it through a decorating bag fitted with a small round tip.

2. To make a glaze that you can spread on with a clean new paintbrush, add more liquid so the frosting flows. To color the frosting, divide it among small cups and add a drop or two of different vegetable colors.

Nutritional Analysis (per scant teaspoon): 16 calories; 0 g protein; 0 g fat; 0 g satfat; 4 g carbohydrate; 1 mg sodium; 0 mg cholesterol

Light Touch

This fat-free icing can be freely used on all types of cookies.

LIGHT CREAM CHEESE FROSTING

Yield: About 1³/4 cups; enough to cover 2 cake layers (not the sides) or one 9-inch tube cake

Here is a moderate cream cheese icing which I include for diehards like me who can't live without it.

1¹/2 cup (12 ounces) light cream cheese, at room temperature

¹/2 cup sifted confectioners' sugar

2 teaspoons vanilla extract

1. In a food processor or blender, combine all ingredients and process until smooth. Or combine the ingredients in a bowl and beat with an electric mixer.

2. If made ahead and chilled, bring to room temperature and beat before spreading.

Nutritional Analysis (per scant 3 tablespoons): 94 calories; 4 g protein; 6 g fat; 0 g satfat; 8 g carbohydrate; 192 mg sodium; 12 mg cholesterol

Light Touch

Although made with light cream cheese (which has half the calories of regular), this is hardly light with 57% of its calories coming from fat; nevertheless, this recipe is an improvement on the original. Although proportions vary, one of my old favorites blends ¹/2 cup butter and 8 ounces cream cheese with 4 cups confectioners' sugar; it has more than three times the fat and four times the cholesterol per serving.

ORANGE BUTTERCREAM FROSTING

Yield: 2 cups; enough to frost top and sides of a 2-layer 8- or 9-inch cake

This is a fine ivory-colored creamy frosting for any festive layer cake; in addition to the vanilla, use 1 teaspoon of any flavoring extract you wish to complement the flavor of your cake. Use this frosting for the Fresh Orange Wedding Cake on page 168; you will need five times the basic recipe (use 1 teaspoon orange extract per batch in addition to the vanilla). If using a hand-held beater, avoid making more than three times the recipe (6 cups) in one bowl. This recipe was developed with Cooking Light *magazine and is used with their permission.*

Advance Preparation

Best made no more than 1 day in advance, covered, and refrigerated. If made ahead, bring to room temperature, add a teaspoon or two of low-fat milk and beat until spreadable before using.

$^{1}/_{3}$ **cup unsalted butter, softened but not melted**

2 tablespoons light cream cheese, at room temperature

1$^{1}/_{2}$ teaspoons vanilla extract

1 teaspoon orange extract (for wedding cake) or other extract

Pinch of salt

4$^{1}/_{2}$ cups sifted confectioners' sugar

5 teaspoons skim milk

1. In a large mixing bowl, cream together the butter and cream cheese with an electric mixer on medium speed. When light and fluffy, add both extracts and salt and beat well.

2. With the mixer on lowest speed, add the confectioners' sugar and milk, beating until blended. Increase the speed to medium and beat until spreadable. Cover and refrigerate until ready to use.

Nutritional Analysis (per 3 tablespoons): 241 calories; 0.4 g protein; 7 g fat; 4.0 g satfat; 46 g carbohydrate; 32 mg sodium; 18 mg cholesterol

Light Touch

It won't surprise you that my classic wedding cake frosting, French egg yolk buttercream, weighs in at 79% calories from fat. By removing all the yolks and nearly all the butter, I have reduced the fat by 68% to 25% and dropped 100 calories and over one quarter the fat per serving. I have kept a little butter and added some light cream cheese, to give the proper texture and taste. Flavor is further enhanced by adding vanilla with another flavoring agent or extract.

ORANGE-CHOCOLATE FROSTING

Yield: 2 cups; enough to frost top and sides of a 2-layer 9-inch cake; 12 servings

This frosting will remind you of childhood birthday cakes; it is sugary, but has a strong orange-chocolate flavor to balance the sweetness.

1/4 cup low-fat sour cream (not fat-free)

3 tablespoons unsalted butter, softened but not melted

1 tablespoon vanilla extract

1 1/2 teaspoons orange extract

1/4 cup fresh orange juice or water, or as needed

3/4 cup sifted unsweetened Dutch-processed cocoa

4 cups sifted confectioners' sugar

Advance Preparation

Frosting can be made a day or two ahead, covered with plastic wrap, and refrigerated.

1. In a large mixing bowl, cream together the sour cream, butter, both extracts, and orange juice or water with an electric mixer on medium speed.

2. With the mixer on low speed, slowly beat in the sifted cocoa and sugar, blending until thick and creamy. Add a teaspoon of additional liquid if too thick to spread. If frosting has been made ahead and chilled, bring to room temperature, add a drop of liquid if needed, and beat until smooth before using.

Nutritional Analysis (per generous 2 1/2-tablespoon serving): 200 calories; 1 g protein; 4 g fat; 2.5 g satfat; 42 g carbohydrate; 44 mg sodium; 8 mg cholesterol

Light Touch

With just 19% calories from fat, this recipe is a flavorful substitute for a classic (80%) chocolate buttercream that has an extra 100 calories and about 20 g fat per serving.

SEVEN-MINUTE ICING

Yield: 3 cups; enough to fill and frost a 2-layer 8- or 9-inch cake

This white satin whipped meringue makes a fluffy cake icing or filling. It is easier to make than Boiled Icing (page 279) because the ingredients are whipped together in a double boiler, making it unnecessary to cook a sugar syrup to pour over whipped whites. Although this is called Seven-Minute Icing, it can take 5 to 8 minutes to reach the ideal consistency, depending upon heat, type of beater, and size of eggs. Variations follow for Maple, Orange, Lemon, and Seafoam (caramel) Icings and Honey Cream Clouds.

In my tests with this technique, I found that the whites were heated to a sufficiently high temperature for a long enough time to destroy any possible bacteria; in fact, this method is slightly safer than the Boiled Icing method because the heat is more direct. Don't try to freeze cakes coated with this icing; the icing tends to break down and get runny when it thaws.

Special Equipment

Double boiler or saucepan with round-bottomed metal bowl that fits over it; hand-held electric mixer

2 large egg whites

1¹/₂ cups granulated sugar

5 tablespoons cold water

2 teaspoons light corn syrup

¹/₄ teaspoon cream of tartar

1 teaspoon vanilla extract (optional)

1. Set up the bottom of a double boiler, or a saucepan, with just enough water in it that the top part or a bowl can sit above it without getting wet. Bring the water to a simmer.

2. Combine all the ingredients except the vanilla in the top of the double boiler or a metal bowl. Place it over the simmering water. Immediately begin beating with a hand-held electric mixer on medium speed. (You can whip with a rotary beater or whisk, but it may take up to 14 minutes.) Whip on medium-low speed for 3 minutes, then increase to high and whip about 3 minutes longer, until the icing is a satiny foam that holds soft peaks and mounds on the beater.

3. Remove the pan from the heat, stir in the vanilla if used, then beat for 1 full minute longer, until the icing is thicker, satiny, and holds stiff peaks.

4. When using this for cake icing, beat a full 7 minutes; if you will be adding this to a meringue or a mousse, whip for only about 6 minutes. Use immediately, before the outer surface air-dries.

Nutritional Analysis (per ¹/₄ cup): 12 calories; 0 g protein; 0 g fat; 0 g satfat; 3 g carbohydrate; 1 mg sodium; 0 mg cholesterol

continued

MAPLE SEVEN-MINUTE ICING

Prepare recipe as directed, but replace the granulated sugar with $^3/4$ cup pure maple syrup. This whips to stiff peaks in about 6 minutes.

ORANGE SEVEN-MINUTE ICING

Prepare recipe as directed, but substitute $^1/2$ teaspoon orange extract for the vanilla and add 2 teaspoons grated orange zest to the finished icing.

LEMON SEVEN-MINUTE ICING

Prepare recipe as directed, but use only 3 tablespoons water plus 2 tablespoons fresh lemon juice in the pan. Add 1 teaspoon grated lemon zest to the finished icing.

SEAFOAM SEVEN-MINUTE ICING

Yield: 4 cups

Caramel flavored. Prepare recipe as directed, but replace the granulated sugar with $1^1/2$ cups packed dark brown sugar, and add $^1/2$ teaspoon almond extract along with the vanilla.

HONEY CREAM CLOUDS

Yield: 4 cups

Prepare recipe as directed with these changes: Omit the water, corn syrup, and cream of tartar. Combine the egg whites with $^3/4$ cup honey. Whip up to 9 or $9^1/2$ minutes for stiff peaks. The color will be pale beige, with a smooth satin texture. Flavor with vanilla extract if you wish, or use $^3/4$ teaspoon orange extract.

Light Touch

This is what Pure Light means: zero fat, zero cholesterol, just a few calories.

BOILED ICING

Yield: About 3¹/₂ cups; enough to fill and frost a 2-layer 8- or 9-inch cake

This thick, shiny white satin icing (also known as Divinity or White Mountain) is an old-fashioned favorite. It is basically a classic cooked-syrup Italian meringue with a slight adjustment in the cooking temperature of the syrup poured over the whipped whites. Try the many variations following the master recipe: Beige Mountain, Lemon, Orange, or Cocoa.

¹/₃ cup water

³/₄ cup plus 2 tablespoons granulated sugar, divided

1 tablespoon light corn syrup or ¹/₈ teaspoon cream of tartar

3 large egg whites, at room temperature

1 teaspoon vanilla extract

Special Equipment

2-quart heavy-bottomed saucepan; candy thermometer; pastry brush

1. In a 2-quart heavy-bottomed saucepan, stir together the water, ³/₄ cup of the sugar, and the corn syrup or cream of tartar. Set over medium heat and cook until the sugar is dissolved; don't stir again, but swirl the pan several times.

2. To prevent crystallization, wash down the pan sides with a pastry brush dipped in cold water. Clip a candy thermometer to the pan and increase the heat to medium-high. Bring the syrup to a boil and cook without stirring for 7 to 8 minutes, until the thermometer reads 239° to 242°F, or when a little syrup will form a soft ball when dropped into ice water.

3. Meanwhile, when the syrup is almost cooked, begin to whip the egg whites. In a grease-free mixing bowl with an electric mixer on medium speed, whip until the whites are foamy. Add the remaining 2 tablespoons of sugar, and whip until *nearly* stiff.

4. As soon as the sugar syrup registers the specified temperature, remove it from the heat and gradually pour it over the whites while whipping them on medium-low speed. Pour the syrup in a steady stream between the bowl side and the beater; do not scrape in the hardened bits of syrup. Continue whipping until the whites are stiff and satiny and feel cool, about 5 minutes. Whip in the vanilla or other extract and use immediately.

Nutritional Analysis: (per 5²/₃ tablespoons): 74 calories; 1 g protein; 0 g fat; 0 g satfat; 18 g carbohydrate; 18 mg sodium; 0 mg cholesterol

BEIGE MOUNTAIN BOILED ICING

Prepare recipe as directed, but substitute 1¹/₂ cups packed dark or light brown sugar for the ³/₄ cup granulated sugar.

continued

LEMON BOILED ICING

Prepare recipe as directed, but substitute 1 tablespoon fresh lemon juice for the vanilla extract and add $1/2$ teaspoon grated lemon zest. If you like a stronger flavor, add $1/2$ teaspoon lemon extract.

ORANGE BOILED ICING

Prepare recipe as directed, but substitute 1 tablespoon frozen unsweetened orange juice concentrate, thawed but undiluted, for the vanilla extract and add 2 teaspoons grated orange zest.

COCOA BOILED ICING

Prepare recipe as directed, but sift $1/4$ cup unsweetened cocoa into 1 cup of the finished and cooled icing. Stir this back into the entire batch, then whip a few seconds just to blend.

Light Touch

Besides a few calories, there's not much in this: a few calories but zero calories from fat. The variations have slight changes in ingredients, but the fat content varies very little.

MARBLEIZED SOUR CREAM TOPPING

Yield: 1¼ cups; enough for one 8- or 9-inch cake

This quick and easy topping is thick enough to cover any number of problems with a cake top, from cracks to a rough surface. The topping does not need to be cooked, but it should be refrigerated.

Topping
2 tablespoons granulated sugar
1 cup low-fat sour cream

Chocolate Mixture
1 ounce semisweet chocolate, melted
2 tablespoons low-fat sour cream

In a bowl, whisk the 2 tablespoons of sugar into the 1 cup sour cream. Spread this over the cake top, covering any irregularities in the surface. In a cup, stir together the melted chocolate and 2 tablespoons of sour cream. Spoon this mixture into a self-sealing plastic bag, cut a tiny hole in one corner, and squeeze the chocolate mixture onto the cake top, making a design.

To create a marbleized pattern, draw S-shaped lines, then pull a knife tip through the lines.

Special Equipment

Pint-sized self-sealing Baggie

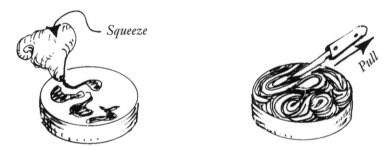

Marbleized top

To make a feathered pattern like the top of a napoleon pastry, draw parallel vertical lines about 1 inch apart across the top of the cake, then turn it 180 degrees so the lines are now horizontal. Draw a knife tip through the lines in a series of parallel motions, each line going in the opposite direction.

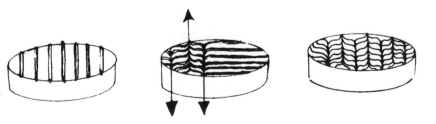

Straight feather

continued

To make a feathered spiral, draw a spiral of chocolate lines, then pull a knife tip through the spiral like spokes in a wheel, with each line going in the opposite direction either toward or away from the center.

Spiral feather

Nutritional Analysis (per 2 tablespoons): 55 calories; 1 g protein; 2.5 g fat; 0 g satfat; 7 g carbohydrate; 21 mg sodium; 0 mg cholesterol

Light Touch

This topping is meant to accompany a reduced-fat cake, so the above figures would never be taken alone. However, by itself, the recipe contains about 41% calories from fat. Note: This recipe is gluten free if the stabilizers in the sour cream are not made from cereals (check label or call manufacturer).

OAT STREUSEL TOPPING

Yield: About 1 1/2 cups; enough for an 8- or 9-inch cake, crisp, or pie

This all-purpose crumble mixture provides taste and texture for the top of any coffee cake, fruit crisp, or pie.

1/2 **cup all-purpose flour or whole-wheat flour**

1/8 **teaspoon salt**

1/2 **teaspoon ground cinnamon**

1/2 **teaspoon ground nutmeg**

1/2 **cup packed dark or light brown sugar**

1/4 **cup old-fashioned rolled oats (not quick-cooking type)**

2 **tablespoons toasted wheat germ (optional)**

2 **tablespoons Grape-Nuts cereal**

1/2 **teaspoon vanilla or almond extract**

2 **tablespoons canola or walnut oil**

1 **tablespoon plus 1 teaspoon skim milk or apple or orange juice, or more if needed**

1. In a bowl, combine and toss together all the dry ingredients.

2. Add the extract, oil, and milk or juice and blend with a fork. If necessary, add more liquid a drop at a time until the mixture forms crumbs. Use as directed in recipe, piling crumbs on top of fruit mixture before baking.

Nutritional Analysis (per scant 2 1/2 tablespoons, with wheat germ): 108 calories; 2 g protein; 3 g fat; trace satfat; 18 g carbohydrate; 40 mg sodium; 0 mg cholesterol

Advance Preparation

Crumbs can be prepared 1 day in advance, covered, and refrigerated. Crumble before spreading.

Light Touch

This nutritious recipe gets 26% calories from fat; the predominant source of fat is the oil. Grape-Nuts substitute for high-fat walnuts but a nutty flavor can be brought out by using nut oil and almond extract. For more flavor, you could crumble into the mixture 1 tablespoon unsalted butter, but that would add 11 calories and 1 g fat per serving.

FINISHING TOUCHES

—❧—

Fat-reduced cakes are not meant to be laden with elaborate embellishments and rich frostings. Nevertheless, they must be presented in their loveliest aspect, appealing to all the diner's senses. The ideas for quick finishing touches that follow are free of fat but loaded with appeal and easy to prepare. Decorate with fresh fruit, cut in unusual designs. Model Apricot Roses by simply rolling up petals cut from commercial apricot roll-ups bought in any deli; you can make your own sheet apricot from dried fruit if you prefer. Sugared Rose Petals and Sugared Grapes dry to a crisp finish and add a romantic touch to any cake top. For high drama on top of a rich cheesecake, pile up a mound of caramelized Amber Sugar Beads or stand up a series of dramatic gleaming shards of Cracked Caramel. Chocolate Curls and Shavings are a cinch to make, as are molded Chocolate Plastic Decorations, yet they give a professional finishing touch to any cake.

DECORATING WITH FRUIT

Instead of frosting, use fresh fruit and berries arranged in a variety of patterns on top of a layer of fruit preserves to decorate the top of a reduced-fat cake, tart, tartlets, or pie.

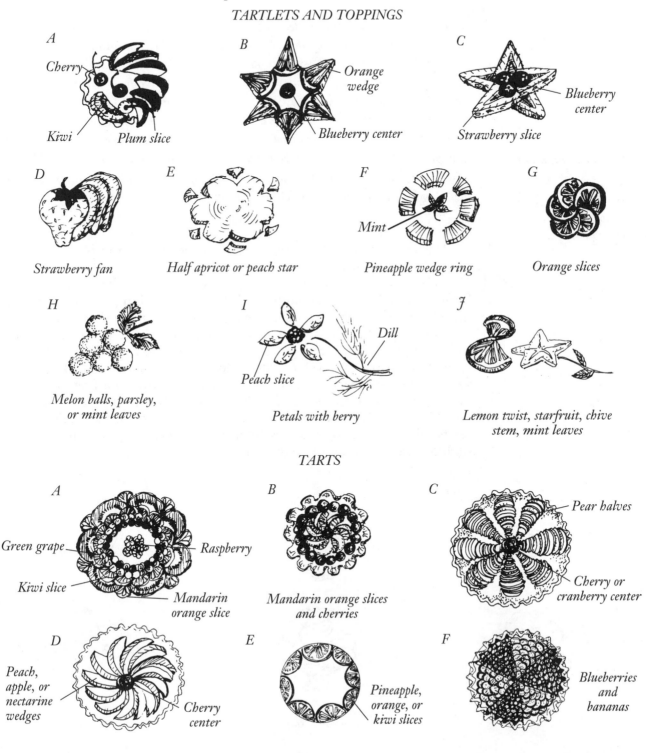

TARTLETS AND TOPPINGS

A
Cherry
Kiwi
Plum slice

B
Orange wedge
Blueberry center

C
Blueberry center
Strawberry slice

D
Strawberry fan

E
Half apricot or peach star

F
Mint
Pineapple wedge ring

G
Orange slices

H
Melon balls, parsley, or mint leaves

I
Dill
Peach slice
Petals with berry

J
Lemon twist, starfruit, chive stem, mint leaves

TARTS

A
Green grape
Kiwi slice
Raspberry
Mandarin orange slice

B
Mandarin orange slices and cherries

C
Pear halves
Cherry or cranberry center

D
Peach, apple, or nectarine wedges
Cherry center

E
Pineapple, orange, or kiwi slices

F
Blueberries and bananas

Glazes, Frostings, Toppings, and Finishing Touches   285

APRICOT ROSES

Yield: One average-sized fruit roll (about 7-inch diameter) makes 1 rose with 12 petals; a 4-inch roll will make a rosebud; 2 will make a full rose. Use additional fruit rolls to cut out flat leaf shapes. If using dried apricots, you need 12 to 15 halves to make 3 full roses.

An apricot rose is an elegant decoration for any flavor cake, and nothing is easier to make if you use sheets of store-bought apricot leather (also called fruit rolls or roll-ups or fruit strips). They are sold in natural food stores and supermarkets, sometimes in the candy section. The best flavors, and colors, are plain apricot, strawberry, and cherry; you may also find a variety of bright (quite unappetizing) colors embossed with cartoon designs. If the latter are all you have to work with, they do fine (the designs get lost when the roses are formed); select the most attractive color to complement your cake (yellow or pink, for example, not bright blue).

If you don't have fruit leather available, you can make apricot roses from moist, halved dried apricots as described below.

Special Equipment

Scissors or kitchen shears; wax paper or plastic wrap; toothpicks; tray; rolling pin, if using dried apricots

Procedure Using Fruit Leather

It is easiest to cut the leather with its paper backing in place. To make the cone that forms the rose center, cut one rectangle of leather about $1\frac{1}{2} \times 3$ inches (*A*) and fold it in the center, wrapping the ends around to form a cone (*B*); pinch the bottom edges in and hold in place for a minute; the warmth of your hand is usually enough to make them stick; if not, use a drop of water. Follow the diagrams to cut shapes about $1\frac{1}{2}$ inches square with rounded tops for the petals (*C*); position them in overlapping rows around the central cone (*D, E*). After adding enough petals to make the correct-size rose, roll back the top edge of each petal with your fingertip. Pinch the base to be sure all the petals adhere, then cut away any excess base and set the rose on the cake top or a tray. Use scissors to cut flat leaf shapes to set beside the rose. The leaves look more lifelike if placed in irregular, slightly raised positions (*F*) rather than flat.

A   3"

$1\frac{1}{2}$"

B

← *Pinch* ←

C

Petal

D

E

F

Apricot Rose

Procedure Using Moist Dried Apricot Halves

Arrange a layer of moist apricot halves, sticky side down, between 2 sheets of plastic wrap or wax paper sprinkled lightly with granulated sugar. With a rolling pin, roll the apricots very thin, but stop before they get holes in them (about $1/16$ inch). To make the central core rosebud, peel off one apricot half and roll it up, sticky side in, forming a cone shape. Press the base to adhere. To add the first petal, peel one rolled apricot half off the paper and wrap it around the center bud, sticky side in, pressing at the base. Add another petal overlapping the first by about half. Continue positioning the petals in overlapping rows. After the first three, stop and use your fingertip to gently roll back the top edge of each petal, giving it a natural shape. Squeeze the base to hold the petals together; if they don't adhere, stick a toothpick through them all. Place finished roses on a tray and freeze for 30 to 60 minutes, until firm. Roses can be kept in a protective carton covered with plastic wrap and refrigerated or frozen up to a week. Before setting roses on a cake, cut the excess apricot off the base, making it flat. You can also use scissors to cut oval-shaped apricot-colored leaves to accompany the apricot roses, or use chocolate leaves.

SUGARED ROSE PETALS AND SUGARED GRAPES

This is one of the loveliest and easiest ways to add a decorative touch to a festive cake. One cautionary note: Be sure the roses have been rinsed clean of any pesticide and blotted completely dry with tissues.

1. Spread individual rose petals on a piece of wax paper or foil. Set nearby a bowl containing 1 egg white stirred into a teaspoon of water and a small bowl containing granulated sugar.

2. With a small, absolutely clean or new paintbrush, brush egg white over both sides of each petal, then sprinkle generously with the sugar and set on the wax paper to air dry. Petals are ready to use as soon as they dry, in about 1 hour.

SUGARED GRAPE CLUSTERS

Small clusters of sugared grapes on stems look very decorative when set on top of tartlets or used as a garnish beside a slice of cake.

To prepare the grapes, simply rinse well, then blot dry thoroughly on paper towels. Prepare a bowl of egg white glaze and a bowl of granulated sugar as for the roses above. Dip the grapes into the egg white, then into the sugar, coating them well. Set the grapes on the wax paper to air-dry. Use when crisp.

CHOCOLATE CURLS AND SHAVINGS

Chocolate Curls can be made with either dark or white chocolate. White curls look dramatic on a chocolate cake, and dark chocolate curls can be highlighted with a faint sifting of confectioners' sugar. Since solid chocolate is high in saturated fat, it is a good idea to use the curls for the cake presentation, then serve only a small single curl or piece of a curl with each portion.

Chocolate Shavings make a decorative cake topping or they can be pressed onto cake sides. In the interest of reducing fat, you can brush melted apricot preserves over the outside of a cake instead of covering it with buttercream icing, then press on a thin layer of shavings. Any unused shavings can be stored in the refrigerator or freezer in an airtight container.

To make Chocolate Curls, use a chocolate bar or block of a size that comfortably fits in your hand. Bring the chocolate to room temperature if it is a warm day, or set it into a barely heated oven for 5 to 10 minutes. Once the chocolate is at the correct temperature, it is a simple matter to draw a swivel-type vegetable peeler across the surface in long slow strokes, letting the resulting curls fall onto a piece of wax paper below. If the chocolate is too cold, the curls will crumble; if too soft they will collapse. Experiment a few minutes and it will be easy. Lift the fragile curls with a toothpick inserted in one end, and pile the curls on the cake top.

Special Equipment

Vegetable peeler or box grater; wax paper

Chocolate Curls

To make Chocolate Shavings, take a piece of block chocolate or a chocolate bar (it does not have to be warmed), and draw it across the medium ($1/4$-inch) holes of a box grater, letting the shavings fall directly onto a cake top or onto a piece of wax paper below.

Chocolate Shavings

Glazes, Frostings, Toppings, and Finishing Touches   ❧   289

CHOCOLATE PLASTIC DECORATIONS

Yield: 9 ounces; about 1 cup; makes 8 to 12 roses, depending upon size, or at least two 3-inch-wide strips to wrap around the sides of two 2-layer, 9-inch cakes

This is essentially edible chocolate modeling clay. Roll it out thinly and fashion into roses (see diagrams, page 286), cut thin strips into ribbons to tie around cakes, or fashion into bows to set on top of a cake. Or roll out a layer about ¹/₈ inch thick and stamp with cookie cutters, making designs to set on top of a cake or around the sides, sticking it in place on a base of apricot preserves or thinly spread icing.

To make two-tone designs, use dark or semisweet chocolate for a base and drizzle lines of melted white chocolate over it, or do the reverse: a white base with dark lines.

Chocolate Plastic is made from solid chocolate high in saturated fat; theoretically, this recipe does not belong in a reduced-fat baking book. However, it is a lovely decorating technique and you will not, in fact, be eating very much, if any, of it. Most of the time the chocolate rose or bow or ribbon will trim a cake top. If it wraps around the sides of a cake and becomes part of each slice, be sure to roll it very thinly first so the amount per serving is scant. If eating it at all is of concern, simply advise your guests to set the chocolate to one side before eating the cake. Note: If using white chocolate, read pages 327–328.

7 ounces semisweet chocolate or imported best-quality white chocolate, chopped

¹/₄ cup light corn syrup

Unsweetened cocoa (for use with dark chocolate)

Confectioners' sugar (for use with white chocolate)

Advance Preparation

Chocolate Plastic can be stored, refrigerated, up to one year. Roses or decorations should be stored airtight in a protective box covered with plastic wrap or a plastic bag.

Special Equipment

Double boiler; instant-read thermometer (optional); wooden spoon; rolling pin

1. Melt the chopped chocolate in the top of a double boiler set over (not touching) simmering water. Note that white chocolate may solidify if heated over 110°F (test with an instant-read thermometer or keep the water warm, not hot, in the pan below). Stir the chocolate until absolutely smooth.

2. Remove the pan from the heat, cool about 2 minutes, then pour in the corn syrup and beat hard with a wooden spoon until the mixture looks dull and forms a ball that pulls away from the pan sides. If some of the syrup looks separated, ignore it. Turn the chocolate ball out into a piece of plastic wrap, cover, and press into a flat package. Let it cool, or refrigerate to set and firm the chocolate.

3. After firming, the chocolate must be kneaded to develop its plasticity. Break off one small piece at a time and work it in your hands until it is soft enough to knead on a work surface dusted with some cocoa or confectioners' sugar (depending on the color of chocolate you are using). If the chocolate is absolutely hard, you can warm it in the microwave (just a few seconds at a time) until pliable. Knead the entire piece of chocolate, then re-form it into a flat package and rewrap to store in a heavy-duty plastic bag.

4. To form shapes, first bring the chocolate plastic to a pliable consistency. Sprinkle the work surface with cocoa (or confectioners' sugar), break off a portion of the "dough," and roll with a rolling pin or model it like clay. See diagrams below for decorating ideas.

Chocolate rose

Chocolate ribbon with rose

Chocolate ribbon wrap

Chocolate cookie cutter shape on tartlet

AMBER SUGAR BEADS AND CRACKED CARAMEL

Yield: About 1 cup caramel; enough to make about 1 cup of beads or decorations for several cakes

For a sophisticated anniversary or birthday celebration, make a silken Orange Cheesecake (page 160) topped with a cascade of brilliant Amber Sugar Beads. Add a bottle of chilled Dom Pérignon and a single yellow rose, and I promise you the event will be long remembered.

Amber beads are lovely but utterly simple to make—just caramelized sugar dripped from the tines of a fork. Cracked Caramel is the same cooked sugar spread into a thin sheet, then broken into shards to be set dramatically upon a cake or tartlet.

Advance Preparation

Caramelized sugar beads and sheets can be made in advance, but in hot or humid weather they become sticky and need to be set into a protective carton in the freezer, where they keep their flavor for about 1 week.

Special Equipment

Jelly roll pan or cookie sheet; 1¹/₂-quart heavy-bottomed saucepan; candy thermometer; pastry brush set in a glass of ice water

Butter-flavor no-stick cooking spray

1 cup granulated sugar

¹/₄ cup water

Pinch of cream of tartar dissolved in 1 teaspoon water

1.   Lightly coat a jelly roll pan or cookie sheet with cooking spray and set aside, with a table fork nearby.

2.   Combine the sugar, water, and dissolved cream of tartar in a small heavy-bottomed saucepan. Set over moderate heat, swirl the pan once or twice, and cook until the sugar dissolves. Do not stir.

3.   Raise the heat to medium-high, and fasten the candy thermometer to the pan side. Cook the syrup, washing down the pan sides several times with a pastry brush dipped in cold water to prevent crystallization. Boil the syrup, unstirred, for 10 to 14 minutes, until it turns a pale yellow color and reaches 300°F on the thermometer: the hard-crack stage. If you drop some syrup into a glass of ice water, it should form a brittle ball or a thread that will crack. If you want the beads to be a darker amber color, cook the syrup to almost 340°F and watch the color carefully so it doesn't darken too much.

4.   At once, remove the pan of syrup from the heat and set it on a heatproof surface or in a pan of ice water (to halt cooking) beside the prepared pan.

To make beads, simply dip the tines of the fork into the syrup, then, holding the fork with the tines pointing down directly over the pan, allow the beads to drop onto the prepared surface. You may find it easier to shake the syrup-coated fork, moving it sharply up and down right over the pan to coax down the dripping beads of syrup. Try to move the fork around so the beads do not drop on top of each other. As they fall, they will harden. After they are completely cold, they can be scooped up and set into a bowl.

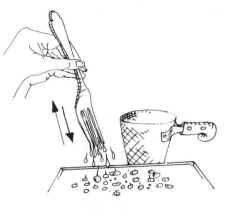

Amber beads

5. To make a sheet of caramel, cover the jelly roll pan or cookie sheet with a piece of aluminum foil pressed flat and sprayed lightly with cooking spray. Pour the cooked amber syrup directly onto the surface and tilt the pan to spread the syrup into an even sheet. When completely cold, lift the foil and peel off pieces of the caramel, breaking it into shards or slivers. Alternatively, just before the caramel has hardened on the pan, lift and pull the pieces apart with two forks, creating dramatically curved irregular segments. Store in a stiff-sided container.

Bend

Caramel slivers

CREATIVE STENCILS

Any object can be set on a cake top and covered with sifted-on confectioners' sugar, cocoa, or cinnamon. When the object is lifted, its silhouette is left, making a decorative pattern. Wheat sheaves, flowers, stiff leaves (nontoxic), knives, forks, spoons, and other lightweight household objects can be used.

- The simplest stencil is a store-bought lacy doily. Set the doily on the cake top, sift on the confectioners' sugar (on a dark-colored cake) or unsweetened cocoa (on a white cake) then lift off the doily.

- You can use a stiff piece of plain paper or oaktag to cut your own stencil. Set the paper on scrap cardboard, sketch a simple design, and cut it out with an X-Acto or other sharp artist's knife.

- Or cut the paper to fit the cake, then fold it in fourths or eighths and cut little designs into the folded edges to create snowflakes. Folded and cut paper can also become valentine hearts, paper dolls, or a flower chain. Open paper flat to use as a stencil.

- Strips of paper, or fabric lace, can be set on the cake top in crisscross patterns before sifting on successive layers of sugar or cocoa or cinnamon. Carefully remove and reposition the strips to make a plaid or complex striped pattern.

Understanding

INGREDIENTS

Baking is an art as well as a science. Give two bakers the same recipe and they will produce two different cakes. You will know that both are chocolate; they may even be moist and well risen (the ingredients' chemistry at work); but each will have its own personality—dense or airy, lopsided or perfectly shaped, overtones of cinnamon or hazelnut (the baker's touch of creativity and kitchen style shining through). Some cooks have a natural instinct for putting ingredients together and seem born knowing their way around a kitchen; others feel awkward at first and need to be shown. Fortunately, baking is a skill that can be taught and, good recipe in hand, good results can be achieved. All that is really required is a willing heart, ready hands, and some simple equipment. It is true that if you can read you can follow a recipe. But if you can also follow directions with intelligence and understanding, the results can be sublime; understanding the nature and function of each ingredient helps greatly in determining the results. Good recipes are careful formulas that balance a variety of elements to produce specific chemical reactions.

Each ingredient has a particular function. In the professional baking guide *Practical Baking*, author William J. Sultan devised a convenient system for characterizing baking ingredients. I have modified it slightly, but find it a useful guide, particularly when working to remove fat from baked products.

- **Binders and tougheners** (provide structure and bind ingredients): Flour, milk solids, egg whites
- **Tenderizers** (soften the crumb by cutting the development of gluten in wheat flour; prevent toughness): Sugar; fat; egg yolks; chocolate; acidic foods such as yogurt, sour cream, buttermilk, and vinegar; honey; molasses
- **Moisteners** (moisten the crumb, lengthen storage time): Milk, water, and some other liquids, such as eggs; sugar syrups; honey; brown sugar
- **Dryers** (absorb and retain moisture, provide body): Flour, milk solids, starches, egg whites
- **Flavorers** (enhance or provide flavor): Chocolate/cocoa; butter; eggs; fats; specific flavoring agents, including extracts, citrus zests, coffee, and nuts

The following section explores in depth the basic baking ingredients and their relation to low-fat desserts.

FLOUR

There are three main types of wheat grown today: hard, soft, and durum. From these, many different types of flour are milled; for the purposes of this book, we will concentrate on bread, all-purpose, cake, pastry, and whole wheat flour.

Flours differ obviously because they come from different types of wheat, but other variations are due to the climate and conditions in which they were grown and the process by which the flour was milled. All factors affect wheat's characteristics, particularly the amount of liquid which it can absorb, a vital factor in baking.

A kernel of wheat is composed of a hairy outer husk, removed during milling, the bran layers, the endosperm, and the germ, or fatty portion of the wheat berry, which is its seed. The bran adds dark color, fiber, and many nutrients to flour. The finer portions closer to the center of the endosperm contain a variety of fine starch particles and gluten-forming proteins. Varying amounts of the highly nutritious bran and germ are retained in dark or whole grain flours or are removed by milling to make highly refined light flours.

The hardness of the outside kernel of the grain determines its ultimate purpose. Hard wheats are high in protein and suitable for breads and other yeast products, while soft wheat is low in protein and best for pastry, cookies, and cakes.

Wheat of the same type can vary in composition and quality from year to year because of rainfall, climate, and temperature. Newly milled flour contains about 15% moisture, the maximum allowed by law, and has a beige or yellowish color due to xanthophyll and other naturally occurring carotenoid pigments.

Many types of flour are bleached or conditioned. When flour is exposed to air, oxygen combines with yellowish pigments and whitens them; historically, the time-consuming air-drying process was the only method used. Today, air may still be used as a bleaching agent, but the use of chemical bleaches and oxidants speeds up the natural oxidizing process. Some chemical bleaching compounds, such as potassium bromate or iodate, are used to improve dough quality. Chlorine dioxide or similar compounds bleach pigments from flour and mature or soften the gluten. Whatever method is used today, oxidation improves baking quality by strengthening the stretching and bonding characteristics of the gluten to create better qualities than are found in freshly milled flour. So-called unbleached flour may actually be oxidized or contain dough conditioners, but it will probably not have been treated to remove the yellowing pigment. It may also be a little heavier or higher in protein than bleached flour and thus less desirable for use in very delicate cakes. Notice whether your flour package is marked "bleached" or "unbleached," and check protein content if using the flour for cake baking.

Since 1940, all retail flour and baker's bread have been required by law to be enriched with iron as well as with vitamins lost during the milling process: thiamin, riboflavin, and niacin.

The ability of flour to absorb liquid and retain moisture depends upon the amount and quality of the protein in the flour. It takes about 2 cups of high-gluten (high-protein) flour to absorb 1 cup of liquid but about 2½ cups of low-gluten flour to absorb the same amount of liquid. There are actually several proteins in wheat, but the main ones are glutenin (located in the outer layer of the kernel) and gliadin (found in the endosperm, the core of the wheat kernel). Glutenin provides strength and gliadin provides elasticity; both are necessary to give flour the characteristics required for successful

baking. When flour is mixed with water and then kneaded and worked, glutenin and gliadin grab onto the water to form strong elastic strands called gluten. Gluten is the focus of this story, because it is the property which gives yeast dough its elasticity. The amount of gluten-forming proteins in flour increase as the total protein levels of the flour increase; the flour with the highest protein content will also absorb the most water. This is essential in bread doughs where you want structural strength to support expanding gases as bread rises. The exact opposite qualities, low protein and little moisture, are wanted for creating tender delicate pastries. The type of flour used should be specific to the baker's needs. Be sure to notice the protein content on the label of the flour under the nutritional information, in grams of protein per serving. The recipes in this book are developed to maximize the qualities of specific types of flour; it is important for successful fat-reduced baking to use the type of flour specified.

The hardest type of wheat is durum (*Triticum durum*). It is milled into a high protein (12.3 to 13 g) yellowish flour (semolina flour) used for making pasta, as well as a coarse granular product known as semolina, sometimes used for specialty desserts.

Whole wheat flour (15% to 16% protein) contains the vitamin- and fiber-rich wheat germ and bran which increase nutritional value but cause it to bake into a heavy product when used by itself. For lighter results, it is often combined with a portion of white flour. Whole wheat flour, an excellent product for bread and rolls, is sold in 5-pound bags like white flour in most supermarkets and is also available from specialty mills and natural food stores.

A relatively new grain called white whole wheat flour is made from a strain of high protein wheat milled with the bran and germ included so that its nutritional value approximates that of regular whole wheat flour; its protein content (13%) is lower than ordinary whole wheat flour, but is similar to bread flour.

Bread flour, milled from hard wheat, has a high protein content, 12% to 15%, that makes it strong and stretchy.

All-purpose flour is sometimes milled from one single type of wheat and sometimes blended from hard and soft wheats; it contains approximately 10% to 13% protein. It is good for most general baking, especially when there is enough fat in the recipe to tenderize the protein (fat coats protein strands, making them slippery, impeding their tendency to grab each other and become elastic).

Pastry flour, milled exclusively from soft wheat, has a protein content of 8% to 12% and generally is neither chlorinated nor bleached. Pastry flour is often sold in smaller bags than all-purpose, and can be found in specialty mills and natural food stores and some supermarkets.

Cake flour usually is milled from 100% soft wheat. It has even less protein, 6.5% to 10% with 8% the average. Because cake flour has less protein, it develops less gluten and thus creates more tender baked goods. Usually sold in 2-pound boxes in supermarkets, cake flour is finely milled and almost powdery. The particular method of bleaching cake flour not only gives it a very white appearance but increases its acidity slightly, helping a cake set faster and have a fine grain. Bleaching also enhances the ability of the flour to absorb liquid quickly and retain moisture during baking. The higher moisture content allows the flour to tolerate more sugar, resulting in even greater tenderness. During the process of creaming a shortening cake, for example, this chlorinated starch clings especially well to the surface of the whipped-in air bubbles, giving good distribution of air pockets and a finer texture than would be obtained with other types of flour.

In low-fat baking, cake flour is preferred for other reasons as well. For many products, it is more successful than all-purpose flour because it contains substantially less gluten-forming protein; it follows that less fat is needed to tenderize what little protein there is. In most low-fat baking, the solution is to cut the fat back and use cake or pastry flour. I prefer to use Gold Medal® Softasilk® cake flour because it consistently produces excellent results.

Self-rising cake flour (8 to 10 g protein) is altogether different, containing added baking powder (leaveners such as calcium acid phosphate or monocalcium phosphate and bicarbonate of soda) and salt. Do not substitute self-rising for other types of flour without adjusting for the presence of leavening in the product; amounts vary depending on the manufacturer but average about 1½ teaspoons leavening and ½ teaspoon salt per cup of flour. I prefer not to use self-rising flour for cakes because I like to control the amount of salt and leavening in my recipes.

You can approximate the texture of cake flour by replacing 2 tablespoons of all-purpose flour with 2 tablespoons cornstarch in every cup. Cake flour actually weighs a little less per cup than all-purpose flour; to substitute cake flour for all-purpose flour, use 1 cup plus 2 tablespoons cake flour for each cup of all-purpose.

Instant-blending flour is processed to be granular so it will mix easily with water without lumping. It is useful for gravy and some biscuits but not generally suitable for baking cakes; do not substitute it for all-purpose or cake flour.

Flour should be stored in a well-ventilated cool location, off the floor and away from excessive moisture. It can absorb strong off-odors as well as excess moisture. Flour stored for any length of time in hot weather or a warm location can become a haven for insects. The best solution is to store flour in the freezer or refrigerator. Flour will keep for about one year at 0°F.

Sifting and Measuring Dry Ingredients

It is important to remember that too much flour can toughen baked goods. Therefore, it is important to use just as much as a recipe requires but no more. To this end, it is necessary to sift and/or carefully measure. This is not as easy as it sounds, because if you measure by volume, as most Americans do, you can pack as much as 2 extra tablespoons of flour into a cup by tapping it as you handle it. A scale is the most accurate tool for measuring because 100 cannot be anything else no matter how it is tapped; many, however, find weighing a cumbersome technique.

When a recipe in this book calls for "½ cup *unsifted* flour," you can stir the flour in the canister to loosen it, then spoon the flour into the cup and level the top with the back of a knife, or you can use the scoop-and-sweep method, dipping the dry measuring cup into the flour canister, then sweep off the excess with the knife. In neither case should you tap the cup or the flour will compact.

When the recipe calls for "½ cup *sifted* flour," pass the flour through a medium-fine mesh strainer set over a piece of wax paper or a bowl. Spoon this sifted flour into the dry measuring cup, heaping it slightly and taking care not to tap the cup. Finally, take the back of a knife and sweep off the excess, leveling the top.

LIQUIDS

For the baker, liquids include eggs, water, milk, cream, sour cream and yogurt, fruit juices, alcohol, honey, molasses, oil, melted butter, and coffee. Liquids have many functions in a batter: They dissolve salt and sugar, create steam to push apart cells and aerate the structure of the product, they moisten the leavening agent to begin production of carbon dioxide gas, causing rising.

Liquids should be used with caution because too much can activate the gluten-producing proteins in wheat flour and cause extra elasticity, resulting in toughness in cakes and pastries. Acidic liquids such as citrus juices, vinegar, sour milk, and buttermilk inhibit production of gluten and thus tenderize baked products. Honey, molasses, sour cream, and yogurt are all acidic and will alter the pH balance of a batter;

when these are present, baking soda (an alkali) is added to neutralize some of the acidity. Liquid quantities must be adjusted when baking at high altitudes (ask your county Agricultural Extension Service for recipe adjustments).

Dairy Products

MILK: Milk products contribute moisture, color, and richness to baked goods and also prolong their freshness. Milk products derive from an animal source, so they contain cholesterol and about 64% of their fat is saturated. However, they also contain protein, calcium, and a variety of vitamins and minerals. Note that as you remove fat from milk products, you reduce the amount of saturated fat and cholesterol, but *increase* the proportion of calcium.

Milk is generally identified by its fat content. Whole milk contains 3.3% to 3.5% butterfat (milk fat) by weight. This is a significant amount when you realize that one cup of whole milk receives 49% of its total calories from fat. To reduce fat in baking, use skim milk or low-fat milk (1% or 2% fat) or nonfat instant dry milk reconstituted with water (see manufacturer's directions for quantities).

Buttermilk is the liquid by-product of churned milk or cream; because the solids and most fats are removed, regular buttermilk is low fat; you can also purchase nonfat buttermilk. Cultured buttermilk is pasteurized skim milk mixed with a lactic-acid bacteria culture. Cultured buttermilk powder, available in cans in the baking sections of supermarkets, is a dry mix that must be reconstituted with water. I use this frequently and always try to keep a container in the pantry.

If substituting buttermilk for whole or skim milk in a cake or other baking recipe, remember to add a little baking soda to neutralize the acidity. Buttermilk is a welcome ingredient for the low-fat baker because it is naturally low in fat and also because its acidity slows the development of gluten in a batter, tenderizing baked products. Many brands of buttermilk lack the label "nonfat" or "low-fat"; check the carton to see whether the buttermilk was made from skim, low-fat, or whole milk. If you cannot tell exactly what type you have, use any buttermilk; all are basically low in fat and the variation in the recipe will be small.

As a substitute for buttermilk (though lacking its rich flavor), you can make your own sour milk by adding 1 tablespoon white vinegar or lemon juice to 1 cup of 1% or 2% milk; let it stand about 3 minutes before using it. Or blend 1 cup of skim milk with 2 to 3 tablespoons nonfat yogurt.

Shelf-stable (boxed) milk, sold in Europe for many years, is now available in most American supermarkets. It is both ultra-high-temperature-pasteurized and aseptically packaged, two important parts to the processing of this product. First, the milk, which must by regulation be labeled UHT (ultra high temperature), is heated to 284°F for 3 seconds to kill bacteria. Second, the packaging process is conducted aseptically, meaning that all packaging material is put through a sterilization bath in a sterile environment to ensure that the milk and its carton are sterilized and free of micro-organisms. This two-phase technique allows the sealed product to remain unrefrigerated for six months, though it must be refrigerated after opening. Shelf-stable milk is available as whole, low-fat (1% and 2%), and skim, but not as buttermilk. It may be substituted by the home baker for any fresh milk product, though its taste is very slightly different.

Canned evaporated skim milk is fresh skim milk minus about half its water content; the resulting liquid is heat-sterilized so it will have a long shelf life. The high temperature of the sterilization process slightly caramelizes the lactose (a disaccharide, also called milk sugar), causing its characteristic sweet taste. This may be used in place of cream in some low-fat recipes. Once opened, evaporated skim milk must be refrigerated, covered, and used within a week.

Sweetened condensed milk is made by using a vacuum system rather than heat to quickly evaporate about half the water from whole or skim milk. The resulting liquid is sterilized and homogenized to prolong shelf life. In sweetened condensed milk, the sweet taste is even more exaggerated because extra sugar is added, about 2 pounds per 10 pounds of condensed milk. This level of sugar makes the liquid uninhabitable for microbes.

Low-fat sweetened condensed milk is a relative newcomer to this line, and a big help to the low-fat baker (for making unbaked cheesecakes or Key lime pie, for example). It is made from a blend of whole and skim milk, with sugar and vitamin A palmitate added, and contains half the fat of regular sweetened condensed milk, from 3 g down to 1.5 g fat per 2 tablespoons. Leftover low-fat sweetened condensed milk can be refrigerated, covered, for no longer than three days; freezing leftovers is not recommended because the sugar crystallizes and will not smooth out when thawed, changing the texture.

Powdered milk is milk with virtually all its water evaporated, so that it is inhospitable to microbes and has a stable storage life. Most powdered milk is made from low-fat milk because fat goes rancid quickly when in contact with solid salts and atmospheric oxygen; in addition (according to food chemist Harold McGee, in *On Food and Cooking*, Scribner's), fat coats the particles of protein, so it would make the powder difficult to mix with water. The resulting neutral-tasting powder keeps several months when stored in a cool, dry location and is a good product for the low-fat baker's pantry.

Bakers can use a little dry milk powder (added with dry ingredients) in dough or batter as a nutritional supplement (extra calcium, for example) or reconstitute it with water and use as ordinary milk in any recipe.

Lactose intolerance is a physiological inability to digest and absorb lactose in many dairy products. The symptoms of this disorder can usually be alleviated by using **lactose-free milk.** Made from either whole, skim, or low-fat milk with the lactose removed, it is sold alongside regular milk in the supermarket, and may substitute for regular milk in all baking.

1 cup	Calories	Percentage of calories from fat	Total grams of fat	Grams of saturated fat	Cholesterol (mg)	Calcium (mg)
COMPARATIVE TABLE OF WHOLE AND LOW-FAT MILK, BUTTERMILK, EVAPORATED SKIM MILK, AND LACTAID						
Whole (3.3%) milk	150	49	8	5	33	291
2% milk	125	37	5	3	18	313
1% milk	119	23	3	2	10	349
Skim milk	86	4	0.4	0.3	4	302
Buttermilk (low-fat)	99	18	2	1	9	285
Buttermilk (3 T powder + 1 cup water)	79	0.3	1	1	5	176
Evaporated (skim/canned)	199	2	1	0.3	10	740
Lactaid (lactose-reduced low-fat milk)	102	unknown	3	unknown	10	300

SOURCE: Anna dePlanter Bowes and Charles F. Church, *Food Values of Portions Commonly Used*, rev. by Jean A. T. Pennington, 15th ed. (New York: Harper & Row, 1989); *USDA Agricultural Handbook 8–1*, 1976.

CREAM: The word "cream" comes from the Latin *chrisma*, ointment or anointing oil. Rich fat, or oil, in ancient ritual was sacred and used to anoint. Surely food for the gods, cream deserves to be on a pedestal; unfortunately, the low-fat baker should leave it there.

There are many types of cream on the market, defined by their butterfat content. Labeling information is often lacking, but **heavy** or **heavy whipping cream** (not the same as whipping cream) has, by law, between 36% and 40% butterfat, enough to whip stiff and hold its form. **Whipping cream** has 30% butterfat; it will whip, but not hold its form for very long. **Medium cream** has 25% butterfat and **light cream** has between 18% and 20%; both medium and light are becoming difficult to find in supermarkets because of lack of consumer demand. You can make your own by blending half fresh heavy cream with whole or skim milk. **Half-and-half** has 10.5% to 12% butterfat and will not whip. Fresh milk and cream refrigerated and maintained at 40°F have a shelf life of no more than twelve days; check the package expiration dates.

Because of its clean clear taste, fresh cream is preferable to **ultrapasteurized**, which is widely available and fine for all uses but has a slightly different flavor; it has been heat-processed to 280°F for at least 2 seconds to kill bacteria. (Normal pasteurization heats cream or milk to 161°F for 15 seconds or 145°F for 30 seconds.)

Obviously, in low-fat baking, any type of heavy cream is a no-no. One cup of 36% heavy whipping cream obtains 95% of its calories from fat, contains 821 calories, 88 g fat (of which a whopping 55 are saturated) and 326 mg of cholesterol (more than a day's allowance, according to the American Heart Association). That said, there are always times when nothing else will substitute; if you are looking for the essential flavor of creaminess, the cream to choose is "heavy cream," but use the minimum possible to add the effect or the flavor desired.

Use a chilled bowl and beater and whip the cream extra stiff. To make a thick, rich-but-reduced-fat sauce, fold this whipped cream into a meringue or Seven-Minute Icing (page 277), or well-drained yogurt.

As a substitute for heavy cream (for a sauce, not to whip) you can use "light" ricotta (which has a slightly tangy or nutty flavor) or low-fat cottage cheese, whipped *absolutely* smooth in a blender, then stirred into a little low-fat vanilla or plain yogurt.

SOUR CREAM: Sour cream is basically fermented heavy cream. Commercially marketed sour cream is cultured sour cream, a rich, tangy product made from 18% butterfat cream that is injected with a bacterium, *Streptococcus lactis*, and allowed to thicken. For the low-fat baker, there are now several brands of low-fat and fat-free sour cream to be used as alternatives to the fat-rich original; save 342 calories with a cup of nonfat sour cream (see accompanying table). Choose brands made from cultured skim milk (read the label); do not use imitation or nondairy sour creams because they frequently contain highly saturated tropical oils or are made with hydrogenated fat. If you cannot find one of these substitutes, use low-fat or non-fat yogurt or Homemade Yogurt Cheese (page 251). If you cannot locate a low-fat or nonfat sour cream, you can substitute plain nonfat yogurt (a saving of 366 calories over 1 cup of cultured sour cream).

YOGURT (YOGHURT, YOGHOURT): One of the oldest foods known to man, yogurt has been made for thousands of years; it may have originated as a deliberate method for preserving milk or been a happy accident resulting when a desert nomad left milk in the hot sun and it combined with airborne cultures and turned into a custard. Yogurt can be made from the milk of cows, horses, sheep, goats, camels, and buffaloes; most of the yogurt in America today is made from cow's milk, though some small producers use sheep's and goat's milk.

While yogurt is neither a cure-all nor a perfect food, as sometimes claimed, it is a nutritious, low-fat, low-cholesterol product containing, among other virtues, high levels of calcium, protein, and B-vitamins.

Yogurts play the numbers game, ranging from one relatively spartan cup of "light" yogurt with 90 calories or plain nonfat yogurt with 127 calories and trace amounts of fat and saturated fat to heavily sweetened creamy fruit yogurt offering up to 250 calories and 9 to 12 g fat. On average, an 8-ounce serving of nonfat yogurt contains about 125 calories.

The Food and Drug Administration defines yogurt as follows. Nonfat: less than 0.5 g milkfat per 4 ounces (100 g); low fat: between 0.5 and 2.0 g milkfat per 4 ounces (100 g); whole milk: approximately 3 g milkfat per 4 ounces (100 g).

Yogurt is made from skim milk, sometimes enriched with extra nonfat milk solids, that is homogenized, pasteurized, and injected with live bacteria—*Lactobacillus bulgaricus* and *L. thermophilus* plus, in some but not all cases, the most highly valued *L. acidophilus*. These bacteria feed on the milk sugar to produce lactic acid. At this point, the milk is incubated, or allowed to ferment, in order to coagulate into yogurt and develop its characteristic tangy flavor. To keep the cultures alive and active, yogurt at this stage must be kept refrigerated during distribution. Live cultures are required in the yogurt sold in Europe, but not in the United States. Here, some companies pasteurize the product once more, killing the bacteria. Read the label to tell the difference. The most desirable yogurts contain "live, active cultures"; better yet, look for those labeled as containing "live, active *Lactobacillus acidophilus* cultures."

Yogurt that has been injected with bacteria in the individual tub or retail container is considered superior to that injected in a huge vat, then transferred to smaller containers. Transferring breaks the coagulation, or set; for this reason, some brands add vegetable gum, modified food starch, or gelatin to hold or reset the yogurt.

For low-fat baking, it is preferable to use yogurt without added gums so that excess liquid (whey) can be drained off. I like to use Colombo® yogurt, widely available in the Northeast and Midwest. It is made with live and active cultures, contains no added gums or starches, and has a clean, creamy consistency that works well in all my recipes.

Yogurt offers many health advantages. Yogurt containing live *Lactobacillus acidophilus* culture has the ability to replace beneficial bacteria wiped out by illness or antibiotics and may help prevent yeast infections. The lactic acid that transforms milk into yogurt also turns lactose into lactase, an enzyme that enables individuals who suffer from lactose intolerance to consume and digest dairy products. Thus, they can eat most brands of yogurt while they cannot eat other milk products.

Low-fat or nonfat yogurt is a good substitute for sour cream or heavy cream. Low-fat Homemade Yogurt Cheese (page 251) may be used in place of cream cheese, though the flavor is less sweet and more tangy.

FROZEN YOGURT: Frozen low-fat yogurt contains roughly half the calories and fat of butterfat-rich ice cream. Like other forms of yogurt, the frozen varieties supply calcium, minerals, vitamins, and amino acids. The frozen version also adds emulsifiers and stabilizers to create a creamy consistency, and some also contain active cultures. However, the fat content can vary considerably.

COMPARATIVE TABLE OF HEAVY CREAM, SOUR CREAM, YOGURT, FROZEN YOGURT, AND ICE CREAM					
8 ounces/1 cup	Calories	Total grams of fat	Grams of saturated fat	Cholesterol (mg)	Calcium (mg)
Heavy cream (36%)	821	88	55	326	154
Cultured dairy sour cream	493	48	30	5	268
Light sour cream (Land O Lakes)	293	15	ND*	ND*	ND*
Nonfat "Free" sour cream (Light n' Lively)	151	0	0	0	ND*
Low-fat yogurt with fruit	225	3	2	10	314
Low-fat (1.5%) vanilla yogurt	194	3	2	11	389
Plain whole yogurt	139	7	5	29	274
Plain low-fat yogurt	144	4	2	14	415
Plain nonfat yogurt	127	0.4	0.3	4	452
Frozen yogurt (Colombo low-fat chocolate)	260	4	4	10	ND*
Ice cream (rich vanilla; 16% fat)	349	23.7	14.7	88	151

*ND—no data available.

SOURCE: Anna dePlanter Bowes and Charles F. Church, *Food Values of Portions Commonly Used*, rev. by Jean A. T. Pennington, 15th ed. (New York: Harper & Row, 1989); *USDA Agricultural Handbook 8–1*, 1976.

EGGS

Eggs are vitally important in baking: They add richness, proteins, vitamins, and minerals, and contribute to the texture, color, and flavor of baked goods. Eggs also help bind a batter together. When a cake rises during baking, the proteins in the egg combine with the proteins in flour to support the structure. And when whole eggs and/or egg whites are whipped, they incorporate air, which expands in the heat of the oven, leavening the product.

One large whole egg weighs 50 g and contains 75 calories (of which 62% come from fat).

The yolk, which weighs 17 g, contains all the egg's fat (5.5 g, of which 1.6 g are saturated) and 59 calories (of which 79% come from fat). The yolk also contains all the egg's cholesterol (213 mg). Because of the yolk's saturated fat and cholesterol content, the American Heart Association currently recommends that the adult diet include only 4 whole eggs or 4 yolks per week, or any number of whites. However, recent research shows many Americans can eat more eggs without effecting blood cholesterol adversely.

The egg white is more friendly to the low-fat baker. One large egg white weighs 33 g, has 17 calories, 3.5 g protein, and zero fat. Obviously, in low-fat baking, one uses more whites and fewer yolks; for cholesterol-free baking, one must eliminate the yolks entirely. In general, as a substitute for one whole egg, use two whites; for two whole eggs, one egg plus one extra white or three whites. Be aware that too many egg whites in a cake batter can have a drying effect; use them judiciously.

If you are trying to reduce fat in a conventional recipe and can tolerate cholesterol, often you can improve the taste and texture of a low-fat recipe by using some yolk, one whole egg, or one egg plus one or two whites. Think of it this way: The yolk does contribute fat, but only 5.5 g. If you divide this among eight servings, each one contains only about 0.7 g fat.

Whole eggs and egg yolks tenderize baked goods because their fat content helps to inhibit the development of potentially toughening gluten in wheat flour in a batter or dough. In addition to fat, yolks also contain natural lecithin, an emulsifying agent which helps yolks whip into a stabilized foam.

To the cook, there is no nutritional difference between brown and white eggs, but eggs do vary in freshness, size, and whipping qualities. For use in cake batters, eggs should be at room temperature to blend smoothly with other ingredients. If they are very cold, set them, in the shell, in a bowl of warm water for about ten minutes.

STORING AND FREEZING EGGS: Egg whites can be stored, refrigerated, for up to a month. Egg yolks can be refrigerated in a covered jar for 2 or 3 days. (I like to put a drop or two of water on the yolks to prevent a skin from forming.) The best way to store eggs is in the freezer; whole eggs or egg whites should be stirred to blend with a few grains of salt or sugar, then frozen in ice cube trays (1 cube equals 1 whole egg). According to the USDA, egg yolks should be stirred together with 1/8 teaspoon salt or 1½ teaspoons sugar or corn syrup per ¼ cup yolks (4 large yolks) and frozen. Eggs, whole or separated, can be frozen for up to 1 year if in an airtight container at 0°F. Eggs should be thawed overnight in the refrigerator before use. Never refreeze thawed frozen eggs.

WHAT TO DO WITH LEFTOVER EGG YOLKS: Since low-fat bakers use whites with impunity, the question always arises of what to do with all the leftover yolks. Here are a few ideas to get you started: Blend them with pure pigment to make egg tempera paint as the fourteenth- and fifteenth-century Old Masters did; cook the yolks and feed them to your dog or cat—the lecithin in yolks is believed to make animal coats glossy; or mix an egg yolk into your shampoo—the lecithin makes human hair shine too. Or toss out the yolks; save them for a few days because you feel guilty about wasting them and then toss them out. Or save them up until you cannot stand another low-fat dessert and make yourself a yolk-rich crème caramel! Remember, I do not suggest a total deprivation diet.

EGG GLAZES: Whole egg or egg yolk glazes are often used in classic baking to give a sheen or gilded appearance to breads and pastries. For low-fat baking, substitute a lightly beaten egg white, or brush the top of a pie with skim milk and sprinkle with some granulated sugar.

MEASURING EGGS: Egg size is very important in baking. In this book, all eggs are U.S. Grade A Large, weighing 2 ounces in the shell. By U.S. law, one dozen large eggs must weigh 24 ounces, although the eggs can vary individually within that dozen. In low-fat baking, this is a critical point. When you are already cutting down on eggs, you need to have full value when you do use one. Keep a sharp eye out; if an egg looks especially small, select a larger one or weigh it or measure its volume.

> 4 to 4½ whole eggs = 1 cup
> 1 large egg yolk = 1 tablespoon
> 1 large egg white = 2 tablespoons = ⅛ cup
> 4 large whites = 8 tablespoons = ½ cup
> 4 large whites whipped with some sugar until
>   stiff = approximately 4 cups meringue

WHIPPING EGG WHITES: Egg whites foam because of the combined action of several proteins. Albumin is thick and viscous, made up of large molecules that resemble loosely coiled strands of twine. When whipped or heated, these strands unwrap and stretch out. When stretched around whipped-in air bubbles, they make a strong self-bonding skin. Ovomucin and globulins increase the viscosity of the albumen, helping it make a fine foam with many cells. Together with conalbumin, these proteins help stabilize the foam at room temperature and prevent it from draining liquid.

When meringue is exposed to heat in the oven, the molecules of air in the foam cells get warm, expand, and enlarge the cells; they might actually grow so large that they would burst if not for the ability of the protein, ovalbumin, to coagulate around and strengthen each cell wall. This prevents the collapse of the cell walls, even when the meringue is baked and the water in it evaporates.

Stabilizers are often added to egg whites. Acidity (in the form of cream of tartar, vinegar, lemon juice) lowers the pH of the albumen slightly and slows down the unfolding of the protein strands, helping them to resist over beating and leaking of liquid. When whites are whipped in a copper bowl, the copper ions interact molecularly with the albumen to do the same thing, just as an acid would.

There are several important things to remember when whipping whites into meringue. First, keep all utensils scrupulously clean; the smallest speck of fat prevents the whites from beating to full volume because the fat becomes suspended in the natural moisture of the whites and softens the proteins, weighing them down. Avoid whipping whites in plastic bowls, which never wash completely grease free. To rid any bowl of a hint of grease, wipe the bowl and beater with a paper towel dampened with white vinegar.

Eggs separate most easily when cold, but whip to greatest volume when at room temperature (about 68°F). This paradox can be solved if you separate the eggs as soon as they come from the refrigerator, placing yolks and whites in separate bowls. Place the bowl of whites into a pan of warm water for about 10 minutes, stirring until the whites feel lukewarm to the touch.

To hold its shape, meringue must be properly whipped. For best results with least effort, use an electric mixer with a balloon-type wire whip that fits the bowl. The point is to keep the entire mass of whites in constant movement. To begin, add a pinch of cream of tartar (or other acid if called for) and salt to the whites and whip on *low* speed, working up to medium. Whipping on low to medium speed gives smaller bubbles which are more stable than the large bubbles produced if whipped only on high speed. When the whites are foamy, but not before, begin to add sugar (if used) gradually, while continuing to whip. If sugar is added too soon, it will dissolve into the whites and hinder the development of the meringue.

Continue to whip until the meringue looks glossy and smooth, and forms slightly droopy peaks. To test this, turn off the machine and scoop out some whites on a spoon or turn the (hand-held) beater upside down. Then continue to beat a few seconds longer (some bakers prefer to do this final stage by hand with a whisk for better control) until almost-stiff peaks form and you see beater or whisk tracks on the surface of the meringue. This is the moment just before the maximum volume is reached. At this stage, you should be able to turn the bowl of whipped whites completely upside down (over a sink if you are nervous) without the whites moving at all. This is the point referred to in the recipes as "stiff but not dry."

Avoid overbeating the egg whites. Overbeating occurs when the albumen strands are bonded and stretched so tightly that they squeeze the water molecules right out of the foam. Overbeaten meringue looks lumpy and dry, and a film of water forms in the bottom of the bowl. If turned upside down now, (this time you need a sink), the mass of whites would slide around precariously.

You can try to salvage and revive overwhipped whites by gently whipping in one extra egg white for every four in the meringue.

About the Safety of Eggs and Meringues

Egg safety and the possible health hazards of eating uncooked eggs and meringues are significant issues for cooks. Some incidents of bacterial contamination, from the bacterial organism *Salmonella enteritidis*, have been attributed to raw, improperly cooked, or undercooked eggs. The cause and cure are not fully understood. Until the hazard is eliminated, it is prudent to be cautious in baking although the likelihood of a problem is slim. According to the American Egg Board, studies indicate the chances of a home cook finding an infected egg are about 0.005%. Here are a few simple guidelines:

When shopping, open the cartons and look at the eggs; avoid eggs that are cracked or unclean. Be sure the store has well-refrigerated egg cases. At home, refrigerate eggs promptly,

storing them inside the refrigerator, where it is colder than on the door. Wash any container or food preparation surface that has come into contact with raw eggs before reusing it. Avoid eating raw eggs or raw egg whites.

Refrigerate cheesecakes and all baked goods containing custards or meringues. Keep cold foods cold (at or below 40°F) and hot foods hot (above 140°F) to prevent growth of salmonella bacteria.

While the bacterium causing the common food poisoning salmonellosis is sometimes present in egg whites, it has also been found on the skins of fruits grown in contaminated soil; its origin is the subject of some debate. Washing produce carefully helps; there is no question, however, that the bacteria cannot survive high temperatures. Commercial food handlers and many restaurants avoid problems by routinely cooking with pasteurized liquid eggs instead of fresh eggs.

To cook raw yolks for use in uncooked recipes: If a recipe for an unbaked soufflé, sauce, or pudding calls for raw egg yolks, they may be prepared as follows to remove any danger of bacteria: Blend each yolk with at least 2 tablespoons of liquid and cook in a heavy saucepan over very low heat, stirring constantly, until the mixture coats a metal spoon or reaches 160°F on an instant read thermometer. Cool quickly (over an ice water bath if desired), and proceed with the recipe.

To make cooked meringues and egg white icings: For the baker, egg white caution means following instructions carefully when preparing meringues, boiled or seven-minute icing, or other preparations such as mousse. While it is highly unlikely that eating a small amount of icing will make you sick, you should at least be informed.

According to the American Egg Board, to destroy the bacteria, egg whites must be held at a temperature of 140°F for 3½ minutes, or 150°F for 2 minutes, or at some point should reach 160°F. I have done some testing on temperatures of cooked meringues. My experiments began with seven-minute icing; the bottom line: this is an easy solution to the safety problem. When I started the tests, the whites were at room temperature (68°F). My first trials were over direct heat, but I found the double boiler easier and more reliable to use. I whipped the meringue over simmering water with a hand-held beater on medium speed for 4 minutes (1 minute longer than over direct heat) and the temperature reached 140°F; then it rapidly climbed to 150°F and stayed there for the next 3 minutes. This technique produces the most silken icing texture. Unfortunately, seven-minute icing cannot be used for all desserts requiring meringue because the ratio of sugar to egg whites must be high enough for the cooking meringue to foam properly before it poaches; in my tests, it poached too soon if the sugar dropped below 3/4 to 1 cup per 2 whites. Food scientist Shirley Corriher explains that sugar prevents coagulation of the egg white proteins; when you cut sugar, the whites coagulate (in this case poach) faster.

To test Boiled Icing (Italian meringue, page 279), I prepared a sugar syrup and heated it to 242°F, the temperature recommended by the American Egg Board. I whipped the egg whites to soft peaks in the electric mixer, then poured the 242°F syrup in a steady stream into the egg whites as they were being whipped. As soon as all the hot syrup was incorporated, the meringue reached 145°F and held this for 45 seconds.

Then, as the whipping continued (per the recipe), the temperature started to descend; after 60 seconds, it plummeted to 125°F. After 2 minutes, it was at 100°F and falling. I conclude that seven-minute icing is easier to make, gets hotter, and stays hot longer than boiled icing, but boiled icing is the only solution for certain recipes.

POWDERED EGG WHITES: To avoid any danger of salmonella bacteria in raw egg whites, many home bakers, like commercial bakeries, are substituting powdered pasteurized egg whites. There are several products on the market, some available in specialty gourmet shops or baker's catalogues, others in supermarkets. One that I use currently is Wilton Meringue Powder, made by Wilton Industries and sold wherever cake baking supplies are available. For this product, Wilton recommends using 2 teaspoons meringue powder plus 2 tablespoons water to make the equivalent of 1 egg white; sugar can be added as desired. The King Arthur Baker's Catalogue (see page 372) offers similar products, including Chefmaster's Meringue Powder and plain unsweetened Powdered Egg Whites packaged with the King Arthur label.

EGG SUBSTITUTES: I have not used commercial egg replacements in any of the recipes in this book because I prefer fresh, natural products. The replacements (such as Eggbeaters) are safe and work well if you wish to use them; follow manufacturer's instructions for quantities to use.

CHEESE

CREAM CHEESE: Cream cheese is a soft, rich, fresh unripened cheese with a mild but slightly acidic flavor made from milk and cream. The whey is first separated and drained from milk curds, then milk and cream are added back to the curds. The fat content of regular cream cheeses range from 35% to 40%. Kraft's Philadelphia Cream Cheese, one widely available brand, is sold in 3- and 8-ounce foil-wrapped blocks that are freshness-dated (see the table on page 312 for nutritive values).

"Light" or low-fat cream cheese is regular cream cheese minus part of the fat. One widely available brand, Philadelphia "Light" Cream Cheese, sold in tubs, is similar to the regular style in texture and taste but contains half the fat. Buyer beware: Kraft also packages "soft" regular cream cheese in the identical tub; it does *not* have the same properties for baking and should never be substituted. Both Kraft and Eater's Choice sell "fat-free-*for-baking*" cream cheese in blocks; results vary depending upon the brand, in my experience. Sometimes it does not completely blend when creamed and may leave tiny white flecks in the baked goods; if overwhipped, it has a tendency to liquefy. Work with it before you bake for company.

Philadelphia also sells "fat-free" cream cheese in a tub; it looks like the "light" version but is greasier, does not taste as good, and should *never* be cooked. Avoid it. My choice is the "light" or low-fat Philadelphia brand, even though it has some fat.

As a substitute for cream cheese, you can use Homemade Yogurt Cheese (page 251), although it is less sweet. Or you can substitute nonfat or low-fat cottage cheese that is drained and pressed dry in a strainer, then whipped absolutely smooth in a blender or food processor.

Neufchâtel cheese is creamy, made from milk, and similar to regular cream cheese in texture. It originated in Normandy, France, and in its original form is cured for a period of several weeks, which gives a particular flavor some perceive as slightly tangy. It is often softer and not quite as mild as cream cheese. There are several low-fat Neufchâtel cheeses on the market. The most widely available brand in my area is packaged by Kraft/Philadelphia, wrapped in a foil brick looking remarkably like the regular Philadelphia cream cheese, but has a third less fat than regular cream cheese, though it is not quite as calorie- and fat-reduced as the Philadelphia "light" cream cheese (see table, page 312). You can use Neufchâtel or light (low-fat) cream cheese interchangeably unless the recipe is specific about the type.

RICOTTA CHEESE: Fresh, unripened, and similar to cottage cheese, ricotta has fine moist clumps and a bland but faintly bitter or nutty taste. Italian ricotta is often made from sheep's milk drained from the curds when provolone cheese is made. In the United States, ricotta is usually made from cow's milk whey, which contains a protein called lactalbumin that, when heated, causes the whey to coagulate, or set. At this point, acids are added, and sometimes extra milk as well. Because ricotta is a fresh cheese, it does not have a long shelf life and should be used when purchased; watch the date on the package. Ricotta can also be frozen, but its texture changes slightly; this does not harm it for baking use. Regular ricotta has between 4% and 10% fat and about half the calories of cream cheese per ounce.

Low-fat ricotta is made from skim milk. There are several low-fat brands with about half the calories, fat, and saturated fat of the regular type. Part-skim ricotta is made from partially skimmed milk, and while it is lower in calories and fat than the whole-milk variety, it has slightly more of both than the "lite" type.

The low-fat ricottas are a bit blander than the whole-milk in taste, but there is not enough difference to affect use in baking. When drained well and blended smooth, ricotta may be substituted for cream cheese, although you should compensate for the difference in sweetness.

COTTAGE CHEESE: A fresh, unripened cheese, one of the oldest types known to man, cottage cheese originally was made from naturally soured milk, probably left in the sun until

COMPARATIVE TABLE OF CREAM CHEESE, RICOTTA, COTTAGE, AND CHEDDAR CHEESE

Type	Amount	Calories	Total grams of fat	Grams of saturated fat	Cholesterol (mg)	Calcium (mg)	Protein (g)
Philadelphia Regular Cream Cheese	8 ounces	784	76	43	224	160	18
Philadelphia Light Cream Cheese	8 ounces	496	38	22	128	304	23
Neufchâtel	8 ounces	592	53	34	176	168	23
Ricotta (whole milk)	8 ounces	432	32	21	126	514	28
Ricotta (part skim)	8 ounces	340	20	12	76	669	28
Ricotta (lite)	8 ounces	280	16	8	40	ND*	32
Cottage cheese (cream-style whole milk)	8 ounces	217	10	6	31	126	26
Cottage cheese (1% low-fat)	8 ounces	164	2	2	10	138	28
Cheddar (medium sharp)	1 ounce	114	9	5	28	208	7
Cheddar (low-fat)	1 ounce	72	4	3	12	192	6

*ND—no data available.

SOURCE: Anna dePlanter Bowes and Charles F. Church, *Food Values of Portions Commonly Used*, rev. by Jean A. T. Pennington, 15th ed. (New York: Harper & Row, 1989); *USDA Agricultural Handbook 8–1*, 1976.

it curdled. Today, milk is set with a lactic starter, then cut, drained of whey, and packaged. Cottage cheese is a lumpy white cheese with either small or large curds and a mildy acidic flavor. Because of the rounded curds, it is also known as popcorn cheese. Cream is often added to give more moisture and flavor; this is called creamed cottage cheese.

The fat content of cottage cheese varies. The richest can have up to 15% fat, while the average has 4% and low-fat can contain only 1% or 2%; dry curd varieties contain 0.5% fat.

Low-fat (1%) cottage cheese is similar to regular cottage cheese in taste and texture, but has about one quarter fewer calories, one fifth the fat, and one third the saturated fat. It also has more calcium and more protein than the regular version; use this type for baking. When the curds are pressed dry in a strainer, then puréed absolutely smooth in a blender or food processor, the smooth paste can substitute for cream cheese. Some brands contain gums that inhibit release of the whey; if you are trying to drain this type, just press out as much liquid as possible. If you are on a gluten-free diet, check the label to be sure additives are not cereal-based.

FARMER OR POT CHEESE: This cheese is similar in taste to cottage cheese but has a much drier texture. As a substitute, use cottage cheese pressed in a sieve to remove most of the excess liquid (whey). Farmer's or pot cheese is often bulk-packed and is not as widely available as cottage cheese. Look for it in specialty delicatessens and supermarkets with large cheese departments. Farmer or pot cheese can contain as much as 8% fat, according to the National Dairy Board.

CHEDDAR CHEESE: Cheddar cheese is named for a village in Somerset, England, where it originated. The word "cheddar" also refers to a step in the manufacturing process (cheddaring), during which blocks of cut cheese are continually turned and stacked for a period of about one and a half hours. A firm aged cheese that varies in color from white to orange, Cheddar is made all over the world. The taste varies depending on the aging and manufacturing technique. American Cheddars range from mild to extra sharp. Regular Cheddars contain about 45% fat.

Reduced-fat Cheddar has about half the calories and fat of regular, and the taste is almost the same. Use it in low-fat baking, especially in muffins and quick breads.

FATS FOR BAKING

Baking fats include butter, margarine, vegetable shortening, lard, and oil. In baked goods, fats tenderize, moisturize, add flakiness, and carry flavors, aromas, and nutrients. Fats also add smoothness to the texture. Different fats have different melting points and contain different percentages of water. For these reasons, the type of fat used affects the tenderness, texture, taste, and shape of baked products.

Types of Fats Used in Baking

Fats can be either saturated or unsaturated; unsaturated fats tend to be liquid at room temperature (oils) and saturated fats tend to be solid. In addition to differences in saturation levels, solid and liquid fats differ in moisture content, melting points, and additives. These qualities affect their uses in baking, and should be considered when choosing fat substitutes. In low-fat baking, remember that the preferred choice for fat is always the one lowest in saturation and monounsaturates are the best.

The type of fat used in baking affects tenderness. Soft or liquid fats (including oils) coat the proteins in wheat flour more completely than solid fat; coating prevents development of the gluten and contributes to tenderness. Since solid fats are more highly saturated than soft or liquid fats, it is important for the low-fat baker to know that a light flavorless vegetable oil such as canola (primarily monounsaturated) can often be substituted for (or combined with) solid fat in a recipe calling for "creaming butter (or shortening) and sugar." The grain of the cake will be denser, but acceptable. When a recipe calls for melted butter or melted shortening, oil can also be substituted. The result will be similar to the original, except in flavor, unless the recipe depends on the eventual hardening of the melted butter for texture, as in certain icings.

For aeration of cake batters, solid fat at room temperature (68°F) or semisolid shortening gives best results. When these types of fat are beaten, creamed, or whipped with sugar, the rough-edged sugar crystals cut air bubbles into the flexible fat, which then stretches and expands, enveloping the bubbles. If the fat is too cold, the walls around the air bubbles will be brittle, cracking and releasing air, causing the cake to fall. Shortening contains no water and thus has the capacity to absorb air to its full volume. It can whip in more air than either butter or margarine, both of which contain milk solids, salt, and water and thus can only contain beaten-in air in their fat portions. In low-fat baking, the aeration is accomplished by using a reduced quantity of fat with the addition of stiffly whipped egg whites or a viscous substance like fruit purée, applesauce, or certain syrups which will hold the air bubbles.

For flaky pastry a cold, solid fat is desirable. The colder it is, the less it soaks into the flour and the more separate it stays, creating little flakes or layers as it is pinched into the flour. In the heat of the oven, the liquid in the pastry dough makes steam that pushes up the layers while the heat sets them firmly; this action creates the quality of flakiness in a pie crust. In contrast, oil blends right into flour, tenderizing the crust but never making it flaky. Solid fat does not have to mean highly saturated butter-fat; you can combine low-fat milk and oil with a little flour and freeze it, then work this into your flour for a low-fat flaky pastry.

The amount of water released by the fat contributes to the total liquid of a recipe. In baking, a fat that contains a lot of water can require more flour and thus toughen the product. Some margarine *spreads* (as opposed to solid margarine) contain well over 50% water. Light or diet margarines have so much water (and occasionally additives or air) that they are not reliable for use in baking unless specifically called for in a recipe developed for that product.

Butter and hard stick margarine contain roughly 20% water. The presence of so much liquid means that an all-butter cookie will utilize more flour, and will usually be less tender, than one made with 100% fat such as oil or shortening.

Butter and margarine are designed as food spreads to melt in the mouth; they have melting points near body temperature (approximately 92°F). Some brands of margarine stay solid a little longer, melting near 100°F. Hydrogenated vegetable shortening has the highest melting point: 110° to 120°F.

If you baked the same batch of cookies with each of these fats, you would see that butter and margarine doughs soften in the oven and spread relatively quickly, before their starches are set; the cookies are usually thin and crisp. Shortening cookies stay puffed up and thick because they set up before the fat melts. For low-fat baking, oil can be successfully used in soft, moist, or bar-type cookies, particularly those made with fruits. It is difficult to make crisp buttery cookies without some solid fat blended with the oil. Let's face it—sometimes you just need butter, in combination with oil or shortening or margarine. Use it; just don't eat the whole batch in one sitting.

BUTTER: Butter has the best flavor of all baking fats. Besides its taste, unsalted butter is preferred because it is (or should be) dated or sold frozen, and should be fresher than salted butter. Salt (0.5% to 6%) is added for flavor, but also to prolong shelf life; it often masks off-flavors in old butter. Made from pasteurized sweet cream, butter is an animal fat and thus contains cholesterol (33 mg per tablespoon). It is a solid fat and thus also saturated (7.1 g saturated fat per tablespoon). Its fat content ranges from 80% to 86%. Water content varies from 18% to 20%, plus 2% milk solids. For cake baking, select the butter with the least water; melt a variety of brands and compare the liquid that settles out upon cooling. The low-fat baker must consider butter a luxury: always tempting, often to be lived without or blended with a less-rich ingredient, but sometimes absolutely essential to spiritual and gustatory life.

MARGARINE: Margarine was invented by a French chemist during the late nineteenth century to provide an inexpensive fat for the army of Napoleon III. It is made from a variety of oils and solid fats that are blended, heated, and combined with water, milk or milk solids, emulsifying agents; flavorings, preservatives, coloring, and vitamins. Margarine is partially hydrogenated (see below) to make it solid. Soft margarine "spreads" usually list water as the first ingredient; they contain unspecified quantities of water and air and about 60% fat. Diet imitation or reduced-fat spreads can contain about 40% fat and at least 50% water; they, as well as soft tub margarines, are absolutely unreliable for baking.

While it lacks the good taste of butter, solid margarine has roughly the same fat content, around 80%, but is much lower in cholesterol. Many brands in fact contain no cholesterol, a big plus. To satisfy kosher dietary laws, one can select a brand made without milk solids or animal fats; read labels. Select a margarine in which the first ingredient on the label is a liquid oil high in polyunsaturates (such as liquid safflower oil); limit products where the first ingredient listed is a hydrogenated or partially hydrogenated oil.

SOLID SHORTENING AND HYDRO-GENATION:

To transform liquid vegetable oil into a solid or spreadable form (margarine or solid shortening), the oil must be hydrogenated. This is a commercial process by which hydrogen molecules under pressure are forced through the oil. In addition to hardening the fat, hydrogenation increases its stability and prolongs its shelf life. During this process, the molecular structure of the oil is changed; the more an oil is hydrogenated, the greater the change and the more solid the product.

Squeeze-bottle or soft tub margarines are changed less than hard stick margarine, and thus may be somewhat more "heart healthy." Many margarines and shortenings maintain a high percentage of unsaturated fatty acids (oils). For example, Crisco contains 80% liquid soybean oil suspended in a honeycomb matrix of 20% hardened (hydrogenated) oil. It is 100% fat, contains no water, and has high levels of emulsifiers (mono- and diglycerides) added to stabilize the structure of baked goods and increase their absorption of moisture. Crisco, like most shortening, is made of highly polyunsaturated vegetable oil; its contains about half the saturated fat of butter and can be helpful to the low-fat baker.

Solid shortening is designed to go in, not on, food. It does not have to taste or feel good in the mouth, so it can contain a generous quantity of emulsifiers to preserve the suspension of the fat in liquid, to hold more air, and to stabilize the moisture content of batter.

Trans fatty acids: During hydrogenation, some of the oil's fatty acid chains, particularly those that are monounsaturated, are transformed into something called trans double bonds. The new structure is called a trans fatty acid (TFA), and contributes to the stability of the hydrogenated fat, helping it to avoid rancidity. Trans fatty acids make up a very small proportion of the total dietary fat intake in the United States. Research on the subject of TFAs has been ongoing for years. Some studies recommend that individual TFA consumption be limited because TFAs seem to act like other saturated fats in the body, raising the level of low-density lipoproteins (LDLs) in blood cholesterol while simultaneously lowering the levels of the good high-density lipoproteins (HDLs). While TFAs occur naturally in small amounts in animal products like beef, lamb fat, butter, and milk, researchers now question whether levels are excessive in hydrogenated fats such as hard margarines, partially hydrogenated vegetable oils, and commercial shortenings and frying oils.

From the point of view of dietary health, margarine—once considered the perfect alternative to the cholesterol and saturated fat in butter—is now being scrutinized along with other hydrogenated shortenings. Confusion for the consumer arises because study results vary. We are told that monounsaturates are desirable, yet some of these are trans fatty acids, which may not be beneficial at all. Similarly, we are advised that saturated fats are unhealthy, yet stearic acid, a saturated fat found in beef, butter, and chocolate, for example, does not appear to raise serum cholesterol levels, so all saturated fats may not be so bad after all. Looking at the whole picture, it is clearly more important to lower overall amounts of saturated fat in the diet than to be alarmed about drastically cutting trans fatty acids.

SHOULD I BAKE WITH MARGARINE OR VEGETABLE SHORTENING OR OIL INSTEAD OF BUTTER?

Butter has all the taste, but also all the cholesterol and most of the saturated fat. The bottom line is that solid margarine is not a perfect butter substitute. It lacks butter's flavor and contains some saturated fat—slightly less than one third that of butter. Its advantage is that it does not (usually) contain cholesterol. You certainly can bake with margarine. Solid shortening has a neutral (or an artificial butter) taste, is reliable for achieving certain qualities in baked goods, has about half the saturated fat of butter, and no cholesterol. But for best health and culinary reasons, I feel that vegetable oil plus a small amount of butter is often the best alternative.

LARD: Lard is rendered pork fat, plus a very small amount of water. It is 100% animal fat and has 14 mg cholesterol per tablespoon. It is 39.2% saturated fat—less than one might think. Lard seems to be less harmful to the diet than previously believed, but, nevertheless, is not really an option in low-fat baking.

COCOA BUTTER: Cocoa butter, once prized for cosmetic use, is a highly saturated fat created as a by-product of processing cocoa beans to make chocolate. As a vegetable fat, it contains no cholesterol. Most of the cocoa butter is removed during the processing of cocoa powder, which is thus extremely low in fat and saturated fat.

OILS: All liquid oils (see table, page 318) have almost the same caloric content. Vegetable oils contain no cholesterol. Oils contain primarily unsaturated fats and are liquid at room temperature; they are predominantly of vegetable origin (although fish oil is also unsaturated). Vegetable oils contain different amounts of mono- and polyunsaturated fatty acids. Oils high in polyunsaturates include safflower, sunflower, corn, soybean, and cottonseed. Research has shown that polyunsaturated fat can lower harmful serum cholesterol LDLs, but large amounts in the diet can also lower the desirable HDLs. Monounsaturated oils may be the most desirable of all oils. Research has shown these oils have the ability to lower levels of undesirable LDLs without affecting the levels of HDLs, high-density lipoproteins. Predominantly monounsaturated oils include canola oil (58% monounsaturated), peanut oil and other nut oils, and olive oil (77% monounsaturated), the most highly praised member of this family. New oil blends regularly appear in the marketplace; among the "healthy" contenders are olive and canola blends (about 60% monounsaturated).

VEGETABLE OIL SPRAY: To grease pans in low-fat baking, use the minimum amount of fat possible. I use no-stick vegetable oil cooking spray. For baking, my personal preference is for a butter-flavored spray such as those made by Crisco or Pam. They are recommended for use with the recipes in this book because they leave no unpleasant aftertaste on delicate cakes and other baked goods. Crisco No-Stick Cooking Spray contains no alcohol and is made from a blend of canola, sunflower, and soybean oil, plus butter flavor and beta-carotene, added for color. Pam is made from canola oil, contains grain alcohol, butter flavoring, and annatto for color.

Both contain a natural antistick soy lecithin, which is an excellent release agent; with this product, cakes and muffins are easily removed from their pans. When I use this, I do not need paper or foil muffin cup liners; however, to facilitate removal of certain types of cakes, I recommend that the pan be coated with cooking spray or brushed with oil and then dusted with flour.

Another pan-greasing alternative is to coat with a light vegetable oil (canola, safflower, and corn are my choices) brushed onto the pan with a pastry brush, or put it into a new pump-type spray bottle (bought in the hardware store). Or you can select any one of a number of commercial pump-type nonstick vegetable cooking sprays.

I am often asked about the safety of aerosol spray propellants. According to the Aerosol Education Bureau, since 1978, nearly all United States aerosol manufacturers have discontinued using chloroflurocarbon propellants (CFCs), which are thought to injure the ozone layer, in compliance with bans by the Environmental Protection Agency, Food and Drug Administration, and Consumer Product Safety Commission. One common propellant is a blend of propane, isobutane, and n-butane, gases that I am assured are "environmentally safe." The small percentage of CFC users exempted from the ban are in the medical and pharmaceutical industries. If you are unsure about a particular product, contact the manufacturer.

HOW TO STORE FATS: Fats have a tendency to absorb strong odors; all fats should be stored covered, away from strong-scented ingredients. Special care must be taken in storage to prevent rancidity, which not only alters taste but is potentially toxic. It can result when fats are exposed to air and combine with oxygen and water. Research shows that by-products of rancid fats can cause damage to the lining of blood vessels, which may later lead to cardiovascular disease.

In general, unsaturated fats (oils) have a less stable molecular structure than saturated (solid) fats. They are more vulnerable to changes from exposure to heat and light and moisture. Oils should be stored in opaque containers in a cool dark location or refrigerated. Cold sometimes turns oil cloudy; this is not harmful and clarity returns as the oil returns to room temperature. Dark-colored specialty oils, such as walnut and hazelnut, are the least stable, with a shelf life of 4 to 6 months. Refined vegetable oils (such as canola, safflower, and corn) should be stored away from air, heat, and light in a cool, dry location; they generally stay fresh for 6 to 10 months.

Some home cooking oils and all commercial cooking oils contain silicones, added to inhibit foaming during frying. These should be avoided; because some cake batters require foaming, use silicone-free oils.

Saturated fats such as butter and cream contain enzymes that can affect and accelerate rancidity. Because the salt in salted butter may mask the smell of rancidity, it is best to use unsalted butter. Butter and margarine should be refrigerated or frozen for short-term use; for long-term storage they should be frozen.

Fats that are rancid or are being reused present a safety hazard. Vegetable oils used at home for frying should never be reused. The high temperatures required for frying cause chemical changes in the molecular structure of the oil, releasing free fatty acids and lowering the flashpoint, or burning temperature, of the oil. Reused home cooking oils may burst into flame when reheated to normal temperatures. Commercial frying fats contain a variety of additives including some to prevent the lowering of the flashpoint and allow reuse of the oil.

HOW TO MEASURE FATS: Oil is a liquid fat: it is measured in a liquid measuring cup. Solid fats such as butter and margarine usually

LIQUID AND SOLID FATS LISTED FROM BEST FOR HEALTH (LOWEST AMOUNT OF SATURATED FAT) TO WORST

Fat	Amount	Percentage of fat	Calories	Total grams of fat	Grams of saturated fat	Grams of monoun-saturated fat	Grams of polyunsat-urated fat	Cholesterol (mg)
Vegetable oil spray	2.5-second spray	—	6	0.7	0.1	—	0.4	0
Canola oil	1 T	100	120	13.6	0.9	7.6	4.5	0
Safflower oil	1 T	100	120	13.6	1.2	1.6	10.1	0
Walnut oil	1 T	100	120	13.6	1.2	3.1	8.6	0
Hazelnut oil	1 T	100	120	13.6	1.0	10.6	1.4	0
Sunflower oil	1 T	100	120	13.6	1.4	2.7	8.9	0
Corn oil	1 T	100	120	13.6	1.7	3.3	8.0	0
Olive oil	1 T	100	119.3	13.5	1.8	9.9	1.1	0
Sesame oil	1 T	100	120	13.6	1.9	5.4	5.7	0
Soybean oil	1 T	100	120	13.6	2.0	3.2	7.9	0
Peanut oil	1 T	100	119.3	13.5	2.3	6.2	4.3	0
Margarine (corn/stick)	1 T	80	101.4	11.4	1.8	6.6	2.4	0
Margarine (corn/tub)	1 T	80	101	11.4	2.1	4.5	4.5	0
Crisco	1 T	100	106	12.0	3.2	5.7	3.3	0
Lard	1 T	100	116	12.8	5.0	5.8	1.4	14
Palm oil	1 T	100	120	13.6	6.7	5.0	1.2	0
Butter, salted	1 T	80	102	12.2	7.15	3.3	0.4	33
Cocoa butter	1 T	100	120	13.6	8.1	4.5	0.4	0
Palm kernel oil	1 T	100	120	13.6	11.1	1.5	0.2	0
Coconut oil	1 T	100	120	13.6	11.8	0.8	0.2	0

SOURCE: Anna dePlanter Bowes and Charles F. Church, *Food Values of Portions Commonly Used*, rev. by Jean A.T. Pennington, 15th ed. (New York: Harper & Row, 1989); *USDA Agricultural Handbook Series 8–4.*

are conveniently sold in quarter-pound sticks, marked on the wrapper to indicate tablespoon and cup divisions. One stick = 8 tablespoons = 1/2 cup; 1/3 cup = 5 1/3 tablespoons; 1/4 cup = 4 tablespoons. If your butter comes in 1-pound blocks, cut it into 4 equal quarters, or sticks, and use the measurements above (1 stick = 8 tablespoons) as a guide. To measure solid fat using measuring spoons or cups, pack it into dry (not liquid) measuring cups or measuring spoons, taking care not to trap air pockets in the bottom. Level the top with a straight edge before use. I prefer not to use the water displacement method—in which solid fat is added in increments to a specific amount of water in a measuring cup until the water reaches the desired level—because water left clinging to the fat may disrupt the balance of liquid in the recipe.

COMMERCIALLY PREPARED FAT SUB-STITUTES: Although I have not used any fat, egg, or sugar substitutes in the recipes in this book, I am often asked about them and feel a brief description is necessary. Some of the new substances vary on a molecular level and the differences between them are highly technical. In some cases, products replace fat successfully but introduce other, often less desirable, qualities, such as rubbery texture. Baking is a complex process, and the function, reliability, and baking qualities of each element are closely related; when one is altered, the end result is altered as well. If you wish to use these new substances, I advise you to be judicious in altering your recipes. Try several versions until you find a balance of taste and texture that you like.

The majority of fat replacements fall into three categories: protein-based, carbohydrate-based, and fat-based substances. Some are available for home use and are sold in supermarkets or specialty food catalogues, while others are only used in commercial food production and will appear on product labels. The following information is abbreviated and intended to be an overview.

Protein-based products made from micro-particulated protein include Simplesse®, a reduced-calorie ingredient made from whey protein or milk and egg protein. Other products in this category include modified whey protein concentrate such as Dairy-Lo®. Carbohydrate-based fat replacers include those made from microparticulated cellulose; gums (guar gum, arabic gum, locust bean gum, carrageenan, pectin, and xanthan gum); dextrins; and fiber (such as Oatrim®), made from soluble oat starch and fiber); fruit purée products such as Lighter Bake® (Sunsweet); maltodextrins such as Maltrin® derived from corn, potato, wheat, and tapioca; starch and modified food starch products such as Amalean I & II® and Pure-Gel®; and polydextrose water-soluble polymers such as Litesse®.

Among the many new fat-based substitutes are emulsifiers, such as: vegetable oil mono- and diglycerides used commercially to replace all or part of the shortening in baking mixes; Caprenin, with the characteristics of cocoa butter and used in confections; Salatrim, a fat-based ingredient, used in confections, baked goods, and dairy products; and sucrose polyesters such as Procter & Gamble's Olestra®, a calorie-free ingredient made from sucrose and edible fats and oils.

SUGARS AND OTHER SWEETENERS

Functions of Sugar in Baking

In baking, sugar provide sweetness, aids the creaming and whipping of air into batters, and contributes grain, tenderness, texture, and color. In addition, sugar's ability to caramelize adds flavor to baked goods. Sugars, particularly sugar syrups and honey, have the ability to attract and absorb moisture, which helps keep baked goods moist and fresh. In fat-reduced baking, since flavor is also often reduced, sugar is needed to retain or enhance flavor and cannot be drastically cut back. As a general rule, I cut about one quarter to one third of the sugar out of my traditional recipes, more if fresh or dried fruit or fruit purée or sauce can be added.

In the creaming process, the sharp edges of sugar crystals bite into the fat and open up pores that grow into air cells which ultimately expand during baking to leaven and lighten a product. Sugar thus contributes to structure and volume.

In fat-free or low-fat cakes, and particularly angel food and chiffon cakes with their large proportion of egg whites, the leavening agent is the air whipped into the whites. Sugar interacts with the egg proteins to stabilize the whipped foam. This makes the foam more elastic so air cells can expand more. In addition, the presence of sugar molecules among egg proteins tends to raise the temperature at which egg proteins set, thus slowing the coagulation, or set, of the egg proteins until the maximum amount of air has developed in the oven to leaven the product. This ensures good texture and volume. This same process aids in the making of seven-minute icing; in the presence of a sufficient amount of sugar the egg whites do not coagulate, which prevents the egg proteins from clinging to each other so the whites can mount and set before they poach. With insufficient sugar, the whites clump and cook too quickly.

Sugar has the potential to slow down the development of gluten in a batter or dough. If there is a lot of sugar in the dough, it causes the gluten-forming proteins to cling to it rather than to each other, thereby inhibiting the building of the stretchy network needed to hold expanding gases. Thus, breads with more than 2 tablespoons of sugar for each 1 cup of flour (holiday sweet breads, for example) tend to be denser than breads with little or no sugar.

With cakes, cookies, and pastries, the interaction between sugar and proteins is beneficial: the more sugar, the less gluten is developed, and the more tender and delicate the texture of the product. A moderate amount of sugar in a cake batter, for example, causes the cell walls to stretch slowly so a cake can rise to the maximum before it is set by oven heat. High-ratio cakes are those with more than 1 cup of sugar per cup of flour; these cakes have an especially fine texture because of the slowness with which their cell walls have stretched.

In low-fat baking, where fat cannot be counted on for tenderizing the gluten, sugar's role as a tenderizer is essential, and for this reason (as well as for enhancing taste) it cannot be drastically cut back without resulting in a rubbery, tough product. As substitutes for some of the sugar, low-fat bakers use applesauce, pear and prune purée, and corn syrup—ingredients that replicate sugar's ability to impart sweetness and add tenderness.

During baking, oven heat causes starch to absorb liquid and swell. This is called gelatinization. The quicker this process, the faster the cake becomes set. Sugar slows this process by competing with the starch to absorb the liquid. As sugar liquefies, the batter remains viscous longer, allowing time for the maximum amount of leavening gases to develop before the batter sets. This gives a fine-grained product with a smooth crumb and good volume.

About Sifting Sugar

Granulated sugar needs to be sifted only if it has been stored for a long time and is lumpy or caked. Confectioners' sugar should always be sifted before use.

Types of Sugar

Sugars are the simplest carbohydrates. Many different types of sugar exist in nature, but only three are primarily used in cooking: glucose, fructose, and sucrose.

The sugar most commonly used in baking is sucrose, a natural sugar found in plants. It is a complex sugar, or disaccharide, composed of one fructose and one glucose molecule joined to form a simple carbohydrate; it can be rapidly absorbed by the body to provide quick energy.

For the baker, sucrose is available as white sugar, brown sugar, or molasses. Each type comes from a different stage of the refining process. Granulated sugar is available in a variety of different crystal sizes, providing unique characteristics that suit the baker's special needs.

White sugar comes in crystal sizes that range from regular granulated to superfine or bar sugar, plus 4, 6, and 10X confectioners' sugar. The size of the crystal is related to the amount of air it can incorporate into a batter when creamed or beaten with fat. Obviously, granulated sugar will cut open larger holes in the fat than powdered sugar. Also, the size of the crystals determines how quickly the sugar will dissolve in a batter. Superfine (also called ultrafine or bar sugar) crystals dissolve much more quickly than regular granulated, so they are best for drinks and meringues. You can make your own superfine sugar by pulverizing granulated sugar in the food processor. Extrafine sugar is slightly finer than regular granulated and is used primarily by professional bakers. Baker's Special sugar is slightly finer than extrafine and is used by commercial bakeries. Pearl sugars, available in granulated and confectioners' style, is a rough-cut coarse grind that remains raised and visible after baking; use it to decorate baked goods. It is available in some gourmet shops, bakers' supply houses, and from mail-order catalogues (see pages 372–373). British castor sugar is similar to Baker's Special; superfine sugar can be substituted. British icing sugar is the same as confectioners' sugar.

Confectioners' sugar is granulated sugar that has been ground to a specified degree of fineness. For home use, powdered 10X is generally used, but 4X and 6X are also available. A box of confectioners' sugar usually contains about 3% cornstarch to prevent caking and crystallization. This gives the sugar a raw taste that is best masked by adding flavorings if the sugar is not to be cooked. Confectioners' sugar dissolves almost instantly, so it is good for meringues, icings, and confections. It is sometimes used for tenderness in cookies and can even be added to cake batters to produce a denser, more silken texture than that created by granulated sugar. Confectioners' sugar must always be sifted before using.

Brown sugar, whether turbinado, dark, or light brown, is less refined than white sugar. The darker the sugar, the more molasses and moisture it contains. Turbinado (usually sold in natural food shops) has a coarser grain than granulated white and a variable moisture content which makes it unpredictable for use in baking, although it can be sprinkled on top of cobblers or cookies. Brown sugars, both light and dark, add color, flavor, and moisture to baked goods. Brown sugars also tend to make baked goods heavy and should be avoided in light fragile cakes. In general, the darker the color, the more intense the flavor. Both dark and light brown sugar have the same sweetening power as an equal weight of white sugar; however, white sugar is more dense. To achieve an equivalent degree of sweetness, brown sugars must be firmly packed before measuring.

To avoid lumping, store brown sugar in a covered glass jar or heavy plastic bag in the refrigerator or a cool dry cupboard. To make 1 cup of your own brown sugar, add 4 tablespoons of unsulfured molasses to 1 cup of granulated sugar.

Molasses is the liquid separated from sugar crystals during the first stages of refining. The color and strength of the molasses depend on the stage at which it comes in the separation process during a series of spinnings in a centrifuge. The first liquid molasses drawn off is the finest quality; the second and later drawings contain more impurities. The third, called blackstrap (from the Dutch word *stroop*, or syrup), is the blackest and has the strongest flavor. The most common types available for cooking blend the finest molasses with some cane syrup to standardize quality.

Some processors treat their sugar cane with sulfur dioxide to clarify and lighten the color of its juice. This produces a sulfur taste in molasses that many find distasteful, so it's best to use only "unsulfured" molasses that has not been treated.

HONEY: Honey is the only sweetener known that needs no additional refining or processing to be utilized. Its color ranges from nearly colorless to dark brown and its flavor from mild to bold, depending on the type of flowers from which the bees gathered nectar. There are over 300 floral sources for honey bees in the United States and over 3,000 worldwide. Honey is composed of fructose (38% to 42%), with lesser amounts of glucose, sucrose, and other sugars, along with water and small amounts of vitamins, minerals, and acids; the ratios of these components vary depending on the honey's floral source. The high percentage of fructose, which is more hygroscopic (moisture absorbing and retaining) than other sugars, is what makes honey baked goods stay moist longer (for longer shelf life), become soft on standing, and feel chewier in the mouth. Honey has a slightly higher sweetening power than sugar and has somewhat different properties in baking. Honey's caramelizing properties cause baked goods to brown more quickly, therefore oven temperature should be reduced by 25°F. It is naturally acidic and should be used in conjunction with ¹/₂ teaspoon of baking soda for each cup of honey used in baked goods. Because of honey's water content, the amount of liquid called for in the recipe should be reduced by approximately ¹/₄ cup for each cup of honey used. To substitute honey for sugar, use ⁷/₈ cup honey per 1 cup sugar or experiment with your individual recipe to achieve best results.

Over time, honey naturally crystallizes—it does so because it is a supersaturated sugar solution. This means that the water in honey contains an extra amount of sugar—more than what it could normally hold. In time, the sugar comes out of solution and into a semi-solid state. To delay crystallization, honey should be stored at room temperature or can be stored in the freezer. Crystallized honey can be reliquefied easily by placing the container in warm water until the crystals dissolve. Or, microwave 1 cup of honey in a microwave-safe container on high for 2 to 3 minutes, until the crystals dissolve, stirring every 30 seconds.

MAPLE SYRUP: Pure maple syrup comes from the boiled-down sap of the sugar maple tree. Avoid imitation maple syrups, which are basically corn syrups with artificial flavoring and coloring added. Use maple syrup as a sweetener in baked goods as you would honey (being conscious of the fact that syrup is sometimes more liquid and proportions may need adjustment). Also use maple syrup as a low-fat sauce on top of cobblers, pancakes, and waffles of course, and yogurt, or homemade yogurt cheese.

CORN SYRUP: Corn syrup has been produced in the United States since the mid-nineteenth century. Starch granules are extracted from corn kernels and then treated with acid or various enzymes to break them down into a sweet syrup. Corn syrup, made up of glucose from the corn sugar plus some added fructose and about 24% water, is valued because of its sweetness and various physical properties. By controlling the thoroughness of the enzymatic action on the starch, the chemical structure can be altered, affecting the sweetness and viscosity of the syrup. Corn syrup has several characteristics that are useful to the low-fat baker. In carefully formulated cake batters, for example, corn syrup can replicate some qualities of oil. For example, because corn syrup is viscous, it tends to hold some air when whipped and it has a tenderizing effect on gluten. In addition, corn syrup imparts a chewy texture to baked goods and, because it is hygroscopic (moisture-retaining), it helps baked products remain moist, increasing their shelf life.

SUGAR-FREE AND LOW-SUGAR SWEETENERS: For low-fat bakers who are concerned about reducing sugar in their diets, there are a variety of specialized products on the market.

One all-purpose sweetener that I have tried with success is Vanilla Nature Sweet, made by Steel's (see page 373). This syrupy sugar-substitute with a good vanilla flavor and no aftertaste is made from Maltitol syrup, a natural sweetener derived from corn that is hydrolyzed (its molecules are split) and hydrogenated to create a substance (polyol) that tastes sweet but is absorbed by the body in a different manner than sugar. Steel's also makes a honey-flavor Nature Sweet and a variety of low-fat, sugar-free or low-sugar Maltitol-based sauces.

LEAVENING AGENTS

Leavening agents are added to batters to make baked goods rise and to produce a light and porous structure. Air, steam, and carbon dioxide gas (produced by baking powder and baking soda) are the principal leaveners.

In reduced-fat baking, egg whites are sometimes used as a substitute for all or part of the whole-egg content of the original recipe; often the egg whites are stiffly whipped, both to contribute to the leavening and to lighten the texture that, without fat, might be too dense.

Baking Powder

Baking powder is a chemical leavening agent. It is made up of acid-reacting materials (tartaric acid or its salts, acid salts of phosphoric acid, compounds of aluminum) and an alkali (bicarbonate of soda). Most brands of baking powder have a starch filler (corn or potato starch) added as a stabilizer to keep the acid salts from reacting with the bicarbonate of soda and to act as a buffer in case any moisture gets into the mixture.

There are three main types of baking powders: **single, fast-acting tartrate** baking powder, which releases gas quickly, as soon as it is mixed with liquid; slow-acting or **phosphate** baking powder, usually used in commercial bakeries; and **double-acting** baking powder, also referred to as SAS. The last is the one I recommend and the one most widely used in home kitchens. It is composed of cream of tartar, tartaric acid, sodium aluminum sulfate (hence "SAS," or sodium acid pyrophosphate), and the mono-calcium phosphates. It produces two separate reactions. When double-acting baking powder is mixed with the liquid in a batter, it forms a solution, causing a reaction between the acid and the alkali, which begins to let off carbon dioxide gas. When this batter is placed in a hot oven, a second reaction occurs, releasing about 12% to 14% carbon dioxide.

Baking powder absorbs moisture from the air, causing it to deteriorate and lose its power after three months. The average shelf life of an opened can is about one year. (Yes, that is one reason why your cakes are falling!) Remove this item from your list of bargains at the buy-by-the-case food warehouse. Unless you do high-volume baking, purchase small containers of baking powder and write the date purchased on the can so you can keep track. Store baking powder in a cool, dark place.

If you suspect you are dealing with an antique product, perform this simple experiment: Combine 1 teaspoon baking powder with $1/2$ cup hot water; if it bubbles vigorously, it is still usable. If it sits in stern silence, toss it out.

If you run out of baking powder, you can make this single-acting substitution in an emergency (but do not try to store this mixture): For every 1 cup flour in the recipe, combine 2 teaspoons cream of tartar, 1 teaspoon baking soda, and a few grains of table salt. Noted chef and food writer Edna Lewis recommends a blend of 2 tablespoons cream of tartar, 1 tablespoon baking soda, and $1^{1/2}$ tablespoons cornstarch; use 1 to $1^{1/4}$ teaspoons of this mixture per 1 cup flour.

For high-altitude baking where the air pressure is lower and gas expansion in the batter is increased, the quantity of baking powder must be adjusted.

Baking Soda

Baking soda, also known as bicarbonate of soda, is another common leavening agent. An alkaline product, it is used in baking when there is an acid agent present (such as buttermilk, sour milk or yogurt, molasses, honey, chocolate, or cocoa) in order to neutralize some of the acidity as well as to provide leavening. The alkaline soda needs an acid in order to react and release carbon dioxide gas. This reaction is similar to fast-acting baking powder, for it reacts just once, as soon as it blends with liquid when the batter is mixed. For this reason, baked goods that use baking soda alone must be placed in the hot oven as soon as they are prepared, before the rising action begins to dissipate.

Bicarbonate of soda has other properties as well. Because it is an alkali, it darkens the color of chocolate or cocoa in a cake. It also causes reddening of cocoa, giving devil's food cake its name.

Be judicious when using baking soda. An excess in baked products results in off odors, a soapy taste, and a darkened or yellowed white cake.

Old cookbooks often instruct the cook to mix the soda with boiling water before adding to the batter. This is because baking soda originally was very coarsely ground, known as saleratus. Today, however, it is very fine and may safely be sifted into the other dry ingredients.

Occasionally, a recipe will call for both baking powder and baking soda. The reason is that the baking powder is needed for leavening and the baking soda acts as a neutralizer for the acidity of certain ingredients.

Yeast

Since ancient times, people have used yeast to raise their breads. The first raised doughs fermented spontaneously from ubiquitous airborne wild yeast spores which lodged felicitously in a batch of dough sitting on rocks in the sun. The word "yeast" (from the Old English *gist*) originally referred to the foam or sediment on fermenting liquid. Beer froth was a common ancient leavener. In the nineteenth century, French chemist Louis Pasteur first explained the nature of yeast, actually a group of about 160 species of single-celled microscopic fungi or living organisms, which feed on sugar and change it into alcohol and carbon dioxide, a "rising agent." Bakers' and brewers' yeast are the most important types for food preparation. Most of the yeasts used in bread baking are members of the genus *Saccharomyces* (sugar fungi); these strains are selected for flavor and the ability to produce enough carbon dioxide to leaven dough; brewers' yeast by itself will not raise bread dough.

The home baker has several types of yeast to choose from: compressed and granulated dry, as well as a fairly new rapid-rise strain. Compressed and granulated dry yeasts are two different genetic strains of the same species, though they have different qualities. Fresh compressed yeast is partially dried (70% moisture), and sold pressed in solid cakes (usually ⅔ ounce). It must be refrigerated (for up to 4 weeks) or frozen (for up to 4 months). It should be a light tan color and have a clean aroma. When old, it is dark brown. To test freshness, crumble equal parts compressed yeast and sugar; they should liquefy at once. To use, allow compressed yeast to dissolve in lukewarm liquid, before combining it with other ingredients.

Dry yeast (8% moisture) can be stored at room temperature or frozen. Because yeast is a living organism, it needs certain temperatures to be comfortable and productive. In general, compressed yeast starts to activate around 50°F and is best around 80° to 95°F. Dry yeast prefers warm liquid (105° to 110°F) plus a little sugar for rehydration. If temperatures are too high, yeast organisms can be disabled or killed, preventing rise of the bread.

Compressed and active dry yeasts can be used interchangeably. One package of dry yeast (1 scant tablespoon; ¼ ounce; 7 g) equals one 0.6-ounce cake of compressed fresh yeast.

Yeast designed to make bread rise in half the conventional time is a different, highly active strain with a finer particle size. It is sold in dry granulated form, in envelopes of ¼ ounce (7 g), and can be stored at room temperature in a cool place until the expiration date on the package. Unlike other types of yeast, this is designed to be added to the other dry ingredients in the recipe, then mixed with a hotter liquid (120° to 130°F). See "Quick-Rising Sweet Yeast Breads," page 217.

SALT

"Sodium," often confused with salt by the layperson, actually means sodium chloride, a chemical that accounts for about 40% of a salt molecule. In other words, salt is just a little less than half sodium. Nevertheless, too much is not good. The National Academy of Sciences recommends a daily sodium limit of 2,400 milligrams, the equivalent of about 6 grams of salt, or roughly 1 teaspoon.

In low-fat baking, removing fat results in removing some flavor. To make the recipe taste good, it is nearly impossible to cut salt drastically, although it is always possible to cut back. Sometimes flavor can be sparked by adding extra grated citrus zest or more flavoring extract. Nevertheless, an absence of salt leaves baked products tasting flat; salt also has the ability to combine with sugar to bring out and balance its sweetness. In this book, every attempt is made to reduce salt and sodium while maintaining flavor.

CREAM OF TARTAR

An acidic by-product of winemaking, cream of tartar is a white powder used in baking to help prevent overbeating of whipped egg whites and to stabilize egg white foam during baking. In addition, it is used when making sugar syrups to inhibit crystallization of the sugar.

Mixtures containing cream of tartar should not be cooked in an unlined aluminum pan because the tartaric acid reacts with the aluminum, turning the food being cooked a gray color.

GELATIN

Gelatin is a natural product derived from collagen, the protein found in bones and connective tissue. In the United States, unflavored gelatin is most commonly sold in dry granulated form; in Europe, it is often sold in leaves or sheets that are reconstituted by being soaked in water for 1 to 2 minutes, then squeezed and dissolved in hot liquid. One envelope of Knox unflavored gelatin has the same jelling strength as five sheets ($2^7/8$ inches by $8^1/2$ inches) of leaf gelatin. Knox granulated gelatin is available in bulk or packaged in small envelopes. Bulk packages are usually freshness-dated (this is helpful because very old gelatin often does not work) but envelopes are not dated. Each envelope contains 1 very scant tablespoon (actually a generous 2 teaspoons), or $1/4$ ounce (7 g). This is enough to set 2 cups of liquid or $1^1/2$ cups of solids.

To dissolve granulated gelatin, sprinkle it on top of a small amount of cold liquid (it does not have to be water) in a small saucepan, and let it stand for a few minutes so the granules swell. Then set it over moderately low heat and stir just until the granules dissolve completely; test by rubbing a drop of the mixture between your fingers—it should feel absolutely smooth. Do not let the gelatin boil, or it will lose some of its setting strength. Another method is to stir the swollen granules into boiling water until dissolved. Although it is not my preferred method, many cooks like to dissolve gelatin in a microwave. To do this, sprinkle one envelope over $1/4$ cup cold water in a glass measuring cup. Let stand 2 minutes to soften, then microwave at full power (high) for 40 seconds; stir thoroughly, and let stand until the gelatin is completely dissolved, about 2 minutes longer. If some granules remain, repeat at 5-second intervals, stirring after each to test the solution.

For the low-fat baker, gelatin is a totally friendly product. One envelope has 25 calories, 6 g protein, 8 mg sodium, and not a bit of fat, carbohydrates, or cholesterol.

Some fresh fruits, such as fresh figs, kiwifruit, papaya, pineapple, and prickly pears, cannot be used with gelatin because they contain protease enzymes that soften gelatin and prevent it from setting. However, if these fruits (except kiwi) are boiled for five minutes, their enzymes are destroyed and they can be added to gelatin without harming its jelling properties.

CHOCOLATE

Chocolate is an important ingredient in any dessert cookbook, even one focused on reduced-fat baking. A glimpse at the Index will show that chocolate recipes are presented here in number and in depth. Chocolate is certainly used in low-fat baking, but it is used with caution—and with cocoa.

Chocolate is processed from pods of the *Theobroma cacao* tree, which is native to South and Central America, and cultivated in Africa and Southeast Asia. The pods are cut from the tree and the inner beans and pulp are scooped out, dried, fermented, and cured. Different beans from different geographical areas have particular characteristics; many manufacturers blend them to combine the best taste, texture, and aroma. At the factory, the beans are roasted, their hulls are removed, and the inner nibs, containing up to 54% cocoa butter, primarily a saturated fat, are crushed and ground, or rolled between steel disks. The heat from this process liquefies the cocoa butter, most of which is removed. The dark brown paste remaining, called chocolate liquor, is further refined by conching (working it back and forth with rollers), to evaporate moisture and volatile acids, mellow flavor, and enhance its quality.

Unadulterated chocolate liquor is molded, solidified, and sold as unsweetened or bitter chocolate. Varying amounts of sugar and cocoa butter are combined with this liquor to create blends known as bittersweet, semisweet, and sweet; each type has a different percentage of calories from fat, and a large portion of the fat is highly saturated cocoa butter.

In this book, you can use either bittersweet or semisweet chocolate interchangeably; unsweetened chocolate (pure chocolate liquor) imparts the most intense chocolatey flavor but has no sweetness. In low-fat baking, since only a small amount of solid chocolate is used, select the best-tasting brand to impart the richest flavor and aroma. Domestic chocolates such as Hershey, Nestlé, Maillard Eagle, Ghirardelli, and Baker's are widely known and work well. For exceptional flavor, I like imports such as Lindt, Tobler, Callebaut, and Valrhona.

To reduce fat, and particularly saturated fat, in your baking, use as little pure solid chocolate as possible. One ounce of solid unsweetened chocolate has 15 g fat, 8.7 of them saturated. To give the illusion and some of the complex depth of flavor of solid chocolate, you can add a small amount of it, grated or melted, to a cocoa-based dessert; however, as a general rule, substitute cocoa (see below) for solid chocolate.

Another way to reduce solid chocolate in a low-fat recipe is to use fat-reduced semisweet chocolate baking chips, a relatively new product available to the low-fat baker. Made by Hershey, the reduced-fat baking chips contain half the fat and 25% fewer calories than regular semisweet baking chips. I have not recommended these in my recipes because they have a different, less chocolatey taste in my opinion; however, they can be substituted for pure solid chocolate if one is on an extremely cautious diet. The fat reduction and flavor come from the use of Salatrim (see page 319), a type of fat that is only partially digested by the body.

White Chocolate

White chocolate is not a true chocolate because it contains no chocolate liquor. It is a blend of whole milk and sugar, cooked, condensed, and solidified, with some cocoa butter added to enhance flavor. Whey powder, lecithin, vanillin, and sometimes egg whites and nuts are also added. The finest-quality imported white chocolate brands (Tobler and Lindt, for example) contain the highest proportion of cocoa butter and thus have the best flavor and smoothest melting quality. In low-fat baking, since only a tiny amount of white chocolate is used, be sure to select the best quality. I prefer Tobler Narcisse, Lindt, Callebaut White, or Van Leer White, available through baking supply houses, some gourmet shops, and specialty food catalogues (pages 372–373).

TO MELT WHITE OR DARK CHOCOLATE: Chocolate is an emulsion; unless handled carefully and melted over a very low heat, the cocoa butter (which melts at a low temperature) will separate out. For this reason, it is best to melt chocolate in the top of a double boiler set over hot (125°F) water. To expedite the process, the chocolate should be chopped fine. Ideally, melt one half or two thirds of the chopped chocolate in the double boiler, then remove it from the heat and stir in the remaining chocolate until melted. Dark chocolate should never be heated above 120°F because it will turn grainy; milk chocolate will become grainy if heated above 115°F. To melt white chocolate, see below.

Chocolate can also be melted in a microwave. For each ounce of chopped dark chocolate, heat on medium-low (50%) power for 2 to 3 minutes (for milk or white chocolate use 30% power), then stir until smooth. Repeat for a few more seconds if needed.

Beware of getting a drop or two of any liquid into melting chocolate. A drop of water can cause the chocolate to seize, or harden. This is not always salvageable, but you can try smoothing it out by stirring in 1 teaspoon solid white shortening for each ounce of chocolate. Curiously, adding a lot of liquid does not harm melting chocolate. For example, you can add a minimum of 1 tablespoon liquid to each 2 ounces of melting chocolate, whisk briskly, and have a smooth product. The rule: the weight of added liquid should be at least 25% of the weight of the chocolate.

When melting white chocolate, keep in mind that excess heat transforms the proteins in the milk additives and causes the chocolate to lump; at between 110° and 115°F the chocolate will start to recrystallize and become grainy. If using a double boiler, set chopped white chocolate over warm (125°F) water and stir until smooth.

TO STORE CHOCOLATE: Store chocolate in a cool, dry location at about 60°F. When the temperature is warmer, a gray or white bloom may develop on the surface; this does not affect flavor, and will disappear when the chocolate is warmed or melted.

COCOA: To make cocoa, chocolate liquor is pressed to remove over half of its remaining cocoa butter. The dry cake of residue is pulverized and sifted into a fine powder containing very little fat. Actual fat content of cocoa varies by brand; for different purposes, manufacturers can alter the exact amount of cocoa butter removed from the chocolate liquor. Typically, one ounce of alkalized cocoa has about 63 calories and 4 g fat.

In reduced-fat baking, cocoa is an essential product; it imparts the intense taste of chocolate with only a trace of its saturated fat. There are different types of cocoa, each treating the natural acidity of the cocoa in a specific way. To neutralize some of the acidity and darken the color, some cocoas are Dutch-processed, or factory-treated with alkali (for example Fedora, Droste, Van Houten, and Hershey European). "Natural" cocoas, such as Hershey and Baker's, are not Dutch-processed. These have higher acidity and are used in recipes in conjunction with baking soda to neutralize some of the acid. The soda darkens and reddens the color and mellows the flavor. There is a wide variety between brands; select cocoa with care, comparing color, depth of flavor, fragrance, and taste. This is especially important in fat-reduced baking, where the quality of the cocoa will determine the flavor of your dessert.

Although cocoa is, by definition, low in fat, Bensdorp Nonfat Dutch-Process Cocoa (containing only 1% fat) has the least fat I know of in a baking product; it is available through the King Arthur Flour Baker's Catalogue (page 372).

Do not mistake instant cocoa mixes for pure cocoa; the mixes are for blending into drinks and have dry milk solids and sugars added. Products such as WonderSlim Low-Fat Cocoa, though low-fat and nearly caffeine-free, are more successful as dietary aids than as a baking ingredient.

To substitute cocoa powder for solid unsweetened chocolate, use 3 level tablespoons cocoa plus 1 tablespoon vegetable oil for each ounce of chocolate. For mail-order suppliers of chocolate and cocoa, see pages 372–373.

Finally, it appears that there may be good news for those chocoholics (I count myself among them) who dream about mountains of creamy bittersweet chocolate oozing cocoa butter from every pore. It turns out that stearic acid, one of butter's primary saturated fatty acids, makes up about half the saturated fat in cocoa butter. Research has shown that stearic acid does not raise the levels of blood cholesterol. The bad news is that it is still fat that makes you fat; in other words, a 4-ounce bar of milk chocolate contains about 588 calories and 36 grams of fat.

COMPARATIVE TABLE OF CALORIES AND FAT IN CHOCOLATE AND COCOA

Ingredient	Amount	Calories/ ounce	Total grams of fat	Grams of saturated fat	Percent of calories from fat
Unsweetened baking chocolate (square)	1 ounce	148	15.7	9.2	89
German sweet	1 ounce	143	9.6	5.6	58
Semisweet or bittersweet	1 ounce	135	8.4	4.9	53
Milk chocolate	1 ounce	145	8.7	5.2	52
Cocoa, unsweetened nonalkalized	1 ounce	64.9	3.8	2.2	50
Cocoa, unsweetened Dutch-processed	1 ounce	62.9	3.7	2.1	49

SOURCE: *USDA Agricultural Handbook 8–19.*

FLAVORINGS

Flavoring agents are especially important in reduced-fat baking because flavor is lost when fat is cut. Use fresh aromatic spices, pure extracts, fresh gingerroot, full-flavored zests and fruits to enhance the taste and bring baked goods to life.

Spices

The aroma of any spice is volatile and fades once the spice is ground. It also fades if the container is exposed to air, heat, or sunlight for a period of time. Ground spices should be stored in airtight containers in a cool, dark location. Whole seeds and spices keep better, but should be stored the same way as ground. If you have the choice, always use freshly ground spices—they give greater flavor.

Check the strength of spices by smelling before tossing them into your perfect batter. A dash of pallid old nutmeg is useless; a grating of fresh nutmeg is pungent.

Extracts

Extracts are the concentrated natural essential oils of a flavoring agent, commonly dissolved in alcohol. Some flavors are made from the oils found in the rind of citrus fruits, others are made from the pulp of the fruit.

Most essential oils are volatile and thus dissipate when exposed to the heat of baking. To have good flavor in your finished product, you must start with the best flavoring agent. Pure extracts cost a little more than imitation flavorings but really are worth it. The difference is critically important in reduced-fat baking, where flavor is lost when fat (especially butter) is cut. You need a strong replacement. For this reason, in many of the recipes in this book, you will see that vanilla extract is double that of the original recipe, and other extracts are usually added along with it. Some essences and extracts (maple, for example) are generally unavailable in pure form; if you cannot find a pure extract, use the imitation or artificial if you must. The "artificial" flavorings are synthetic, sometimes weaker in flavor, and often impart a chemical taste.

There are several suppliers of fine pure extracts in this country, Cook Flavoring Company in Washington State, for example, or Nielsen-Massey. These and others are available mail order from Williams-Sonoma and King Arthur Flour Baker's Catalogue (see page 372); they are also sold in gourmet shops.

Vanilla extract varies greatly in quality and strength. The vanilla bean is the fruit pod of a variety of tropical climbing orchid. Some bakers believe the finest extract is made with the vanilla bean from Tahiti, while others prefer beans from Madagascar (my favorite) or Mexico.

For the purest vanilla extract, make it yourself; it's easy. Buy four fresh pliable aromatic vanilla pods (in a gourmet shop) and slit them lengthwise. Soak the pods in two cups of vodka in a covered glass jar for at least two weeks. After this time, you can remove the pods and strain the liquid if you wish, or just leave them in; the extract is ready to use. Store all liquid extracts in dark-colored containers, tightly closed, in a cool, dark place.

Pure ground vanilla bean powder, used as a substitute for liquid extract, has long been available in Europe and is now imported to this country. A different product, called vanilla powder (Nielsen-Massey), is a blend of ground vanilla bean extractives and maltodextrin that can be sifted onto the tops of cookies and cakes. Both powdered products are available through the King Arthur Flour Baker's Catalogue.

I like to keep a canister of vanilla sugar on hand for baking. Simply stick a vanilla bean into a jar of granulated sugar and use as needed. The flavor perfumes the sugar and can be used in any baked product complemented by vanilla.

Zests

Zest is the brightly colored part of the peel of citrus fruit. The white pith beneath the zest can be bitter and shouldn't be used. Zest contains all the essential oils or flavors of the peel. Usually the fruit is grated on the small holes of a box grater or mandoline to remove the zest. Alternatively, a zester—a small tool with a sharp scooped "eye"—is used to remove shallow strips of peel that are then finely minced and substituted for grated peel.

The hardest part of grating zest is removing the pieces that are caught on the sharp teeth of the grater. A trick that solves this problem is to wrap a piece of baking parchment tightly over the toothed surface before grating. As the fruit is grated, the zest is caught on the paper. When the paper is lifted off, the zest is easily scraped into your batter.

Fresh Gingerroot

Fresh gingerroot is available in Asian markets and many supermarkets. Look for plump smooth-skinned pieces that are heavy for their size; you should be able to peel the skin with the gentlest scrape of your fingernail. Avoid dried, wrinkled pieces as they will be fibrous and lack juice. To use gingerroot, peel it with a paring knife or vegetable peeler, then either grate it on the finest holes of a grater or rub it across the teeth of a porcelain ginger grater (available in Asian markets) or cut the pieces across the grain into very thin rounds, then chop as fine as possible. Ginger juice can be extracted most easily with an electric vegetable juice extractor.

Dried Fruits

Dried fruits add flavor and their natural sugars provide sweetness. Chopped dried fruit can be a useful substitute for the texture supplied by nuts, which are much higher in fat. Fresh and dried fruits are not only low in fat; they are also a valuable source of vitamins, minerals, and fiber. There are a few exceptions to the rule that fruits are low fat, notably avocados (16% fat) and ripe olives (30% fat).

When purchasing dried fruits, look for those with good color and plump, full shape; avoid those that are hard as rocks. The chances are that in a natural food store the product will be good, but it is best to taste one piece (ask first, please) before buying. Dates and prunes are sold pitted or with pits. Pitted are easier to work with and can easily be chopped. I prefer whole pitted dates to the packaged prechopped, which often seem to be either covered with crystallized sugar or dried out. In any case, dates are easy to chop by hand.

Dried prunes are also available slightly moist (for snacking); some brands are good, others too gooey. Test these before adding to a cake.

FRUIT PURÉES

In my experience, fruit purées cannot successfully replace all the fat in low-fat baked goods, but they are excellent as a partial substitute. Generally low in calories (if unsweetened) and virtually fat free, commercially prepared or homemade applesauce, fruit butters (apple butter, pear butter), mashed bananas, and prune purée, for example, all replicate some of fat's desirable characteristics. They are viscous, have the ability to trap some air when whipped, contain some cellulose which traps moisture and acts as a stabilizer, and contain some natural pectin (especially applesauce), which tenderizes the protein in wheat flour. In addition, all fruit purées add flavor. When using purées, it is essential to match the choice of fruit with the primary flavor of your cake; bananas, for example, are too strong a taste to be used in a chocolate cake, while prune purée is a good match. Apple and pear purées blend with most fruit and spice flavors. There is no hard and fast rule for substitution; experiment with type and amount of fruit if you want to alter your own recipes. In this book, use the exact type and amount specified to achieve optimum results.

To make your own purée or fruit butter, simply peel, pit, and cut up the fruit of your choice (pears, apples, peaches, plums, for example) and place it in a pot with a small amount of water. Cook over medium-low heat, taking care that enough liquid remains to prevent scorching, until the fruit is soft, then purée in a food processor or put through a food mill, or mash. For cleanest flavors and fewest calories, do not add sugar.

The low-fat baker has two choices when using prune purée. You can make your own, which I generally prefer: Combine 1 cup dried pitted prunes (about 18) with 1 cup water in a heavy-bottomed saucepan. Cover, bring to a boil, then reduce the heat and simmer until the prunes are soft, about 5 minutes. Add ½ cup more water and purée the mixture in a food processor; this makes about 1½ cups purée. The second choice is to use a commercially prepared prune butter called lekvar, sold in 1-pound or 17-ounce jars and available in many supermarkets and Eastern European specialty food shops. Lekvar usually contains corn syrup, water, sugar, pectin, and citric acid. Because of the additives, it is both sweeter and more viscous than homemade prune purée.

Commercially prepared fat replacements based on fruit purée have begun to appear on the market with some frequency; if you're tempted to use these, try them out cautiously to be sure that you like the resulting taste and texture.

NUTS

❧

The good news is: Nuts impart unique flavor and texture to baked goods. The bad news is they are high in fat—walnuts are 64% fat, pecans 65%. However, some recent studies on both walnuts and almonds (75% fat) have indicated that eating increased quantities of nuts (added to a healthy already low-fat diet) actually had the effect of lowering the overall blood cholesterol levels of the volunteers. This may appear to be just another dietary contradiction, but one fact emerges: the type of fat you eat is just as important as the amount. Nuts are very low in saturated fat and higher in polyunsaturated and monounsaturated fats, which are more "heart-healthy."

In low-fat baking, one of the easiest ways to cut fat is to cut out or cut back on the nuts. I prefer not to cut them out because I want to retain the flavor and texture. You can reduce the amount in the original recipe by as much as three quarters without fear of failure. Ask yourself if you can replace them with a crunchy low-fat cereal such as Grape-Nuts, or with a low-fat chopped dried fruit such as apricots, or raisins. In some of the recipes in this book, I have used nut oils (hazelnut and walnut) to impart the flavor of the nut without the high fat. This works in certain formulas, but the oil must be absolutely fresh. Walnut oil, particularly, has a tendency to become rancid quickly; smell the oil before using it. Always store nut oils in the refrigerator.

If you use nuts, see how little you can get away with and still retain some nut flavor and texture. Put the nuts on top of a cake or muffin, rather than in the batter. The exposed nuts will toast during baking, so their flavor will be enhanced. Also, they are visible and so more noticeable.

Be sure the nuts you use are fresh. Nuts keep longest when stored in their shells; next best are whole nuts rather than chopped. Store nuts in sealed bags in a cool, dry place or in the refrigerator or freezer (though I have found that nuts stored in the freezer lose some of their flavor after about a month). Purchase your nuts from a reliable source to be sure they are flavorful and fresh.

Because nuts, particularly walnuts, contain a lot of oil, they often become pasty when ground. To prevent this problem, *dry out the nuts* before grinding. Bake the nuts in a shallow pan in a preheated 300°F oven for about 10 minutes, tossing them occasionally. *To toast nuts* instead of simply drying them out, increase the oven heat to about 325°F. Toast the nuts, tossing or stirring several times, until they are aromatic and begin to turn golden in color, 12 to 15 minutes. Nuts can also be toasted in a heavy-bottomed frying pan set on medium heat for 3 to 5 minutes; stir or toss continually to avoid burning.

NUTS AND SEEDS, LISTED FROM LOWEST IN SATURATED FAT TO HIGHEST				
Type	**Amount**	**Calories**	**Total grams of fat**	**Total grams of saturated fat**
Chestnuts, roasted	1 ounce	70	0.6	0.1
Poppy seeds	1 ounce	90	8	1
Black walnuts	1 ounce	172	16	1
Sesame seeds	1 ounce	165	14	1
Almonds, blanched	1 ounce	166	15	1
Hazelnuts, unblanched (filberts)	1 ounce	179	18	1
Sunflower seeds, dry	1 ounce	165	14	2
Pistachio nuts	1 ounce	164	14	2
Peanuts, dry roasted	1 ounce	161	14	2
English walnuts	1 ounce	182	18	2
Pecans	1 ounce	190	19	2
Cashews, dry roasted	1 ounce	163	13	3
Peanut butter (Skippy chunk)	1 ounce	190	17	3
Macadamia nuts	1 ounce	199	21	3
Brazil nuts, unblanched	1 ounce	186	19	5
Coconut (dry, sweet, flaked, canned)	1 ounce	126	9	8

SOURCE: Anna dePlanter Bowes and Charles F. Church, *Food Values of Portions Commonly* Used, rev. by Jean A.T. Pennington, 15th ed. (New York: Harper & Row, 1989); *USDA Agricultural Handbook 8–12*, 1984.

To remove the skins on hazelnuts after toasting, wrap the hot nuts in a coarsely textured towel and allow to stand for a few minutes. Then rub the skins off with the towel. *To remove the skins from almonds or pistachios*, blanch the shelled nuts (skins still on) for about 2 minutes, then drain and drop them into cold water. Pinch off the skins with your fingers; they pop right off.

All nuts are high in total fat and saturated fat; if using nuts at all, stick to walnuts, almonds, peanuts, hazelnuts, pecans; watch out for fat-rich Brazil, cashew, macadamia, and coconut (see the table on page 333).

Equipment

The recipes in this book are written with the assumption that your baking pantry includes the basic equipment described below. While creative substitution is often a virtue to be admired, there are times in baking when only the correct equipment will do. Read through the following notes before beginning to bake. Baking pans are described first, then the additional baking essentials.

BAKING PANS

Baking pans are available in an amazing array of materials, sizes, and shapes. For the basic pantry, a few sizes and shapes will suffice; to substitute pans, see the chart on pages 340–341. When buying pans, select the best quality you can afford. Look for sturdy, durable pans with smooth seams. An important factor in pan selection is the pan size. Maddeningly, every manufacturer uses a different system. Some measure a pan from rim to rim, others across the lip to the outer edges, others across the bottom. I measure across the top inner edge. I also measure the volume of a pan by noting the number of cups of water needed to fill the pan to the brim (see Pan Volume and Serving Chart, pages 340–341). Many cakes can be baked in pans of a variety of shapes and sizes; recipes that are flexible in this regard have the volume of batter noted in cups in the Yield section of the recipe. Select alternate pan sizes from the chart by comparing volumes. Note that pans should be filled about two thirds full so there is room for the batter to rise. Something as simple as the wrong pan size may result in baking failure. Batter that is too thin when poured into a large pan bakes into a cake that is too flat; if the pan is too small, the batter may overflow when it rises.

For low-fat baking, Teflon, Silverstone, and other nonstick pans are a great help because they require less fat to prevent baked goods from sticking; however, they are not essential. If you use them, avoid the cheapest nonstick products because the coating will be thin and wear off quickly. A more important problem with nonstick coatings is accidental superheating. When nonstick products are used according to manufacturers' directions, there is no danger and they are FDA-approved for safety.

Nevertheless, accidents happen. Cooks (and pet canaries in the kitchen) should be aware of the fact that when *empty* nonstick pans are left *unattended* over *high direct heat* for too long (it is impossible to estimate time) the pan may attain temperatures above 400°F, at which time fluorocarbon polymers in the nonstick surface may begin to burn, breaking down into toxic gases—compounds which can be hazardous to human health and fatal to small birds. Food Scientist Harold McGee believes these fumes are unhealthy at 400°F. DuPont says nonstick cookware can emit toxic fumes at temperatures exceeding 500°F. Whatever the toxic temperature, the way to avoid the problem is to pay attention and not leave the stove when an empty pan is over a hot burner. Or, use seasoned cast-iron pans or other pans without a nonstick surface. There is little danger in baking with nonstick pans, however, because baking pans are filled with batter before being set into a moderately hot oven. One of the few exceptions is in making popovers, where the empty (or pregreased) pan is preheated, but temperatures in this case are still within safe limits.

For cake baking, you need a few basic pans. Buy **layer cake pans** in pairs or threes in 8- or 9-inch rounds. Also select one or two 8- or 9-inch square pans at least 1½ to 2 inches deep. Look for sturdy aluminum or heavy-gauge tinned steel; for cakes, avoid dark or black pans, which give a dark crust undesirable in delicate cakes. **Springform pans** have two pieces: a flat, fluted, and/or tubed bottom panel made of metal (some manufacturers use heatproof glass) and a surrounding hoop fastened with a spring latch. Opening the spring releases the pan sides and the cake can remain on the pan bottom; these cakes do not have to be turned upside down. Springform pans are used for delicate tortes, cheesecakes, and constructed layer cakes built up, then chilled and unmolded.

Tube pans vary in manufacture, size, shape, and name. Whether they are called plain tubes, rings, Bundts, or kugelhopf molds, all have a central tube designed to conduct heat to the center of the batter, allowing the dough to rise and bake evenly. When selecting a tube pan, remember that the heavier the metal, the more evenly the cake will bake. Select the sturdiest pans, such as tinned steel (I like the Kaiser pans imported from Germany). Teflon-lined Bundt pans are made of aluminum as well as heavy cast aluminum; both give good results.

Angel food cake pans are also tube pans, but most have removable bottoms as well as small feet sticking up around the rim so the baked cake can be inverted and suspended as it cools. Some pans lack the feet but have a long tube for the cake to rest on when inverted. If your pan lacks both, simply invert the pan over the neck of a tall bottle and let it hang upside down until the cake is thoroughly cooled.

A **jelly roll pan** for home baking commonly measures $10\frac{1}{2} \times 15\frac{1}{2} \times 1$ inch (not to be confused with a professional "half-sheet" pan $12\frac{1}{4} \times 17\frac{1}{2} \times 1$ inch); it should be of sturdy construction with a good lip all around. Use this for thin sheet cakes and petits fours, or turn the pan upside down and, in a pinch, use it as an extra cookie sheet. It also makes a fine tray to catch drips when icing a cake or cookies placed on a wire rack.

Sheet cakes can be baked in oblong or rectangluar pans $1\frac{1}{2}$ to $2\frac{1}{2}$ inches deep. I often use a lasagne pan or turkey roasting pan for a sheet cake.

Pie plates can be made of metal or Pyrex heatproof glass or pottery. If you prefer metal pie plates, select pans with sloping sides in 9- and 10-inch diameters in aluminum with a dull or dark finish, which absorbs heat quickly. Avoid highly polished metal pans, because the shine tends to deflect heat, causing the crust to bake more slowly. I prefer Pyrex pie pans because they conduct heat quickly and brown crusts nicely, and I can see the color of the bottom crust as it bakes. I could not do without my 10-inch Pyrex pans in regular depth and deep-dish, both purchased in the hardware store. (These are not always available in cookware shops; I don't know why.)

Tarts are generally baked in fluted-edged metal or ceramic pans. The ones I prefer are imported from France and have a removable flat bottom. They are available in a range of sizes, and also in rectangular and specialty shapes; for home baking try the 7- to 11-inch rounds to begin with. To unmold a tart, set the center of the baked tart on a wide-mouthed canister and press lightly on the edge of the pan. The edging ring will drop away, leaving the tart to be carried and served on its metal bottom. Individual tartlet pans made of the same material as the full-size pans or of heat-proof glass are also available in cookware shops and from bakeware catalogues.

Use **cookie sheets** made of heavy metal with a shiny surface. The best designs have only one narrow lip, for a handle, so the hot air can easily circulate around the cookies. Avoid cookie sheets with full edges that block the heat. If you notice cookies browning too fast on the bottom, slide a second flat sheet beneath the first, to insulate it slightly from the heat.

Muffin pans come in a variety of sizes, from mini-muffin tins with $1\frac{3}{4}$-inch-wide cups to giant $3\frac{1}{3}$- to 4-inch diameters. The average size, called for in this book, is $2\frac{1}{2}$-inch diameter. Select a pan with a dark, dull finish that absorbs heat rather than a shiny surface that deflects it. Muffins bake well in heavy or thin pans; weight does not seem critical. Teflon or nonstick coatings can be a great help in baking low-fat muffins.

Charlottes are made in tapered molds. Nearly any wide-mouth pan will do. The classic charlotte mold, imported from France, is a slightly tapered cylindrical form made of tinned steel. It is available in graduated sizes from 6 ounces to 2 quarts. Avoid molds made of aluminum because the metal can interact with certain fillings and/or acidic fruits, causing the fillings to darken. If you do have an aluminum mold, line it with plastic wrap before filling it. For nonbaked charlottes, simply use a round plastic freezer container (1- or 2-quart capacity).

Note: To allow for even circulation of oven heat, be sure all baking sheets or pans are allowed 2 inches of clear air space between them and the oven walls.

PAN VOLUME AND SERVING CHART

Pan shape and size	Maximum cups fluid to fill to capacity	Maximum cups batter (allowing for rise)	Approximate number of servings
Round Layers			
6 × 2 inches	4	2 to 2½	6
7 × 2⅝ (springform)	7½	4 to 5	8
8 × 1½ or 8 × 2	4½ to 5	2	8 to 10
9 × 1½ or 9 × 2	6 to 6½	3 to 3½	8 to 10
10 × 2	10	4½ to 6	14
12 × 2	14	7½ to 9	22
14 × 2	19½	10 to 12	36 to 40
Square Layers			
8 × 2	8	3½ to 5	9 to 12
9 × 1½	8 to 9	4½ to 5	9 to 12
9 × 2	10	5½	9 to 12
10 × 2	12⅓	6	20
12 × 2	16	10 to 12	36
14 × 2	24	12 to 14	42
Rectangular (Sheet Cakes)			
8 × 12 (7½ × 11¾ × 1¾)	8	4 to 5	12
9 × 13 (8¾ × 13½ × 1¾)	16	8 to 9	20 to 24
11 × 17 (11⅜ × 17¼ × 2¼)	25	14 to 15	24 to 30
10½ × 15½ × 1 (jelly roll pan)	10	4 to 5 for butter cake or 8 for génoise	24 to 35
12¼ × 17¼ × 1 (professional half-sheet)	12	5 to 6	25 to 35
Heart			
6 × 1¾	3½	2	6 to 8
9 × 1½	5	3 to 3½	16
9½ × 2¾ (springform)	12	8 to 9	16 to 18
Tube, Ring, Bundt, and Kugelhopf			
8 × 3¼ (plain tube)	9	5 to 6	8 to 10
9 × 2¾ (plain tube)	6 to 7	4 to 4½	8 to 10
9 × 2 (springform)	9 to 10	6 to 7	10 to 12
9¼ × 3¼ (fluted tube or Bundt)	9 to 10	5 to 6	10 to 12
9½ × 3¾ or 10-inch (plain tube or springform)	12	6 to 7	12 to 14
9 × 4 (kugelhopf)	10	5 to 6	10 to 12
9¾ × 4¼ (kugelhopf)	12	6 to 7	12 to 14
10 × 3½ (Bundt)	12	6 to 7	14
10 × 4 (angel cake tube)	16	8 to 8½	12 to 14

Pan shape and size	Maximum cups fluid to fill to capacity	Maximum cups batter (allowing for rise)	Approximate number of servings
Loaves			
$5\frac{1}{2} \times 3 \times 2\frac{1}{8}$	$2\frac{1}{4}$	$1\frac{1}{2}$ to $1\frac{3}{4}$	6 to 8
$6 \times 3\frac{1}{2} \times 2$ (baby)	2	$1\frac{1}{4}$ to $1\frac{1}{2}$	6 to 8
$7\frac{1}{2} \times 3\frac{1}{2} \times 2$	5 to 6	3	7 to 8
$8\frac{1}{2} \times 4\frac{1}{2} \times 2\frac{3}{4}$ (average)	$5\frac{1}{4}$	$3\frac{1}{2}$ to $3\frac{3}{4}$	7 to 8
$9 \times 5 \times 3$ (large)	8 to 9	4 to 5	9 to 10
Charlotte Molds			
$5\frac{1}{2}$-inch base, $3\frac{1}{2}$-inch height	6	—	8
6-inch base, 4-inch height	8	—	10
Soufflé Molds			
$6\frac{1}{2}$-inch base, $3\frac{1}{4}$-inch height	6	4 to 5	8
7-inch diameter, $3\frac{3}{4}$-inch height	8	6 to 7	10
Muffin Pans/Cupcakes			
$1\frac{3}{4} \times \frac{3}{4}$ (baby)	4 teaspoons	3 teaspoons	1
2×1	3 tablespoons	2 to $2\frac{1}{2}$ tablespoons	1
$2\frac{1}{2}$-inch diameter	$\frac{1}{3}$ cup	$\frac{1}{4}$ cup	1
$2\frac{3}{4}$-inch diameter	$\frac{1}{2}$ cup	$\frac{1}{3}$ cup	1
$3 \times 1\frac{1}{4}$	$\frac{1}{2}$ cup	$\frac{1}{3}$ cup	1
$3\frac{1}{2}$-inch diameter	1 cup	generous $\frac{3}{4}$ cup	1

OTHER BAKING ESSENTIALS

The following items include baking essentials as well as gadgets. Clearly the electric mixer, food processor, oven, thermometers, and cooling racks fall into the first category, while others, like a nut grinder and goose-feather pastry brushes, may seem frivolous to you but are essential to me.

The Special Equipment note preceding each recipe lists only the specific pan recommended and any out-of-the-ordinary items needed, such as baking parchment, but not bowls or measuring cups.

Wax Paper and Baking Parchment

Wax paper is useful for collecting sifted dry ingredients or grated zests, or for lining baking pans for cookies and cakes. It will brown in the oven, but (in my experience) will not burn. When pans are lined with wax paper, the paper should be greased, and sometimes dusted with flour, if the recipe so specifies.

Baking parchment is a specially formulated paper designed for lining baking pans to prevent baked goods from sticking. The paper does not generally have to be greased; exceptions in this book are so noted. You can draw on baking parchment with a pencil, for ease in following guidelines when making cookies or meringue shapes. Parchment is more durable than wax paper and thus ideal for making paper decorating cones (page 348). It is available from some supermarkets, restaurant supply houses, and baking specialty shops (see pages 372–373) in dispenser rolls, in precut triangles (for decorating cones), and in rounds to fit various cake pans.

Aluminum Foil

Aluminum foil is very useful when making pastry. It can be used to protect the bottom of the oven from juicy pie fillings, and small pieces can be shaped into tents to set over browning pie pastry decorations. Foil is also used to line "blind-baked" pie shells that are lined with rice or pie weights during baking.

The most useful foil gadget, however, is the foil frame I have devised to prevent overbrowning the pastry around the edges of a pie. To make this one-piece, easy-to-handle frame to fit a 9-inch pie plate, cut a 10-inch square of foil and fold it into quarters. Tear out the center, leaving about a 2-inch edging (A). Unfold the foil (B) and set the opened frame over the pie or tart after about half the baking time, before overbrowning has begun. Gently crimp the edges to the pan rim. Remove the frame during the final few minutes of baking to even the color of the top.

A

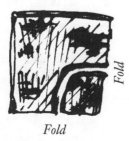

Fold

B

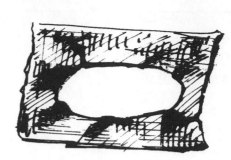

Unfolded foil frame

Mixing Bowls

You cannot have too many bowls in too many different sizes. However, you *need* only a few. I recommend heavy pottery for hand mixing or stainless-steel bowls with flat bottoms (so they don't tip) for use with an electric mixer. Metal bowls are not subject to thermal shock; these are best for mixtures such as mousses that you whip over heat, then set into an ice bath to chill.

For general use, you need a set of bowls sized 1, 1½, 2, and 3 quarts. Life will go on without a copper bowl for whipping your egg whites, but it is a classy (and surprisingly efficient) addition to your pantry. Pyrex bowls are useful; one of my favorites is a 2-quart measuring cup/bowl marked in increments. Use it to measure the total volume of cake batters, a help when you are not sure which cake pan to use. Do not use plastic bowls for mixing batter or whipping egg whites; it is virtually impossible to remove all odors and grease from plastic, and the merest trace of fat will inhibit whipped meringue.

Measuring Cups and Spoons

Dry measuring cups are designed specifically for measuring dry ingredients (e.g., flour, sugar). Fill the cup to the top, then level the ingredient off by passing a straight edge over it. Dry measuring cups are commonly available in nesting sets, in graduated sizes from $1/8$ to 2 cups. They do vary in quality, and cheap plastic cups will not be as accurate as sturdy metal. My favorites, available from specialty cookware shops such as Williams-Sonoma (see page 372) are heavy-duty stainless steel and precisely calibrated in $1/4$-, $1/3$-, $1/2$-, 1-, and 2-cup sizes.

Liquid measuring cups are very different. They have pouring spouts and are commonly available in 1-, 2-, and 4-cup sizes. The best are made of Pyrex. To use, you simply fill the cup to the desired mark, set the cup flat on the counter, and bend down so you can check it at eye level. Don't fill a liquid measuring cup up to the brim or you will have too much; there is a small extra space above the top measuring line so the measured liquid can be poured or carried without spilling. Dry and liquid measuring cups should not be used interchangeably.

Measuring spoons come in graduated sizes from $1/8$ teaspoon to 1 tablespoon; metal spoons are more accurate than those of flimsy plastic. My favorite type is similar to the heavy measuring cups; they are stainless steel, sturdy, and relatively expensive.

Electric Mixers

While most batters can be beaten by hand with a wooden spoon, and some are best done that way, electric mixers save time and whip in more air than one can incorporate by hand. There is a wide variety of mixers on the market: hand-held electric (cord) and (battery-operated) cordless mixers; stand-type home-style mixers of moderate price having two or more bowls; and heavy-duty professional mixers with stainless-steel bowls of various sizes and several beaters (balloon whip, flat paddle, dough hook) such as the English Kenwood Stand Mixer and the American KitchenAid. Remember that hand-held and home-style mixers do not have the power of the professionals, so will take longer to achieve the same result but often give better

results because they incorporate less air; adjust your technique and recipe times to your appliance. In my kitchen, I use the heavy-duty KitchenAid Model K45SS, with a head that tips back to raise the beater, making it easy to scrape the bowl and beater or add ingredients. For whipping cream, I often use the half-size KitchenAid bowl, or simply a small deep bowl and a hand-held mixer. If you use a heavy-duty mixer be sure to adjust the beater so it reaches into the bottom of the bowl (see the manual).

Food Processors, Blenders, and Mincers

A blender does a good job of chopping and mixing and puréeing, but overall is not as versatile as the processor. The ubiquitous food processor is a great time-saver for making bread crumbs, shredding carrots, apples, or potatoes, chopping nuts or dried fruits. The processor also does a fine job of mixing creamed icings and glazes that do not need air incorporated. In general, I do not recommend the processor for cake batters unless the recipes are specifically designed for its use, as are several in this book. The speed and power of the processor blade can quickly overwork the mixture and overdevelop the gluten in the flour, producing a tough product. In my kitchen, I use a Cuisinart DLC 7 Superpro and an 11-cup KitchenAid Ultra-Power Food Processor.

To grind herbs and poppy seeds, I recommend an electric herb mincer such as the one made by Varco (see suppliers, page 372). It consists of a small cup with a set of thin sharp blades that sits on a base containing the motor. One adds the herbs or seeds to the cup, places the cover on top, and pushes down to engage the motor on contact. The electric blender will grind poppy seeds, but you can add only $1/2$ cup of seeds at a time and must stir them down once or twice. The food processor, on the other hand, will not grind poppy seeds because they are too small and just fly about the blade.

Sifters/Strainers

The distinction between a sifter and sieve is often as fine as the mesh that distinguishes them. In theory, a sifter has from one to three screens of medium-fine wire mesh. It is used for dry ingredients (flour, baking powder, confectioners' sugar). A sieve has a slightly coarser single-screen mesh and is used for draining fruits and straining sauces. I have several of these in my kitchen, each slightly different in mesh size. For most of the sifting operations in this book, I use a single-screen sifter with medium-fine mesh. None of the recipes in this book requires a triple-tier sifter. A handy addition to the pantry is a 3-inch-diameter, medium-fine sifter with a 3- or 4-inch handle. I use this for sifting (dusting) flour or cocoa onto greased pans; the sifter can reach into a tube pan to direct powder onto the sides of the greased tube, normally a difficult task. For decorating cake and cookie tops, I also use a stainless steel shaker with a fine-mesh strainer top.

Wire Whisks

Wire whisks are used for whipping or folding certain ingredients together. The multiple wires have the effect of opening the batter and incorporating a lot of air when beating. Whisks come in a variety of sizes, from about 3 inches long for whipping melted butter in a measuring cup to enormous whisks for oversized commercial bowls. Select a whisk that is all metal, molded into a metal handle. The whisks with wires poked into a wooden handle are impossible to clean, and eventually old unmentionable food particles collect in the tube and begin to discolor your meringue or your batter.

Rubber Spatulas

Rubber spatulas (often made of plastic) are invaluable for mixing, stirring, and folding ingredients together. The blade is a flexible tongue perfect for scraping down bowls and beaters or turning batters out of bowls into baking pans. They come in all sizes, from 4 or 5 inches to 18 or more for the professional kitchen. I prefer the type with a wooden handle affixed to a flexible blade which is acid- and high heat-resistant and will not stain or deteriorate. Williams-Sonoma carries a type that is made of silicone rubber developed for medical equipment, so it is especially durable. For many scooping/stirring tasks, I use a spatula with a scooped head, a cross between a spatula and a spoon (Rubbermaid calls its version the Spoonula).

Graters

I recommend a stainless-steel box grater or a flat mandoline with a variety of hole sizes. For grating citrus zest I use the finest holes; for grating carrots, apples, or potatoes, I use the medium-sized holes. I also have a 4- × 8-inch flat panel grater with a handle at one end; this is useful for citrus zest and hard cheeses. Fresh gingerroot can be grated on the panel grater or on a beautifully designed Chinese porcelain ginger grater sold in Asian markets.

Nut Grinders

For European nut tortes and some other pastries, nuts must be ground into a fine, dry powder rather than chopped fine. The easiest method is to use a hand-held food or nut mill in which a presser bar pushes down on the nuts, forcing them onto a rotating cutting disk. A blender or food processor can also be used, if some of the sugar used in the recipe is added, but the nuts will never be as light or fine as when shaved with a nut mill. Before grinding walnuts (or other oily nuts) to a fine powder, they should be dried out in the oven (see page 333).

Pastry Brushes

A pastry brush is used for applying egg washes and jelly glazes to tarts. It is also useful for spreading syrups and preserves on cake layers.

For the most delicate tasks, I prefer an imported European goose-feather brush with a handle of braided quills. This lovely tool, available from fine cookware shops and catalogues, lasts a long time, is very inexpensive, and can be washed in warm water and air-dried. For ordinary tasks such as brushing glazes and also for brushing oil on baking pans, I use a natural or nylon bristle brush, available in sizes from 1 to 2½ inches wide. Keep a sharp eye out for fallen bristles in the glaze. No matter how thoroughly you wash them, brushes tend to hold a trace of past flavors. Since I also use a pastry brush for savory purposes such as spreading garlic butter on bread, I have learned to use an indelible pen to mark the handles of my brushes "SAVORY" and "PASTRY." This keeps my icing glaze from smelling like garlic.

Cake Testers

One of the tests for doneness for many baked products is to stick a cake tester into the cake; if it comes out clean, the cake is done; if covered with wet crumbs, the cake needs more baking time. Theoretically, this is a fine test, but you need to watch for other signs as well because an overbaked cake will also produce a clean testing pick.

In my grandmother's day, the preferred cake tester was a clean broom straw. My favorite is a thin bamboo satay skewer—inexpensive and available at Asian food markets and gourmet shops—but a toothpick can also be used. Special metal cake testers that look like long hatpins with a looped handle are sold in hardware and bakeware shops. In general, I prefer a wooden pick because metal heats up quickly and batter may cling to it even when the cake is completely baked.

Cooling Racks

Cooling racks are essential for baking. When a baked cake or sheet of cookies comes from the oven, it should be set on a raised rack so it can cool with air circulating all the way around it. The rack prevents condensation of moisture on the bottom of the baked goods and promotes even cooling. Most cakes have a fragile structure and need to cool in the baking pan for 10 to 15 minutes before unmolding. After unmolding, cakes should continue cooling on a wire rack so air circulation will draw off the moisture or steam. If the steam remained inside the cake, it would become soggy. Other baked products benefit from cooling on a rack for the same reasons.

Racks range from flimsier ones of thin wire to heavy-gauge, and from 8-inch rounds perfect for a single cake layer to broad rectangular racks made for the professional kitchen, holding a dozen layers. Select racks slightly bigger than you think you will need; the best racks are the most sturdy and have the mesh close enough together to prevent cookies from sliding between the wires.

Cardboard Cake Disks

Corrugated cardboard rounds are invaluable for supporting cakes and cake layers. They are sold in disks ranging from 6 to 18 inches in diameter. They are available in plain brown paper or with one side covered with white, gold, or silver foil; bakers' supply houses carry disks with fluted edges. Basic disks are sold in restaurant supply or party and paper goods shops. If you cannot find them, you can make your own by drawing around a cake pan on a piece of stiff or corrugated cardboard; cut them out and cover them with aluminum foil, pressed flat.

Thermometers

Specialized thermometers are important for accuracy at different stages of baking and in general food preparation. Take care of your thermometers. Do not put a cold one directly into boiling syrup, but rather warm it in hot water first; thermal shock can crack the glass tubes.

For making candy, sugar syrups, and pastry creams, I use a candy–jelly–deep fry thermometer with a mercury-filled glass tube fastened to a stainless-steel casing.

For instant read-out temperatures for sauces, soufflés, meringues, melting chocolate, and so forth, I use a special small thermometer with a stainless-steel stem and a large round dial mounted on top (with a shorter temperature range than regular thermometers). Instant-read thermometers are not meant to be left in food throughout the cooking time, but rather inserted from time to time to check the temperature; the thermometer reacts within seconds, then is removed. Called Instant Bi-Therm thermometers, they are made by Tel-Tru and Taylor, among others, and are available in hardware stores and cookware shops. The King Arthur Flour Baker's Catalogue (see page 372) also sells two types of digital instant-read thermometers. These battery-operated instruments (more sensitive, more accurate, and much more expensive than the simpler bi-therm) are useful for measuring the temperature of baked bread as well as candy or for chilling sorbet.

Ovens and Oven Thermometers

Even heat is essential for accurate baking. Both electric and gas ovens produce good results, but you must know your ovens well and watch them carefully, for even the best seem to lose accuracy easily and often. While it is a good idea to have the calibration checked occasionally, and certainly if you suspect it is off, it is also important to be sure the doors close tightly, that their gaskets are still flexible, the vent filters are clean, and hot spots (which most ovens have) are monitored. Hot spots mean that baked goods color more in one spot than another on the oven shelf. If this happens, turn the item or transfer it to another shelf or move it front to back on the same shelf halfway through the baking time. I have two new Maytag electric wall ovens that are remarkably accurate, and two old gas ovens that have distinct personalities of their own; we have a decided love/hate relationship, though we tolerate each other and have learned how to work well together. The secret of our success, and it can be yours too, is that in the unreliable ovens I rely on auxiliary thermometers placed in the interior; in some cases I use two, one in front, one in the rear.

The two most widely available oven thermometers are the spring type, which has two metal strips that expand or contract to move a dial, and the mercury-type thermometer, which is more accurate. I prefer the latter, available mounted on a metal stand or in a folding metal case. Both are sold in hardware and cookware shops. Set the thermometer in place on the oven rack, then adjust the outer oven thermostat so the interior thermometer is correct. If a recipe fails, don't blame the cookbook, or yourself, until you have your oven temperature checked.

For accuracy when baking, always preheat your oven at least 15 to 20 minutes before placing the baked goods inside. Ingredients will react in unexpected ways if set into the wrong temperature and results can be disastrous. Check the interior auxiliary thermometer before putting in the baking pan.

POSITIONING OVEN SHELVES: Recipes in this book specify the position of the oven shelf upon which the cake is to be baked. This is important because the heat circulation varies within the chamber. Different types of baked goods bake better in different temperatures; some prefer the hotter area, some need a moderate heat. The topmost shelf is hotter than the middle, the oven floor the hottest spot of all. Single-layer cakes can be baked in the lower third of the oven or the middle, where the heat is moderately hot. Thicker cakes, with more than two inches of batter, or cakes with delicate structure should be baked in the center where the heat is more even and moderate. If you have doubts, use the middle. If you are baking cookies or several cake layers at one time, position two racks to divide the oven evenly into thirds. Allow an inch or preferably two between baking pans to allow heat to circulate properly. If baking several layers or cakes at one time, stagger them on two shelves so they are not directly in line with one another.

CONVECTION AND MICROWAVE OVENS: Convection ovens contain an interior fan to blow the heat around. This constant circulation causes them to cook about 25% faster than regular ovens; it produces a nicely browned crust on pies and breads and a fine interior crumb in breads and cakes. However, the rush of air produced by the fan is too gusty for fragile meringue cookies, for example, and may blow them right off the pan. Convection ovens are preferred by many professionals and are used by many bakeries. I personally feel that I do not need a convection oven because I bake delicate cakes more often than breads. When converting ordinary recipes for regular ovens to use in a convection oven, lower the baking temperature about 50 degrees.

I use my microwave for melting butter and chocolate, defrosting and warming baked goods. But I continue to feel that my conventional ovens give me more control, produce a better texture, and are generally better for baking.

Pastry Bags and Decorating Tips

Pastry bags are used for piping icing, meringue, or soft doughs like pâte à choux for eclairs. Bags are available in materials ranging from cotton canvas to nylon and in sizes from 7 inches to nearly 24 inches long. Select the bag fitted to the task: small bags for delicate designs and melted chocolate, large ones for piping meringue and batter. For all-purpose use, I use a 16-inch nylon bag. I prefer the nylon for ease in cleaning. It is also flexible, comfortable in the hand, and will not leak fat from the fabric as cotton will. Wash the bags in hot water and air-dry them after use.

To fill a decorating bag, fold back a 4- or 5-inch cuff and set the tip down into a 2-cup measure for support. Fill the bag, then squeeze the icing down into the tip and twist the bag closed. To use the bag, hold the twist-closure between the thumb and fingers of one hand. In this way, you hold the bag closed while applying pressure to squeeze out the icing. The other hand guides the bag and helps support its weight.

Decorating tips made of metal are the best; avoid flimsy plastic tips because they crack easily. Tips and bags manufactured by such companies as Ateco and Wilton are available from cookware shops. Select tips that fit the bags—small tips for small bags, extra-large tips for the long bags. When you have a new bag, you must trim the tip so a decorating tip can fit inside. Drop the decorating tip into the bag, allowing the nose to peek out, so the icing will be forced through it. Or use a plastic 2-piece coupler (sold with the tips); this device allows you to fasten the tip on the outside of the bag, so you can change it for another design without changing the bag.

The simplest decorating bag of all is a heavy-duty plastic bag with a small hole cut in one corner. Add the icing or melted chocolate, roll the top closed, and squeeze it out through the hole. Discard the bag when done; no cleanup. To achieve a finer design using the plastic bag, drop a metal decorating tip into the bag (or attach it to the bag with the plastic coupler so the tip can be changed from the outside) and force the icing through the tip. Save the tip before discarding the used bag. The plastic bag method is ideal for children to use when decorating cookies.

PAPER DECORATING CONES: Disposable paper decorating cones can be purchased pre-cut or homemade out of wax paper or baking parchment. To make a cone, cut a triangle about 12 × 15 inches (*A*). Pull the long side of the paper around its midpoint, making a cone (*B*). Hold the cone tight while wrapping the second point around (*C*); tuck in all the ends (*D*) to hold the cone in place. Use a piece of tape to fasten the side, securing the shape. Cut a tiny piece off the cone tip, or cut a hole that permits the nose of a metal tip dropped into the cone to peek out. Fill the cone, fold down the top, and squeeze out the icing (*E*).

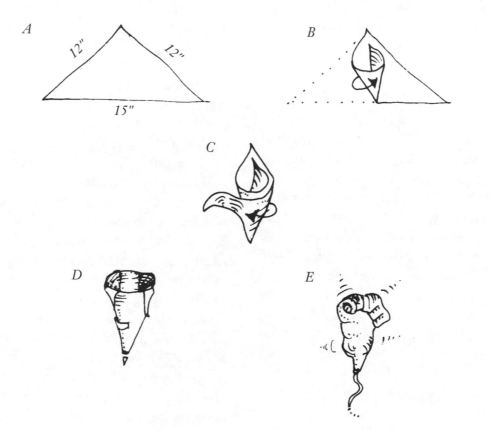

Appendices

RECIPES FOR SPECIAL DIETS AND/OR SPECIAL OCCASIONS

Consult the Index for page numbers.

TOTALLY FAT FREE
(1% calories from fat or less)

Apricot Mousse

Steve Keneipp's Coffee-Spice Angel
Food Cake

Meringue Pie Shells and Individual
Meringue Nests

Burgundy Poached Pears in Meringue
Shells

Marshmallow Fluff

Brandied Cranberry-Maple Sauce

All-Purpose and Firm Fruit Glaze

Vanilla and Orange Icing Glaze

Cookie Frosting

Seven-Minute and Lemon Seven-
Minute Icing

Boiled Icing

Apricot Roses

Sugared Rose Petals; Sugared
Grapes

Amber Sugar Beads and Cracked
Caramel

Tropical Dreams (fruit only)

CHOLESTEROL-FREE
(trace amounts of cholesterol)

Vanilla, Cocoa, Orange, or Lemon
Icing Glaze

Seven-Minute Icing

Boiled Icing

Cookie Frosting

Marshmallow Fluff

All-Purpose and Firm Fruit Glaze

Amber Sugar Beads

Apricot Roses

Berry Sauce

Raspberry Sauce

Plum Sauce

Steve's Spa Chocolate Sauce

Chocolate Sauce

Blueberry-Honey Sauce

Brandied Cranberry-Maple
Sauce

Piña Colada Sorbet

Margarita Sorbet

Strawberry Daiquiri Sorbet

Spiced Cranberry Sorbet

Chilled Cantaloupe Soup

Burgundy Poached Pears in Meringue
Shells

Ginnie Hagan's Vermont
Blueberry Pie

Passover Apple and Honey Crumble

Tortilla Tarts

Steve Keneipp's Coffee-Spice Angel
Food Cake

Walnut Crumb Bars

Berry Bars with Streusel Topping

Apricot Mousse

Claire's Fruit Pudding Cake

LACTOSE-FREE RECIPES

(May contain yogurt, indicated with *; use yogurt with live active enzymes, per label. No milk products; replace any skim milk in recipe with alternatively listed juice or water or use Lactaid milk per personal dietary needs)

Burgundy Poached Pears in Meringue Shells

Chilled Blueberry-Raspberry Soup with May Wine*

Chilled Cantaloupe Soup*

Piña Colada Sorbet*

Margarita Sorbet*

Strawberry Daiquiri Sorbet*

Spiced Cranberry Sorbet*

Apricot-Orange Cake Filling (omit butter)

Apricot Mousse

Chocolate Sponge Roll

Almond Sponge Roll

Tortilla Tarts

Steve Keneipp's Coffee-Spice Angel Food Cake

Ginnie Hagan's Vermont Blueberry Pie

All-Purpose and Firm Fruit Glaze

Vanilla, Cocoa, Orange, or Lemon Icing Glaze

Boiled Icing

Seven-Minute Icing

Marshmallow Fluff

Lemon Curd

Berry Sauce

Blueberry-Honey Sauce

Raspberry Sauce

Plum Sauce

Brandied Cranberry-Maple Sauce

Steve's Spa Chocolate Sauce

Chocolate Plastic Decorations

Apricot Roses

Amber Sugar Beads and Cracked Caramel

GLUTEN-FREE RECIPES

(*See adjustments indicated in individual recipes. Check labels or call manufacturers to be sure flavoring extracts as well as modified food starches, stabilizers, and gums in reduced-fat dairy products are gluten-free; avoid all spirits or liqueurs made from cereal grains)

Gluten-Free Orange Biscotti

Liz's Gluten-Free Bionic Bars

Homemade Chocolate Pudding

Piña Colada Sorbet

Margarita Sorbet

Strawberry Daiquiri Sorbet

Spiced Cranberry Sorbet

Meringue Shells

Apricot Mousse

Apricot-Orange Cake Filling

Marshmallow Fluff

Cookie Frosting

Light Cream Cheese Frosting*

Seven-Minute Icing

Boiled Icing

Orange Buttercream Frosting*

Marbleized Sour Cream Topping*

Vanilla Cream

Vanilla Custard Sauce

Blueberry-Honey Sauce

Praline Sauce (made with rum)

Berry Sauce

Raspberry Sauce

Plum Sauce

Brandied Cranberry-Maple Sauce

All-Purpose and Firm Fruit Glaze*

Chilled Cantaloupe Soup

Chilled Blueberry-Raspberry Soup with May Wine

Burgundy Poached Pears in Meringue Shells

Vanilla, Cocoa, Orange, or Lemon Icing Glaze

Amber Sugar Beads and Cracked Caramel

Chocolate Curls and Shavings

Chocolate Plastic Decorations

REDUCED-SUGAR

*(Reduced sugar or no sugar added; for those who may wish to limit sugar intake. *Replace jam or preserves with sugar-free all-fruit preserves)*

Chilled Cantaloupe Soup
Chilled Blueberry-Raspberry Soup with May Wine
Low-Sugar Apple Pie
Low-Sugar Graham Cracker Crumb Crust
All-Purpose Pie Crust (omit sugar)
Apple-Pear-Plum Low-Sugar Fruit Crisp
Peaches 'n' Cream Pie
Tortilla Tarts*
Peach Pizza*
Blueberry-Honey Sauce
All-Purpose and Firm Fruit Glaze*
Plum Sauce
Steve's Spa Chocolate Sauce

FUN FOR CHILDREN

(with adult supervision)

Marshmallow Fluff
Chocolate Chip Cookies
Cowboy Crunch Cookies
Peanut Butter Cookies
Chocolate Sandwich Cookies
Fudge Brownies with Vanilla Cream and Praline Sauce
Chocolate-Caramel Turtle Tartlets
Valentine Heart Tarts
Jack-o'-lantern Cups
Pumpkin Cream Bombe
Chocolate Curls and Shavings
Chocolate Plastic Decorations
Apricot Roses
Tortilla Tarts
Burrito Blintzes
Peach Pizza
Mother's Day Peach Melba
Father's Day "Tie" Cake
Chocolate Tulip Shells

HOLIDAY GIFTS FROM THE KITCHEN

All quick holiday yeast breads
All cookies, brownies, and bars
Orange Bundt Cake
Pumpkin Pound Cake with Maple Glaze
New Year's Honey Cake
Belgian Honey Cake
Orange Layer Cake
Drop-Dead Chocolate-Espresso Mousse Cake
Cocoa Cake
Chocolate–Sour Cream Cake
Brandied Cranberry-Maple Sauce
Blueberry-Honey Sauce
Plum Sauce
Father's Day "Tie" Cake
Praline Sauce
Chocolate Sauce; Steve's Spa Chocolate Sauce
Marshmallow Fluff

SPECIAL DESSERTS FOR HOLIDAYS

Christmas/New Year's/Chanukah

Santa Lucia Saffron Buns and Braid
Panettone
Favorite Christmas Bread
Steamed Fig-Date-Apricot Pudding
Holiday Cranberry Upside-down Cake
Trifle
New Year's Honey Cake
Belgian Honey Cake
Pear-Prune-Brandy Cake
Spiced Cranberry Sorbet
Burgundy Poached Pears in Meringue Shells
Rugelach
Walnut Crumb Bars

Easter/Passover/Spring

Sticky Honey Buns
Cherry-Raisin Bread
Pineapple-Apricot Crown
Swedish Cardamom Braids

Easter/Passover/Spring (continued)

Orange Cheesecake with Amber Sugar Beads

Nectarine Cheesecake with Blueberry-Honey Sauce

Chocolate-Flecked Cheesecake with Chocolate Curls

Almond Sponge Roll with Apricot Mousse and Apricot Roses

Lemon Sponge Roll with Lemon Curd Filling

Mother's Day Peach Melba

Father's Day "Tie" Cake

Trifle

Tiramisù

Lemon Meringue Pie

Fresh Cherry Clafouti

Peach Pizza

Orange Bundt Cake with Orange Glaze

Lemon Pound Cake

Passover Tulip Cookies with Fruit

Double Chocolate Passover Sponge Cake

Tortilla Tarts

Mandarin Mousse Pie (in Meringue Pie Shell)

Tropical Dreams

Chilled Blueberry-Raspberry Soup with May Wine

Chilled Cantaloupe Soup

Strawberry Mousse Pie

Thanksgiving/Halloween/Fall

Pumpkin Frozen Yogurt

Pumpkin Cream Bombe

Pumpkin Frozen Yogurt on Walnut Crumb Bars

Spiced Sponge Roll filled with Pumpkin 'n' Spice Cream

Pumpkin Pound Cake with Maple Glaze

Holiday Cranberry Upside-down Cake

Orange Bundt Cake with Brandied Cranberry-Maple Sauce

Jack-o'-lantern Cups

Chocolate-Caramel Turtle Tartlets

Chocolate Sponge Roll with Apricot-Orange Cake Filling

Steamed Fig-Date-Apricot Pudding

Belgian Honey Cake

Chocolate Mousse Tartlets

Upside-down Apple Bread Pudding with Bourbon Cream Sauce

Valentine's Day

Valentine Heart Tarts

Strawberry Cream Pie

Drop-Dead Chocolate-Espresso Mousse Cake

Chocolate Mousse

Madly Moka Cheesecake

Holiday Cranberry Upside-down Cake

Chocolate Tulip Shells with Strawberry Mousse and Brandied Cranberry-Maple Sauce

Other Holidays: Fourth of July/Mother's and Father's Days/April Fool's Day

Fourth of July Firecracker Pie

Red-White-and-Blue Fourth of July Pie

Mother's Day Peach Melba

Father's Day "Tie" Cake

Raspberry-Rhubarb Fool in Chocolate Tulip Shells with Raspberry Sauce

Oops! what do i do now?

Quick-Fix Cover-up Tricks

Relax, it happens to everyone. When you most want it to be perfect…the cheesecake cracks, the cake top slopes so much the frosting would slide off if it wasn't so lumpy; the cake edges are as misaligned as a dropped deck of cards; the pie pastry is full of holes. What should you do? Here are a few tricks to keep under your toque for just such emergencies.

First, remember that your guests are not reading this book, and don't know what the dessert was supposed to look like. They will know only what they see at the final presentation, and it will taste delicious even if its appearance has been modified. So, no apologies. Smile and act as if you planned it to be this way. Be forthright, positive, and proud of your creation. After all, you exercised your creative and culinary skills here even if things went awry. In fact, you should get extra credit for dealing with it, so I'll give it to you.

IF THE CHEESECAKE CRACKS OR THE CAKE TOP IS BUMPY:

- To cover cracks in the top of a cheesecake, spread fruit preserves on top. If the preserves are too thick, warm them until they're spreadable. If the cracks are deep, use preserves with pieces of fruit, and gently place the pieces into the gaps. If you want smooth preserves, strain out fruit pieces.

- Spread warm fruit preserves over the cake, then scatter toasted almond slices on top (just a few, for decoration, because nuts are high in fat).

- Brush a thin layer of warm fruit preserves on the cake top, then cover with finely crushed vanilla or chocolate wafer crumbs. They can be pressed onto the cake sides as well (or you can simply pick up the cake between your hands and roll or dip the cake into the crumbs). For the final touch, sift 1 scant teaspoon confectioners' sugar over the crumbs on the cake top; the sugar should be a very light dusting. Unsweetened cocoa can be used in place of sugar.

- Fresh berries or fresh sliced fruit (or canned fruit slices completely drained and blotted dry) can be arranged in concentric circles all over a jam-coated cake top as if making a fruit tart. Melt some apricot preserves, strain out the fruit pieces, and use a pastry brush to coat the fruit with the shiny glaze. Chill the cake to set the glaze.

- Cracks, discolorations, and other distortions on the surface of a cheesecake are easily disguised with the Marbleized Sour Cream Topping on page 281. Or spoon some seedless raspberry preserves into a small self-sealing plastic bag with a hole cut in one corner. Squeeze the bag to force jam onto the sour cream to make a design. Refrigerate the cake to set the glaze.

- If a layer cake top is rippled or just plain uneven, the first and easiest line of defense is to cover it by sifting on a generous layer of confectioners' sugar or unsweetened cocoa, thick enough to hide bumps.

  Another way to disguise an uneven cake top is to make a paper stencil with an abstract design and sift on powdered sugar or cocoa in a jagged or zigzag pattern that confuses the eye. Alternatively, set a paper doily over a plain layer of cocoa and sift on a tiny bit of confectioners' sugar. Lift off the doily, leaving a design.

  Chocolate Curls or Shavings (page 289), Sugared Rose Petals (page 288), or Apricot Roses (page 286) cover a multitude of sins when scattered over the layer of sifted confectioners' sugar on top.

- If your cake top has a particularly ruinous or cratered surface, title it "Mountain Top Cake" or "Alpine Cake" and disguise it as follows: For a two-layer cake, use a serrated knife to slice off (horizontally) about one third of the irregular top layer. Break this piece into $1/2$- to $3/4$-inch chunks and toss them lightly with any preserves or melted chocolate (to lightly glue the chunks together). Brush the same preserves or melted chocolate over the sliced cake top, then pile on the chunks and cover them with sifted unsweetened cocoa topped with a tiny bit of sifted confectioners' sugar on the peaks. Voilà…a snow-dappled mountaintop! Note: For a four-layer cake, you can use the whole fourth layer for the chunks.

IF THE CAKE CAREENS OR THE LAYERS LEAN:

- You have two choices. The quickest fix is to prop up the offending area by working between the layers: Stick more frosting or cake filling or a little wedge of cake dug out from the bottom surface between the layers in the low spot. Or fill in the dips or sloping areas on top with more frosting, blending it out until the top looks level. If the cake is not yet frosted, use a serrated knife to level off the domed or sloped surfaces. Or slice a narrow wedge from the top of the inner layer and set this on the top to build up a low spot before covering it with frosting.

IF CAKE SIDES ARE UNEVEN OR THE FILLING OOZES OUT:

- My favorite save for uneven and/or oozing cake sides is to wrap the whole thing up in a band of Chocolate Plastic (page 290). You can cut a ribbon of chocolate to fit the width of your cake and wrap it around the sides, leaving the top untouched, or you can make a wider piece and drape it over the top edge as well (see page 291). You can even gather small pieces of the chocolate into ruffles and cover the entire cake top. Note, however, that this is made from solid (high-fat) chocolate. Lift off the chocolate decorations before cutting the cake and set just a little piece of the chocolate on each serving (to cover up the blemished area).
- Another trick for covering up unsightly cake sides: press on vanilla or chocolate wafers or animal crackers (for a kids' cake) or sections of other neatly sliced cookies, covering the frosting, which should hold them in place. If the frosting is dry, mix up a little confectioners' sugar and skim milk to use as a glue. If the cake is not yet frosted, cover the sides with jam before pressing on the cover-up cookies.

IF PIE PASTRY IS PALLID OR DEVELOPS HOLES AND CRACKS:

- If the pie crust is baked blind (unfilled) and you notice cracks or holes developing in the pastry, use a little extra unbaked pastry (I try to hold a small ball of dough in reserve for this purpose) to stick over the holes, using egg glaze (1 egg white beaten with 2 teaspoons water) or water as glue to hold it in place. If you don't have pastry left over, mix flour and water into a paste and press it over the cracks.

- After baking your fruit pie, test the doneness of the fruit with a sharp knife tip. If you feel it is still hard, put the pie back in the oven for another 20 to 30 minutes. Cover the top with foil. Watch carefully and retest for doneness.

- Even if it is home-baked, nothing is less appealing than a white, doughy-looking pie filled with nearly raw fruit in runny juice. If your pie pastry looks pallid in spite of your best efforts, simply sprinkle grated nutmeg or cinnamon sugar over the top. If the fruit inside is still unbaked, however, you need to put the pie back in the oven at a higher temperature for another 20 minutes and check it often so it doesn't overbake. To prevent that from happening in the future, brush pastry tops with egg glaze (1 egg white beaten with 2 teaspoons water) and sprinkle it with sugar before baking; the sugar caramelizes into a golden brown color.

IT IS HOPELESS; I'M GOING TO FEED THIS TO THE DOG:

- If it tastes all right but looks hopeless, here's the best trick of all: Break up the cake and bury small pieces of it beneath layers of pudding and fruit to make a very elegant Trifle (page 193).

FAT, DIETARY FAT, CHOLESTEROL, AND CALORIES

In a culture that believes you are what you eat, that skinny is sublime and voluptuous is vulgar, "low-fat" is the most sought-after designer label. Fat food is perceived as sinful and eating is equated with making a moral statement; the fun seems to have gone out of dining. Our society seems to have conspired to make us feel guilty if we crunch a bunch of potato chips and virtuous if we drink a glass of skim milk. Is this really the struggle between good and evil? What's wrong with this picture? Both notions are foolish and extreme when stared at too long; yet paying attention to good nutrition, per se, does make good sense.

For good health, the body needs over forty different nutrients; these are divided into five major classes: fat, proteins, carbohydrates, minerals, and vitamins. Fat is a vital nutrient that the body needs, in some measure, for good health, even for life itself. Second, food would not taste nearly as good without any fat. The question is the amount and type of fat *needed*, as opposed to that *desired*.

Fat belongs to a group of organic compounds called lipids (from the Greek word *lipos*, meaning "fat"). Fat's essential characteristic is that its chemical structure is made up of fatty acid chains composed of carbon, hydrogen, and oxygen, the same three elements found in carbohydrates, though in differing proportions. For the purposes of this book, we are concerned with two basic types of lipids: triglycerides (and the fatty acids they contain) and cholesterol.

Why does the body need fat at all? Fat molecules play many roles: they supply a fuel source for many tissues, they aid in the synthesis of cell membranes, they help the synthesis of cholesterol (which the body makes to fulfill its need for cholesterol) and sterol hormones. Fat in food provides the most concentrated source of energy in the diet, actually $2^1/_4$ times more than an equal weight of proteins or carbohydrates. The body utilizes the fat it needs for energy, then stores the rest in various fatty tissue. Some goes to blood plasma and other body cells, but the majority of the excess is stored in fat cells. Bodily fat also serves as insulation against climatic temperature changes, prevents bodily heat loss, and protects vital organs. Body fat can be made from excess calories either from proteins, fat, or cholesterol in the diet.

Nevertheless, some fat is essential to a healthy diet. A totally fat-free diet is not healthy under normal circumstances. Fat serves as a carrier for four essential fat-soluble vitamins: A, D, E, and K. Without fat, these vitamins could not be absorbed by the body. Fat also helps the body use carbohydrates and proteins more efficiently.

There are many different types of fats, or fatty acids, contained in food; all but three of these types can be made in the body. The three that cannot, yet are essential for good health and necessary in the structural integrity of some cellular membranes must come from dietary fat; these are called the essential fatty acids: linoleic, linolenic, and arachidonic acids.

Those of us who love to eat know that fats play a vital role in cooking and also help to make our food taste good. Fats hold and carry flavors and aromas, contributing to taste appeal. Oil-soluble flavors carried in fats coat our taste buds so they remain on the tongue, lingering to create a complex taste quality scientists call "mouth-feel." Foods lacking fat also lack mouth-feel; they rarely taste as good, or subliminally urge us to take another bite. Oil-soluble aromas also linger, remaining to give pleasure even after food is swallowed. When fats are reduced, flavoring agents have to be added or increased to restore or enhance taste. After dietary fats are eaten and digested, they tend to leave the stomach slowly, thereby contributing to a feeling of satiety, or fullness. In the baking process, fats contribute to flavor, color, texture, leavening, and other factors (see page 313, Fats for Baking).

There is a popular misconception that all products that are low fat are also low calorie and therefore can be eaten in quantity without causing a weight gain. The truth is that some are but most are not; you can't eat the whole cake even if it is reduced in fat. If calories are an issue for you, moderation is still the point. If you consume more calories, especially calories from fat, than are necessary for maintaining good health and optimum weight, you will gain weight.

All calories are *not* created equal; 50 calories of butter is not the same as 50 calories of sugar or starch. The body converts fat calories to bodily fat more easily than it converts carbohydrate calories; in other words, fats are metabolized more efficiently. The body uses less energy for this process and has more energy left over to use for other activities or to store as fat. Thus, excess fat calories make you fat faster than excess carbohydrate calories, although an excess of these will also eventually end up as fat cells.

According to the American Heart Association, the average American diet presently derives as much as 34% to 36% of its total calories from fat. Most health authorities agree this is excessively high. AHA authorities recommend individuals over two years of age cut their total daily fat intake to 30%; more conservative voices look for much less.

Research indicates that diets *excessively* high in fat may be bad for our health. Diets high in saturated fats are the worst culprits, with high-cholesterol diets running a close second, although the danger of high cholesterol has been slightly downrated in certain cases. Cholesterol is a type of fat, or lipid, found in food from animal sources and also synthesized in the body; cholesterol is never present in vegetable or plant fats. Cholesterol is essential for many bodily functions and, within limits, is beneficial to the body. The total amount of cholesterol in the blood depends on the body's natural production, dietary intake, and bodily absorption. This interaction is complex and affected by many factors including genetics. To supply the amount of cholesterol needed, the natural bodily production of this substance changes in relation to diet. The amount and type of fat in the diet also affects the cholesterol level in the blood.

High levels of saturated fat and cholesterol are known to raise blood cholesterol levels, a major risk factor for coronary artery disease: clogging of the arteries leading to heart attacks, inadequate circulation to the legs, and weakening of the walls of blood vessels, leading to strokes. It is also possible that a highly saturated-fat, high-cholesterol diet may be a contributing factor in adult-onset diabetes and certain cancers.

For many people, reducing excessive dietary intake of saturated fat and cholesterol results in a reduced risk of many of these diseases. However, as recent research has shown, some individuals suffer high blood cholesterol levels even when their diets are low in both fat and cholesterol; these cases are generally related to genetic factors.

ABOUT DIABETES

About 13 million Americans have diabetes, a chronic disease that impairs the body's ability to use food properly. During normal metabolism, the process of turning food into energy, a form of sugar called glucose is produced when carbohydrates (sugars and starches) are digested. To utilize glucose, the body requires insulin, a hormone produced by the pancreas. Individuals with diabetes either do not produce enough insulin, or the insulin they have doesn't work efficiently. Without insulin to move the glucose into body cells where it can be used for energy, glucose accumulates in the bloodstream and spills out into the urine. While there is not yet a cure for diabetes, it can be managed by monitoring blood glucose levels, eating a healthful variety of foods, engaging in routine physical activity, and, in some cases, taking insulin or oral diabetes medication.

There are two principal types of diabetes: Type I, or insulin-dependent diabetes, and Type II, or non-insulin-dependent. For both, the three main elements of management are food, exercise, and in some cases, insulin or oral diabetes medications. Food makes blood glucose levels rise; exercise and insulin make the levels fall. Diabetes control is a balancing act of these factors. When out of balance, one risks either hypoglycemia (low blood glucose) or hyperglycemia (high blood glucose).

Type I (insulin-dependent diabetes) affects some 300,000 Americans. It usually begins in childhood and in young adults. In this form, the pancreas produces little or no insulin. Individuals with this type of diabetes must test their blood glucose levels throughout the day and take insulin injections in order to be able to metabolize food.

Type II diabetes affects about 12.7 million Americans. Individuals with this form of the disease produce insulin, but the body is unable to use it effectively, resulting in abnormal blood glucose levels. Type II diabetes is treated through testing blood glucose levels and may require the use of oral diabetes medication or insulin. Individuals with both types of diabetes must monitor their food consumption and include regular forms of exercise.

Each person with diabetes must plan his or her own treatment program in consultation with a diabetes care team (physician, dietician, nurse, and other health care providers). Consultation with a dietician includes a nutrition assessment and development of an individualized eating plan, which will vary from one person to the next.

There is some recent good news for people with diabetes. According to the American Diabetes Association and the American Dietetic Association, the sugar ban has been lifted. This is an important shift in philosophy, setting aside the long-held belief that sugar and sweets raised blood glucose levels faster than complex carbohydrates (starches). New research gives priority to the total amount of carbohydrates consumed rather than to the source of those carbohydrates. This does not mean sugar and sweets can be eaten haphazardly, but rather that an individual has more dietary flexibility and choice; a sweet dessert may be eaten if the sugar it provides is substituted for other carbohydrates in the diet.

Desserts are beloved but bedeviling to persons with diabetes, not only because of the carbohydrates present but also because of the amount and type of fat they contain. The American Diabetes Association suggests that people with diabetes should lower their consumption of saturated fat as well as total fat. This can be accomplished by using low-fat or nonfat cream cheese, yogurt, low-fat salad dressing or mayonnaise, low-fat sour cream, less butter or margarine, only low-fat or nonfat dairy products, and fewer foods with hydrogenated fat such as packaged mixes or store-bought baked goods. Further recommendations include eating smaller amounts of lean meat, poultry, and fish or, as an alternative, dried beans, peas, and lentils.

Working with a dietician, one can create an eating plan that includes the use of desserts in moderation. The recipes and notes in this book are not intended to be medically specific for any particular health regimen. Rather, they are lower in fat and cholesterol, as low in calories as good taste will permit, and in many cases extremely low in sugar (see page 353 or the Index for reduced-sugar recipes). Although the nutritional analysis (including total fat, saturated fat, and carbohydrates) is listed for each recipe in the book, I did not include food exchanges. I hope readers with diabetes will adapt my recipes to their own needs within the context of their own specific nutritional programs.

I have tried to present a variety of dessert options, while using only natural ingredients. I have not used any artificial sugar substitutes or fructose; I do use nutritive sweeteners such as granulated sugar (sucrose), honey, brown sugar, and sugar-free all-fruit preserves. Many recipes use these sweeteners in minimal amounts. One tablespoon of brown sugar in a recipe with 8 servings means that each serving yields only $1/8$ tablespoon sugar (and remember, it is the total carbohydrate that counts, not its source). As an alternative to sugar in certain cases, I recommend syrups containing isomalt (see Steel's products, page 373). Note that all nutritive sweeteners add carbohydrates and calories. Of course, you can use any nonnutritive sweetener (a sugar substitute that contains minimal calories) in the recipes following the manufacturer's directions for use. But be aware that flavor, texture, and appearance of baked goods will vary depending upon the type of sugar substitute selected.

How can I reduce fat in my old recipes?

The special qualities of fat are hard to replicate, and successful substitutions, especially for baked goods, are tricky. Generally, when you cut back or cut out fat, you need to readjust a whole range of elements in a carefully balanced formula. You must enhance flavors by increasing or adding flavoring agents such as zests, extracts, and sometimes sugar. To maintain the desired texture in baked goods, a suitably viscous aerating and moisture-holding fat substitute is needed: fruit purées (prune, apple, banana), corn syrup, various vegetable oils, whole eggs, whites, and/or stiffly whipped egg whites. Sometimes, for successful baking, a little butter must be used to achieve the proper taste. To restore the tenderness contributed by the fat in the original recipe, cake flour often is used instead of higher-protein all-purpose flour. But cake flour absorbs a different quantity of moisture than all-purpose flour, so then liquids must be adjusted; acidic dairy products such as yogurt or buttermilk may be added, as they inhibit gluten development. Sometimes when acids are added, they must be balanced by the addition of neutralizing baking soda.

Remember that this book focuses on low-fat, *not totally fat-free*, baking. With very few exceptions (meringues and a few unusual cakes, for example), totally fat-free baked goods taste unspeakably rubbery, pasty, and boring beyond endurance. You can, however, reduce fat with some success in many cases. Beware of tinkering too much when reducing fat in your own baking recipes. Baking recipes are carefully balanced formulas; eliminating fat drastically upsets this balance. The recipes in this book have all been carefully tested and are reliable. Study their proportions if you want to alter another recipe. As a general rule, it is possible to cut fat from a "traditional" recipe by about one quarter to one third; the resulting texture may be more dense because solid fat creamed with sugar will incorporate more air than will oil.

PERSONAL FAT MATH

To determine your own personal health requirements and actual weight and/or desired weight loss, you must evaluate such factors as how much you exercise, the state of your present health and/or risk of illness, and your family hereditary patterns. You should consult with your doctor and/or nutritionist to prepare a suitable dietary program. The information following is intended to be a general guideline, not an individualized program.

According to the American Heart Association, the average American adult derives about 34% to 36% of his or her daily total of calories from fat. Most authorities agree that this is too high and recommend 30%, while more conservative voices look for 20% or even less.

Calories are a measure of food energy. Thus, a woman weighing 125 pounds and leading an active life requires approximately 1,800 calories per day. If 40% of these calories were from fat, she would consume 720 calories (40% × 1,800) from fat per day. If the same individual cut-down to 30%, she should derive no more than 540 calories from fat (30% × 1,800).

Pure fats all weigh the same amount and contain the

same number of calories of fat. For example, all oils—including canola and peanut oils—are 100% fat. One tablespoon of any one weighs 13.6 g, usually rounded off to 14 g, and contains 14 g fat. (These fats do, however, differ in their degree of saturation: Canola oil is approximately 6% saturated, while peanut oil is 17%.)

Every gram of every fat (solid or liquid) provides 9 calories (more exactly, kilocalories, kcals), a measure of energy. Thus, 1 tablespoon (13.6 g weight) of any type of oil equals 13.6×9/kcal, or 122 calories (usually rounded to 120). One tablespoon of butter weighs 14.2 g. Butter is 80% fat. Therefore, $80\% \times 14 = 11.2$; 11×9/kcal = 99 calories per tablespoon of butter.

How to Calculate Fat Grams

There are three easy ways to calculate the total number of grams of fat (fat grams) allowed per day.

1. Simply divide the number of calories required to maintain your ideal weight (or your goal for percentage of calories from fat per day) by 30%. For example, say 1,800 calories: $1,800 \div 30\% = 60$ g fat per day.)

2. Another method is to calculate the number of calories per day derived from fat—in our example, 30% of 1,800 = 540—then divide this figure by 9, the total number of calories in each gram of fat. Thus, $540 \div 9 = 60$ g fat per day.

3. The third (less accurate) method is to divide your ideal weight in half. If you weigh, or wish to weigh, 125 pounds, you should consume no more than 62.5 g fat per day ($125 \div 2 = 62.5$). If you weigh 180 pounds, you can consume 90 g fat per day and still meet the 30% goal.

How to Allocate Your Daily Fat Grams

Pay attention to three factors: the total quantity of fat, the type of fat, and the amount of cholesterol you consume. The American Heart Association Dietary Guidelines for Healthy American Adults recommends that your total daily intake of fat grams (60 in the examples above) be divided roughly in thirds by type of fat, to provide a ratio of one third monounsaturated fat, one third polyunsaturated, and one third saturated. Each third should be no more than 10% of the total daily caloric intake, for a total of 30% calories from fat.

USDA FOOD LABELING STANDARDS

"Cholesterol-free vegetable oil," light, lite, low-fat, fat-free…more hype than help? Packaging terms at one time seemed to do little but confuse consumers. In an attempt to clarify and standardize meaningful commercial product label information, the Food and Drug Administration and the U.S. Department of Agriculture's Food Safety and Inspection Service in 1994 issued new regulations for nutrient content claims. I present a summary of these guidelines here to clarify the issue and help readers select reduced-fat ingredients needed for dessert-making. However, it should be perfectly clear to the reader that the definition of terms and specific regulations apply to product labels, not to the nutritional analysis, text, or titles of recipes in this or other cookbooks.

The 1994 FDA regulations focused on eleven core terms: free, low, lean, extra lean, high, good source, reduced, less, light, fewer, and more. Certain terms and regulations are particularly relevant to ingredients used in low-fat baking and desserts. Some examples of new definitions:

"Sugar free": less than 0.5 g per serving. "No sugar added": zero sugar added during processing or packaging (including ingredients that contain sugars such as dried fruit). "Reduced sugar": contains at least 25% less sugar per serving than the reference food. "Calorie free": fewer than 5 calories per serving. "Low calorie": 40 calories or less per serving; if a serving is 30 g or less, or 2 tablespoons or less, then 40 calories per 50 g food. "Reduced calorie": at least 25% fewer calories than the reference food. "Fat free": less than 0.5 g fat per serving. "Low-fat": 3 g or less per serving; if a serving is 30 g or less, or 2 tablespoons or less, then 3 g less per 50 g of food. "Saturated fat free": less than 0.5 g per serving, and the level of trans fatty acids (TFAs) must not exceed 1% of total fat. "Low saturated fat": 1 g or less per serving and not more than 15% of calories from saturated fatty acids. "Cholesterol free": less than 2 mg cholesterol and 2 g or less saturated fat per serving. "Low cholesterol": 20 mg or less and 2 g or less saturated fat per serving. "Sodium free": less than 5 mg per serving. "Low sodium": 140 mg or less per serving. "High fiber": 5 g or more per serving. "Good fiber source": 2.5 to 4.9 g per serving.

The regulations allow "fat-free" claims for any food with less than 0.5 g fat per serving. "Free" can also be applied to saturated fat, cholesterol, sodium, sugar, and calories. Foods that don't contain a certain nutrient naturally must be labeled to indicate all foods of that type meet the claim—for example, in the case of applesauce, which never contains fat, a fat-free claim would have to read: "Applesauce, a fat-free food."

In the past, products containing a relatively small percentage of fat based on total weight or volume could be labeled "% fat free," as in "98% fat free." In terms of percentage of calories from fat, however, the food could actually be high in fat. This is because fat contributed most of the calories in that food independent of its weight or volume. With the new regulations, products with "% fat free" claims must really be low in fat and thus useful in maintaining a low-fat diet. The claim must also accurately reflect the amount of fat present in 100 g of the food. If, for example, the food contains 5 g fat per 100 g of food, it must be "95% fat free."

"Light" and "lite" can refer only to nutritionally altered products that contain one third fewer calories or half the fat of the reference food. If the food derives 50% or more of its calories from fat, the reduction must be 50% of the fat.

Items labeled "low calorie" or "low fat" in general must have 50% or less sodium than the reference food. As stated above, "sodium-free" items must have less than 5 mg per serving; "low sodium" must have 140 mg or less per serving; "reduced sodium" must contain at least 25% less per serving than the reference food.

"Light" is allowed to describe color or texture of a product only if qualifying information is included, but "light brown sugar" is permitted because it has a long history of acceptance and use.

"Healthy" claims on a food can be used if the product is low in fat and saturated fat, one serving does not contain more than 480 mg sodium or more than 60 mg cholesterol, and contains at least 10% of the Daily Reference Intake of Vitamin A, Vitamin C, calcium, iron, protein, or fiber.

"Fresh" foods must never have been frozen or heated, and contain no preservatives. Low-level irradiation is, however, allowed. Foods quickly frozen while still fresh or blanched (briefly scalded before freezing to prevent nutritional breakdown) can be called "fresh frozen." Traditional uses such as "fresh milk" and "freshly baked bread" are not affected by the regulations.

The statement "contains no oil" can apply only to food that is really fat free, not one containing a source of fat other than oil, such as an animal fat. A label stating "made with canola oil," implying it is low in saturated fat, must meet the definition of "low saturated fat." "Made only with vegetable oil" implies that, unlike animal fat, it contributes no cholesterol and is low in saturated fat. Therefore, this use is allowed only if the food meets the definition of "cholesterol free" and "low saturated fat."

Implied claims are controlled as well. Statements such as "contains oat bran" implies things about nutrient content and is allowed only when the food actually contains a meaningful level of that nutrient and is prohibited when wrongfully implying the food does or does not contain a meaningful level of a nutrient. These claims are allowed if the food's nutrient content meets the exact content implied by the claim.

The new regulations establish "standards of identity" and define many foods' composition and the ingredients they must contain. Such standards have long been in place, originally conceived to protect consumers from deception. Today's nutritionally aware consumers require new protections. For example, original standards of identity for sour cream required that it contain 18% fat; anything less had to be called "imitation" or "substitute." New regulations allow fat reduction of products labeled "low fat" or "light" as long as that food is still nutritionally equivalent to the original version. Light sour cream can now have just 9% fat content as long as vitamin A is added back to replace the amount lost when fat was cut; sour cream lacking added vitamin A must be called "imitation light sour cream."

Infants and children under two years of age need dietary fat for good health and normal development. For this reason the FDA is not allowing nutrient content claims of foods for children under two unless with special permission. However, current dietary guidelines do not specify limits for salt and sugar in diets of children under two so the FDA prohibits phrases implying low or reduced amounts of sodium or calories ("no salt or sugar added") in baby foods.

"Unsweetened" or "unsalted" claims on foods for adult consumption are permitted because they are considered to refer to taste rather than nutritive content.

MAIL-ORDER SOURCES AND SUPPLIERS

GENERAL BAKING NEEDS

Betty Crocker Savings Catalog
P.O. Box 5371
Minneapolis, MN 55460-5371
612-540-2212
Baking pans, sheets, racks, and utensils, specialty muffin and cake molds, and mixing bowls; catalogue is 50¢

Bridge Kitchenware Corp.
214 East 52nd Street
New York, NY 10022
212-688-4220
212-838-1901
Domestic and imported baking pans, cooking equipment, utensils

The Broadway Panhandler
477 Broome Street
New York, NY 10013
212-966-3434
Wide variety of baking and cake decorating utensils; no catalogue

Dean & DeLuca
560 Broadway
New York, NY 10012
212-226-6800
Catalogue: 800-221-7714

3276 M Street, NW
Washington, DC 20007
202-342-2500
Baking supplies, special flour, utensils, chocolate and cocoa, dried fruits, dried cranberries and cherries, baking equipment

King Arthur Flour Baker's Catalogue
P.O. Box 876
Norwich, VT 05055-0876
800-827-6836 (orders)
802-649-3717 (Baker's Hotline)
Flour, chocolate, cocoa, nonfat cocoa, hard-to-find pure extracts, nuts and seeds, powdered egg whites and meringue powder, baker's equipment and utensils, including goose-feather pastry brushes and instant-spot thermometers

Sweet Celebrations
7009 Washington Avenue South
Edina, MN 55439
800-328-6722
Cake decorating and baking supplies, utensils, chocolate

Williams-Sonoma
Mail Order Department
P.O. Box 7456
San Francisco, CA 94120-7456
800-541-2233
Baking equipment and utensils, baking ingredients, fine chocolate and cocoa, flavoring extracts, thermometers; catalogue

Community Mill & Bean Inc.
267 Route 89 South
Savannah, NY 13146
800-755-0554
Complete line of packaged and bulk "certified organic" grains, baking mixes, and fresh-milled flours, including whole wheat pastry flour; catalogue

Wilton Industries
2240 West 75th Street
Woodridge, IL 60517
708-963-7100
800-772-7111
Wilton Meringue Powder, plus full line of cake decorating products and utensils; catalogue

SPECIAL DIET AND GLUTEN-FREE INGREDIENTS

Steel's Gourmet Foods
D 175 Continental Business Center
Bridgeport, PA 19405
800-6-STEELS
610-277-1230
Low-fat and sugar-free products including fruit and fudge sauces and maple syrup; "Vanilla Nature Sweet, a sugar substitute for baking"

Gluten-Free Pantry
P.O. Box 840
Glastonbury, CT 06033
800-291-8386
860-633-3826
Gluten-free and wheat-free baking mixes and ingredients including xanthan gum and alcohol-free vanilla and almond extracts; catalogue

Dietary Specialties
P.O. Box 227
Rochester, NY 14601
800-544-0099
Gluten-free and wheat-free foods, including xanthan gum, gluten-free flours

Ener-G Foods, Inc.
P.O. Box 84487
Seattle, WA 98124-5787
800-331-5222
Catalogue for gluten-free and wheat-free products

SELECTED BIBLIOGRAPHY

Bowes, Anna dePlanter, and Charles F. Church. *Food Values of Portions Commonly Used*. Revised by Jean A. T. Pennington. 15th ed. New York: Harper & Row, 1989.

Braker, Flo. *Simple Art of Perfect Baking*. Updated and Revised. Shelburne, VT: Chapters Publishing Ltd., 1992.

Cunningham, Marion. *Fannie Farmer Baking Book*. New York: Alfred A. Knopf, 1984.

Jamieson, Patricia, and Cheryl Dorschner, eds. *Eating Well Recipe Rescue Cookbook*. Charlotte, VT: Camden House Publishing, 1993.

McGee, Harold. *The Curious Cook*. San Francisco: North Point Press, 1990.

———. *On Food and Cooking*. New York: Charles Scribner's Sons, 1984.

Martin, D. W., P. A. Mayes, and V. W. Rodwell. *Harper's Review of Biochemistry*. 18th ed. Los Altos, CA: Lange Medical Publications, 1981.

Netzer, Corinne T. *Encyclopedia of Food Values*. New York: Dell Publishing, 1992.

Purdy, Susan G. *Have Your Cake and Eat It, Too*. New York: William Morrow, 1993.

———. *A Piece of Cake*. New York: Macmillan/Collier Books, 1989.

Sax, Richard. *Classic Home Desserts*. Shelburne, VT: Chapters Publishing Ltd., 1994.

Sultan, William J. *Practical Baking*. 3rd ed. Westport, CT: AVI Publishing Co., Inc., 1982.

Ulene, Arthur, M.D. *The NutriBase Nutrition Facts Desk Reference*. New York: Avery Publishing Group, 1995.

INDEX